No Mercy Here

No Mercy Here

Gender, Punishment, and the
Making of Jim Crow Modernity

Sarah Haley

The University of North Carolina Press CHAPEL HILL

© 2016 The University of North Carolina Press
All rights reserved
Manufactured in the United States of America
Set in Espinosa Nova by Westchester Publishing Services

The paper in this book meets the guidelines for permanence and durability
of the Committee on Production Guidelines for Book Longevity of the
Council on Library Resources. The University of North Carolina Press
has been a member of the Green Press Initiative since 2003.

Cover illustrations: photograph of prisoners with horses, courtesy of the Georgia
Archives, Morrow, Ga.; background, detail of prisoner Eliza Cobb's dress, courtesy
of the Georgia Historical Society, Savannah, Ga.

Library of Congress Cataloging-in-Publication Data
Haley, Sarah, author.
No mercy here : gender, punishment, and the making of Jim Crow modernity /
Sarah Haley.
     pages cm. — (Justice, power, and politics)
Includes bibliographical references and index.
ISBN 978-1-4696-2759-5 (cloth : alk. paper)—ISBN 978-1-4696-2760-1 (ebook)
1. Women prisoners—United States—Social conditions. 2. African American
prisoners—United States—Social conditions. 3. Women prisoners—United States—
History. 4. African American prisoners—United States—History. 5. Sex discrimination
in criminal justice administration—United States. 6. Women prisoners—Abuse
of—United States. 7. African American women—Abuse of—United States. 8. Race
discrimination—United States. 9. Sex discrimination against women—United States.
10. Prison sentences—United States—History. I. Title. II. Series: Justice, power,
and politics.
HV9471.H25 2016   365'.4308996073—dc23
2015032183

Portions of this work appeared earlier in somewhat different form as " 'Like I Was a Man':
Chain Gangs, Gender, and the Domestic Carceral Sphere in Jim Crow Georgia," *Signs* 39,
no. 1 (Autumn 2013): 53–77; reprinted here by permission of the publisher. Fred Moten's
"fugitivity is immanent to the thing but is manifest transversally" from *Hughson's Tavern*
(Leon Works, 2008) is used courtesy of the author and publisher.

In memory of Catherine Elizabeth Rice Haley.
And for the struggle to free black women and girls.

Contents

Acknowledgments xi

Introduction 1

CHAPTER ONE
Carceral Constructions of Black Female Deviance 17

CHAPTER TWO
Convict Leasing, (Re)Production, and Gendered Racial Terror 58

CHAPTER THREE
Race and the Sexual Politics of Prison Reform 119

CHAPTER FOUR
Engendering the Chain Gang Economy and the Domestic
Carceral Sphere 156

CHAPTER FIVE
Sabotage and Black Radical Feminist Refusal 195

Conclusion 249

Notes 259
Bibliography 299
Index 319

Illustrations and Tables

Photograph of Eliza Cobb 19

Photograph of Martha Gault 23

"Lively Scenes at Police Matinee as Depicted by
Gordon Noel Hurtel" 37

Dolly Pritchett 48

Women at Milledgeville State Prison Farm 83

Image of Mattie Crawford 96

"Social Conditions of Southern Negroes" 99

Black children described as the worst features of the
convict labor system 112

"Confronted by Woman's Edition Reporters,
Police Chief Beavers Breaks Long Silence" 145

Bars at Chastain Arts Center 250

Table 1. Female population range in Georgia's felony
convict camps, 1868–1905 33

Table 2. Georgia's misdemeanor prison population,
1899–1907 33

Acknowledgments

This book's long and winding road was paved with colleagues, friends, and family whose imprint is indelible. I was incredibly fortunate to have guidance from three exceptional scholars from its early incarnations. Hazel V. Carby pushed me to expand the intellectual horizons of this book, to be braver and bolder than I could imagine. Her brilliant insights have shaped my ideas immeasurably and have made me a better scholar; many of the book's critical frameworks emerged from her guidance. Glenda E. Gilmore taught me to find seemingly lost voices and modeled a research and writing practice that honors them, grounding me in methods that opened historical worlds. Joanne Meyerowitz introduced me to critical fields of historical inquiry with both patience and rigor; her example and the knowledge she imparted have profoundly influenced me ever since.

At the University of North Carolina Press I was incredibly fortunate to be part of the Justice, Power, and Politics series and to work with Heather Ann Thompson, Rhonda Y. Williams, and Brandon Proia. I thank Heather and Rhonda for their encouragement, groundbreaking scholarly model, and keen vision. Brandon's deep engagement and commentary enhanced this book, and his enthusiasm helped it come along. I cannot thank him enough for his important role in this book's long trajectory. I am also very grateful to the entire exceptional UNC editorial, production, and marketing team. A portion of chapter 4 of this book was published in *Signs: Journal of Women in Culture and Society*, and I am appreciative of the exceptionally helpful feedback from anonymous reviewers and editor Mary Hawkesworth.

I received critical research support from the Gilder Lehrman Center for the Study of Slavery, Resistance, and Abolition; the Beinecke Rare Book and Manuscript Library; the Ford Foundation; the Woodrow Wilson Foundation; and Dean Alessandro Duranti and the Social Sciences Division at UCLA, for which I am grateful. Archivists at numerous institutions were critical to the development of my research, including the staff of the Robert W. Woodruff Library, the Hargrett Rare Book and Manuscript Library at the University of Georgia, the

Manuscript, Archives, and Rare Book Library at Emory University, and the Fulton Superior Courthouse. I am particularly grateful for the assistance of exceptionally rigorous and dedicated archivists, including Wesley Chenault at the Auburn Avenue Research Library on African American Culture and History; Beth McLean at the Kenan Research Center; Dale Couch, Steven Engerrand, and Allison Hudgins at the Georgia State Archives; Lynette Stoudt at the Georgia Historical Society; and Lauren Rogers at the University of Mississippi Archives and Special Collections Division. I am also very grateful to Sa Whitley for providing important research assistance, deftly facilitating requests for permissions and materials in the late stages of this book. Finally, I am especially grateful to Ricardo Bracho for his outstanding editorial and indexing work.

I have benefited meaningfully from exceptional scholars who have provided insight in many settings as this book has developed: Dan Berger, Felice Blake, Jordan Camp, Aaron Carico, Erin Chapman, Brian Chung, Craig Gilmore, Ruthie Gilmore, Frank Guridy, Emily Hainze, Claudrena Harold, Christina Heatherton, Rebecca Hill, George Lipsitz, Nancy MacLean, Natalia Molina, Bethany Moreton, Khalil Gibran Muhammad, Alondra Nelson, Naomi Paik, Sherie Randolph, Dylan Rodriguez, Jason Ruiz, Judah Schept, Micol Seigel, Emily Thuma, and Pamela Voekel. I am grateful for invaluable insights from Saidiya Hartman and Thavolia Glymph as well as Cheryl Hicks's generous and incisive comments, which were pivotal, profoundly shaping this book. C. Riley Snorton has also been extraordinarily generous, offering insights that have critically shaped my thinking as well as abundant support. Thank you for your generosity, inspiration, and knowledge.

Conversations with C. Riley Snorton have been indispensible, teaching me so much, shaping my thinking, and helping to keep me grounded. Cheryl Hicks's comments on the manuscript were invaluable; her astuteness profoundly improved this book. I am grateful for postdoctoral support from the Center for African American Studies (CAAS) at Princeton University. I wish to thank CAAS staff members Carla Hailey Penn, April Peters, and Jennifer Loessy and the remarkable community of guests, fellow visiting scholars, and faculty who I had the great fortune to meet including Daphne Brooks, Eddie Glaude, Tera Hunter, Carina Ray, Noliwe Rooks, and Aishah Shahidah Simmons, Valerie Smith, and Salamishah Tillet. Discussions with Imani Perry and Lyndon K. Gill were particularly helpful, their brilliance matched only by their warmth.

Over the years colleagues, friends, and teachers have influenced this book in profound ways from graduate school to the final days and weeks of my writing. Gretchen Holbrook Gerzina, Diane Harriford, Matthew Frye Jacobson, Gerald Jaynes, Jennifer Baszile, and Michael Denning trained me to think in new ways. I am also indebted to Janet Giarratano, Geneva Melvin, Pat Cabral, and Liza Cariaga-Lo for their consistent encouragement and tremendous work. W. Chris Johnson, Mike Amezcua, Dan Gilbert, Amanda Ciafone, Dara Orenstein, Andrew Friedman, Kenise Lyons, David Huyssen, Suzy Newbury, Tammy Ingram, Calvin Warren, Aaron Carico, Sam Vong, Karilyn Crockett, Tisha Hooks, Adom Getachew, Shatema Threadcraft, Jane Ptolemy, Lara Weibgen, Lindsay Rogers, Lucia Cantero, Zsofia Jilling, Theresa Runstedtler, Brandon Terry, Evans Richardson, and Melissa Stuckey—I so appreciate the vision you offer to the world, not to mention the conversations that sustained me in the rough-and-tumble grad school years.

I am grateful to the Graduate Employees and Students Organization and the New Haven labor movement, especially Anita Seth, Jeffrey Boyd, Stephanie Greenlea, Melissa Mason, Mandi Jackson, and Barbara Vereen, for more organizing lessons than I can count. Thank you for the innumerable pushes and for your transformative work. Working with David Saunders, Mary Reynolds, Ariana Paulson, Eddie Camp, Jackie Kaifesh, Lou Weeks, Latoya Steel, Stephanie Mosley, Brandice Ratliff, Tamika Barton, Sheena McIntosh, Kessha Hughes, Chardé Baggett, and Shirley Lawrence was an incredible honor.

Uri McMillan has been there for the *longue durée* and cross-country moves. I am very grateful for his scholarly voice and friendship. My dear comrade David Stein has taught me so much about justice, trust, and friendship. I am lucky to have benefited from such meaningful scholarly exchange over the years. Friendships with Brandi Hughes, Kimberly Juanita Brown, and Nicole Ivy have made me a better thinker and person. I am always in awe of their grace and genius. My immense gratitude goes to Jennifer S. Leath for loving encouragement, brilliant insight, and no small amount of adventures. Thank you to Stephanie Greenlea for a most powerful friendship on many shifting terrains of struggle.

As a New Yorker who found herself transplanted across the country, it was my good fortune to have encountered exceptional friends and colleagues in Southern California. I am grateful to colleagues in the Gender Studies, African American Studies, and History departments at UCLA, as well as members of the rich community of scholars in the University of California system and beyond including Mishuana Goeman, Michelle Erai, Aisha Finch, Grace Kyungwon Hong, Purnima Mankekar, Kathryn Norberg, Jenny Sharpe, Sharon Traweek, Juliet Williams, Robin D. G. Kelley, Scot Brown, Yogita Goyal, Peter James Hudson, Jemima Pierre, Darnell Hunt, Uri McMillan, Mignon Moore, Melvin Rogers, Mark Sawyer, Chandra Ford, Christine Littleton, Caroline Streeter, Richard Yarborough, Brenda Stevenson, Kelly Lytle Hernandez, Mireille Miller-Young, Noah Zatz, Chris Tilly, Ellen DuBois, Rachel Lee, Jessica Cattelino, Sara Gualtieri, and Diana Williams. I am grateful to have had the opportunity to meet Angela Y. Davis during her visiting lectureship at UCLA, since without her scholarship, this book would surely not exist. Many thanks to Eboni Shaw, Jenna Miller-Von Ah, Richard Medrano, Van Do-Nguyen, and Samantha Hogan for the innumerable ways their exceptional and tireless work has made this book possible. A special thank you to Belinda Tucker, Beth Marchant, and Cheryl I. Harris, for their intellectual vision and institutional work to create and support a very special community of scholars.

I am grateful to Grace Hong, Maylei Blackwell, Yogita Goyal, Dayo Gore, Mishuana Goeman, Kara Keeling, Tiffany Willoughby-Herard, Arlene Keizer, Mignon Moore, Jodi Kim, Sara Clarke Kaplan, and Sarita See for reading my work and strengthening it with suggestions, discussions, and critical questions about this book's major ideas.

In Los Angeles, Lalaie Ameeriar, Lauran Jackson, Kai Green, Claudia Peña, Shana Sojoyner, and Jamila Webb have been great colleagues and friends, supporting this work and keeping me in good spirits along the way. Special thanks to Ashon Crawley, Priscilla Ocen, and Damien Sojoyner for their friendship and beautiful and urgent work. Grace Kyungwon Hong and Aisha Finch have been extraordinary colleagues, valued friends, and brilliant intellectual models. I am profoundly grateful for their mentorship, support, and camaraderie.

Tera Hunter, Dayo Gore, and Robin D. G. Kelley have been especially generous with their time and genius; there are really no words to express my appreciation to them. Thank you for indispensible insights, scholarly visions that have influenced this book profoundly, and for your exceptional kindness. Conversations with Dayo about the practice of history in general and black feminist history in particular have pushed my thinking in important directions. Robin shared his worlds of knowledge, helped me to arrive at critical conclusions, and is a constant source of inspiration. Tera's work is the prized model that changed my trajectory as a scholar; she has given time when her time was precious and her commentary altered this book, sharpening it in ways that would not have been possible without her exacting eye.

My deep thanks to family and friends who have meant so much to me over the years: Victoria Bond, Billy Carey, the Fraziers (Kevin, Reece, and Shane), Sean Fields, Queen GodIs, Sylvia Harris, Shaka King, the Redmonds (Sheryl, Jessie Sr., Jessie Jr., LaDonna, and most especially Alani and Akari), Nicole Sanders, Kristan Sprague, Emma Taati, and the divine Valerie Ann Tuttle have motivated me with their talents and kept me laughing for years and years. I am fortunate to know Deborah Vargas and Erica Edwards, brilliant scholarly models as well as treasured, steadfast friends.

My sisters, Yasmin Cader and Lauren Roberts, bring so much to my life from near and from far; words fail to express how much I adore you and admire your courage, wisdom, and kindness. Thank you to Ellen Glick for having modeled an extraordinary devotion to political transformation.

Shana L. Redmond's brilliance and fearlessness make me imagine new possibilities. Her vision and care make me smarter and more courageous. Thank you for many revelations about love and justice, and for sticking with this book and with me. My family has taught me perseverance and integrity and sustained me with years of love and sacrifice. My father, Michael Haley, has always awed me with his deep commitment to justice and encyclopedic knowledge of political history and literature (not to mention sports). This book is indebted to his teaching and tenacity. Without my aunt, Linda Haley, I would be lost. Thank you for being the sun in dark hours and the swing in my step. This book is for the incomparable Catherine Haley, the strongest, smartest woman I ever did meet; thanks for still listening when I call.

No Mercy Here

Introduction

Let me tell you girls it ain't no mercy here
Lord catching this long line is killing me
It's so many women
Here and so many different kind
Some high yellows but I'm a chocolate Brown.
This long line is killing me.

—ALMA HICKS

I begin by directing the court's attention to the fact that as the
accused in this case, I find myself at an enormous disadvantage.
As a Black woman, I must view my own case in the historical
framework of the fate which has usually been reserved for my
people in America's halls of justice.

—ANGELA Y. DAVIS

"Lula Walker is my name . . . I have a niece who married a drunk and
trifling husband."[1] It was a loving aunt's authoritative assertion, the beginning of a thorough defense predicated upon the possibility of reunion. Lula Walker's niece, Emma Johnson, was convicted of murder
in 1901 and sentenced to a life term in Georgia's Milledgeville State
Prison Farm. Walker kept the grief and desperation she must have felt
during the eight years of her niece's imprisonment out of her correspondence with the state prison commission. Instead, she explained that
there was a "feeling of hatred for the Negro of many of the Whites"
that accompanied the "Freedom of the Negro." This hatred manifested
in the treatment of black women under the law, since "the poor Negro
Woman had no judgement of the lawyers interlect or any control of
a jury and well you know all Jury's are not considered Perfect."[2] Her
scathing critique of U.S. jurisprudence centered its role in the rule, justification, and maintenance of white supremacy and its impact on black
women; yet she offered a layered analysis of jury misjudgment, citing
the case of Vince Sanford, a white man who was acquitted despite ample
evidence that he murdered his wife's lover.[3] If white men enjoyed the
presumption of innocence, Walker wanted the prison commissioners

1

to understand "how often the unfortunate Negro Women may suffer at the hands of a jury." But she hoped "at the hands of the Ga. Pardoning Board she will receive a *fair and just* investigation of her case."[4]

Lula Walker explained in no uncertain terms that Emma Johnson's husband "*often* threatened her life and when he attempted to *kill* her (*She killed him*) and was sent to the State Farm for life."[5] Given this acute and chronic violence, Johnson should have been found not guilty under "Ga. laws [that] plainly says when your life is threatened and you are assaulted with anything the sise of an ordinary marble you may make the fatal blow and it will be Justified Homicide."[6]

In response to her letter Walker received assurance from the secretary of the prison commission that they would "give the same as careful consideration as if you were as white as snow and possessed all of Rockefeller's wealth." Walker was clearly acutely aware of the magnitude of white supremacy and its impact upon black women in particular; still that response had to provide her with some hope that her deliberate and painstaking appeal might free her beloved niece. Perhaps she imagined the day Emma would come home, how they would make up for the eight years they had been apart. Perhaps she envisioned a perfectly set dinner table; perhaps she prepared funny stories from Emma's childhood or thoughtful plans for the future to dull the pain of years of captivity. Lula Walker's careful petition on her niece's behalf suggested that she was a woman of preparation, but all such plans would have to wait. Emma Johnson's petition for parole was denied in 1909; she would not be released on parole until 1915 when her trial judge, W. M. Henry, offered a picture of Johnson that was starkly different from the one Walker had presented. While her aunt described her as a young woman who reasonably acted in self-defense against her husband's potentially deadly violence, Henry opined that she was an "ignorant country girl scarcely more than a child in moral and mental development."[7] Johnson's ignorance was, according to Henry, a mitigating factor, and he supported her release; citing his letter, the prison board granted Johnson's parole after she had served fourteen years in a place that might aptly be called Miseryville. On parole she would have to work as a live-in domestic servant for a white family, still under the custody of the prison authority; she would not escape the clutches of carceral supervision until her sentence was commuted in 1916.

Lula Walker's letter and Emma Johnson's case highlight how black women's experiences within Georgia's punishment system constituted them as subjects outside of the protected category "woman." The maintenance of this racial-gendered order is vital to a nuanced understanding of the southern carceral regime and the history of Jim Crow modernity. The state institutionalized gendered racial terror as a technology of white supremacist control, and often this state violence compounded intraracial intimate abuse that they faced in their homes. State violence alongside gendered forms of labor exploitation made the New South possible, not as a departure from the Old, but as a reworking and extension of previous structures of captivity and abjection through gendered capitalism.

This book reveals how the criminal legal system crafted, reinforced, and required black female deviance as part of the broader constitution of Jim Crow modernity premised upon the devaluation and dehumanization of black life broadly. Moreover, *No Mercy Here* excavates black women's confrontations with the carceral state, challenging the knowledge it produced and, in some cases, dismantling its infrastructure. This sabotage practice was more than a reaction against the convict labor regime's physical and symbolic violence. Through letters, blues creations, and everyday acts of resistance they established a vision of a different world. Lula Walker hoped that by exposing how black women's claims to vulnerability and the bodily autonomy were denied through racial bias and the deprivation of legal resources she might convince a hostile audience that her niece deserved reprieve. Her careful but brazen letter is but one of many freedom transcripts that this book excavates in order to illuminate both the mobilization of ferocious state violence and the vigorous efforts to reject the world that such violence sought to create. This book blends a history of ideology with social history in order to shed greater light on the development of systems of terror, structures of economic and political subordination, and hidden dimensions of working-class African American women's lives.

No Mercy Here traces criminalized women in legal proceedings, in jails, in mixed-gender and all-women's convict camps, in chain gangs, at Milledgeville State Prison Farm, on parole, and in the popular imaginary. Following the Civil War prisoners were contracted out to private individuals and companies to labor under heinous conditions on railroads, turpentine farms, plantations, brickyards, sawmills, in coal mines, and in broom-making camps. State authorities also forced women and men convicted of violating local laws to clean, pave, and maintain city streets. There was virtually no oversight of convict camp conditions and private individuals charged with managing these camps had full reign to abuse and exploit prisoners and their labor. Violence abounded, imprisoned women and men suffered injuries and died of beatings, disease, neglect, and overwork.

This system of convict leasing was eliminated in 1908 and replaced with a successor, the chain gang, and the apple did not fall far from the tree. On chain gangs women and men convicted of crimes were forced to labor on county roads under the direct control and supervision of county authorities. There was no longer a diverse array of convict labor industries in Georgia, yet infrastructural development continued to depend upon the labor of prisoners and conditions for imprisoned women and men remained atrocious. On the chain gang death was ubiquitous, brutality and illness were omnipresent, and prisoners were forced to work from sunup to deep dark. Private individuals and companies continued to benefit from the labor of prisoners, as commerce was supported through modernized roads. Moreover, a gendered system of labor exploitation emerged in 1908, under which imprisoned women were forced to work for private white families before their prison sentences were complete. This system of gendered and racialized economic exploitation and social control helped to maintain the notion that a white woman's social and economic role was as domestic manager, a position perceived to be necessary for capitalist expansion. The new system established a public-private partnership whereby both state employees and ordinary women became wardens, controlling the social lives, labors, and futures of imprisoned African American women.

In addition to municipal, county, and state convict camps and a privatized regime of domestic prisons women and men in Georgia were also sent to Milledgeville, in the central part of the state. There, hundreds of women were imprisoned and made to perform grueling agricultural labor and endured rampant violence and subhuman conditions. While black women were imprisoned far less often than black men, they, unlike their white female counterparts, were not shielded from the punishment regime. White women were rarely imprisoned in Georgia and almost never sent to convict lease camps or chain gangs. In the rare instances in which they were given such punishment they often received special treatment, better conditions, and earlier release. From 1908 until 1936 black women were virtually the only female prisoners on the chain gang.[8]

To understand such staggering violence, this book investigates the role of gender ideology in the development of gendered racial capitalism. *No Mercy Here* examines the mutually constitutive role of race and gender in constructing subject positions, technologies of violence, understandings of the social order, and the construction and application of the law. Put another way, this book seeks to excavate the carceral life of race and gender ideology, how such ideas produced, and were produced by, the southern penal regime. The mutually constitutive role of race and gender is evidenced at every historical turn. Illuminating the experiences of previously marginalized historical actors is undeniably and inherently important; however, the intention of this book is not merely to add to the history of convict labor by centering women, but rather to discover how black women's experiences and gendered logics of punishment nuance the history of southern economic, political, and social life. Imprisoned women are important to the history of white supremacy and the southern penal regime, not merely because they were there, but because their cases and lives represented the terrain of an ideological contest that transcended the penal world.

At stake in this conflict was gender ideology, the maintenance of white supremacy, the shape and substance of modern southern identity after 1865, the development of Jim Crow, and black women's freedom. Gender ideology created the condition of possibility for the existence of the chain gang, as white women's protection was codified in the law establishing chain gangs. This penal legislation reinforced prevailing cultural ideas about gender roles and social positions, and in exposing black women to extreme violence the singular status of white womanhood—indeed the racially specific definition of womanhood—was reasserted. The carceral system exposed and enforced the radical otherness of the black female subject, thereby solidifying white women's particular gender formation.

The late nineteenth and early twentieth centuries were critical periods in the development of gender and sexual ideology. The emergence of new modes of sexual classification, the continued deployment of white feminine sexual vulnerability as the most explosive sign of white supremacy, narratives of racial-sexual excess as justification for lynching and political subordination, all mark the period's complex and calcifying gendered-racial-sexual order.[9] But ideas about imprisoned black women were also significant in this long moment of ideological and social development, specifically with regard to notions of sexual antinormativity. As "queer" came to mean "Queer," the black female body's arrested and arresting deviance was reinforced through the carceral political domain. As chapter 2 reveals, imprisoned black women were labeled queer in the years immediately preceding the word being used to describe homosexual desire and homosexuals.[10] The imprisoned black female subject was, in some ways, one vestibule to queerness; she was "the principal point of passage between the human and the non-human world" or "the route by which the dominant modes decided the distinction between humanity and 'other.'"[11] Gender and sexual categorization were critical to this project of human categorization, and this study examines the discursive and material process by which imprisoned black women became a point of passage between what was normative and what was queer.

In this moment, the invert was a "newly created object of study" in sexology, which increasingly focused on examinations of the body to determine sexual normativity and deviance. In this medical discourse, black women's sexual organs were consistently characterized as abnormal, less sexually differentiated than white women's, and therefore evolutionarily retrograde.[12] If the black female body was rendered queer in medical discourses, carceral understandings of black women also positioned her as a social, cultural, and political invert. Through policing, legislation, and judicial enforcement, black women were made juridical inverts: perverse, primitive, and pathological, and therefore unentitled to protection or freedom. Carceral institutions and concomitant ideologies evacuated the black female subject of her claim to the body, much less bodily protection, and in so doing produced a codified white female subject defined by bodily sanctity.[13] Carceral gendering reveals that gendered knowledge is produced not merely through male/female binaries but also through a complex of material and discursive knowledge projects; normative female gendering was produced through the spectacular cultural and legal production of the black female invert as a relational and trammeled social category defined by deviant motherhood, physical grotesqueness, the capacity for hard labor, the impossibility of sexual, emotional, and physical injury, mental inferiority, and disposability. Carceral practice contributed significantly to modernity configured through complex, relative, and relational gendered and sexual positionalities.[14] Perhaps the most salient and predictable feature of black female categorization was the "locus of both unredressed and negligible injury," raising the question of whether "unredressed injury" is itself a gender category and to what extent it is constituent of queerness.[15] If we consider the possibility that unredressed injury constituted a gender category of its own, black women's resistance to violation was more than a movement for bodily protection (although the importance of that cannot be overstated); such resistance was a contestation and re-shaping of gender categorization, a recognition of black female queer-ness as a structuring logic of American society. While unredressed and negligible violation plagued black women's lives, the attributes of black female categorization were incoherent. At once considered sexual and asexual; ideal objects of domestic, industrial, and agricultural labor; shrewdly criminal and daft; maternal and infanticidal; domestically ser-vile and disruptive, docile and irreverent, the black female subject was constituted through a series of contradictions that throw stable subject categorization into chaos.[16] Yet this instability was a resource for the con-solidation of an opposing stable, coherent, legible juridical subject—"white woman"—in popular and legal contexts; this was constantly managed and reproduced through prosecutorial discretion, judicial decision making, and penal policy.

The chapters that follow demonstrate the role of the southern pe-nal regime in the construction of racially determined and defined gen-dered subject positions during a long historical era in which segregation took hold. As a history of ideology, *No Mercy Here* demonstrates that the legal cases of black women like Emma Johnson represented a cul-tural battleground in a contest over gendered and racial constructions of humanity. Where Lula Walker asserted her niece's status as a human being with a right to protect her own life in the context of domestic violence, W. M. Henry represented her as morally and intellectually un-derdeveloped and lacking the characteristics of full humanity. Emma Johnson was not an anomaly. Her depiction and her experience of the most intimate terms of patriarchal and state violence will become all too familiar as the chapters that follow unfold. Like slavery, convict labor "configured and structured social and legal boundaries of both race and gender," physically and epistemologically, as knowledge about black women assumed the character of property, material through which to politically and economically structure the modern South.[17]

In this regime women's lives were profoundly altered by their expe-rience of punishment. They faced violence of an order that is unrepre-sentable. I do not claim (or attempt) to be able to depict the magnitude or depth of pain that black women endured. Yet this book does seek to ex-plain (more than describe) the necessity of violence against black women's bodies in the maintenance of white supremacy as an ideological, economic, and political order during a period of rapid historical transition. Recent historical work has engaged cultural theorist Hazel V. Carby's powerful claim that "the institutionalized rape of black women has never been as powerful a symbol of black oppression as the spectacle of lynching" by providing historical analyses of the ways in which violence against African American women was central to U.S. history.[18] Yet new insights about this history remain to be uncovered. In so doing this study fits within a vital scholarly conversation about the centrality of women and gender in histories of racial violence.[19] Gendered racial terror encompassed a range of violent practices that were routinely inflicted upon black women's bodies, but from which white women's bodies were almost always exempt. The history of gendered racial terror contains slippages and contradictions. There were instances of white women being sentenced to convict lease camps, for example, a fact that distinguishes incarceration from slavery. However these cases were rare, fleeting, and immediately became the source of outrage in popular discussion. In such instances in which white female bodies were violated the situations were "rectified." White women were released early, prison authorities were scandalized, special living quarters were offered, and laws were changed. Gender ideology was constructed and reiterated through discourses of protection.

No Mercy Here does not argue that white women were the ultimate beneficiaries of the racial constructions of gender that shaped punishment policy, since their protection from the regime's worst features also made their captivity at the state farm (albeit in very small numbers) socially acceptable. However "woman" did become a property right and a privilege in the context of southern punishment. I am also not arguing that the fundamental problem of this history was black women's exclusion from womanhood, as if to say that the course of historical events would have been more just if normative femininity had been able to encompass blackness. Far from contending that woman is a category into which more people should have been included, the goal of this book is to demonstrate that gender is constructed by and through race, and that the production of woman and other stable gender categories required violence. Carceral institutions shaped constructions of gender not merely by distinguishing women from men, but by sedimenting invented taxonomies of female subjects with race as the vestibule of absolute difference, a fixed dividing line that constructs gender.

In popular discourse, newspapers, courtroom testimony, legislation, and clemency rulings the black female juridical invert was given a range of labels including ignorant, violent, criminal, lascivious, negligent, and grotesque, all of which defied the animating characteristics of woman-hood. Black female subjects were produced outside of the binary cat-egories of woman and man. This does not mean that they were always treated as men; in fact they specifically were forced to end their prison terms as domestic servants for white families. Yet black women's dispro-portionate presence in spheres of domestic carceral servitude did not place them closer to normative femininity, since the relation of servant to employer also served to expose black women's difference from the white women for whom they worked. Moreover, as part of their prison sentences black women were consistently positioned in proximity to masculinity, forced to perform hard labor that was rarely mandated for white women, even those few white women who were in convict camps alongside black women. The flexibility of the black female subject, the ability of white patriarchs to relegate her into the harshest labor spheres both in and outside the home but always under the condition of violence, helped define modern social relations under Jim Crow. The malleabil-ity of the black female subject in the white imagination reinforced the fixity of the white female subject and her traditional social role as po-litically, economically, and socially subordinate to white men.

This analysis traces women's experiences of imprisonment, the racial construction of gender, and gendered racial terror over space and time. The convict camp is perhaps the most discrete place of all, a site of con-tainment predicated upon the certainty of borders. This analysis focuses on specific places: jails, prisons, convict camps, and chain gangs; follow-ing theorist Dylan Rodriguez this book explores the prison as a regime, "a dynamic state-mediated practice of domination and control, rather than a reified 'institution' or 'apparatus.'"[20] Carcerality was a practice and, often, a performance. At the core of this conception of prison as re-gime is the understanding that it generates "a technology of domination that exceeds the narrow boundaries of that very same juridical-carceral structure."[21] The parameters of subjection technologized through the carceral state reached far beyond "its announced material boundaries and juridical limits," instead structuring and constituting the state writ large through a regime of neoslavery.[22] Assault and destruction of the body in specific contexts (riots, scaffolds, penal camps) were fundamen-tal tools in the construction of white civil society, white human value, and white personhood more broadly.

Time in this account is marked by the creation of a new, industrial-ized, and urban South. The New South was a political, economic, and cultural formation shaped by disfranchisement, a rapid increase in white women's participation in the paid workforce, labor unrest, black migration, extralegal violence; and segregation. Gender's strange career contributed to the development of Jim Crow. Under slavery black women were legally designated as property, not women, and gender was elusive and unstable. Emancipation brought a shift in the legal status of black people marked by a moment of limited enfranchisement that was followed soon after by conflagrations of extralegal violence, disfranchisement, and the retrenchment of blacks as noncitizens. The disavowal of black citizenship and humanity following Reconstruction was both a legal and cultural development, and gender was central to the process of establishing black inhumanity after the Civil War.

While African American women were a minority of prisoners in Georgia's convict lease camps and chain gangs, their very presence there, along with the regimes of violence and popular representations to which they were subject, reveals the gendered logics and imperatives of southern punishment.[23] The time of this history then, is the long moment of black women's political, legal, and social transformation from de facto deviants to de jure nonwomen, which occurred, like segregation, in response to shifts and strains in the cultural and political economy of the South, which made legal clarity a necessary feature for the maintenance of white supremacy. Between 1880 and 1920, rigid cultural, legal, and social structures of segregation were systematically imposed in cities and towns across the South, ultimately consolidating into an entrenched racial caste system. C. Vann Woodward's *The Strange Career of Jim Crow* grounds much of the discussion about the development of segregation in the South, arguing that Jim Crow was neither inevitable nor immediate, but rather developed in the last two decades of the nineteenth century as a response to key factors, most importantly economic depression and the threat of interracial populist cooperation and sociopolitical movements. Historians including Neil McMillen, Howard Rabinowitz, Grace Hale, Leon Litwack, and Glenda Gilmore have built upon Woodward's now classic thesis by demonstrating that Jim Crow was also profoundly a response to black political and social movements for equality.[24] Gilmore's intervention is critical to this book as she situates African American women as central actors in this era, demonstrating that gender ideology and resistance to black women's activism undergirded white supremacy.

No Mercy Here centers black women's experiences of southern punishment as part of the process of consolidating Jim Crow, understanding the period as a specific (albeit long) moment bounded by the late nineteenth and late twentieth centuries as well as an order; modernity refers less to a specific geopolitical location or historical period than to a contested and complex process of becoming that is linked to an imagined social and political future. Modernity, in this context, was characterized by the cultural, economic, and social formation constituted by the experience of living amidst rapid change or discontinuity, shifts in class relations brought about by the transition from agrarian to industrial economies, and the attendant ruptures or fragmentations of identity that these shifts produced. If modernity can be defined, at least in part, as the tension between autonomy and fragmentation, this definition applies to the Jim Crow South, where black political organizing, white women's increased independence, black migration, and labor conflict challenged assertions of absolute white collective autonomy.[25] White women's burgeoning participation in the paid labor market at the turn of the century figures prominently in this analysis, as it threatened traditional patriarchal relations in the industrializing South and made it necessary to reify their traditional roles through a discourse and penal practice that emphasized their absolute difference from black women. Working white women in the South, "it seemed, were threatening family life; wage-earning daughters were prone to promiscuity or vulnerable to abuse."[26] In short, southern white women's participation in the paid labor force threatened the white patriarchal status quo grounded in ideals of domesticity and chastity. This development, alongside black women's migration to the urban North, was a profound threat to white supremacist patriarchy, and legal and cultural discourses of protection for white women convicted of crimes responded to these tensions.

Black women's treatment under the carceral state was critical to these racial and gendered political, social, and economic contingencies.[27] Jim Crow modernity was produced through a nexus of the material and ideological, the appropriation of bodies and the consolidation of gendered and racially specific notions of the human. Modernity, a structure of power "shaping material and epistemological conditions of life and thought" into which black people were conscripted, "coercively obliged to render themselves its objects and its agents," had to be perpetually reasserted and reinforced precisely because of imprisoned women's contestation of their conscription.[28] As Georgia developed from an agricultural, plantation-based economy to an industrial one, gendered racial terror fortified white patriarchal control over economic, political, and social relations, thereby enshrining Jim Crow modernity.

Convict labor provided the resources for southern modernization, the development of its public and private infrastructure.[29] After 1908 the chain gang literally paved the way (through massive county road construction) for perhaps the most significant icon of American modernity: the automobile. The percentage of surfaced roads in Georgia increased from 3 percent to 7.27 percent between 1904 and 1909, and would increase to 15.5 percent by 1914.[30] This rapidly expanding infrastructure-building process was continued, indeed escalated, through the 1930s and early 1940s through the Works Progress Administration infrastructure projects.[31] The criminalization of black women and their use as labor resources for the development of the infrastructure of the modern Jim Crow state built by convict labor has received little scholarly attention. However in recent years historians have produced exciting new work on economic development, urbanization, and the criminalization of African American women, constituting a critical field of black feminist carceral history.[32]

Kali Gross's groundbreaking analysis of African American women and crime in Philadelphia unveiled new facets of working-class women's material and social lives through the lens of the penal system, examining the crimes for which they were arrested in order to provide new knowledge about both popular representations of black women, their political and economic marginalization, and their resourceful participation in illicit economies in order to improve their living conditions and acquire greater autonomy over their lives.[33] Cheryl Hicks's seminal work also interrogates the social and economic lives of black women who faced arrest and imprisonment, while examining the inner lives of working-class black women, providing dramatically new insight into their ideas about respectability, morality, and "feminine dignity."[34] Hazel V. Carby's influential analysis of black women as the subject of "moral panics" in the industrializing North has shaped the conceptual framework of this project, which considers such panics in the development of modernizing Georgia. No Mercy Here contributes analyses of the South to a broader and growing field of black feminist carceral history.[35] Such scholarship delineates a gendered carceral landscape, offering new interpretations of the experience of carceral violence, the contours of black women's historical lives, and the role of gendered racial regulation in historical regimes of punishment.

The symbolic centrality of Georgia to New South economic progress narratives was displayed through the International Cotton Exposition in 1881 and at the 1895 Cotton States and International Exposition. The latter aimed to facilitate and exhibit interstate southern trade and economic infrastructure, but perhaps it gains greatest historical significance as the site for Booker T. Washington's "Atlanta Compromise" speech that touted the dignity, even glory, of African American "common labour" and a future in which the races could be "as separate as the fingers, yet one as the hand in all things essential to mutual progress."[36] Washington's capitulation to market forces and racist ideologies situates Georgia as a beacon of both the Old and New South: the slave state that becomes the glittering symbol of economic advancement premised upon segregation. Dominant gender ideology would also configure Georgia's status as a symbol of Old and New South via a model of white femininity that extended through the early twentieth century, with its ultimate representation in Margaret Mitchell's bestselling novel, *Gone With the Wind* (1936), seared in the American consciousness through its Oscar-laden smash-hit film adaptation. W. E. B. Du Bois turned to Georgia as the focus of his trenchant critique of convict labor and the southern legal system in his 1904 study *Some Notes on Negro Crime Particularly in Georgia* and in *The Souls of Black Folk* he argued with respect to Georgia, "In many other respect, both now and yesterday, the Negro problems have seemed to be centered in this State."[37]

The point is not that Georgia is exceptional or that it holds a uniquely important place in southern history, but that it figured centrally in ideas about the economic, social, and political future of the South. African American women were critical to Georgia's economy, as Atlanta "held the distinction of employing one of the highest per capita numbers of domestic workers in the nation" from the late nineteenth through the early twentieth century.[38] Beginning in the late nineteenth century white women entered the paid labor market in rapid numbers and while black women remained relegated to domestic service work well into the twentieth century, new opportunities for white women emerged in various industries including garment, candy, box making, and textile mills.[39] As a study concerned with working-class black women's interior lives, social and material experiences, refusals of white supremacy, and knowledge production, *No Mercy Here* is profoundly indebted to Tera

Hunter's *To 'Joy My Freedom: Southern Black Women's Lives and Labors after the Civil War*. Not only does this account rely on Hunter's detailed exploration of all of these themes but it is conceptually indebted to the book's definitive demonstration of black women's economic, social, and political centrality to southern modernity. Georgia's prominence in the southern imaginary makes its ideological infrastructure as important as its political economy. Development was figured and configured through black female deviance and violation, undermining "a theory of modernization that equates the development of a society's productive forces with the notion of progress" and instead illuminating the grounding of modernity in unfreedom.[40] African American clubwomen recognized the importance of imprisoned black women in a New South premised upon the violences of the old, and they focused their attention on Georgia to make their case that a southern economy that relied upon convict leasing was a form of gendered and racial barbarism. Indeed, it was the vigorous agitation and urgent analysis of clubwomen including Selena Sloan Butler and Mary Church Terrell that led me to Georgia as the site through which to examine women's experiences under the convict lease system. Their searing critique of gendered racial terror and state violence in Georgia, in the place meant to epitomize a new era of southern economic and political relations, introduced me to this study.

Despite the considerable record of convict labor abuses, examining the lives of imprisoned black women entails incredible challenges. The hundreds of clemency cases, whipping ledgers, medical and police dockets, and annual prison reports that referenced black women's imprisonment in chain gangs and convict camps, which comprise the foundation of this book, present a brutal conundrum. Saidiya Hartman has argued that "to read the archive is to enter a mortuary," since it reproduces the social death of certain subjects through the erasure of interior desires, beliefs, sentiments, and thought pathways, relegating them to objects of torture, annotations on a ledger.[41] The archive circumscribed the knowledge I was seeking; documents written by imprisoned women were mediated by their audience, largely prison authorities; other historical actors (judges, penal authorities, police, journalists) who produced the reports, legislation, observations, and rulings that constitute much of my evidence disregarded or perpetrated violence against the subjects of this book. The practice in this book is to read along the archival grain of death and destruction, as well as against it, to uncover and imagine black women's social and interior lives and intellectual contributions. This task will necessarily be incomplete.

The chapters that follow proceed chronologically, but are also organized around several themes including popular representation, patterns of arrest, labor and punishment conditions, reproduction, gendered racial violence, reform, domestic violence, domestic servitude, and a range of imprisoned women's carceral sabotage practices. The first two chapters deal primarily with the period from 1868 to 1908, during which Georgia maintained the convict leasing system as its primary method of punishment. Chapter 1 traces patterns in the popular representation of criminalized black and white women alongside the criminalization of particular acts they were alleged to have committed. Chapter 2 also focuses on the convict leasing era, and analyzes productive and reproductive labor, and the logic and practice of gendered racial terror. Georgia's convict labor system was a complex web of city, county, and state convict camps, and in each of these domains black women faced a double burden of both labor and violence. Chapter 2 details women's experiences within all of these carceral realms.

Chapter 3 turns to the sexual politics of black and white women's anticonvict-leasing activism at the turn of the twentieth century. The significance of imprisoned women in the ideologies of black and white clubwomen is illuminated through the strategies of three women and their organizations: Selena Sloan Butler and Mary Church Terrell of the National Association of Colored Women and Rebecca Latimer Felton of the Woman's Christian Temperance Union (WCTU). In their anticonvict-leasing activism black women constructed a critique of state violence that highlighted the rape of black female prisoners. Rebecca Latimer Felton and the WCTU performed evangelical prison work and lobbied the state legislature, calling for the elimination of convict leasing. Yet Felton's sexual politics and attention to imprisoned black women were filtered through a greater concern and outrage about the issue of interracial sex and her conception of black female lasciviousness and inherent amorality.

Chapter 4 is organized around watershed change in Georgia's criminal legal system, albeit change that did not bring better conditions for those in its convict camps. The abolition of convict leasing in 1908 gave way to the chain gang, implemented through several key penal reforms that codified the preexisting racial definition of womanhood. Chapter 4 also traces black women's experiences of domestic violence and follows those who were paroled from Milledgeville State Prison Farm to the domestic carceral sphere, where they were forced to labor as servants for private individuals. Women were subject to reimprisonment at Milledgeville for any transgression; their letters are profound elucidations of parole as carceral space, demonstrating the carceral state's reach beyond the discrete institution of the prison.

I end with a consideration of women's sabotage praxes both in and beyond Georgia as well as their conceptual and physical practices of dismantling the punishment regime. Blues created by imprisoned and nonimprisoned women are central to this consideration as critiques of punishment imbued black women's popular blues as well as a rare set of recordings by black women imprisoned at Parchman Penitentiary in Mississippi. The women in this chapter reimagined modern society, positioning punishment not as a natural or necessary prerequisite for its development, but as an obstacle to their independence, sexual, and economic freedom. Their critiques of the legal system were incredibly complex precursors to critical race feminism that would emerge more than forty years later. Black women's punishment-themed blues contested dominant southern narratives about the nature of modernity and the nature of punishment. While this chapter reveals that imprisoned black women sometimes escaped, waged work slowdowns, and other forms of defiance, their contestation of the meaning of modernity was, perhaps, their most significant sabotage practice.

Summary
chapter

CHAPTER ONE

Carceral Constructions of Black Female Deviance

> It was early this mornin' that I had my trial
> It was early this mornin' that I had my trial
> Ninety days on the county road and the judge didn't even smile.
>
> —GERTRUDE "MA" RAINEY

Eliza Cobb was born at the dawn of emancipation in 1866, yet in her life there was little respite from captivity or the agony of conditions wrought by white supremacy. At age twenty-two Cobb was raped and became pregnant, and when she felt the pangs of childbirth one early November morning in 1889 she fled to the outhouse of the home where she lived with her mother, terrified and alone. She gave birth "at stool" on the floor of the outhouse, between sharp devices, tools, and debris.[1]

Police alleged that she killed her baby, and as a result she was arrested and convicted of infanticide in 1889.[2] She was sent to Du Bois sawmill camp situated in the southern pine belt, a region which produced a third of the nation's lumber laborers. At the Du Bois camp, workers had to cut down trees and saw lumber from sunup to sundown. Eliza Cobb would have the dubious distinction of being one of the very few female lumber workers in the South.[3] Eventually, Cobb was transferred to Georgia's Milledgeville State Prison Farm where black women performed arduous field labor. Many of the women with whom she lived at the prison farm had experienced the deprivation, violence, and agonizing labor of plantation life under slavery. Now they now found themselves under the gun, lash, and debilitating grind of farm labor under white control in freedom's aftermath. In their younger fellow prisoners, like fourteen-year-old Mary Lou Fears, they saw dashed dreams of a future in which black girls would never know such deadly relations of violence and exploitation.[4]

From the beginning Cobb maintained her innocence. Her mother had a violent temper and died in a mental institution while Cobb was in prison. To avoid her mother's fury Cobb hid her pregnancy, so when the contractions came she went into the outhouse to give birth alone. What happened next was the source of contestation at trial. She said the baby was stillborn, but the state garnered a conviction based upon one piece of evidence: the coroner's testimony that the baby had died of a stab wound to the head. Although the "evidence against her was wholly circumstantial," she, like other black women in Georgia, was imprisoned because she could not combat the burden of guilt that guided all-white juries in infanticide cases.

Cobb was convicted and spent the better part of her youth cutting and hauling lumber and driving carts and plowing under the most heinous conditions imaginable until she was "hardly able to be of much more service to the state."[5] After her body was so badly injured from the work and "a growth upon the back of her neck" was "gradually getting larger and larger" so that it would "eventually cause her death unless something [was] done to check it," the coroner who had testified during her trial reemerged.[6] He admitted in an affidavit to the Prison Commission that "he had thought about it since the trial," and was unsure about his original conclusion. Now he believed that Cobb was likely telling the truth: the baby was probably stillborn and the wound he found could have been imposed postmortem, inflicted perhaps by a nail in the outhouse where the child was found.[7] Armed with this new evidence along with verification of her unprofitability, favorable letters from prison administrators attesting to her model behavior, and supportive petitions from the original jurors who convicted her, Cobb submitted requests for a commutation of her sentence. But her clemency petition was denied in 1907 and again in 1909.

Finally in 1910 her advocates crafted a different clemency strategy and submitted a new application. The audience for her request was G. R. Hutchins, chairman of the Prison Commission of Georgia, and Governor Joseph M. Brown, who took office in June 1909 and who had to approve the chairman's clemency recommendations. Although prison guards and administrators aided in Cobb's attempt to be pardoned from Milledgeville, these actions could not redress the harm of her twenty years of captivity, the harm of physical, psychic, and sexual violation she endured during her imprisonment as a penal laborer. Redress was not even at issue in the production of her clemency case. If will and intent were the central issues in her conviction, these considerations would emerge again in her clemency struggle. Various officials presented Cobb as daft and hopeless, lacking the capability and even the will required in order to kill her child, and appealed for leniency based

Photograph of Eliza Cobb. Courtesy of the Georgia Archives, Morrow, Georgia, RG 1-4-42, image ah00962.

upon diminished capacity. To prove this they provided a new piece of evidence in her 1910 materials: a photograph.

In their joint letter to the state Prison Commission the warden, matron, guards, and prison physician wrote that they hoped her likeness, "recently taken," would give some idea of her facial defect. J. Matthews, the ordinary of Upson County where Cobb was convicted, in his list of mitigating issues noted that she was "very badly burnt about the face" and "her mind was not as strong as the average negro's."[8]

Although officials went to unusual lengths to document deformity in Cobb's case, the discourse about her deviance, ugliness, and ignorance was not exceptional. Her description as a "horrible-looking person" may have been attributed to an accident, but it was part of a larger pattern of black female representation.[9] Black women's bodies were similarly portrayed in letters from convict lease guards and overseers as well as journalistic descriptions and cartoons. Perceived ugliness was one attribute that defined black women's deviance from the category "woman" and justified their imprisonment and assault during the nadir of American race relations, from the end of Reconstruction through the Progressive Era. Black women's perceived status as deranged subjects proved to be the fertile ideological ground upon which constructions of normative gender positions flourished.

Eliza Cobb was only legible to white authorities as an imbecilic, monstrous body, and the success of her application for pardon from the state penal farm depended upon the ability of her advocates to appeal to this preconception. According to her advocates she lacked the essential traits of personhood and normative femininity—a capacity for language (her clemency records do not include documents in her own words), beauty, consciousness, submissiveness, maternalism, purity, and moral deliberation.[10] Degrading discourses about Cobb's alleged lack of intelligence and homeliness were key to her clemency case, inflicting grave injury as part of the process of her "freeing." White lawyers and prison officials crafted her application for pardon based upon the attributes that, to them, made Eliza Cobb intelligible as a racialized subject— disfigurement and idiocy. Her sex was invoked but in the carceral narrative she bore no resemblance to woman, "True" or not. Convict labor was a system through which to prove black female deviance from these characteristics; ironically this proof was deployed toward the end of both conviction and clemency. Cobb's freedom depended on an appeal to white supremacy that reinforced her position as "other," specifically, other-than-woman. Her experience provides evidence that juridical power actually produces what it seems to represent.[11]

The iconic image of convict labor is a photograph of a group of men at work. Cobb's portrait encourages a different understanding of convict labor in which the fraught and contradictory category of gender is central. Her representation raises perhaps more questions than answers about the production of gender categories in the postbellum South. Her long dress, which might generally signify conformity to normative standards of modest womanhood, is prominently marked by stripes that reflect the hyperimprisonability of black women and their gender deviance. Cobb's position as captive and utterly abject is emphasized by her location and backdrop. Her back is literally up against the brick wall of a prison that held black people almost exclusively and she is holding a work-related tool, reinforcing her status as disposable laborer.

The ambiguity of her expression reinforces the strategy of her final, successful appeal, which was that she was meant to evince only ugliness, not sentience. Her sentence was commuted in September 1910.

The discourse surrounding Cobb's image illustrates the limits of human legibility for black female subjects, who could be both literally and figuratively captured because they were perceived to so profoundly deviate from the norms of white femininity. In the white imaginary "black woman" was an oxymoronic formulation because the modifier "black" rejected everything associated with the universal "woman." The black female subject occupied a paradoxical, embattled, and fraught position, a productive negation that produced normativity. She was an invention of a white supremacist imaginary defined in part by subjection to extreme violence and terror. In popular press accounts black women were often referred to as negresses, female but altogether distinct and anathema to the construction of normative womanhood. The terms "negro woman" and "negress" were often used in the same article, sometimes in the same paragraph, and reflect an uneasy, antagonistic relationship between blackness and femininity in the white popular imagination.

It was rare for prison administrators to take photographs of women inside Milledgeville as evidence for clemency applications. However the representation of abjection in Cobb's photograph is rendered even clearer when considered alongside the image of a white female prisoner named Martha Gault, also contained within her clemency record and also mobilized for executive leniency.

Wanton Meets Woman

In 1923 Martha Gault was charged with assault with the intent to murder, theft of an automobile, and an offense so grave it colloquially signifies the worst sort of theft and criminal behavior: she committed highway robbery. She was given a five-year sentence to be served at Milledgeville. No one denied that she beat the driver of the car with a pipe before she and her male accomplice stole the vehicle. According to the judge, the crime was so grave that it was "impossible for the human intelligence to entertain any idea of clemency or even leniency after reading the record in this case."[12] In fact, he had never "prosecute[d] for a more deliberate and wanton offense than this was."[13]

This was damning judicial commentary, and therefore her case for clemency required strong mitigating evidence. Martha Gault's photograph provided decisive proof of her submissive character necessary to counter the aggravated nature of her crime. Her likeness is clear, and her smile is apparent. The partial figure of a companion situated her sentimentally within the realm of feminine friendships and her proximity to a pet reinforced, through distinction, Gault's humanity.[14] Although the photograph was taken at the state farm, the shot makes it difficult to ascertain whether she is inside or outside of the prison, an ambiguity that signaled her fitness for freedom. It was unassailable femininity rendered visually. Although the photograph may have been worth a thousand words, the rich narrative of subjectification was there as well. Despite the judge's indicting statement about the aggravated nature of the offense, he reflected, "it remains only for an appeal to conscience and to the sense of humanity that we all have, to avail anything in the interest of this party." Although he knew nothing of her parentage, the judge conceded that she was worth redeeming on the grounds that it might be possible to make her a "good and useful woman."[15] What was once "wanton" became "woman" and in order to rehabilitate her womanhood, freedom was in his opinion "far better for society than to keep her in servitude at her age, consequently if you determine from the showing made before you that such would be the probable result of the exercise of the pardon to her, I recommend that the same be done."[16] Milledgeville's warden J. E. Smith offered his opinion that she was "not in class with the girls who are serving sentences here and she stays away from them as much as is possible for her to do," while the prison matron argued in a four-page letter to the Prison Commission and governor that she was "bright," "deserved to be in school," and had "no bad habits."[17] In fact, she was "of a very modest and refined nature" and with a bit of training would make "a splendid woman and good citizen."[18] Her sentence was commuted to present service in December 1825, after she had served two years of her five-year sentence.

Eliza Cobb was Martha Gault's antipode. The judge's assessment of Gault powerfully exposes the polarity between black and white women, categorically opposed yet entangled in constructions of reason, freedom, and subjectivity. In the cases of Cobb and Gault, both crimes were perceived as heinous, but while Cobb's crime was associated with innate qualities and physical depravity—monstrosity and idiocy—Gault was cast as the victim of bad male influence. It was the trial judge's opinion that "this girl was more or less under the dominion of her companion and that but for him she could not have planned and executed

Photograph of Martha Gault. Courtesy of the Georgia Archives, Morrow, Georgia, RG 1-4-42, image ah00964.

this crime."[19] Cobb's distance from womanhood was at the heart of her alleged crime, the murder of a child whose sex is never mentioned. Yet this distance remains since her innocence (and possibility of redemption as a true mother) could not be the premise for her pardon. Instead, it was her inability to care and her physical repugnance that provided the discursive material for a legitimate clemency claim. In sharp contrast, Gault's redemptive femininity is constituted through her relationship to a domineering man. She is infantilized through a discourse of innocence, as the victim of an older man and as a girl whose future was uncertain but potentially auspicious. Her future environment mattered. Circumstances, conditions, and domination all mattered in Martha Gault's case, while the relevant facts of Eliza Cobb's case consisted of corporeal attributes. Gault's plight appealed to the "conscience and sense of humanity that we all have." The judge's invocation of concern in terms of a universal "we" and a presumed universal sense of humanity both masks and creates the possibility for a production of personhood understood in specifically racial and gendered terms. The assumption of universality forged bonds of commonality between the judge and his white male audience, the governor and prison commissioners. Although race was never mentioned the justification for concern was white feminine vulnerability and the expression of concern in Gault's case was white masculine chivalry, ideas that linked her freedom to societal progress.

The photographs were cast to demonstrate the facticity of Eliza Cobb's monstrosity and Martha Gault's humanity.[20] The victim of Gault's assault offered his support for her pardon by humanizing her plight. He told the Prison Commission that "she seemed hardly more than a child and scared to death."[21] By contrast, Cobb's fear and injury were summarily disregarded. After remarking upon her burnt face, J. Matthews's letter to the Prison Commission explained, "although it might not have amounted to rape some people thought that she was possibly forced to commit the act which caused her pregnancy."[22] Matthews's letter reveals much about the logic of white supremacist patriarchy. The only "fact" presented in the letter is that Cobb's face was burnt. Her rape is presented as rumor, a veiled insinuation submerged in the relevant "facts" of her grotesque appearance and idiocy. Moreover, white supremacist patriarchy endowed Matthews with the authority to measure the degree of force that would have constituted, or "amounted to," rape. He offers no explanation of why force did not amount to rape in Cobb's case and his account (the only account) of her rape was laden with such doubt, qualification, and equivocation that it was rendered null.

Eliza Cobb's advocates represented rape as innuendo and they erased all reference to her second child, conceived and born while she was imprisoned at Du Bois sawmill camp. The camp's medical ledgers indicate that she was hospitalized for "labor/giving birth" on December 5, 1889, eleven months after she was convicted of infanticide.[23] It is possible that

Eliza Cobb "consented" to have sex with another prisoner only two months after arriving at a predominantly male convict camp, barely a year after being raped and forced to hide her stillborn child from her mother. Yet because of these traumas and the prevalence of rape by prison guards whose technologies of force included the lash, the pressure to be an inconspicuous model prisoner in order to receive a pardon, and the gun, it is more likely that she was raped. Force pervaded every moment of prison time in southern convict camps. The convict camp was a location ruled by the sovereignty of the prison administration, its overseer and guards, a sovereignty that was enforced by the unfettered power to injure. Eliza Cobb's story is representative of the experience of black women in general, whose sentences to convict labor included gendered forms of racial terror including rape and the attendant violence of compulsory childbirth and familial estrangement.

Eliza Cobb was real and she was also an invention.[24] She was the deviant body required to make Martha Gault's idealized body real, to give it political, cultural, and social meaning. Eliza Cobb's body was inordinately useful. It served the economic project of white supremacy by performing physical labor in both the fields and the home. The South's economy was built upon the cultural project of racial differentiation, and Cobb's representation provided the material otherness upon which the iconography of white supremacy and white womanhood rested. The juridical representation of her monstrosity is part of a broader cultural representation of alarming others. In the nineteenth century a gothic literary monster emerged to distinguish racialized and gendered bodies, representing a "peculiarly modern emphasis upon the horror of particular kinds of bodies" that "condenses various racial and sexual threats."[25] What writers inscribed in fiction through the gothic monster, jurists and politicians in the postbellum era invented in the courtroom, through the figure of the black female subject. The transition from slavery to a "free" southern economy based upon coerced wage or contract labor was a historical process in which the hierarchy of bodies had to be reconstituted, reconsolidated, and reasserted, and the threat of black political or economic advancement needed to be thwarted. While not all black female bodies were described with the discourse of grotesquerie that marked Cobb's description, the mainstream stories herein about black women and crime reveal that they were popularly depicted as excessive, disfigured, and incorrigible. This meant they could be disproportionately arrested, forced to work under heinous conditions, and subjugated, but also that white women would be forced to remain in their subordinate roles through a perennial association with fragility and domesticity. While the Civil War might have produced an opportunity for new definitions of gender and gender roles, the narrative of exceptional white feminine vulnerability became critical to the maintenance of white supremacy through the dissemination of discourses of virtue and domestic order.[26] For black women, the construction of their bodies as monstrous meant not only that their political and economic power would be limited, but also that they would be subject to disproportionate arrest and imprisonment.

The official term for Georgia's convict system was the penitentiary, but the penal system was in fact a diffuse conglomeration of convict labor camps owned and managed by private companies or individuals that won leases from the state. The company or individual paid the state for the labor of its convicts. In the convict lease camp the lash was central to everyday life and the goals were twofold: to extract extreme amounts of labor from imprisoned women and men, and to reinforce their location at the bottom of the cultural economic hierarchy of southern society. Brutal conditions meant that illness and injury were perennial features of life under imprisonment.

State prisons were established in the United States in the nineteenth century, and Georgia built Milledgeville State Prison Farm in the early part of that century. The first prisoner was confined at Milledgeville in 1817 and in the antebellum era there were never more than 245 prisoners in the penitentiary at any given time. Virtually all of the prisoners at Milledgeville in the antebellum era were white.[27] Where penitentiaries existed in Georgia and across most of the South they were abandoned as the primary vehicle for punishment after the Civil War in favor of the convict lease system under which prisoners were forced to labor in various industries including mining, turpentine, lumber, farming, brickmaking, and railroad construction. Whipping, rape, medical neglect, and exposure to death by egregious living and work conditions were some of the system's defining features. Georgia's convict lease system began in 1868, three years after abolition, and was replaced in 1908 by the chain gang system in which women and men worked on various county public works projects. Although the chain gang system ostensibly eliminated the use of convict labor for private profit, inhumane conditions and violence persisted, and the state became the recipient of its profits.[28]

The convict lease and chain gang systems combined public terror and discipline in a modern technique of southern punishment. Michel Foucault charts a genealogy of punishment that locates the late eighteenth century as a dramatic turning point in penal history and in the history of human relations. It is, in Foucault's analysis, the transition, or "technical mutation between one art of punishing to another," between the public execution and the timetable.[29] According to Foucault in the era of torturous public executions extreme pain served as the main mode of punishment and the body was the primary vehicle through which to deliver punishment. In the era of the timetable, or modern penitentiary punishment, the soul serves as a vehicle through which to impose a punishment that primarily consists of the deprivation of rights, property, and privileges. Foucault argues that the transition from the chain gang, which was "linked with the old tradition of the public execution," to the penitentiary was a significant marker of the transition to modernity. According to Foucault, the French monarchy abolished the chain gang in 1836 because it was a hideous public display. Although some white southerners pushed to reform the convict lease system, that reform actually took the form of the establishment of the chain gang, and a continuation of the public display of black bodies in pain and at hard labor. In France prisoners in the traveling chain gangs wore insignias of their crimes, such as tattoos, and provoked the disdain of crowds of onlookers. In the United States the insignia was blackness, and the chain gang was normalized as an ordinary part of southern racial and gendered caste. Moreover, as I will detail, the arrest and criminalization of black women was sensationalized in the press, a spectacular discursive display that rendered their difference and unassimability.

Foucault's genealogy has heavily influenced theoretical and historical understandings of the nature of modern punishment. As Eliza Cobb's and Martha Gault's cases demonstrate, his analysis of the emergence of biopower is essential to understand modern punishment. In the U.S. South, the production of knowledge about the body was marshaled to determine who could live or die, or live in conditions arguably worse than death, and who could be set free. The prison regime, judicial authorities, and juridical logic was key to the functioning of biopower. Although biopower was critical, in the South it was deployed to normalize white subjects, rather than to rehabilitate black ones inside. Public terror was not usurped by disciplinary power; instead discipline and public terror coincided in postemancipation America. In the South, carceral torture was often flamboyant.[30] Atlanta's residents remarked about the inconvenience of the local chain gang in the middle of the bustling city center, and it was not until 1885 that officials removed the "spectacle of woman convicts" from Atlanta's streets to the more secluded Fulton County almshouse convict camp, where they performed a debilitating combination of brickmaking and agricultural labor.[31] In convict-leasing investigations officials sometimes subpoenaed local residents to testify about their observations of whippings and general conditions in the camps.[32] The supremacy of the white body was on display on the chain gang through the figure of the overseer armed with a lash and the black body in chains. Just as slavery served the inextricable cultural and economic purposes of white supremacy, convict leasing perpetuated both the white South's acceleration of industrial capitalism and its attendant development of Jim Crow modernity.[33]

Molly Kinsey was only ten years old when the Civil War ended in 1865 but she remembered both the perils of slavery and the threat of captivity under Jim Crow. In the years following the Civil War she lived in Sparta, Georgia, where she met her first husband. She was a lifelong member of the African Methodist Episcopal Church (AME Church) even though both of her husbands were Baptists. Her history, especially her spiritual development, was also marked by the precariousness of freedom and the ubiquitous threat of captivity in the South. Although Kinsey had been a member of the AME Church for more than thirty years by 1914, an experience that year precipitated a special call to God, a call to preach. At age fifty-nine she was working in her restaurant. Tired, she sat on the steps where she saw a young boy whom she had known since he was a baby, in stripes and chains. He was with "some more mens, in stripes, chained tergether, from the chain gang. I sot there, my heart bleedin' fer that boy, my heart wus so heavy and I had so much sorrow in my heart fer him, and I prayed for him."[34] Kinsey went home, opened her Bible, and prayed, "God, I don't want to go to the chain gang and I don't want to go to hell, I want to be your servant, take me and use me as you will."[35]

Molly Kinsey describes being lifted by God that night, being carried through the sky and dropped in the churchyard. She told her husband about her call to preach but economic adversity prompted her to move to Atlanta where she worked as a nurse and as a laundress for Chevrolet, never formalizing her ministry and instead institutionalizing her call in her private life: "I preached and I'm still preachin'. I'm preachin in my home."[36] Her experience reveals the spectacle of convict leasing as a mode of terror and the omnipresent threat of carceral terror for black women in Atlanta. She describes her religious experience in terms of sympathy, dread, and fear. The sight of young boys in stripes and chains left her brokenhearted and fearful of God's judgment in the afterlife. But she was also terrified of what might happen to her in this life, terrified that although she was a woman and although she was then fifty-nine years old, she too might face a physical hell, the chain gang.

Unbecoming Women: Criminalization and Gender Making

It was a reasonable fear. Despite inadequate record keeping, it is clear that throughout the nineteenth and early twentieth centuries black women in Georgia were arrested and imprisoned in far greater numbers than white women. Ascertaining the precise rate of imprisonment for women in Georgia is difficult. From 1868 until 1897 Georgia's principal keeper was the public official appointed by the governor and charged with visiting the lease sites, communicating with the lessees, and issuing annual or biennial "penitentiary reports" to the governor. These reports included imprisonment rates and descriptions of the conditions of the state's felony convict camps. Until 1899 Georgia only maintained statistics for state felony prisoners. However its convict lease infrastructure also included city and county misdemeanor camps, documented by scattered registers. Centralized state reporting of misdemeanor populations began in 1899 and in 1900 there were more than twice as many black women in misdemeanor convict camps than in the state penal system. This suggests that black women's representation in convict camps was far higher than official numbers suggest because they were disproportionately sent to poorly documented local or county camps. Although statewide comparative data for the early period does not exist, local dockets help fill the void in state documentation of rates and patterns of policing and arrest for black women.

Records from the Atlanta recorder's court reveal that police arrested hundreds of black women annually in that city after the Civil War. One year after emancipation, women accounted for 17.4 percent of city arrests. Of the women arrested, 776 were black and 195 were white.[37] By 1888 female prisoners still represented less than a quarter of the total arrests, yet black women were 5.8 times more likely to be arrested than white women.[38]

Between June and July 1886, eighty-six black women appeared in Atlanta's city court. Thirty-eight of them received chain gang sentences because they were unable to pay their fines, which ranged from $1.75 to $25.75. Whether the court-imposed fine was high or low, it was often beyond the means of black women, who during this period were mostly employed in domestic service, earning between $4 and $8 per month.[39] During the same months in 1886 twenty-two white women appeared in city court, and all but four paid their fine; the four who did not pay received chain gang sentences.[40] Black women and men in recorder's court were disproportionately charged with public quarreling and using profane language. Forty-five of the eighty-six black women arrested in the summer of 1886 were charged with arguing or using profanity, compared with nine white women. Of those charged with that offense twenty-two black women and three white women were sent to the chain gang.[41] Other common charges for both white and black women in city court included drunk and disorderly conduct and occupying/keeping a house of ill repute. Less often women were arrested for other violations including failing to abate a nuisance or dumping dirty water in the streets. Women were sometimes arrested for vagrancy, although not nearly as often as black men. In some cases the charge of vagrancy referred to prostitution. On August 21, 1873, four black women, Sarah Stubbs, Emma Davis, Lizzie Patterson, and Bettie Wilson, and one white woman, Pauline McCarthy, were convicted of vagrancy for prostitution offenses in city court. They were sentenced to fines ranging from $20 to $25 and court costs, and if they could not pay they would be forced to serve out their time on the city chain gang.[42]

If the South arguably "capitulated to racism" by consolidating Jim Crow in the 1890s, black women in Atlanta experienced this reality in a boom in arrests and imprisonment that compounded the impact of the grave economic depression that began in 1894.[43] Those who could not pay the fines imposed as punishment in city court were sentenced to labor on local chain gangs. Each year between 1893 and 1900 more black girls and young women between the ages of fifteen and twenty were arrested than white boys and white girls in the same age group combined.[44] In 1893 black men were 1.4 times more likely than white men to be arrested in Atlanta, while black women were 6.4 times more likely than white women to be arrested.[45] That year, black male youth were three times more likely to be arrested than young white males while young black girls were nineteen times more likely to be arrested than their white female counterparts.[46] Even after arrest it was unusual for white women who had been convicted of municipal offenses such as quarreling or disorderly conduct to serve out their time because they were usually able to pay their fines.[47] Although the fines were usually comparable across race and gender lines, there were vastly differential outcomes for black and white women in both city violations and misdemeanor sentencing.

COAL CAUGHT THE EYE of twelve-year-old Lucinda Stevens as she passed a railroad yard in Atlanta, Georgia. She picked up a few pieces, perhaps as a random gesture of a girl wandering about; perhaps she hoped to take a couple of pieces to use as fuel for a stove, the action of a girl who had recently lost her mother, hoping to help her adoring father. As soon as she put the pieces in her hand she was apprehended by police and carried to the stockade. Devastated at the incarceration of his "baby girl" for a few lumps of coal, her father, John Stevens, convinced a few reputable white men to submit a petition asking for the child's release from the city stockade. Despite the petitioners' characterization of John as "a hardworking negro who seems to want to do right" and who could not afford to pay his daughter's fine, the application for clemency was denied within one day of its receipt.[48]

The prevalence of municipal convict labor sheds light on the reach and depth of punishment in the lives of black women and men, a reality that is masked by incomplete state penal records. Penal authorities bemoaned the difficulty of obtaining accurate numbers of prisoners from camp overseers. Often county law officers sent prisoners directly to the convict camps rather than sending them to the principal keeper's custody at Milledgeville, where they could be counted before being sent to a camp to work out their time. As a result Principal Keeper John Darnell believed in 1870 that there were "a good many convicts in the lessees of whom no record can be found."[49] Despite this, in that year Darnell came prepared to answer questions about his record keeping before the committee appointed to investigate the condition of the penitentiary. He described the problem of obtaining accurate numbers from the lessees but provided approximate counts for the overall penitentiary population and for white men and women. He was not questioned about the numbers of black males in the camps but when asked how many black females there were in penal custody he answered, "I am not prepared to answer at this time."[50] Darnell's lack of accountability for black women and men in the prison system reveals the institution's casual disregard for black life and the primacy of white life. According to Hubbard Cureton, a black man who served twelve months on the lease for sleeping with a white woman sometime between 1868 and 1870, there was only one white woman imprisoned with him. Soon after she arrived at the convict camp Thomas Alexander, co-owner of Grant, Alexander, and Co., released her. Cureton was working when he overheard Alexander explain that he turned her loose because "his wife was a white woman, and he could not stand it to see a white woman worked in such places."[51] Extant records document only two white women in state convict camps from 1870 to 1880.[52]

The statewide female prisoner population increased in the late 1880s. In 1888, a 20 percent jump in women's imprisonment caused the principal keeper significant concern. He noted that the net increase in the overall prison population from 1886 to 1888 was eleven. The "remarkable feature of this increase" was that "ten of the eleven are females."[53] The *Atlanta Constitution* covered his findings, posing the question of whether crime was increasing among the female population, and highlighting the principal keeper's shock that "the net increase . . . has been entirely in women."[54]

The Georgia State Prison Commission was established in 1899 and began keeping statistical information on misdemeanor convict camps. Prior to that year there was no annual report of Georgia's misdemeanor prison population, however two special investigations of misdemeanor camps were conducted that provide additional information about women's imprisonment. R. F. Wright's special investigation of 1895 was incomplete. Although he visited and inspected thirty-three convict camps, at the time of his report he had yet to visit approximately fifteen of the convict camps located in the most populous counties in the state. Excluding these highly populated areas, he found that there were nineteen black women and no white women in misdemeanor camps. Two years later Phillip Byrd conducted a special investigation of misdemeanor camps for which he visited fifty-one misdemeanor convict camps and found that there were ninety-five black women and four white women. Neither Wright's nor Byrd's estimations of female misdemeanor prisoners were accounted for in the principal keeper's report, which only documented felony convicts. In each year from 1900 until 1908 (when statewide prohibition was passed) numbers of black women equaled or exceeded white men in county convict camps and on chain gangs.[55]

TABLE 1 Female population range in Georgia's felony convict camps, 1868–1905

Year	1868–1875	1876–1880	1881–1885	1885–1890	1891–1895	1896–1900	1901–1905
Black	13–30	30–40	30–33	40–52	54–68	57–75	75–81
White	0–1	1–2	1	0–1	2	2–3	5–7

Source: Principal Keeper's Annual Reports, 1868–1905 and Annual Reports of the Georgia Prison Commission, Record Groups 21-1-1 and 21-1-40, Georgia Archives, Morrow, Georgia.

TABLE 2 Georgia's misdemeanor prison population, 1899–1907

Year	1899	1900	1901	1902	1904	1905	1906	1907
Black women	116	148	170	103	133	208	165	206
White women	1	7	11	5	1	5	1	2
Black men	2135	2192	1786	2010	1725	1923	1789	1946
White men	132	105	117	103	105	152	88	144

Source: Annual Reports of the Georgia Prison Commission, Record Group 21-1-40, Georgia Archives, Morrow, Georgia. Data for the year 1903 is unavailable.

Black newspapers including the *Savannah Tribune* focused on unjust punishments meted out to black women and men for petty crimes, reporting on horrific legal abuses such as the sentencing of a black woman to ten years in a convict camp for snatching $5 from a child in 1876. While the white press was sympathetic toward imprisoned white women, criminalized black women were vilified for public disorder, especially quarreling and using vulgar language. When reporting about white women prisoners, journalists invariably emphasized the fact that the woman in question was either "the only white woman" or one of two in the convict system.[56] One article begins, "A white woman in jail! Not only that—a widow and a mother, a woman whose hair is turning gray."[57] Their assertions that a white woman was the only woman in state or local convict camps were often, but not always, true yet the reiteration of the exceptionality of white female imprisonment upheld the legitimacy of the entire system. The mainstream press tended to present imprisoned white women as subjects in need of rescue and accounts often emphasized ongoing efforts to secure their pardons. White women prisoners' beauty was also often invoked in popular reports.[58] Because white women's imprisonment was rare, a fact that journalists invariably noted alongside appeals that they be released, discourses about convict labor upheld the gender and racial order of the late nineteenth- and early twentieth-century South.

Writers for the *Atlanta Constitution* would prove themselves very adept at propagating cultural logics of white supremacy both in their daily coverage and in their broader literary impact. Joel Chandler Harris was associate editor of the paper, in which his creation Uncle Remus and the tales that bear his name were first published, "redefining what counted as culture and what counted as politics."[59] The paper's regular reporting was often as vivid and outlandish as the Uncle Remus stories of Brer Rabbit and Tar Baby that depicted black people as primitive tricksters. In 1876, the same year that the *Savannah Tribune* bemoaned the horrible sentence of a black woman for petty theft, the *Atlanta Constitution* printed a story about five black women and one black man from "Crowfoot Alley." Crowfoot Alley was described as an "interesting street [that] is not laid down on any map that we have ever seen, and is never found by a visitor, unless by accident."[60] The *Constitution*'s "Crowfoot Alley" article described a pathetic neighborhood filled with clothing lines and houses in "every state of decay" as a preamble to the story of Mamy Jones, Ella Wallace, Alfred Willoughby, Lucy Willoughby, Mattie Williams, and Ann Thomas, who were brought into court for disorderly conduct and quarreling. An argument that had grown to include several residents was allegedly the cause for the arrests. Alfred Willoughby and the five women from "Crowfoot Alley" were described as a "solemn set of darkeys."[61] The women, according to the reporter, were raucous, rancorous beings who had mouths and knew how to use them. He opined that they were being arraigned for blowing off steam, "which might have been utilized at the wash tub," naturalizing their status as washerwomen.[62] Black women's perceived unruliness, propensity to fight, inability to control their children, and general vulgarity were policed as an infringement upon their ability to perform their natural duties as washerwomen and domestic servants.

In Atlanta the entrenchment of black women in domestic service work was particularly severe and had a particularly long reign. In 1890 four out of five black women in the city worked in domestic service. By 1930 nine out of ten black working women in Atlanta still worked in domestic service *alone* while nine out of ten black women nationally worked in service or agriculture.[63] In 1880, 30 percent of black women lived with white employers, working as cooks and domestic servants. While white employers attempted to maintain the space as a domain of black female obedience, black women working in domestic service contested the authority of their employers. As Tera Hunter's masterful work has revealed, these strategies for resistance included quotidian individual practices such as feigning illness, slacking at work, quitting, and refusing to live in their employers' homes, as well as collective action, including organized labor strikes.[64] Black women's contestation of the oppressive conditions of the white home was essential for their independence, yet their resistance practices and personal lives were vilified in the press. Arrest for public quarreling was a technique to control black working-women's independence, public image, and community life.

Reporters conveyed an absolute polarity between the white and black home, which respectively represented order and disorder, decorum and salaciousness, wealth and poverty. The subservient black female subject in the white home was an ideal reinforced by structures of exclusion from other industries. The sight of black women on the streets in black neighborhoods, perhaps with their voices raised, was an assault on the model of a docile black women in the white domestic sphere, and therefore subject to punishment. Arrests of black women for public quarreling often stemmed from police surveillance rather than a complaint by one of the parties or a witness.[65] The black female juridical subject in the courtroom was a deviation from the idealized black female worker in the home. Stories of black women being policed and imprisoned performed necessary work in the white cultural imagination to reinforce their access to black women's domestic labor. When they strayed from the position of domestic worker by stepping out of line in the streets they faced punishment. The street was punishing; it was the landscape of arrest and the site of carcerality as shackled black female bodies were made to construct and maintain the very same roads upon which they were policed, breaking rocks on local chain gangs.

Representations of black women reflect the gendered character of a popular antiblack discourse that permeated the Progressive Era from the 1890s through the 1910s. This era produced a boom in liberal reform initiatives including pressure for governmental regulation of monopolies, increased labor regulations, public health reform, antipoverty organizations and legislation, and women's rights, but was also accompanied by scientific racism, eugenics, antiblack cinema, white supremacist world fairs, a dramatic swell in lynchings, and the consolidation of Jim Crow. David W. Southern argues that there were two types of progressives in the South: agrarian reformers and urban elite reformers. Whether urban or agrarian, most southern progressives espoused either moderate or radical racist ideology. Moderates supported discrimination and disfranchisement but denounced the criminal justice system and opposed lynching. Radicals condemned black education, advocated lynching as well as structural discrimination, and generally leaned toward demagoguery.[66] Journalists, lawyers, and judges in Georgia could fit either of these categories. Yet it is important not to overstate this moderate/radical binary since moderates supported the logics and structures of exclusion that enabled disproportionate policing and arrest. Moreover, as Eliza Cobb's case revealed, advocates often expressed sympathy while denying the humanity of black female subjects by disavowing their experiences of extreme violence such as rape. That disavowal, while different than vocal support for antiblack violence, often enabled terror by upholding a logic of biological difference that justified black women's disproportionately long sentences and a lack of public scrutiny about their experiences of violation. If black women could not be raped, rape could not be justification for their release, and could not serve as the basis for oversight or investigatory reform measures.

By the end of the nineteenth century black women were subjected to increasingly vicious journalistic representations. They were referred to as negresses, crazy negresses, leather-skinned negresses, and jet black negresses. Stories abounded about one-eyed black negresses, or negro women with burns and scars on their faces, who assaulted both innocent white women and men, and other black women and men with whom they were arguing. They were reputed to have carried out immoral, insane, and atrocious acts, such as luring young white girls into sex work and stealing and brutally whipping "blue-eyed" white babies.[67] Sometimes this propaganda revolved specifically around black female maternal deviance. In 1900 an article in the *Atlanta Constitution* depicting "Lively Scenes from the Police Matinee" featured the cases of two black women, one from "Darktown" and the other from "Crooked Alley." Martha Vines was charged with disciplining and cursing at several of her "sixteen or seventeen children," one of whom was serving time in a convict camp. The judge presiding over the case was certain that the charges were severe because "what Darktown can't stand must be intolerable enough."[68] Popular notions of the iniquitous nature of the black neighborhood served as a source of legitimacy for the punishment of its members.

LIVELY SCENES AT POLICE MATINEE
AS DEPICTED BY GORDON NOEL HURTEL

"Lively Scenes at the Police Matinee as Depicted by Gordon Noel Hurtel,"
Atlanta Constitution, August 29, 1900.

Although Vines's arrest was for cursing, her status as a degraded mother, indeed an animalistic subject, was at the core of the judicial decision, according to the press account. After asking Vines to verify how many children she had the judge chastised her for disturbing Darktown with her numerous "offspring." He advised her to send some of them to another locality before asking whether she knew the story of the old woman who lived in a shoe and, in case she didn't, he recited it for her. "Here was an old woman who lived in a shoe. She had so many children she didn't know what to do. She gave them some broth without any bread, then whipped them all soundly and put them to bed."[69] The judge advised that she send some of her children away so that she could more easily deal with the others, the bonds of black maternal affection either irrelevant, invisible, or impossible. The presence of "disorderly" black female subjects on the street, and their excessive reproduction of nefarious black children was a threat, a divergence from their primary function, maintaining the white domestic sphere and the sanctity of the white home.

The *Constitution* reporter included a revision of the nursery rhyme to caption his caricature of Martha Vines. His lyrics were "There was an old woman who lived in a stew; and cussed her young brats till she made the air blue; she was so very wroth and they so badly bred; that the fussy old woman to the chaingang was led."[70] Although many of the children depicted in the cartoon were boys, in the foreground was a depiction of Martha Vines whipping her daughter. If Vines's excessive reproduction and deviant mothering was producing out-of-control children, girls were visibly among the dangerous class that might be created. The judge fined Vines $5.75 and was impervious to her complaint that she didn't have a cent. As the bailiff carried her away to jail the judge commented, "I really believe it would be worse punishment to send her back to her children."[71] The Jim Crow carceral state enforced one of the most consistently stable presumptions of American history, mobilized continuously for the justification of draconian racial institutions—that black women's inherent deviance reproduces (and thereby produces) black cultural pathology, necessitating legal and extralegal control over their bodies and behavior.[72] General charges such as cursing or quarreling mask the precise nature of surveillance and punishment for black women in Atlanta. Beneath the vague charges was the goal of making them good domestics but disassociating them from femininity by presenting them as bad mothers and aggressive beings who were dangerous because they might produce more of their kind.

Black women's incorrigible delinquency meant that they required policing and technologies of management that resonated not only with domestic practices of white supremacist patriarchy, but also with international regimes of colonial management. Black women's images proliferated to familiarize publics with how the intrinsic gender and racial deviance must be governed both within and beyond U.S. borders. An 1897 *Weekly News and Courier* article entitled "A Queer Colony of Female Convicts in Georgia" proclaimed that Colonel Maddox, the operator of the all-female Camp Heardmont, had perfected inmate management.[73] According to Maddox, "there is no longer mutiny or rebellion" because the lash had been replaced by leadership and mastery.[74] Maddox claimed that such benevolent paternalistic modes of carceral rule produced at least two significant results: "the women no longer play sick, but to the contrary are anxious to work at all times," and "there is not a woman in all the camp who would not nurse me day and night if I were ill."[75] Having managed to achieve the twin goals of colonial mastery—labor extraction and docility—Maddox contended that his camp was a model, his female prisoners were "workers that would put strong men to shame" and were "better off today than they were when they came." Camp Heardmont was nothing less than a "panoramic review of antebellum days, where the master was kind and the slave obedient and faithful."[76]

This discursive entanglement of the colonial, queer, and antebellum emerged in precisely the moment when journalistic representations of international statecraft depended upon familiar racial knowledge. Late nineteenth-century industrialization required cheap labor and raw materials, resources acquired through military intervention, occupation, and annexation in Cuba, the Philippines, Puerto Rico, and Hawaii. Old South romanticism was a key frame through which subjects in the Caribbean and Pacific Islands were rendered in order to justify U.S. militarism and undermine claims to self-governance in the zone of American imperial conquest. Journalists and cartoonists circulated depictions of Cuban, Filipino, Puerto Rican, and Hawaiian darkies, even rendering Cuba *as* mammy, whose renowned patience and docility was expended under the horror of Spanish colonial rule. But "one of the most prevalent—if not *the* standard—visual trope deployed by turn-of-the-century US cartoonists to depict the 'natives' of Cuba, Puerto Rico, the Phillippines, Hawai'i, Ladrones (Guam), and other new US tropical 'dependencies' was the image of the '*pickaninny*.'"[77] The proliferation of familiar slavery archetypes and interweaving of the antebellum and colonial was a crucial framing of militarism in a dramatically shifting moment in U.S. foreign policy; this framing resolved intraracial sectional conflict by incorporating southern white supremacy into the national discourse of expansionism, thereby cultivating, consolidating and circulating a narrative of deviance and dependency to reconcile domestic and transnational labor exploitation in the service of industrialization.[78] Gendered temporal frameworks informed a colonial cultural order in which "the merging of the racial evolutionary tree and the gendered family into the family tree of man provided scientific racism with a simultaneously gendered and racial image through which it could popularize the idea of linear national progress."[79] In this instance, national progress was popularized through the reification of antebellum romanticism; white military manhood relied upon black female anachronism and difference. Black women's representation as disorderly but

The caste of slavery in words

productive when subject to forms of carceral management derived from Old South technologies of racial control presented a useful discourse for maintaining white supremacist political and economic relations, and for reinforcing practices of racial governance that could be successfully exported abroad.

These portrayals reveal how "the representation of male *national* power depends on the prior construction of *gender* difference";[80] as the *Weekly News and Courier* headline suggests, black women were *queer* colonial subjects whose enormous strength was presented in opposition to white feminine frailty. Pearl Pendergast, the only white woman in the camp, spent most of her time in the sick quarters and was depicted as an "authority," entrusted with counting the convicts to prevent escape. Being too feeble to work in the field, she cared for the dormitory and did "a large amount of the sewing in the camp," lending idealized domestic credibility to a regime that replicated the division of domestic labor under slavery.[81] Black female inversion was reified through carceral narratives and labor divisions. Although the term "queer" did not come to signify male effeminacy in northeast urban centers until the 1910s or homosexual desire until the middle of the twentieth century, blackness and queerness were routinely linked in Atlanta's discourses in the late 1890s.[82] In 1897, for example, there were at least forty-three articles published describing black life as queer, most of which recounted lurid tales of recorder's court: blind and armless men fighting; two black women, one "big" and the other "featherweight," fighting over men; scantily clad black men wandering intoxicated and, upon arrest, demanding that the judge buy them a shirt; a list of queer terms and phrases such as "doing the dust" and "calling me out my name" delineated with their definition according to police; a black man whom reporters called both a "queer spectacle" and "nothing less than a demon" had to be dragged naked to the prison barracks because he refused to dress for his arrest.[83] "Queer" was used to describe a range of happenings in Georgia, but other than a regular column in which "queer things" (strange objects and animals) were described in the city, "queer" was most consistently used in Atlanta's mainstream press to describe perverse black bodies, ideas, and behaviors that could only be interpreted and governed through police and judicial action. The meaning of "queerness" was constructed through carceral renderings of excessive, uncontrollable, and often naked black bodies. The proliferation of the association between blackness and queerness constituted one of the critical terrains upon which knowledge about gender and sexual deviance was constructed in the years preceding its circulation to describe sexual counternormativity. Representations of the carceral management of black queerness had to be continually reasserted in order to produce racial and gendered knowledge that would justify domestic and international political economies of industrial labor exploitation and resource extraction.

Strange black women serving their time on the city chain gang in Atlanta were subject to the ridicule of the local press. In 1883 the *Atlanta Constitution* ran a series of stories about Lizzie Patterson, a black woman who had been arrested and incarcerated several times. That year she was ordered to serve time at Camp de Emmel, named for its overseer Jack de Emmel, and while en route to serve her sentence she overdosed on morphine. It was unclear whether her death was accidental or suicide. The Atlanta press did not eulogize Lizzie Patterson. Reporters scoffed that she was so notorious that arresting her was part of the criteria for becoming fully qualified as a police officer. She reputedly had a strong grip that she used on police, and it "seemed impossible for her to stay sober."[84] Although Patterson may have been an example of expendable, incorrigible black life, her specter also garnered eager press attention. The *Constitution* ran two stories about Lizzie Patterson's ghost that was rumored to be haunting the women in the stockade of the local chain gang. Violet Jones, who was described in the paper as a "black, ugly hag," was asked if Patterson was haunting the stockade. According to the article, she and the other women in the convict camp cried out, "that's true, as sure as you live."[85] The narrative of Patterson's ghost was a collective one; several women were quoted, all with stories about her phantom. Her zeal for prison life reputedly transcended the physical world, since "in death she was as devoted to the quarry as she was when alive."[86] Lizzie Patterson's death was incidental, only the mechanism through which to invent a convenient narrative of black female transcendent attachment to captivity that reinforced the naturalness and tenability of their disproportionate imprisonment.

Whether the women in Atlanta's chain gang actually experienced the haunting of Patterson's ghost remains uncertain. Perhaps the women contrived the narrative of Patterson's ghost as a strategy of resistance. At least one woman crafted a story that explicitly opposed prison authority, reporting that the ghost threatened to poison the overseer if she was ever assigned cooking duty again. Patterson's ghost represented the possibility of defiance with impunity, and some women imprisoned at

Camp de Emmel mobilized her specter as a source of protection that ranged from threats to appeals to sympathy. De Emmel told the press that the women had told him they were too frightened to sleep in the stockade and requested to be released for the night, promising to come back in the morning. Their fears were disregarded, described as "pitiful as well as amusing."[87]

Some prisoners at the convict camp may have been particularly susceptible to fear of ghosts. Young girls and young women comprised a majority of the overall female prison population. Sixty-nine percent of women with felony convictions whose ages were recorded were twenty-five years old or younger and 18 percent of those serving time for felonies in nineteenth-century Georgia were black girls under the age of seventeen.[88] Unlike in northern states like New York, girls were not prosecuted under separate minor laws, and they do not appear to have been arrested in a specific panic about sexual vice.[89] Black girls were prosecuted for economic crimes under adult laws and incorporated into the black prisoner class as laborers who could perform alongside older women and men. In Atlanta they were nineteen times more likely to be arrested than their white female counterparts and were prosecuted as adults for a range of municipal crimes.[90] In the late nineteenth century, reformers bemoaned the lack of juvenile reformatories in Georgia but even after one was established in 1907 black girls continued to be housed with adults at Milledgeville or sent to the chain gang; the state farm reformatory housed only white and black boys.[91] The Atlanta branch of the Southern Association of College Women advocated for a reformatory for white girls to protect "the purity of womanhood," since pure women were the foundation of the home and the race.[92] A girls' reformatory in Fulton County was hardly in operation a year before it was closed down in 1919, its operators claiming vaguely that it was not a success.[93] As late as 1925 Selena Sloan Butler and the State Federation of Colored Women's Clubs continued to organize for the statewide passage of a bill for a training home for delinquent colored girls.[94]

Young girls were often the targets of arson prosecutions. Fifty percent of black women convicted of arson whose ages were recorded were under the age of seventeen.[95] At age thirteen, Florida Thomas was sentenced to a life term in 1890 for an arson in which no property was damaged.[96] Pleasant Morgan was given a seven-year sentence for attempted arson when she was fifteen years old.[97] Although only a few details are available for the cases of young girls convicted of arson, available information suggests that many of them were accidents, minor crimes, or acts coerced by adults. Regardless of the nature of the crime, arson carried a mandatory life sentence for much of the nineteenth century.

In 1888 police raided Sophia Baker's cabin where they found clothes and a bed ticking that were allegedly stolen from neighbor's burned down house. She was only fourteen years old and although she did not testify at trial, her landlord claimed that Baker had told him that the man she lived with, Joe Johnson, threatened to kill her if she did not participate in the crime. Although the strongest evidence against Baker related to possessing stolen goods, she was convicted of arson, which carried a life sentence.[98] She served time at several camps including Camp Heardmont before she was pardoned in 1894. If the homeowner's account is true, young Baker's life was ceaseless terror; her childhood spent under the ominous dictate of an older man, her adolescence and young adulthood under perennial assault by the lash, backbreaking labor, and imminent rape. Unlike Martha Gault's case, there was no appeal to the "conscience and sense of humanity that we all have," and no notion that she could be innocent under the dominion of an older man.

Although the numbers of women in Georgia's state penal system grew after 1886, aside from prohibition-related offenses the types of crimes for which women were convicted remained generally consistent throughout the nineteenth and early twentieth centuries. Women's crimes were believed to be "proportionately more atrocious" than men's. The principal keeper pointed out in 1897 that more than 50 percent of women were convicted for crimes that were considered especially heinous—arson, infanticide, and murder.[99] Yet in the nineteenth century only a slim majority—51 percent— of women were convicted of violent crimes including murder, attempted murder, or assault, and many of these so-called crimes were acts of self-defense against violence. An additional 5 percent of women were convicted of arson. Although arsons were often accidental, rarely resulted in physical injuries, and often caused only moderate property damage, the crime was considered a violent one. Thirty-eight percent of women were imprisoned for economic crimes including larceny or burglary.[100] The remaining 6 percent of female felony convictions were for moral crimes (selling whiskey without a license, adultery, prostitution, abortion, bigamy, gambling) or escape, perjury, and forgery.[101]

Women in Georgia were regularly ordered to serve years in state convict camps for petty larceny. In 1872 Emma Jones, a washerwoman in Atlanta, was sentenced to two years at Milledgeville for failing to return to her employer clothes that she had been hired to wash. The *Atlanta Constitution* hailed her sentence as a means of asserting discipline and deterring other domestic workers inclined to steal.[102] In 1892 Susan Conyers worked as a cook for a white family under bad conditions; she was said to have quarreled with the male head of household routinely. One night after preparing the family's dinner she returned to her own cabin, which was on the main house property. She made a plate filled with the left over supper she had cooked and brought the plate, along with a chair, to her cabin and proceeded to eat her dinner. Before she could finish she was arrested, accused of stealing a cheap gold ring from her employer's house. She was also charged with stealing the plate and chair she had used while she ate her supper. In total Conyers was convicted of two counts of larceny: one for the ring and one for the plate and chair, each of which carried a twelve-month prison sentence. In total the ring, plate, and chair were estimated to be worth less than $5. Notwithstanding the petty nature of the charges against them, black women like Susan Conyers who had poor relationships with white employers were vulnerable to arrest and had little defense against the word of the white men and women for whom they worked. Conyers's predicament was not at all unusual; black women were regularly charged with stealing jewelry, clothing, or household items of moderate or very small value. Mary Campbell was convicted of burglary for stealing dresses in 1892 and Della Cole was convicted of the same crime the following year. Lucy Gibson received a six-month sentence for stealing an undershirt from her neighbor in 1894. The following year Rosa Thomas was convicted of stealing inexpensive jewelry from her employer. In 1904 Hattie Trawick, a young black woman "just of age," was charged with stealing a range of household items including six towels, a cream pitcher, three pictures, tablemats, a bed spread, and a dress shirt. She was sent to work the roads of Baldwin County for twelve months when she could not pay her fine of $20. In 1906 Maria Cobb was convicted of stealing $5 worth of baby clothes and was also sent to the chain gang.[103]

White women were arrested for minor theft less often and they were more likely to serve their time in jail rather than convict camps. In 1901 Emma Wilter, a white woman, was convicted in Atlanta for stealing two garments worth less than 25 cents and received a harsh sentence of six months in jail. In 1909 Susan Morgan was sent to jail for three months for larceny. Her lawyer argued that she was in dire economic straits when she committed the crime, and that she was a mother to several children. She was pardoned after one month so that she could leave Savannah and "return to her country home" where she could care for her family.[104]

The air was thick on the late summer day in 1903 when Wyley Dean meandered through Gainesville, Georgia, attending to various errands in the town square. He moved freely if slowly, a white man from thirty miles away in White County, Georgia, progressing with the help of a crutch to aid his body, which was crippled from rheumatism. His business in the town consisted of purchases at various establishments: medicine from M. C. Brown's drug store, foodstuffs from Red Grocery, a visit to Buffington's stable, perhaps a stop at the local bookstore or jewelry store. Dusk fell and he walked slowly up Washington Street toward Green Street. It is unclear whether Nancy Smith encountered Wyley Dean that evening. She would have had to start out from the colored section of Gainesville, about a mile from the square. Between her segregated neighborhood and the town center were streets aptly named for the landscape of Jim Crow, signposts of the repression, peril, and injustice that she might encounter on any given day: Arbitrary Street led to Fair Street then to Race Street along the route to the public square. Wyley Dean claimed that he saw her as he turned gingerly down Green Street. He claimed that as they passed she brushed against him. He claimed that despite being at the center of town he had not passed anyone else along his route. He specified that he was not drunk at the time, although he did sometimes take a drink. When he felt her brush past him he was "insulted" and had "hollowed at her" but by the time he realized his money was missing she was running far ahead of him and his plodding body could not catch her. He called the police and had Smith arrested. There were no witnesses. Smith claimed that she had never seen the man in her life. The officers searched her but found no money. Although there was "not a particle of evidence against her," under the penal logic of segregation Dean's word was enough to make the charges stick. She was convicted of larceny and sentenced to serve twelve months on the chain gang. After four months in prison Smith filed for clemency on the grounds that the evidence against her was nonexistent, but her petition was denied. The dangers of Jim Crow public life were grave, and black women were subject to arrest for any infraction of political etiquette or for simply being in public. After all, although it was dark when the incident occurred, Wyley Dean managed to send Nancy Smith to the chain gang because he "was able to identify her specially from all other negroes on account of her very large breasts."

Unbecoming Mothers

Some women in Georgia's convict camps had been driven to commit petty crimes by the need to provide for their basic material welfare and that of their children. Yet a number of them were also charged with the crime understood as the gravest rejection of one's status as a woman: infanticide. Georgia's carceral authorities did not mind stealing black children for its convict-leasing modernization project and working them to death; they did not mind if children born to mothers serving time in convict lease camps died during childbirth and they had no regard for what happened to those children if they survived birth. But prosecutors routinely prosecuted black women for killing their children. It is difficult to fully understand the historical experiences of black women charged with infanticide because the evidence for this crime during this period was often so thin, unscientific, and speculative that it is virtually impossible to know if most women were guilty. In the context of extreme violence, poverty, and political repression it is possible that some of the women charged with infanticide did in fact kill their children in desperation to shield them from these conditions or to protect the material survival of their families. Given how rumor-laden the charge of infanticide was, it is very likely that many of the women accused were innocent. Black women with few resources often only had access to inadequate legal representation and were convicted by juries composed of white men. Unreliable witnesses and dubious medical evidence also contribute to the difficulty of retrospective assessments of guilt or innocence.

For black women like Eliza Cobb, a reputedly vexed relationship to normative femininity, and thus motherhood, made them disproportionately susceptible to infanticide allegations. At least 10 percent of the women convicted of murder in Georgia in the nineteenth century had been charged with killing their children. Between 1868 and 1936 there were at least twenty-two women imprisoned for infanticide in Georgia, although the number is likely higher since some undetailed murder convictions may have been related to the deaths of babies. Most of those convictions occurred between 1870 and 1920. Of that number only three were white.[105] Although it was extremely rare for white women to be sent to convict camps for infanticide during this period it was more common for stories about suspected infanticides of white babies to appear in newspapers. There is a significant disparity between the number of stories about white infanticide cases in the press and the number of white women who were imprisoned for the crime. White babies were reportedly found dead in public places in several instances, and there are a number of reports of white women or white married couples being suspected of infanticide but evading punishment or receiving acquittals.[106] In 1895 a white man, Arthur Cole, was arrested and charged with infanticide after he allegedly gave a dead child wrapped in paper to one of his black male servants to discard. He was exonerated, perhaps because the only evidence was the testimony of his black employee. Also in 1895, in Dahlonega, Georgia, a judge sentenced a white woman named Miss Scroggins to a fine of $50 and court costs for attempting to kill her child. The fine "was at once paid by the citizens of the county" and Miss Scroggins was immediately released.[107] In 1899 a white woman named Evaline Hughes was suspected of infanticide but fled authorities before she was arrested and was never imprisoned for the crime.[108] In 1914 a white married couple, Mr. and Mrs. Lanier, were acquitted of infanticide in separate trials.

A young white woman named Dolly Pritchett was at the center of the most famous infanticide trial in early twentieth-century Georgia, the subject of at least fifteen newspaper articles.[109] Described as a poor mountain girl, her plight generated concern from Georgia's most elite social sectors. In an *Atlanta Constitution* article that was published after her conviction Dolly Pritchett's lawyer, E. W. Coleman, extolled her beauty, incorporating it as one of the relevant issues in her case. He described her as "a beautiful girl when fixed up a little ... has a clear, blue eye, a cheerful and attractive face, a kind disposition."[110] These attributes along with her sad past constituted her propensity for reform and the injustice of her imprisonment. Coleman invoked her whiteness and beauty as part of his strategy to achieve a pardon for Pritchett by securing public sympathy and outrage against her persecution. If Eliza Cobb was femininity's "other," Dolly Pritchett was its youthful paragon.

To support his strategy, Coleman included a demure photograph of Pritchett in his article. She is wearing a long dress, signifying modesty, sans the stripes that represented criminality. Pritchett is holding an unidentifiable object that looks similar to the article in Cobb's hands,

By E. W. Coleman, Who Defended Her in Court.

DOLLY PRITCHETT.

"Pitiable Story of Dolly Pritchett; Flimsy Evidence That Convicted Her,"
Atlanta Constitution, January 6, 1901.

suggesting that she, too, might have been at work just before the picture
was captured.

Coleman's closing argument in Pritchett's defense made headlines. It
lasted two hours and according to one observer before he delivered it
"nearly everyone thought the girl would hang" but afterward "nearly
everyone thought she would be cleared or a mistrial made."[111] Nevertheless, in 1900 Dolly Pritchett was convicted of infanticide and sentenced
to Milledgeville for life. The text of Coleman's closing argument is not
available; however, it was probably quite similar to his postconviction
published account of her plight. He explained there that she grew up in a
poor family and worked hard on her father's farm. Her father was cruel,
denying her the opportunity for education and ultimately abandoning
her. Pritchett and her younger sister were thrown out of their father's
house for secretly visiting their older sister, who was estranged from
the family, and upon their eviction the two girls then went to live with
their older sister. At age sixteen, Pritchett was charged with infanti-

cide after she allegedly gave birth to a child that she left in the woods several miles from her sister's house.[112] According to Coleman the evidence against her was completely circumstantial, consisting of witnesses who claimed that she had been pregnant the week before the baby was found, but was not pregnant the following week.[113]

A few days after the *Atlanta Constitution* printed Coleman's article it published another printed editorial, this time by L. Graham Crozier, whose wife was a prominent clubwoman and suffragist. In his estimation Pritchett needed "the shelter of no reform institution. She does need to be placed where her intelligence may be developed and where her pride and spirit of sturdy independence may be conserved."[114] To Crozier, Dolly Pritchett's conviction was so unjust it exemplified the need for reform of the entire American jury system. He quoted her bright and eager answers to questions he posed during a visit he made to her at Milledgeville. When asked if she could sew, she replied with excitement that she could make her own clothes, and when asked how she would earn a living she "replied without a moment's hesitation, 'I will make a crop!'"[115] Pritchett's articulation, industriousness, intelligence, and good nature humanized her, and Crozier was furious that in America, especially "in a section of that country that boasts so long and so loud of its chivalry," Pritchett could be condemned to a life of penal servitude.[116] Unlike Eliza Cobb or the majority of black women whose clemency applications and public representations did not include first-person statements, Pritchett was portrayed as a fully human subject, characterized by the capacity for language and sentience. Her representation as a speaking subject stands in sharp contrast to Cobb's portrayal as idiotic, mute, and by extension animalistic.

The public needed to know about Dolly Pritchett. White women were not supposed to be prosecuted for infanticide, as evidenced by the low numbers of convictions during this period. Crozier and Coleman appealed to tropes of white femininity in order to make Dolly Pritchett legible as a sympathetic subject despite the fact that she was charged with an instance of extraordinary gender-deviating violence. This did not prove to be a difficult task. She received an outpouring of public support that included letters and petitions from several hundred residents of Cherokee County, judges, county officers, and white clubwomen.[117] Mrs. Rebecca Douglas Lowe was featured in the society pages for her vehement advocacy on Dolly Pritchett's behalf. Mrs. E. Horne, of the Georgia Federation of Women's Clubs, spearheaded action to get Pritchett pardoned so that she could be sent to the House of the Good Shepherd for fallen women in Georgetown, Maryland. Clubwomen agreed with Coleman and Crozier that in Dolly Pritchett there was "the making of a good woman."[118] Mrs. Horne claimed to have rescued several young southern women by sending them to the House of the Good Shepherd, where they had a chance to reform. Yet both Dolly and her mother "emphatically denounced" the plan to send her there. Pritchett's pardon might have been granted in 1901 when her first application was recommended and endorsed by a petition from the Georgia Federation of Women's Clubs, but she resisted maternalist attempts to reform her by altering the geography of her incarceration. Instead she said that she would rather stay at Milledgeville until she could secure an unconditional, direct pardon.[119] Despite her objection to being sent to the House of the Good Shepherd, the Georgia Federation of Women's Clubs continued to support Pritchett's efforts to be released.

Propelled by public outcry and appeals from Georgia's elites, Governor Joseph Terrell pardoned Dolly Pritchett in 1902, two years into her life sentence. The efforts to send her to the House of the Good Shepherd and the relatively short prison sentence represented Pritchett as a young white girl adrift rather than a violent criminal. Although her guilt was certainly questioned by those around her, her femininity was not. By the end of the nineteenth century poor white women had become important objects of political concern. They were deployed in electoral politics to make poor white men choose race over class at the polls, despite clear class antagonisms between elite and poor white men. In the view of elites, poor white women's purity was incontrovertible despite differences including "class, manners, and living conditions."[120] This was a distinctly postbellum phenomenon. The Civil War and postbellum poverty transformed gender ideology, which in the antebellum era maintained that poor, laboring white women were deviant. As formerly wealthy white elites faced poverty after the Civil War, poor white women were included under the umbrella of virtuous feminine subjects and were incorporated into the class of vulnerable, protected subjects.[121] Dolly Pritchett had allegedly committed one of the greatest crimes against womanhood—killing her child. Yet even this was not enough to diminish her virtue. An absolute notion of white feminine vulnerability that was not contingent upon wealth or social status was necessary to fortify the ideology of white supremacy that held that racial caste was required to defend the New South against the pervasive threat of rape by black men.

The political necessity of this conception of poor white women's purity is reflected in the history of infanticide prosecution in Georgia. Dolly Pritchett was not alone in garnering such protection under the law. Anna Brock was convicted of infanticide in 1900, and was also pardoned after two years.[122] Annie Darcy was one of only three white women on record for serving time for infanticide during this period, and served a relatively longer sentence of seven years.[123] In infanticide cases, white women's perceived innocence and certain propensity for reform did not always protect them from imprisonment altogether, but did, on average, garner leniency from politicians and legal authorities who either refused to prosecute them altogether or granted pardons after relatively short sentences. With records revealing that only three white women were convicted of infanticide after the Civil War, their average sentence was 3.6 years imprisonment. The average length of imprisonment for a black woman for the same crime was fifteen years.[124]

Occasionally white female vulnerability and black female lechery emerged in representations not of infanticide but of black women's sexual threat to white children. In 1887, newspapers reported that a "Savannah quadroon" and an "Atlanta negress" were imprisoned for "enticing and attempting to entice young white girls away from home for immoral purposes."[125] E. Henderson, who was identified as black through her "kinky hair," was alleged to have passed for white by wearing a blonde wig in order to steal white girls ranging in age from nine to fourteen from their parents. She had allegedly secured at least five girls with promises of nice clothing and good homes, intending to keep them for ostensibly lewd companionship or "lives of sin." Extant punishment records do not contain accounts of this case, and therefore the women's fate remains a mystery, as does any further evidence of the supposed crime beyond the sensationalized journalistic account. Yet this representation of a black queer menace to young white girls coincided with other, more frequent allegations of black female deviance: their inclination to kill their own children. Flora Richardson and Louisa Lindsay, both black women, were convicted of infanticide in 1900, the same year as Anna Brock and Dolly Pritchett. Yet Richardson and Lindsay were forced to serve much longer sentences, and were not pardoned until 1908 and 1909 respectively.[126] Both women denied killing their children and both were convicted by all-white juries. Richardson was working in a field when she felt the first pangs of labor. She ran to her house and found the door locked so she attempted to climb in a window. She fell from the window and could not get up. The child was stillborn and she buried it in the woods. When police came to her house to question her about the child she voluntarily led them to the place where she had buried the baby.

After recounting the story of the crime and asserting Flora Richardson's possible innocence, her attorney added two additional grounds for clemency: she was "a deformed and half-witted girl."[127] Richardson's white neighbors joined her petition for clemency, also arguing that she was "of a low order of intelligence, a little above an idiot" or "what would be classified as imbecile." They noted that she was physically deformed, burnt by a fire when she was a young girl.[128] Despite what they classified as her limited capacity, members of the white community attested that they would like Richardson to be able to care for her mother, father, and brother, because her parents were "worthy old negroes" who paid their debts, and her family members were "still weaker minded than she. It seems to run in the family." Despite several letters from white citizens Flora's first pardon application was denied. She was finally released four years after her first clemency application, in 1908. After losing her child she was forced to serve eight years at Milledgeville for a crime that available evidence suggests she did not commit. While Dolly Pritchett's advocates argued her innocence with conviction, Flora Richardson and Eliza Cobb were presented as possibly innocent; however, the reiteration of the "fact" of their imbecility implied that the more likely scenario was that they were so idiotic that they killed their children. A trend emerged in clemency strategy that reflected broad views of black female subjects, positioning them as repugnant, if childlike, objects. Lawyers and community residents repeatedly described black women as deserving of leniency because they were innately incapable of supporting or protecting the lives of their children. The disavowal of their ability to care for young life was one marker of their exclusion from the category "woman," exemplified in paternalist and maternalist accounts of white women prisoners' innocence, beauty, difficult family and life experiences, and capacity for rehabilitation. Revealing the contradictions inherent to white supremacist gender ideology, black women perennially charged with caring for white children were prosecuted, that is persecuted, as unfit to mother their own.

Like Flora Richardson and Eliza Cobb, Julia Whitfield, Cammie Parks, Maggie Mills, Sarah Robinson, and Ann Winship were all characterized as "weak-minded" and imbecilic in clemency file documents. Julia Whitfield's counsel wrote that she was "stupid . . . to the extent of imbecility," that she did not aid in her own defense, and that consultation with her amounted to nothing.[129] Her lawyer wrote that the commission should grant Julia's pardon if they believed she was either not guilty or "not a fit subject of punishment because of her mental condition." Black women's presumed guilt required that their legal advocates have an alternative ground for leniency. Although the basis for leniency toward white women was feminine purity and the basis for black women was degeneracy, this is not a simple matter of different means to the same end of lenience. As the disparity in lengths of sentences for infanticide demonstrates, black and white women's alterity had severe consequences for black women's lives, subjecting them to much longer periods of imprisonment and exposing them to the violence that plagued the convict camp.

Without trial transcripts and in the context of unreliable witnesses and medical evidence it is virtually impossible to assess the general validity of charges of infanticide. Flora Richardson's experience was part of a larger pattern for black working women who performed arduous field labor. The late nineteenth century brought a decline in black fertility rates and a strikingly high child mortality rate that was due to the poor health of rural women and their families.[130] Both rural field labor and urban domestic manual labor impacted black birth rates, as a black physician observed in 1896. He wondered "why should we be surprised at the great number of still-births among our women, since they do most of the work that is liable to produce this state of things . . . cooking, the sweeping, the lifting of heavy pots, they carry the coal, the wood the water; they carry heavy burdens on their heads."[131]

There is a long history of racial and sexual biases in infanticide cases.[132] Women accused of infanticide had three major not-guilty defenses: that the child was stillborn; that they were not the mother of the dead child; or that their husbands had committed the murder. Usually, infanticide was charged in cases where women gave birth alone, so there were no eyewitnesses. In Julia Whitfield's case the medical examiner could not prove whether the baby had been asphyxiated or choked by the umbilical cord. The evidence against Mollie Farmer must have been very weak because she was convicted after three mistrials.[133] One of Amanda Hill's supporters wrote to the Prison Commission protesting her conviction because her trial was not equal to that received by someone of wealth and influence, arguing "lawyers admitted by the courts hardly ever tear their shirts over a poor unfortunate."[134] Rose Henderson was convicted on the basis that "she was known to be pregnant and a child newly born was found in a ditch with its throat cut, the child being proved by circumstantial evidence to be hers."[135] In 1886 Savannah Veal, described in the press as a mulatto woman, was charged with killing a child she denied was hers. Yet authorities believed they had successfully proved that the baby was of African descent, and therefore must have belonged to Veal.[136] The burden was usually on the woman to prove that she was innocent, and the standards for evidence of innocence were very high.

Although Louisa Lindsay was imprisoned for several years for a crime that she vehemently denied committing, she benefitted from the support of her father. Lindsay was convicted of infanticide during the same year as Dolly Pritchett and Flora Richardson. Her father circulated a petition, got it signed by "all the white men he knew," and submitted it to the Prison Commission. Still, her application for pardon was denied in 1906 and again in 1908. No accounts of the crime remain, except that she pled not guilty and a jury convicted her at trial. In 1909, when she was dying of consumption at Milledgeville and he had heard nothing about the status of her third clemency request, her father contacted prison officials directly; he informed them that he would be arriving from Spaulding County the next day to pick up his daughter. An authority at Milledgeville sent a hurried telegram to the Prison Commission asking, "Louisa Lindsay—father coming for her tomorrow—shall we let her go?" With her father's proactive effort and Louisa's inability to labor any longer, the Prison Commission granted her pardon the same day. The *Atlanta Constitution* ran a short article noting fallaciously that Louisa Lindsay was a white woman who had been pardoned because she was dying of consumption inside Milledgeville.[137] Although she was a black woman, a fact that was mentioned numerous times in her pardon materials, Louisa was transmogrified by the press into the figure of frail and vulnerable white femininity, who was rescued from the state farm by the governor and paternal chivalry only weeks before her death.

Tragedy surrounded the cases of women charged with infanticide. Susannah Gilbert, Elizabeth Pitts, and Sarah Robinson all admitted that dire circumstances led to the deaths of their children, either intentionally or by accident. Susannah Gilbert was fifteen years old when she had her first child in 1868. She was afraid that her mother would beat the child if she heard it crying and covered its mouth with a pillow, accidentally smothering it.[138] Elizabeth Pitts was an unmarried mother and was terrified of her father, who threatened to kill her if she ever became pregnant again. When she became pregnant for the second time she hid her pregnancy from both her father and her employer. She gave birth to her child while she was at work in her employer's garden and attempted to give it away. She left the baby in a visible place in the garden, hoping that someone would find it but that no one would identify her as the mother. The child was found dead in the garden the next day.[139] Sarah Robinson's legal brief for pardon indicated that she was fifteen years old when she killed her child; she claimed that the father of her child, who was older, coerced her into committing the crime.[140]

They were all young women afraid of the violence that plagued their lives and the futures of their children. Impoverishment and pandemic violence, including rape, imbued black women's lives in the late nineteenth century. In this context black women may have been faced with an unlivable choice about whether mercy meant ending their children's lives. Yet the disproportionate imprisonment of black women for the murder of their children reveals the white supremacist logic of the southern penal regime. Many of the women who were imprisoned for various crimes in Georgia's convict lease system were mothers, and their imprisonment imposed grave economic and emotional consequences for their families, especially their children. The southern legal system, which routinely threatened the lives of black adults and children through estrangement, medical neglect, overwork, and whipping, asserted a valuation of black children only when such claims provided the state with a labor resource.

Infanticide prosecutions reveal the degree to which juridical power, ostensibly wielded under the auspices of protection, actually adjudicates the appropriate imposition of death. Black women who cited motherhood and the need to care for their children as grounds for pardon were routinely denied.[141] Martha Link had been convicted of trespassing in 1892, and was sentenced to nine months on the Hancock County chain gang. Her clemency application was denied because the only mitigating factor in her case was that she was the mother of a large family of small children.[142] Black life (the life of the child) becomes legible when it is deployed by white authorities in order to enact violence (imprisonment), but is illegible when deployed by black subjects to defend against violence (motherhood as a ground for pardon). Georgia's legal system disproportionately imprisoned black women thereby destroying their ability to care for their children, but also arrested them when they allegedly caused the deaths of their children. Saidiya Hartman's insight regarding efforts to limit abuse under slavery is relevant to black women's post–Civil War imprisonment. Hartman argues that because of the fragmented identity of the slave, she was recognizable only by measure of degrees of tolerable violence, "the designation of person [under slavery] was inescapably bound to violence, and the effort to protect embodied a degree of violence no less severe than the excesses being regulated."[143] The same regime that foreclosed black life operated under a guise of concern for it, and that concern was deployed in order to imprison black women. Thus, "the violence of subjection concealed and extended itself through the outstretched hand of legislated concern." In a context of profound disregard for black life (young and old), and through an institution that routinely threatened it, juridical concern inflicted what Hartman describes as "a mutilation of another order."[144]

By the turn of the century white middle-class men and women perceived several threats to their economic and political authority and familial security. The late nineteenth century witnessed economic depression, massive labor strikes, the introduction of white women into "public" leisure and commercial spheres, and the emergence of black contract labor. Moreover, the decline of self-employment and small business ownership, and the emergent power of northern corporate interests appeared to threaten white economic independence and independent agricultural households. The protection of white women became a technique for asserting the stability of white manhood in uncertain times.[145] The juridical production of black female deviance meant that black women were arrested more often, and were forced to endure protracted periods of captivity. The invention of Eliza Cobb was a necessary condition for the invention of Martha Gault and Dolly Pritchett, which means she was necessary for the invention of "woman" as a historically specific cultural category. The oppositional qualities ascribed to Martha Gault and Eliza Cobb reveal the essential role of racial alterity in the production of gender categories. Through the legal system powerful white men continually and repeatedly ascribed characteristics to female bodies, which fortified an absolute binary between black and white.

Although guised in a discourse of objectivity and rationality, legal actors joined the press, entertainers, and literary figures to produce popular fictions, contributing to what Gail Bederman describes as the "historical, ideological process" of gender construction.[146] Lucinda Stevens, Mamy Jones, Ella Wallace, Lucy Willoughby, Mattie Williams, Ann Thomas, Sarah Stubbs, Emma Davis, Lizzie Patterson, Bettie Wilson, Martha Vines, Violet Jones, Sophia Baker, Pleasant Morgan, Florida Thomas, Susan Conyers, Della Cole, Mary Campbell, Rosa Thomas, Nancy Smith, Julia Whitfield, Flora Richardson, Mollie Farmer, and Eliza Cobb are among those whose position as gender-deviant subjects was propagated by the press and reflected in judicial decisions. This exclusion from the normative feminine subject position meant disproportionate arrest and prosecution. After the Atlanta race riot black women would be sent to county chain gangs while white women were imprisoned in the state farm. But both before and after that shift from convict leasing to the chain gang, black women would suffer from unrelentingly cruel conditions and medical neglect wherever they were imprisoned— at the state farm, in mixed-gender convict camps, and in all-women's convict camps. The disavowal of Eliza Cobb's experience of gender violence as a legitimate factor in her clemency case by prison authorities was all too common. Black women would face unconscionable acts of gendered racial terror that would virtually always be denied or ignored. The practice of gendered racial terror worked to crystallize the position of the black female subject outside of the normative category "woman."

The following chapter turns to gendered racial terror and the infrastructure of unfreedom that crystallized knowledge about gender through the production of worthy, fully human white citizens and through the violent subjection of black female bodies. A close examination of southern convict camps demonstrates that power at its extremities illuminates and enacts dominant ideology and systems of subordination.

CHAPTER TWO

Convict Leasing, (Re)Production, and Gendered Racial Terror

> It is a story predicated on impossibility—listening for the
> unsaid, translating misconstrued words, and refashioning
> disfigured lives—and intent on achieving an impossible goal:
> redressing the violence that produced numbers, ciphers, and
> fragments of discourse, which is as close as we come to a
> biography of the captive and the enslaved.
>
> —SAIDIYA HARTMAN

> Love is contraband in hell.
>
> —ASSATA SHAKUR

She was already tired by the time she made it to the place where she was sent to work. More than 100 miles from home, Adeline Henderson saw hundreds of other people in her predicament when she finally arrived at Dade County Coal Mines.[1] The journey seemed so long and the place so strange, she wondered if she was dreaming. All men, all striped, faces dirty from the coke ovens and the mines. Where would she sleep? It wasn't until deep dark that she met Nancy Morris, who would stay in the bed next to her. For her part Nancy was relieved that finally, after three months, another woman had come to the camp and they would share sleeping quarters. In arguably the worst camp in the state, it was the worst time to arrive at Dade: 1884 was a cold year and the harvest did not yield, so there were no vegetables to be had. Despite the cold, the air was still stifling in the two scarcely ventilated barracks. Meat was also scarce so they ate only corn bread and syrup for months and months and months.[2] Nancy told Adeline that they would have to get up before the sun, earlier than everyone else to get the camp ready for dawn work. Then they would go to the coke ovens.[3] That first night Nancy told Adeline that soon she wouldn't notice the smell and the dirt so much. The cottons seem less infested when your head is lead heavy.[4] Over the next few days Nancy showed her how to get the water and boil the lye and mend the clothes and make the corn bread and how to help

58

the men in the red-hot fire of the coke ovens. Adeline mentioned that everyone at home called her Addie.

Three months later, with a gleam in her big brown eyes, Addie told Nancy about Moses. Adeline said she wouldn't be here forever because Moses was going to get out soon and he had lots of friends, and they would help her.[5] And then she would help Nancy. When, Nancy wondered. Yesterday was not soon enough because *everyone* was sick. They touched their mouths to check for bleeding, knowing that it was the first sign that the weakness would come and then death. Although they did not catch pneumonia or typhoid or consumption they were consumed with dread and gloom.[6] Four men went to the bathroom and vomited; one never came back. After that the guards screamed, saying that Nancy and Adeline were to blame for the vomiting and the death because they were wretched cooks, venomous women who tried to kill the others. Murderesses. But it was the bread and the syrup and the bugs and the dirt in all of it. They worried at every bite and mourned the others.[7]

For a few minutes each night Addie told Nancy Moses stories. Both Adeline and Moses came from Cobb County and when Moses got her out they would get married and live with the four little ones Addie loved so much and had left behind, and they would take care of her ailing mother.[8] Moses promised he wouldn't treat her bad like her old man back at home. Nancy loved the stories. One night, when she was especially tired she blurted it out: since Adeline loved her babies so, why did she stop the last one from taking a first breath? After that, Adeline refused to speak to Nancy, not even to tell her that the "evidence against her was mostly circumstantial."[9] So Nancy wondered if the baby stopped breathing on its own, or if Adeline couldn't keep the baby, what with all of the others crying and needing. But she realized "it was not a story to pass on" and never asked again.[10] For weeks she feared that Addie would never speak to her, outside of the cooking and the mending and the coke ovens anyway.

But Adeline came around in the weeks before the food stopped altogether and the guards tried to starve them all. Instead of Moses stories they talked about the plan—no more cooking or mending or cleaning or mining or burning coke, no more work at all. The whisper of no more work had been making its way through the camp for weeks, and Addie and Nancy helped stow scraps from each meal until they had enough to last several days.[11] On that hotter-than-hell day in July they would later call "enough day," Enos and A. J. told the guards that no one would work until they had meat and vegetables and until they stopped the whippings. Soon they were surrounded by all of the guards, guns drawn. And things stayed that way all day and all night until the next day it seemed that shooting would begin. The guards forced the blacksmiths out of the stockade first. They made them chisel away, unshackling and reshackling the others until it was all over—everyone chained together, knowing that work would resume at sunup. That night was quiet except for the screams of Enos, A. J., and the others who had dared to make the demands and the sound of the extra-thick lash meeting skin.[12] They cringed when they saw the first man being whipped with the new strap that overseer Kilpatrick had invented, with shoe pegs that tore so deep the wound never really closed.[13]

Despite wounds that would not close, over nine winters and summers at the coke ovens they built a friendship borne of years that felt like lifetimes. There were bad nights: when Moses left and when Adeline got word that even though twenty-nine white men from Powder Springs had signed that letter to the governor, she wasn't getting out.[14] Faithfully, Moses had written to Governor John B. Gordon pleading, "I do hope and trust in the god of Heaven that you will look at the case and consider the case and let me have her for my wife. I love her and I can't help it. I would marry her in there if it was so fit. So I will. Please hoping you will give me that girl Adeline Henderson for a wife."[15] "Governor," he implored, "you know what it is to love."[16] Black love failed to persuade the governor, a former Confederate military leader and the widely acknowledged head of Georgia's Ku Klux Klan. After Adeline learned that her petition for clemency had been denied she wondered when Moses would forget her and if her children already had. Few personal letters got to that corner of hell at the top of Georgia that they called Dade.

A year later Nancy and Adeline learned that they would be moving. Not getting out, just moving, but they would be going together. They held hands and wondered if the next place would be worse. Nancy wondered if there would be coke ovens. This would be the longest journey yet, past Nancy's sister in Newton and Adeline's children in Cobb County; past Atlanta, Stone Mountain, and Athens. It took more than a day until they made it to the smaller camp. When they arrived they looked at each other, stunned to find that the other prisoners were women. For nine years they had thought they might be two of the only women in stripes in all of Georgia. If they made it out of Dade they could definitely make it out of this Heardmont place. Adeline took Nancy's hand again when she saw the look of terror on her face as Colonel Maddox patted Nancy's shoulder. And she covered a shivering Nancy with her own blanket and held her head as she retched on the long night after the guard took his turn with her. And they hugged when Nancy told her three weeks later that she had to put the rags on, both relieved that no baby would be coming, at least not this time.[17]

From then on Adeline suffered with Nancy. Like others in the camp, Nancy caught the debilitating "all overs," and the pain seemed to be everywhere. Her neck was always wet from the tears and she never rested, but the doctor said the pain was in Nancy's mind.[18] Adeline visited Nancy in the sick quarters when she caught fever, and they scowled at the guards for making Nancy leave after only four days when she was clearly still not well. Adeline was the first to notice that Nancy began to slack in the fields when she normally moved so fast. She asked what was wrong but Nancy didn't have an answer. When guards failed to quicken Nancy's pace with lashes she was again put in the camp hospital bed in severe pain from the lacerations and from the jolts in her bones.[19] Adeline came every night with verses and questions and demands, blinking hard and often, determined not to let the tears leave her eyes. "Are you better?" she would ask, on May 17th and 18th and 19th and every day until after two weeks Nancy was better, the pain in her legs now only a dull ache, and the throbbing had subsided. The night she left the hospital, there were no hushed memories of Moses. "Don't get sick again," was all Adeline would say before she went to sleep.

At Heardmont there were women from all over Georgia and Adeline would try to lift Nancy's spirits by recalling the stories of the day. One of the Atlanta women said that before she was arrested, a schoolteacher came to her house talking about domestic virtue and conduct and industrial schools. The paper in her hand had a round circle on it with the words "lifting as we climb." They all thought it was funny; they already knew how to lift. It was practically all they did, lifting and carrying all of the clothes in Georgia. But the words of the lifting and climbing lady remained with them; just before the schoolteacher left the house she said that the colored women's club was wearying the governor about the vicious lease and that one day soon they would get rid of it. As the days went on the women at Heardmont hoped the schoolteachers' wearying was working because plowing and hoeing and pulling carts and having babies who resembled the guards as much as the mothers taxed them, body and soul.

Twelve years of hard labor and captivity exhausted Adeline, who took sick just as the flowers bloomed and days became hotter in 1897. Now it was Nancy's turn to visit the camp sick quarters every single day; they imagined Adeline's oldest daughter, laughing and tugging at her hair to keep it in place. Nancy's "all overs" did not keep her from whispering with Adeline, though she was crushed every time Addie's smile tightened from the sharp, stabbing pains in her stomach. It was a life's love built from the intimacy of two dungeon camps and more than four thousand days filled with agony and affection, fear and fondness, rage and rememories. Nancy ripped a piece from her skirt and wrapped it around Adeline's wrist so she could be with her even when she had to return to work. She thought about the men who had vomited and went to the bathroom all night at Dade, and how one never got well. She thought about how easily people died from going to the bathroom too much or, in Adeline's case, not enough. She prayed that Addie would not die and she visited the spot where they put the cross after Laney Long collapsed next to them in the fields and she asked Laney to keep Adeline alive with her. After two weeks, when it was harder for Adeline to speak, Nancy held the cold cloth at her friend's head. Addie listened as Nancy told her years worth of private things, alone for the first time because, strangely, there were no other women in the infirmary while Addie was sick.[20] On June 6th Nancy held Adeline's hand tight; she was in such a bad way. She cursed the guards who forced her to return to work, knowing that she would not see Addie alive again. As she went back to pulling carts, she planned what she would say about Adeline, about what she meant to her at the memorial huddle that night.[21] Suddenly Nancy realized that everyone would be looking to her to decide what song they would all sing in her memory; she realized then she didn't know Addie's favorite song and she hated herself, tears streaming, plopping onto the shovel.[22] Eventually, when Nancy was released she took Addie's blanket with her, the one that kept her warm when she was so cold on one of those first dark nights at Heardmont.[23]

A SPECULATIVE ACCOUNTING of the lives of Nancy Morris and Adeline Henderson grounded in and elaborated from a range of archival documents is not an attempt to romanticize women's lives or relationships and does not remedy archival gaps or offer a redemptive reading, but instead enables a historical musing upon the emotions, ambivalences, and intimacies that might have marked their experiences in the context of overwhelming violence. Imprisoned women's relationships with each other are mostly buried amid a much more voluminous account of the violence they endured. In municipal camps where black women were imprisoned for shorter periods near their homes they were able to maintain friendships even after confinement.[24] After being released from the Fulton County chain gang in 1884 Matt Clark went back at least once to visit her friends there.[25] Yet felony prisoners like Nancy Morris and Adeline Henderson were often sent to camps far from home, and while distance made relationships more difficult to sustain after they were released, they were incarcerated for longer periods and they had time to develop close bonds. Black women in particular would need each other. Although there is record of only one white woman being whipped in Georgia's prison system, as this chapter reveals black women in Georgia's convict camps were the target of regular, institutionalized physical and emotional violence.

White women distinct/separate

Sarah Autry's isolation and despair in George D. Harris's Bartow Iron Works camp was not documented but it must have been immense. She was only twenty years old in 1875, when conditions at Harris's camp were so miserable that they even tested the tolerance of Principal Keeper John T. Brown, whose nostalgia for plantation labor management made him generally impervious to such atrocities. He remarked that the prisoners' physical condition "was deplorable. Scurvy and other diseases were prevailing with nearly the entire force," which was a problem because "eight [convicts were] entirely unable to perform any labor."[26] Given this lack of productivity he was inclined to shut the camp down.

George D. Harris was determined to keep his camp running and he gave a sworn statement in which he described the ample food provided, consisting of beef, bacon, molasses, and vegetables, and "all the bread they can eat."[27] While he admitted that the prisoners' uniforms were dirty, he argued that they were no dirtier than any laboring man's uniform. He boasted that he had hired doctors to care for the sick and professed that his convicts were "satisfied with their treatment as prisoners."[28] Harris claimed that the prisoners were being kept at work and that production was satisfactory to pay contingent expenses to the state.[29] There was one stain on camp conditions, an existential threat to the heroic industrialist endeavoring to operate his mines in the service of southern progress, and it was the stuff of Homer and Hans Christian Andersen: a mythology of black female pathology offered to warrant the wretchedness of the camp.

During a legislative hearing on conditions at his camp, Harris testified that although most prisoners were "comfortable," Sarah Autry was a contaminant in his camp since it was "utterly impossible to keep her clean." He tried desperately to manage her hygiene, providing her with "suits of clothes for change" and forcing her to wash every Sunday. But on the other days of the week she refused. As she was "perfectly indifferent to her personal appearance, and of the lowest order of humanity," she polluted the camp, infecting the entire environment.[30] Harris rehearsed the tale with his camp overseer Zachariah Penn, as it was the final strategy to save Bartow Iron Works. Penn faithfully echoed Harris's statements, testifying that Autry was "required to wash and dress just as the other prisoners are required to wash and dress" but that it was "impossible with ordinary effort to keep her clean."[31] Harris and Penn's strategy failed, and prison authorities took the extremely unusual action of shutting the camp down.

In the clutches of captivity, where filth and disease and sweat and the lash were rampant, perhaps Sarah Autry conceived of the daily bath as an exercise in futility. Perhaps she refused to bathe as a performative rebuttal to the mobilization of discourses of camp benignancy that allowed for the painful destruction of her body and estrangement from her loved ones. In the imaginary of prison camp authorities Autry was viral, at once incurable and transmissable. Perhaps, given the absence of other recourse, she claimed virulence, withholding the self-labor of purification as an assertion of humanity, contesting the ability of convict camp operators to legitimate carceral starvation and violence through presentations of black contentedness; a most emphatically queer subject's staged corporeal disidentification with the material and representational structures of carceral subjection that were premised upon material starvation and discourses of contentment.[32] If Autry staged this refusal, she would not be the last imprisoned woman to wage such a protest; in 1980, women at Armagh Prison in Ireland held a "dirty protest," refusing to bathe in both support of the Irish nationalist struggle and in protest against their brutalization by prison guards.[33] Conditions being what they were at Harris's "deplorable" camp where six of forty-seven prisoners died, it is likely that Autry was denied basic amenities and her sentence meant suffering without access to clean water in quarters that lacked any barriers to the heat or the cold. Reports of her alleged filthiness likely derive from a combination of malingering by authorities, deprivation, and refusal.[34] It is apparent that she had no protection from the ire of vexed camp owners and guards, who, it is clear, detested her so fiercely that they centered her in a narrative about the future of iron mining meant to appeal to the core principles of black female abjection that defined white supremacy.

Women and men alike faced food scarcity, disease, work injuries, excruciating labor demands, violence, and death. The standards for camp management mandated only the most minimal requirements for prisoners' sustenance and since laborers were so cheap their expiration was tolerable under convict leasing. The specifications varied slightly over time, but the best possible rations in convict camps consisted of beef, pork or mutton twice per week, fresh vegetables three times per week, dried fruit on days that vegetables were not served, molasses two days per week, corn bread five days per week, and wheat bread two days per week. Compliance with such specifications was rare. The camp barracks, which required each prisoner to have five hundred cubic feet of breathing space, were to be cleaned every two weeks. Hours of labor were from sunrise to sunset each day except Sunday. Beginning in the 1880s the state required that on the Sabbath day prisoners were supposed to be "released from their chains" and allowed to worship, and sleeping quarters were to be segregated by race and gender.[35]

Official investigations were sporadic but observers found ample evidence of neglect and brutality. Following the 1870 special investigation of penitentiary conditions Principal Keeper John Darnell had to concede that treatment of convicts in the penitentiary was "not as the legislature contemplated it should be," that prisoners were kept at work until 10:00 P.M., and that they were whipped brutally, sometimes to death.[36] During that investigation Hubbard Cureton, who had recently been released from Grant, Alexander, and Co. convict camp, testified they had been forced to begin work at 5:00 A.M. and ended "about deep dark."[37] They received a half-hour break in the winter and one hour for break in the summer. Cureton received a "wedge of bread and ration of meat" for breakfast and lunch. For dinner he received only a wedge of bread and syrup. He testified that he sometimes could have eaten three or four times the portions of food he was given.[38] James Maxwell, who was imprisoned on the lease at the same time, testified that he seldom had enough to eat.

Although Harris claimed that he did everything possible to induce Sarah Autry to wash, it is clear that cleanliness and comfort of imprisoned women and men was not the primary concern for convict overseers and managers. On the Macon and Brunswick Railroad, prisoners were not allowed to wash their face and hands before working in the morning. They were forced to bathe with other prisoners in only six inches of dirty water. James Maxwell was sometimes forced to use drinking water to clean his face. At other times he felt too dirty to eat.[39]

In 1886 the principal keeper discovered that prisoners in one camp had "no fresh or any other kind of beef" and hardly any vegetables.[40] Almost every prisoner he spoke to complained that he or she did not get enough to eat. At another camp he found that the "buildings" were not appropriate and conditions were very unhealthy. In 1887 in Polk County convict camps there were no religious services offered; the beds for prisoners were inadequate, and prisoners were worked at nearly every hour of the day and night, with only one hour of rest in the middle of the day instead of the recommended two hours.[41] In 1888 at Rising Fawn iron ore mines camp, the bedding and barracks were filthy and sickness was rampant.[42] In 1889 Fulton County prisoners complained of starvation and relentless beatings.[43] In 1895 Principal Keeper Joseph Turner found that in Kramer, Georgia, prisoners were worked at night and on Sunday.[44] The grand juries that observed these camps consistently described abominable conditions, yet determined that the camps were generally acceptable, model even. Neither starvation, nor disease, nor filth, nor flagellation undermined their findings that Georgia's convict lease camps were operating under the law and within the bounds of moral acceptability.

A special investigation of misdemeanor camps in 1895 reveals the persistence of deplorable conditions into the turn of the century.[45] Imprisoned women and men were forced to sleep in hovels without floors, tents on the bare ground with vermin-filled bedding. Sleeping quarters were "veritable sweat boxes" and prisoners were forced to go for weeks without changing clothes.[46] Two years later another investigation found that in some camps prisoners were forced to work as many as twelve to fifteen hours per day and the stench of fecal matter permeated the camp. The special inspector was, however, satisfied with the amount of food prisoners received, noting, "a convict, like a mule, must be fed if you expect paying returns from his labor."[47]

Convict leasing "depended upon the heritage of slavery and the allure of industrial capitalism," the combination of which produced a modern system in which capitalist development was forged through structures of antiblack racism and terror.[48] Convict leasing represented a gendered regime of neoslavery that constituted modernity by extending the gender logics produced under slavery through gendered racial terror and gendered regimes of brutal labor exploitation. Jim Crow modernity premised upon black subordination in the service of southern capitalist development required definitive ideas about gender difference. Whiteness was constituted through gender normativity and therefore black antinormativity had to be continually reasserted for the maintenance of white supremacy. If at the turn of the century lynching increasingly incorporated symbols of industrial and cultural progress (telephone poles, bridges, and photography) as part of its violent apparatus and spectacle, convict leasing also created modernity, constructing infrastructure for southern material development in a system so vicious that black death scarcely mattered as convict labor was so cheap and abundant that individual laborers were easily replaceable.[49]

In George D. Harris's account of the fate of southern modernization and modernity, black female bodies were envisioned as critical to the future of Bartow Iron Works camp—their capacity to labor, their unfitness for civilization, their incorrigibility, their position as anathema to femininity, and their general repugnance were crucial to the prospects of southern development. Sarah Autry's body was positioned then as stain, virus, and threat in order to elide the camp's degraded and inhumane conditions.[50] While it is clear that bondage, deprivation, and psychic and bodily terrorization link slavery and convict leasing as continuous regimes of antiblack violence, labor extraction, and captivity, a gendered analysis of convict leasing reveals additional continuities. As under slavery, black female bodies remained valuable reproductive resources. Black female injury was an ideological resource for the production of white womanhood as the paragon of gender normativity and the exclusive subject of chivalry. The history of slavery reveals that gender ideology was necessary scaffolding for the perpetuation of the peculiar institution, and that black female bodies served as key resources in the economic development of the system.

Although less direct and perhaps less visible, the reproduction of property was still part of the maintenance of convict labor in the aftermath of abolition. As chapter 1 revealed, the production of discourses of bad motherhood was mobilized to punish black women, to send them to municipal and county convict camps, and to classify their children as criminal and therefore imprisonable. The punishing discourses about black women used motherhood as a site through which to demean black humanity and justify the criminalization of "poorly bred" black children, producing a criminalized race of laborers who could be apprehended and worked to the bone. As under slavery, reproduction continued to enable forced labor; in this instance through the notion that the black female body reproduced criminality and, by extension, a class of subjects that could be made captive and worked mercilessly. Indeed, Principal Keeper John T. Brown reasoned that since the war "the poor creatures" had been so "stirred up on the subjects of politics and religion" that without better advising the state would need to invest in "a number of islands, for the time is not distant when these young vagrants will get out of their long shirts and into 'Georgia Stripes.'"[51]

As in the plantation household, black women remained a vital resource in social reproduction. Under slavery black women performed grueling household labor that allowed for the production of white femininity as the creator of a tranquil, warm, and inviting plantation household;[52] under convict leasing black women's reproductive labor allowed the camp to function, albeit as a space of disease and death. As they struggled to use the meager resources at their disposal for the survival of their communities, black women's simultaneous burden of providing for their own family's subsistence and performing grueling domestic and field labor was extended in the experience of convict camp bondage. As under slavery, black women continued to face a double labor burden; they had to cook, mend, clean, and launder and also had to hoe, plow, dig, mine, saw, pull carts, blacksmith, and grade the streets under the demands of each convict camp. Black female labor continued to be conscripted for both production and reproduction, and their bodies were terrain for the consolidation of white supremacist ideology. The rape and sexualized torture of black women signaled that the privileges of white male supremacy continued to consist of unfettered sexual access to black women, and unabated racial-sexual sadism in the carceral neoslavery regime.

Gendered Spheres of Captivity

During the convict-leasing period between 1868 and 1908, private individuals and companies developed a diverse array of convict-leasing industries, beginning with the railroad. There were "no convicts confined inside the walls of the Penitentiary" by 1871 and until 1874 the vast majority of women and men imprisoned in Georgia were forced to work on the railroad.[53] The first state convict-lease contract went to William A. Fort in 1868 but later that year the state legislature passed an act transferring all imprisoned women and men to the camp operated by Grant, Alexander, and Co. for the purposes of constructing the Macon and Augusta Railroad. Between 1871 and 1874 imprisoned women and men worked on the construction of several railroads: the Georgia and Alabama Railroad, Brunswick and Albany Railroad, Georgia Air-Line Railroad, Georgia Western Railroad, and the Northeastern Railroad.[54] As Alex Lichtenstein details, "between 1865 and 1880 five new major rail lines crisscrossed Georgia's countryside, opening up new markets, stimulating the growth of Atlanta, commercializing the Upcountry, and encouraging extractive industry."[55] By 1880 Georgia had increased its railroad track more than any other state besides Texas, and "between 1869 and 1871 alone, Georgia's convicts graded the roadbeds of at least 469 miles of new rail lines."[56] The construction of these railroads was essential for Georgia's manufacturing interests and after 1874, with hundreds of miles of rail line intact, the convict labor industries expanded. The state began contracting people out as forced laborers to brickmaking, turpentine, iron, and coal companies.

Ultimately, Georgia employed convict leasing in myriad industries, however initially the diversification of convict leasing had its skeptics.[57] For some, including John T. Brown who took the principal keeper's office in 1873, the system was becoming too complicated. In 1875 he proposed a simpler plan for the future of convict leasing; the solution was to make convict leasing more slaveryesque. He envisioned a carceral island plantation, located just off Savannah, for the production of "sea island cotton, rice and sugar cane."[58] To Brown the island was ideal because its "liquid walls" prevented escape, thereby easing the hardship of managing convicts. The majority of the convicts could be "managed easily on an island, such as I propose, as we once worked slaves on our plantations, and could be worked profitably."[59] Brown was not alone in his explicit plan to make convict labor an extension of slavery. Oran Roberts, his contemporary and a prison administrator in Texas, "harked back to the antebellum society he had long idealized" by using black field labor to construct an industrialized prison system for the supposed benefit of whites. Like Roberts, Brown hoped to use black prisoners primarily as plantation laborers.[60] But while Texas established a hybrid plantation/penitentiary system, Georgia created a more complex convict labor system that incorporated field labor as one of a diverse array of industries that relied upon prisoners. In 1874 fifty prisoners were leased out to Henry Stevens for "various jobs" around his place and in his neighborhood, and several convict camp plantations including Old Town were established. In addition to agriculture Georgia relied upon convict labor for its modernization industries. By the early 1880s sawmilling and lime quarrying were added to the list of industries that utilized the labor of prisoners. By 1888 there were fourteen permanent state convict camps and three temporary camps. These camps were filled with shackled people who ensured through their captive labor that Georgia would not languish in the dark place of postbellum defeat, but would instead develop, contribute, and integrate into to a modern nation worked by the "free."

Women were usually the minority in convict camps and this likely exacerbated the isolation of punishment. While they may have been in the minority, between 1868 and 1908 women were imprisoned in virtually every single convict camp in Georgia including Fort's and Grant, Alexander, and Co's railroad camps; those administered by the Bartow Iron Works, Bolton broom factory, Central Georgia Land and Lumber Co., Chattahoochee Brick Company, Chattahoochee Lumber Company, Dade County Coal Mines, Du Bois sawmill, Graysville lime quarry, the Jefferson County Railroad, and Rising Fawn iron ore mines; as well as Camp Heardmont, Old Town camp, Smith and Taylor's farm, the Fulton County almshouse convict camp, and Milledgeville State Prison Farm.

The principal keeper's account of women's work changed from year to year, depending on the man in the office. In January 1870 Principal Keeper John Darnell reported that the female convicts "are all colored, but one, and are all worked without any discrimination with the male convicts."[61] In 1870 there was a state congressional investigation of the conditions of William D. Grant's lease that was sparked by a small number of critics, both private citizens and legislators, including the Reconstruction Era's black state legislators. Grant denied the charge that women ever worked side by side with men, stating, "the stouter ones shovel to themselves in a light material."[62] Yet formerly imprisoned men also testified before the committee, contradicting Grant's contention that women did different work and confirming that women did the same work as men. One former prisoner, Thornton Hightower, testified that women "shovel dirt and drive carts. Sometimes there are more women than are needed to drive carts; then they are put to shoveling dirt with the men."[63] Another former prisoner, Stephen Miller, confirmed this account, testifying that in rare cases men were given washing detail even when there were women in camps who could have carried out laundry duties, and that women were routinely worked alongside men.[64] When the investigatory report was finalized, largely dismissing the appalling stories that prisoners recounted, the three black legislators on the committee challenged the senate, and one even called then governor Bullock a murderer.[65] The investigation changed little for women or men, and by the turn of the century R. F. Wright reported in his 1895 *Special Report on Misdemeanor Convicts* that women and men were still "worked together indiscriminately."[66]

In 1874 Principal Keeper John T. Brown observed that the women, "apportioned promiscuously to the several lessees," were "employed as cooks, washer-women, and other light work in the prison quarters."[67] "Apportioned promiscuously" indicated that although Brown did not decide which women were sent where by their specific characteristics, he did ensure that women were sent to each of the convict camps to provide the indispensible domestic labor required to sustain even the most disgusting camp conditions. Ominously and not incidentally, Brown categorized black female "promiscuous" allocation to convict camps and labors in the most sexually suggestive way possible, a labor designation intimating the acceptability of rape. Promiscuous apportionment might characterize the gendered racial labor dynamics of Jim Crow modernity in which sexual and economic violence merged; sexual, industrial, and reproductive labor constituted the field of exploitation and terror. What Brown described as "light duty" was in fact grueling, arduous domestic labor. Cooks were forced to wake up two or three hours before the other workers at Grant, Alexander, and Co camp.[68] Some were required to wake up at 1:00 A.M. or 2:00 A.M. to prepare food for the entire camp, which could be from fifty to 150 prisoners, and to put the food into buckets. Black women who had few options but to perform domestic labor for low pay in the free world were now forced to carry out domestic manual labor without pay, and under the most heinous of conditions as convicts. Domestic work at the convict camp included cooking for mass consumption, washing, and mending prison uniforms that were, according to one lessee, dirty and tattered as the "prisoners often tear their clothes during the week."[69]

John T. Brown's description of "light duty" is part of a patriarchal undervaluation of the difficulty of domestic work for both white and black women. Yet Brown's idea of what constituted "light work" was also informed by his personal history as a slave driver. In 1873 Brown outlined his qualifications for the position of penitentiary keeper: "having spent most of my life on public works, as a contractor, managing large forces of slave and freed labor, I feel competent to judge well organized and well worked forces."[70] His contempt for formerly enslaved women and men was apparent in his 1873 report, which included his history of the penitentiary system. According to Brown the penitentiary was "soon filled to overflowing with negro convicts, as all men of common sense saw would be the case as soon as freedom was conferred to the slave population."[71] He described prisoners as "astonishingly dissolute, profligate and insolent. Some of them will insult the keeper to his face, and laugh at the terrors of their punishment . . . in such cases a more severe mode of punishment should be resorted to."[72] Brown, unfazed by dangerous and unhealthy camp conditions, regularly issued favorable reports about the convict camp, remarking upon the positive diet and health of imprisoned women and men.

Pearl Black was one of the few women in the Sumter convict camp in 1908, and was expected to perform domestic work for the entire chain gang. She was sentenced to twelve months for adultery and was pregnant when she was arrested. Black was "on her feet cooking" in the Sumter chain gang when she was eight months pregnant, and complained to prison camp officials that she was suffering great pain.[73] As Tera Hunter has revealed, in antebellum Georgia even young (six-year-old) girls were expected to "nurse, cook, chop in the fields, chop wood, bring water, wash, iron, and in general just do everything." The life of women imprisoned in Georgia's convict camps mirrored this experience, where there was a distinct expectation that women would perform the domestic work for the camps, but also that they would "in general just do everything."[74]

Imprisoned women faced an extraordinary double burden. While they had to perform domestic duties, they were also expected to carry out the other tasks that each camp industry required. Black women like Lizzie Patterson, whose story was told in chapter 1 and who worked on the construction of the Georgia Air-Line Railroad, were not exempted from hard labor because they were women.[75] Since lessees paid for the labor of women as they did for men, they complained when women were not performing up to the general standard of convict work. In 1893 chain gang authorities refused to pay Walton County for Susan Conyers's labor because her old age and illness prevented her from doing the strenuous work required on the chain gang.[76]

By the late nineteenth century farmwork became a common form of imprisoned women's labor but they were also forcibly employed in the other convict industries. In 1891 45 percent of the prisoners sent to Old Town farm were women.[77] In 1898 black women were imprisoned in turpentine and sawmilling camps across the state, as well as on public roads. There was also one white woman working on the public roads of Floyd County. As chapter 3 details, Lizzie Boatwright's torture and her experience "working as a man" digging ditches at W. H. and J. H. Griffin's camp, would become emblematic of the wrongs of convict leasing for members of the National Association of Colored Women (NACW).[78]

Pregnancy exacerbated the impact of backbreaking labor demands for women in Georgia's convict camps. One woman in Richmond County's brickmaking camp told a Special Committee on the Condition of the Criminals in 1881 that overwork led to the premature birth of her child when she was six months pregnant.[79] She and many other black women including Mamie Cubbo, Hattie Johnson, Lula Johnson, and Annie Lucas were sent to the chain gang despite being pregnant at the time of their sentencing.[80] In 1895 Susan Gardner was pregnant when she was sent to the Muscogee Rock Pile. After serving three months of an eight-month sentence her health was in drastic decline and she was not expected to recover before the end of her sentence. She was released only shortly before she was to give birth, when she could no longer work at all.[81] In 1881 Leta Morris served most of her short sentence on the Atlanta city chain gang despite giving birth during her imprisonment.[82]

Although pregnancy was rarely viewed as a condition that justified judicial leniency, black women were sometimes released early when their bodies were no longer useful to the lessees. In 1884, a twenty-year-old black woman named Ella Gamble was given a life sentence for arson and sentenced to the Chattahoochee Brick Company's convict camp.[83] She was pregnant when she arrived.[84] Twenty years later, when she filed her appeal for pardon in 1904, she had been diagnosed with cancer of the womb, and her lawyer reported that her condition had declined dramatically "on account of the heavy work she has been compelled to do since her confinement."[85] By the time of her appeal she had been transferred from Chattahoochee to Milledgeville, where the prison physician examined her. He was ambivalent about whether she should be released. He wrote to the judge that a trip home might cause a sudden hemorrhage and immediate death. He had explained the risk to Gamble, but she was willing to make the perilous trip anyway. She wrote to Joseph Turner, chairman of the Prison Commission, pleading for his attention:

> Judge Turner I do humble beg you to please if there is any way in this world to stop me from bleeding to death please for the lord's sake Judge I humble beg you to send me home to my brother so he can give me cure and then I will return back to the farm. If you will not agree to let me go otherwise Judge I beg you to please help me save my life for I am bleeding day after day.[86]

It is difficult to know whether Turner was swayed by Gamble's plea for help, or whether he had shrewdly calculated the dramatic decline in her productive value that her condition imposed, but he granted her release in 1904.[87] Florence Rivers was in similarly dire medical straits in 1906, when she submitted a letter to the Prison Commission from the secretary-treasurer of the Chattahoochee Lumber Company's convict camp verifying that she was going blind and was completely unable to work; her sentence was commuted that year. In 1905 Nellie Carpenter, who had been imprisoned for a year and had two remaining to serve, petitioned for a pardon because she was "badly afflicted by disease having suffered for years with womb trouble which renders her physically unable to labor."[88] Joseph Turner recommended that her petition be granted on the grounds that "she is afflicted badly with uterine disease causing frequent hemorrhages which render her incapable of work . . . arduous labor would endanger her life."[89] Yet Turner's recommendation was a perverse interpretation of leniency. Her original sentence was three years; he granted a conditional pardon, ruling that if she could pay a fine of $100 she may be released, but if she did not have the means, he would reduce her sentence by a year, leaving her with twelve months on the chain gang.[90] Nellie Carpenter was made to pay to compensate for her decline in value as a convict laborer, or she would be forced to remain imprisoned despite her profuse hemorrhaging and chronic pain. There is no record of whether her fine was paid or whether she had to remain in captivity. Part of the prison commissioner's power derived from caprice, his complete control over the terms under which mercy was allotted. One year before denying Carpenter an unconditional pardon Turner granted one for Leila Blackman, who was also pregnant at the time of her arrest. She was released two months early because "she has been unable to labor on the chain gang and has been confined . . . owing to her health she will not be able to labor on the chain gang during the term of her sentence."[91]

As under slavery, there were contradictions embedded in prison commissioners' and governors' decisions regarding black female labor. Julia Morton was convicted of arson in 1899 and petitioned for parole in 1908. She submitted a request stating that she had violent fits and fainting spells, and was therefore "unable to perform manual labor."[92] She also submitted a prison physician's letter that affirmed that her convulsions made her "worthless for the time being."[93] Despite the substantiation of her economic worthlessness, her request for parole was denied. From the 1870s through the 1930s authorities approved clemency applications from most white women on the grounds that they were too frail to work.[94] The neoslavery carceral state extended ideas of black female indomitability, namely that "strength and ability to bear fatigue, argued to be so distasteful a presence in a white woman, were positive features to be emphasized in the promotion and selling of a black female field hand at a slave auction."[95] When faced with the threat of grueling convict labor, white women were viewed as sympathetic subjects. For example, W. M. Gammon, chairman of the Floyd County Board of Commissioners of Roads and Revenue, described Mrs. R. B. Hill as an "unfortunate white woman" and a "pitiable object," and advocated strongly for her release.[96] The disproportionate leniency applied to imprisoned white women reveals that under emancipation, the black female body's capacity for labor was in direct contrast with white women's.[97]

Contrary to such assumptions, black women's bodies were battered and broken by convict labor and sometimes none of the carceral physicians could put them together again; often they did not even try. At some camps there were no hospital facilities or arrangements and in others there was not even a physician available to treat sick or injured men and women. Several lessees boasted that they had not used the services of a physician in years and forced prisoners to make up for work that they missed when they were sick by working extra hours.[98] Mattie Black was one of three prisoners who the Sumter County Board of Commissioners of Roads and Revenue believed were burdens on the state. She, Adolphus Kicks, and Joe Green were in such advanced stages of illness that county officials wrote to the Prison Commission, requesting their pardon. The board of commissioners wrote that Black was "worthless as a laborer" because she was suffering from hysterical convulsions as well as fractures of the breastbone and ribs.[99]

As a result of the arduous field labor at Camp Heardmont women suffered lacerated hands, boils, and sprains. Mary Washington's finger was gashed so bad it had to be amputated. Fannie Drinks sustained a cut that became infected with pyaemia, a disease that attacks festering, open wounds. Pyaemia often proved fatal in the nineteenth century, and although there is no record indicating whether or not Fannie recovered, her arm had to be amputated in an attempt to stop the spread of the infection. Rose Henderson, Sarah Johnson, and Annie Marshall were all battered by falling trees. At the Fulton County almshouse convict camp, Sarah Mayes fell and broke her shoulder while she was working and at Milledgeville Anna Hendley was seriously injured after falling off of a wagon.[100] Even those lucky enough to keep their limbs were worked to the bone, sustaining work-related injuries. Amelia Moreland was hospitalized for a foot laceration and Evelyn Brown sprained her knee while at work.[101]

If the actual labor did not pummel the body, disease incapacitated imprisoned women, leaving no one unscathed. At Camp Heardmont and throughout Georgia's convict camps pneumonia, pleurisy, malaria, tuberculosis, and the flu were among the bacterial and infectious diseases made rampant by atrocious camp conditions. Since Georgia did not consistently track deaths in convict camps by gender and records of illness are also incomplete, it is unclear how many imprisoned women died before they were released. At Camp Heardmont at least five black women died between 1894 and 1897 of conditions including cholera, pneumonia, fecal impaction, and sunstroke. Laney Long had been suffering from lung congestion and her body gave out in the fields when she was only thirty years old. Martha Williams, whose previous health had been good, also died suddenly while at work in the fields at Heardmont.[102] At the Fulton County almshouse convict camp Mary Boyd contracted the flu, which weakened her lungs and incapacitated her. Dr. R. L. Hope predicted that the illness would soon progress into consumption.[103] Women suffering from serious illness were, in rare cases, allowed to remain in the hospital for prolonged periods. Sarah Dixon, a white woman who was sent to Milledgeville for murder, spent two years at the prison hospital with a catarrh "or some other dreadful malady" that made it almost impossible for her to swallow. She was anesthetized with opium, and was released early upon the recommendation of the prison physician, who was certain that she would soon die.[104] For white women socialized to fear black men and construct their identities through difference from black women, the convict camp was also a site of intense anguish. In 1890 the emotional pain of convict life was too much for a seventeen-year-old white girl named Callie Bush, who was the only white woman at Graysville lime quarry camp. Indeed she was the only white woman in Georgia's felony convict system at the time. After serving one year of her fifteen-year sentence she told a guard that she "would rather be dead than penned up this way" and committed suicide by drowning herself in the Chickamauga River.[105]

Bessie Robinson, a black woman who was sent to the Fulton County almshouse convict camp for charging goods from a store to the account of her employer, was incapacitated by episodic swelling and intense pain from a burn she had sustained as a child. Still, she was never allowed to recover from the episodic inflammations and throbbing but instead was forced to work through the excruciating pain.[106] Such experiences were common. Neuralgia is a vague diagnosis that describes acute, intense nerve pain; often used to described facial nerve pain, neuralgia pain could result from a wide range of conditions including diabetes, rheumatism, multiple sclerosis, infections, blood vessel inflammations or clots, tumors, trauma, or herpes. The condition takes many forms and targets different areas of the body, and contact with any affected area would cause agonizing pain. Trigeminal (facial) neuralgia pain can be so intense that it has been termed the "suicide disease." Women hospitalized for neuralgia at Camp Heardmont were kept under observation for short periods of time before they were "returned to work." The combination of overwhelming pain and heavy agricultural labor made convict life traumatic for women who suffered from a disease that made even the slightest touch extremely painful.

The hyperimprisonability of black female subjects and the assumption of their deviance led to the establishment of several all-female county convict camps in Georgia beginning in the 1880s, including Camp Bolton, the Fulton County women's camp, and Camp Heardmont. The establishment of all-female convict camps may be seen as an early Progressive reform, one that conformed to the mandate to delineate the boundaries of male and female life and improve public infrastructure and services. Yet in the South the logic and institutionalization of separation meant the perpetuation of ideologies of racial inferiority and structures of subjugation rather than material improvement. The establishment of separate women's camps by white male penal authorities appears to be a response to the perceived incorrigibility and lasciviousness of black female prisoners, rather than an attempt to improve their conditions. The creation of a space of captivity specifically for black women signaled their difference from, rather than conformity to, normative gender categories. The public narrative about the establishment of Camp Bolton was that black women were more trouble than black men, primarily because of their irrepressible libido. As one report put it, "in spite of considerable pains taken to keep the female convicts on good behavior, there has always been more trouble with them than with the men, and a good many scandalous things have happened, in spite of all precautions."[107]

Black women's bodies were relocated but not protected from the harrowing reality of convict labor. The first all-female convict camp was built in Atlanta in 1885, for women convicted of both municipal and state crimes. The female convict camp was to be located on the property for Fulton County's brand new almshouse for paupers and the elderly. Prior to 1885 the almshouse was deemed "entirely inadequate and uncomfortable in the winter."[108] The Fulton County Grand Jury recommended that the facility be moved closer to the city and that a "brick building [be] erected capable of more accommodations and conveniences for the better care and attention to the unfortunate poor and helpless of our county."[109] The city's captive black female labor force weathered the heat with little shelter and made the brick so that the county poor could be transferred from "rude hovels" to a brand new building that would keep out the cold.[110] Dr. R. L. Hope, superintendent of the almshouse and female convict camp recalled years later, "all the bricks that were used in the construction of the almshouse were made by the women convicts. At the time, there were eighteen women who were thus engaged in making brick. They were aided by five men and two brick molders."[111] Women who had been convicted in city court were forced to build the infrastructure for their future captivity.

Like the male and female prisoners who labored for the Chattahoochee Brick Company, the women who made the almshouse brick had to shovel wet clay and transport it back to a plant. There they had to push the clay through rectangular molds, then fire the bricks in coal kilns, where one or more of the brickmakers would have to stand nearby the kiln, enduring the blistering heat of the kiln in order to toss batches of bricks into the top of a large oven.[112] The predominantly female crew made 40,000 bricks in Georgia's summer heat in 1884. They were forced to rush to complete the job before winter interfered with the construction of the new facility.[113] The women at the almshouse convict camp served sentences ranging from six to twelve months. They were required to perform domestic and agricultural labor, cooking and cleaning for the residents of the almshouse, farming, and planting cotton. In 1885 they produced 800 bushels of corn, 700 bushels of potatoes, 100 bushels of peas, 100 bushels of onions, and 2,400 pounds of meat—provisions for the almshouse residents.[114] They were also assigned to grade the roads surrounding the almshouse.[115] By 1897 several other counties including Chatham, Laurens, Glynn, and Richmond had county or almshouse farms for female misdemeanor prisoners, but while some women convicted of misdemeanors in these and other counties were sent to all-female camps, other black women were sent to camps with male prisoners.

The Fulton County almshouse and its convict camp were relocated in 1911. The camp continued to exist until at least the late 1930s, when Thomas Reed wrote a memorandum on the city services of Atlanta condemning the conditions at the almshouse and recommending that it be closed. Reed and other investigators believed that if a new almshouse were to be built, it should not "be allowed to depend for its labor supply on the women's convict camp" because its patients should be cared for by the standards used at hospitals.[116] By midcentury the almshouses were closed and the buildings and surrounding land became what is now the Chastain Park Amphitheater, North Fulton Golf Course, and Chastain Arts Center. The windows of a small back room in the Chastain Arts Center still contain the prison bars used to prevent the escape of imprisoned black women who were kept there.[117]

Working-class white women who were convicted of city crimes including keeping a disorderly house and larceny were usually sentenced to serve terms at the Fulton County jail instead of the almshouse convict camp.[118] Belle Russell was one of the few white women who were imprisoned at the almshouse; she had been convicted of "larceny from person" in 1904 and ordered to pay $100 or serve twelve months on the public works.[119] Unable to pay the fine, she served several months in the Fulton County jail before she was sent to the almshouse convict camp, but once there she remained in bed most of the time with rheumatism.[120]

Despite Belle Russell's experience, it was so rare for a white woman to be sentenced to the almshouse convict camp that it served as grounds for Myrtle Blake's pardon. In May 1897 she and Pearl Harrison were convicted of robbing two men on the street. Harrison fled authorities and Blake was sent to the almshouse camp. After serving six months of a nine-month sentence she received a pardon at the urging of John Berry, an Atlanta city court judge. Berry's logic resembles that of the judge in Martha Gault's case described in chapter 1: he described her crime as an aggravated one but was appealing to the governor for clemency because he feared he had made a severe moral error. He explained that he did not realize at the time of his sentence that "she would be confined in the same room with negro women."[121] Such a punishment was an affront to the ideology of white supremacy and, by 1897, the racial separation that defined Jim Crow modernity. Judge Berry was quite concerned since she was the only white convict there and, to add insult to injury, she was forced to wear the striped uniform. His view of these facts, coupled with her good conduct, was grounds for early release. State officials and reporters often reiterated the exceptionality of a white woman in the convict camp. Mattie White, a "woman of rare beauty," was reputedly the only white woman in Floyd County convict camp in 1896, and her confinement with black prisoners sparked public outrage.[122]

In Atlanta and throughout the state, convict labor was reserved almost exclusively for black women. In June 1900 there were twenty-five women serving time at the almshouse convict camp. All of the women were black and the youngest, Mamie Bowers, was only sixteen years old.[123] By 1904 three of the forty-seven women in the almshouse convict camp were white, but only one white woman lived in the convict camp barracks. Two of them resided in the almshouse building rather than the convict camp in order to receive medical treatment.[124] In fact, almost all of the white women sent to the almshouse convict camp were diverted from the prison barracks to the almshouse itself. With the exception of Myrtle Blake, every white female convict sent to the Fulton County almshouse camp was allowed to live inside the almshouse building. Narcissa Reynolds and Cornelia Rake, two white women convicted of begging in the streets in 1907, were both serving their time in the almshouse rather than the convict camp barracks. They had been convicted of vagrancy together, but only one of them, Reynolds, was ill. Rake was allowed to remain in the almshouse to keep Reynolds company.[125] Although both women were policed for occupying public space in ways that challenged white women's absolute association with domesticity, their behavior elicited a social response that was based upon notions of white feminine protection and domesticity.

The production of Myrtle Blake, Cornelia Rake, and Narcissa Reynolds as subjects deserving of protection required that they be construed in opposition to the imprisoned black female subjects from whom they were separated, and the polarity between black and white female subjects entrenched the meaning of "woman" as a social category. Dichotomous thinking has been integral to the formation of identity positions and categories, especially with respect to the gendered mind/body binary. Binaries construct identity by hierarchizing and ranking two opposing terms "so that one becomes the privileged term and the other its suppressed, subordinated, negative counterpart."[126] This was the foundation of Jim Crow modernity under which moral health and economic progress were defined by difference and separation. Black female bodies performed important cultural labor by serving as the symbolic other against which the iconic symbol of white supremacy—the white lady—could be positioned. Black women at the almshouse convict camp were forced to perform street grading and farming, and also to serve the almshouse residents, including their fellow prisoners who were white women. Black and white women's differential positionality within convict camps is significant because it sheds light on the absoluteness of racial categorizations of gender. This does not mean that white women were not judged for committing crimes or being labeled as prisoners—conviction and imprisonment itself was a severe form of judgment. Still, "white woman" was a fixed, absolute medical-juridical category that was applicable even to its most reviled, ostracized members—those who were deemed convicts and punished by the state.[127]

Camp Bolton was the second all-female convict camp established in Georgia, created as a response to black women's perceived unruliness in the integrated convict camps. Established to control stereotypical black female lasciviousness, the camp was also entangled with the mammy "controlling image," as imprisoned women were forced to create the tools through which other black women would be relegated to domestic servitude, fixing black women's association with subordinated domestic labor.[128] In 1890, thirty women serving sentences at the Chattahoochee Brick Company's convict camp were sent to the newly established Camp Bolton just outside of Atlanta so that they could manufacture "brooms enough to sweep the state of Georgia."[129] That year captive black women were forced to labor without pay, making the tools that would be used in poor black women's low-wage domestic service work. Camp Bolton only remained open for a year and a half. Although the reason for its closure is unclear, by the end of 1891 all of the women at Camp Bolton were transferred to W. H. Maddox's Camp Heardmont in Elbert County. There they worked three thousand acres of his six-thousand-acre plantation along the Savannah River planting wheat, corn, cotton, oats, and grass, and milling flour from sunrise to sunset with one guard for every ten women. At Maddox's Camp their work sometimes also led women to strategies for escape; after doing extensive canal repair work, they used their knowledge of the water and flatboats to evade the bloodhounds that guarded them, "going up and down the river on a boat and the dogs cannot tell which course they have taken."[130] Imprisoned black women were reputedly "as strong as men" and were therefore given arduous sunup to sunset field work.[131] The division of labor at Camp Heardmont was organized by race. There were only between one and three white women imprisoned there in any given year, and they were only made to work in the field as punishment for bad behavior.[132] Pearl Pendergast, a white woman imprisoned at Camp Heardmont, maintained that she was never made to leave her quarters, and was employed in sewing and mending the striped dress uniforms worn by all the prisoners.[133]

By 1898 Camp Heardmont was shut down and women imprisoned there were transferred to Milledgeville State Prison Farm. Milledgeville consisted of separate male and female prison buildings, a dining room in each building, a blacksmith and wood shop, and a hospital.[134] Although Milledgeville's infrastructure resembled a penitentiary, imprisoned women and men were made to perform hard agricultural labor from sunrise to sunset. The prisoners at Milledgeville were women, infirm men, elderly men, and young boys. The vast majority of women at the state farm were black and were, accordingly, excluded from the category of disabled. In fact, they were considered to have a particular capacity for hard labor and assigned a disproportionate amount of the fieldwork at the fledgling state farm. When the newly established Prison Commission assumed oversight of Milledgeville in January 1899 it was described as a disaster, replete with overgrown hedges, obliterated ditches, pine thickets, and cotton lands in disuse. Swamps covered with water had developed, and "not more than one thousand acres of land [was] ready for cultivation."[135] The commission hired some labor to improve the farm; however, black women's labor was viewed as particularly valuable in this

Women at Milledgeville State Prison Farm (circa 1895–1920). Iva Roach Benton Papers, MS 01764. Courtesy of the Georgia Historical Society, Savannah, Georgia.

endeavor. The officers of the Prison Commission observed that since the women had been working at Camp Heardmont for several years they had developed agricultural skills and strength. They described all but five of them as "strong, healthy, and accustomed to this work."[136] Of the 108 men on the farm the Prison Commission surmised that no more than thirty were able to do the work necessary to sustain the farm, and most of the boys confined at Milledgeville were from the city and knew little about farming. At the turn of the century prison authorities believed that the women "having been engaged exclusively in farm work for many years, at Heardmont, under the old lease system, were, when received, the best labor on the farm," and they were primarily responsible for the production and cultivation of crops sufficient to both sustain the prisoners at Milledgeville and be exported for profit.[137]

Whereas Milledgeville held some women convicted of felonies and misdemeanors in captivity, other carceral spaces were designed for those who violated city laws. The geography of Atlanta's municipal convict labor systems shifted over time. By the late 1870s an Act was passed in the city legislature delineating the terrain of convict labor, responding to city residents' objections to the presence of prisoners in the middle of Atlanta's busy streets. Buckhead, which rested on the outskirts of Atlanta but did not become part of the city limits until 1952, became a central location for convict labor. Buckhead's position as both proximate and peripheral to Atlanta made it an ideal terrain for convict labor and both the almshouse convict camp and the Kriese City convict camp were located there. While prisoners in chains could be hidden from view in the bustling center of the city, they would pave the streets surrounding Atlanta, contributing vitally to the city's development. For roughly a decade, from the late 1860s until February 1879, women and men convicted of petty crimes in city court were sent to work ditching, grading, and macadamizing the streets in Atlanta and Fulton County. If the Atlanta station house or Atlanta jail needed cleaning some women would be required to do that labor instead of working the streets.[138] The system of working women and men on city streets existed throughout the state, and did not escape vehement criticism.

In Griffin, Georgia, in 1883 an elderly white woman was spotted working in chains on the city street gang. Local white women were purportedly so moved by this "inhuman spectacle" that they asked a man on the street to try to free her from her chains. Speaking on behalf of the community at large, one resident wrote to the *Griffin News* that white women should be sent to the jail rather than the chain gang because "to make a white woman work with manacles, on the public street, and amongst negro hands, is a crime against that chivalrous regard for the sex which the south especially claims to hold, and we are as much surprised and shocked by this outrage on public sentiment."[139] The crime is not reported in the account of the Griffin woman's injustice, revealing its irrelevance in the popular imagination, yet the fact that authorities chained her in the first place demonstrates that the system was imperfect and fraught with contradiction.

The polarity between black and white women's subject positions was not natural, and therefore had to be reified through reactions to such stories and constant vigilance from judges and prison authorities. A white woman could indeed slip through the cracks, but her humanity was usually recuperated by expressions of outrage and relief from harsh conditions. Such reprieve sometimes came only after experiencing violations, such as being chained and forced to work on the public roads. Still, a white woman in chains regardless of her crime, performing hard labor, represented the absolute decline of the South, and accordingly provided the opportunity for a true act of chivalry. White femininity needed to be liberated from its public "manacles" by any means necessary, legal or not. As with lynching, here white male vigilantism was lauded, since it was perceived to advance the goal of protecting virtuous white womanhood.

In 1879 the city devised a plan to send men and women convicted in city court to serve out their sentences at a rock quarry on Butler Street. Andrew Stewart, the chairman of the Fulton County Committee on Streets, was delighted to finally find a location for the quarry. Prisoners would be transferred there in March, and their labor would be ample for the demands of the city. The corral was fifty by one hundred feet and consisted of several nine-by-nine-foot cells built with the intention of housing up to fifty city court prisoners.[140] A greased sixteen-foot fence with a spiked iron railing surrounded the quarry to prevent escapes. The fence was seen as essential since women and men escaped from the street brigade "almost daily." There were plenty of prisoners in the city stockade to fill the rock quarry cells. Stewart estimated that there were "forty-seven prisoners confined in the cells of the station-house. A good number of these are woman. The idea is to keep the entire force constantly employed with rock hammers breaking up rocks, and then have a hired force on the streets filling up the bad holes . . . with the broken rocks."[141] This new initiative would be a monumental advance toward the cause of constructing good streets in Atlanta. There would be rock enough to pave every street and then build a wall around the city.[142] By 1882 women and men in Atlanta's stockade were divided between the rock quarry and street work. Camp de Emmel, noted for its haunting by Lizzie Patterson in 1883, held forty women and men in 1882.[143]

Black women in Atlanta were consistently forced to perform excruciating rock-breaking work. Just two months before the Camp de Emmel was established, a female rock-cracking brigade was established at the Atlanta stockade composed entirely of women convicted in recorder's court.[144] The number of prisoners working as city convict laborers varied widely from day to day in Atlanta, since the sentences in city court ranged from a few days of street work to twelve-month terms. In June of 1882 there were between fifteen and twenty-five people at work in the quarry at any one time, half of whom were women and children. As a "general thing" they were "nearly all negroes, while now and then a white man or woman is furnished with quarters, where they get plenty to eat and all the work that they can do twelve hours out of every

Convict Leasing and Gendered Racial Terror 85

twenty-four." Two of the women at the quarry were given food preparation detail as part of their daily work.[145]

The Theater of Black Female Abjection

Whether they were held captive in cages at Milledgeville or mobile wagons in convict camps, violence permeated women's experiences of punishment. All violence is, of course, gendered insofar as it is exacted by and against people socially constructed as gendered subjects. Examining violence against black women as gendered racial terror is not meant to reinforce or naturalize the idea that women and African Americans are gendered and racialized subjects while white men are not. Instead, this analysis delineates gendered racial terror as a particularized instrument of state attack against black women and as a mechanism through which gender was constructed in historical, cultural, and political contexts. Recent scholarship has dispelled the narrative of American racial violence that has focused on lynching and race riots and has posited three social subjects of this history: white men (as perpetrators), white women (as foils), and black men (as victims).[146] Yet racial violence exacted upon black women and its meaning for the construction of gender ideology is still underexplored. My analysis of gendered racial terror in Georgia's penal regime builds upon recent scholarly interventions by arguing that specific forms of penal violence operated as cultural tools that reified normative, mutually constitutive, gendered and racial social categories.

Gendered racial terror describes techniques of violence that were inflicted upon black female bodies but were virtually never imposed upon white women. In the extremely rare cases in which such acts of violence were exacted upon white female bodies, they instigated popular outrage and official action.[147] Gendered racial terror was a resource in the production of race as a metalanguage, giving words, in this case "black" and "woman," the power to mean.[148] Its forms included specific psychic, physical, and symbolic acts of violence against black women. Violence exacted upon black women's bodies was useful because the infliction of pain imposes a radical relationship to corporeality and "the association of blacks and females with corporeality excludes and debars them from the public sphere that makes subjectivity possible."[149]

Gendered racial terror should, in this context, be defined by using white female bodies as a barometer for what was tolerable since under the logic of white supremacy. "White woman" was a normative subject position and protection lay at the heart of postbellum politics and the construction of gender categorization during the development of Jim Crow modernity. Moreover, subjects are produced in relation to each other. Just as "the slave is the object or the ground that makes possible the existence of the bourgeois subject and, by negation or contradistinction, defines liberty, citizenship, and the enclosures of the social body," black females as others made white women, and by extension or negation, white normative femininity, possible.[150] For these essential reasons, scenes of gendered racial terror in this chapter must be considered in the context of black women's lack of protection, for these "materialized scene[s] of unprotected female flesh—of female flesh 'ungendered'" reveal black women's position as a radical other to the normative female subject position "woman."[151] Hortense Spillers argues that the reduction of the captive to flesh was produced through its absenting from a subject position, or "a physical and biological expression of 'otherness,'" through which it "translates into a potential for pornotroping and embodies sheer physical powerlessness that slides into a more general 'powerlessness.'" Pornotroping "names the becoming-flesh of the (black) body and forms a primary component in the processes by which human beings are converted into bare life."[152] The southern convict camp was part of an archipelago of pornotropical sites in which black female bodies were rendered flesh for the production of value: the ideological value of the continued relegation of black people to things and, inextricably, carceral value for southern racial capital through the use of such objects for labor. As Gina Dent and Angela Y. Davis have argued, "the prison is itself a border," a tropic defined as a turning point, boundary, or limit, but one that does not merely confine or delineate but produces and reproduces quotidian relations of power.[153] This reproduction is accomplished in part through the mobilization of black women as discursive and material resources for racial subordination and capital accumulation. If "reproductivity names the ensemble of discourses, state and individual practices, and collective fantasies through which modern notions of race, gender, and sexuality have been given form and meaning through the logics and language of reproduction," black female flesh was a reproductive vessel for the state practice of racial imprisonment.[154]

Protection was grounded in the development of a discourse of white female passionlessness and moral purity that construed white women in terms of moral absolutism in order to proliferate a broad political project of racial solidarity over class differences. By the 1880s white female reformers and white male politicians began to argue that even "fallen women" needed to be protected, not castigated.[155] White men carried out acts of gendered racial terror as part of the project of making Jim Crow modernity, which entailed a "sexualized struggle over political power."[156] The construction of gender categories and roles was crucial to the maintenance of white supremacy as a cultural and political institution since white men believed that "black men's attempts to enter the white male domain of politics could seem to foreshadow attempts to enter—and therefore dominate—white men's households, particularly their daughters and wives."[157] The vulnerability of gender categorization meant the attendant vulnerability of political and economic supremacy, and black women had a significant symbolic role to play in this order. While the synonymy between "woman" and "protected subject" became fixed over time, the infliction of violence against black women's bodies and the discourse and practice of protection of white women's bodies was also executed over time, constructing and reifying the meaning of "woman" as a subject position defined by race, and leading to its juridical codification as a social position in 1908.[158] Some of these acts, including whipping, were also exacted against black men, but are still considered gendered racial terror because their infliction upon black women's bodies but not white women's bodies had special significance in delineating the recognizable boundaries of gender categorization.

If enslaved women "fell victim to rape precisely because of their gender," they also fell victim to whipping because of their gendered and raced social position.[159] Indeed, this similitude in treatment only reinforces their proximity to masculinity, rather than to "woman" as a radical "other" to "Man."[160] While there is little evidence to suggest that black women were perceived as men, they were treated and depicted in opposition to normative femininity. They were situated in opposition to the normative gender position, and produced outside of binary oppositional gender categories as something else altogether; that "else" was contradictory and ambiguous but in black women's lives it fundamentally meant exposure to violence. Black women were queered through processes of forced malleability institutionalized under Reconstruction and Jim Crow, through the infrastructure of the courts, convict lease camp and the chain gang.

The modifier "black" indeed repudiated "woman" but was also distinctly different from "man." Black women's subjection to all forms of antiblack violence as well as distinct forms of gendered violence mirrored a historical double burden that has largely been analyzed in terms of labor. If under slavery, in its aftermath, and in the convict camp, black women were forced to perform fieldwork and domestic work, they were also forced to endure antiblack and gender-specific violence.[161] They were caught in double binds, double burdens, and double jeopardy when it came to both labor and violence. It is also worth noting that the violence black women endured under convict leasing was coupled with extreme labor exploitation that rendered them near-commodities, or as some have argued, more expendable than slaves because convicts were so inexpensively replaced.[162] Black women's commodification and violation converges here in a process of gender making in which normative femininity was constituted through its invert, the black female subject.

From the inception of the convict-lease system whipping was part of the infrastructure of control and forced productivity. In 1881 Georgia created the position of whipping boss as a reform for the prevention of excessive violence. In most cases the whipping boss was hired by the lessee, and instead of monitoring or preventing "excessive" violence, he merely legitimized the management techniques and violence carried out by the camp authorities. Along with the investigatory committees of 1870 and 1895, the whipping boss functioned to legitimate the violence of the camp. Investigations created the appearance of concern but produced little change, exposing a stark difference between investigation and oversight. Still, some women attempted to obtain the protection of the whipping boss's ironic stated role as a monitor of excessive violence. In 1890 women at Camp Bolton apparently attempted to diminish the violence they endured there by sending a petition to the governor requesting that a whipping boss be appointed.[163]

Whether a camp employed a whipping boss or not, black women were routinely subjected to punishment by the lash. If they were perceived not to be working hard enough or breaking other rules they were brutally whipped by the camp guards. In 1870 Hubbard Cureton informed the congressional Committee to Investigate the Penitentiary that if prison guards didn't like a particular prisoner they told him or her that they would soon receive medicine. That medicine was the strap. While he was imprisoned he saw women prisoners receive twenty lashes on their naked backsides in front of men for "something they done in the stockade."[164] Thornton Hightower testified at the same investigation that he saw women on the North Georgia Railroad being whipped.

They received fifteen to twenty-five lashes on their bare skin. Thornton saw three women who were accused of driving their carts poorly and quarreling with each other being whipped in front of male guards and prisoners, with their clothes pulled over their heads. James Maxwell, who was imprisoned on the Macon and Brunswick Railroad sometime before 1870, also testified that when women tried to resist whipping they would be held with their clothes pulled over their heads. They would receive between fifteen and fifty lashes, "fifteen was the lowest."[165]

Women were forced to endure the pain of whipping every day in Georgia's camps. Whipping reports, which do not exist across all years or for all camps, document instances of women being whipped from 1885 through 1909. Clemency records account for earlier periods; in 1875 Rachel Crowder was taken to Terrell County jail and whipped by the police officer who arrested her.[166] At Old Town Camp in 1885 women were whipped for bad work, "bad plowing," and neglecting their work.[167] In 1884 Leila Burgess was sent to Chattahoochee at age fourteen after being convicted of murder. The evidence revealed that her father, James Burgess, was beating her unmercifully with an ox whip, when her mother tried to intervene. James turned on Leila's mother and began to beat her. In order to save her mother she picked up an axe and delivered a fatal blow to her father's head. After Leila attempted to save both herself and her mother from the abuse of her father, she was convicted of murder and sent to Chattahoochee. There, she was whipped thirteen times for idleness, and fifteen times for disobeying rules.[168]

Chattahoochee and Old Town were not exceptions. There are records of black women being repeatedly whipped by guards at Greston, Oglethorpe, Dade, Tifton, Bobick, and Bolton camps. Based upon extant (albeit incomplete) "whipping reports" maintained by penal authorities, there is little difference in degree between the punishment that convict guards imposed upon black women and men. At Old Town camp, for example, between July 6 and 20, 1886, ten prisoners were listed on the camp whipping report. Three women and four men received ten lashes for various violations, while three other men received less than ten lashes for their crimes.[169] The crime and the guard's whim, rather than the prisoner's gender, determined the number of lashes a prisoner received.

Yet race and gender did play a role in convict camp punishment in a theater of black female abjection. Forced sexualized performances of domination and submission were meant to enforce black women's dehumanization and display it to all prisoners in the camp as well as any on-lookers on county and city roads. The ritual of whipping black women in convict camps included forcing them to expose their naked backside in front of men and to stand in a sexualized stance, with their head between the overseer's knees. Hubbard Cureton testified before the state legislature that he had seen a woman being whipped "and the overseer standing on [her clothes], with her head between his knees, and he was whipping her on the naked butt. The overseer's name was Captain Potts. She was a chain-gang prisoner from Augusta; cannot call her name—do not know her name."[170] Although men were also whipped "enough to conquer them," as Cureton testified, only black women were forced to adopt the specific head-between-the-knees stance while being whipped.[171] Lizzie Boatwright reported that a young white guard named Cannon at W. H. and J. H. Griffin's camp,

> whipped me and a negro woman convict from Greene county, twice each. Both whippings were to punish us for trivial offenses—one time because our feet were sore and we stopped on the side of the road to fix the rags so as to protect them from the heavy brogan shoes (men's shoes, she said) that we were wearing. He ordered us to take down our trousers. We begged him to take us where the men convicts could not see us exposed, and he answered, "G—d—you, strip." One time I had my monthlies and I told him so but he said it made no difference and so he stripped us down and beat our naked skin with the strap. Several male convicts were all about us when we were whipped.[172]

The most modest request to be tormented in private fell upon deaf ears; black women uniquely faced the experience of being exposed while beaten until they bled, the menstrual blood running down their legs. Boatwright's decision to inform Cannon that she was menstruating reveals that such torture was perceived by the women who experienced it as a form of sexual violation, which they tried desperately to escape by asserting their claims to womanhood. When asked by Special Investigator Byrd, Cannon admitted that he "treated them as men."[173] Not only were black women exposed and whipped in front of male prisoners in sexual poses, they were also forced to go to the bathroom in the ditches in front of men.[174] These sexualized gender- and race-specific rituals of violence mark the convict camp as a pornographic site arranged in part by the spectacle of sex and violence toward the goal of maximized production.[175] The convict camp was constituted as pornographic through the entanglement of performance, sex, and commerce. Sexual imagery circulated widely in the camp: overseers directed and choreographed naked whipping rituals before a mixed audience of other prisoners, producing a spectacle of gendered racial terror. Rape was also sometimes exacted in view of other prisoners in the open structure of the camp. The enactment of sexual terror before the coerced gaze of the imprisoned was pornographic in that the images were affective industrial sexual objects—manufactured and circulated in the camp as a critical element of capital accumulation. Sexual violence, like the whip, was a fundamental technology of carceral control, marshaled toward the creation of a productive and docile labor force critical to southern capitalist development. Guards' performances of sexual violence were part of the job of carceral labor management; the scene of sexual violence was also a product, a tool manufactured to facilitate modern production. Gendered racial terror was not only profitable as a performance and instrument of managerial control over black women. As prison investigation testimony reveals, such acts of violence also clearly influenced imprisoned men, instilling a sense of powerlessness and setting the terms of labor authority in the camp writ large.

To force black women and men to urinate and defecate alongside each other in ditches was, under the racial and gendered ideologies of Jim Crow Georgia, to reduce them to animals by stripping them of gender distinctiveness as well as basic facilities for human hygiene. Black women were whipped as often and with the same force as black men. Yet the pose to which black women in particular were forced to submit during whippings is a gender-specific form of sexual domination to which men, by all accounts, were not subjected. In the very same context and by the very same people, black women were treated as black men, indeed denied fundamental apparatuses of gender consideration (separate bathroom spaces, or bathroom spaces at all). In other proximate moments they were abused in gender-specific ways that evince their perceived difference from both black men and white women. Black women occupied a liminal space of gender ambiguity in a society in which dualistic constructions of gender made humanity legible. Thus black women were construed in a range of related positionalities—masculinized, unsexed, and hypersexualized. Black women embodied what Spillers terms a "paradox of non-being" where the unsexed and supersexed black woman "cast the very same shadow" of exaggerated mythological representations of human subjectivity.[176] This fraught, contradictory gender position meant that they could be exposed to regimes of institutionalized violence from which white female bodies were, except in rare cases, protected.

Eliza Randall was subject to violence both before and after her conviction for murder in 1888. The details of her case, imprisonment, and what may have been an escape or kidnapping executed by one of the guards at Camp Bolton riveted both local and national journalists and their reading publics.[177] In 1888 she killed her father who, according to both black and white neighbors, "made incestuous advances" toward her.[178] Although one press account of her crime referenced the possibility of abuse, most portrayed her as a cruel and calculating murderer who resisted her father's moral discipline and who "ever since her incarceration ... has conducted herself as one wholly indifferent and unconcerned" with the magnitude or moral implications of her crime.[179] She was only a teenager when she and a male accomplice were arrested and sentenced to death by hanging for the murder of Randall's father. Her sentence was commuted to life in the penitentiary in 1888 and she served seventeen years, first at the Chattahoochee Brick Company's camp, then Camp Bolton, and finally at Camp Heardmont. The seventeen years of Eliza Randall's imprisonment were filled with violence and chaos. In 1891 M. M. Bolden, one of the guards at Camp Bolton, took Randall from the camp, although it is unclear whether she went willingly or was forced. After being pursued for two weeks as fugitives they were caught and brought back into custody, chained to each other. Bolden claimed that he wanted to free Randall because he believed she was a good woman and that she was innocent of the charge against her. Randall was returned to Camp Bolton to serve her life sentence and Bolden was sentenced to four years in the penitentiary for aiding an escape.

In a rare case of civil action against a guard, Chattahoochee Brick Company sued Bolden for breach of contract.[180] Eliza Randall and M. M. Bolden were the subjects of six sensational stories in the *Atlanta Constitution*, yet hidden from the public was the fact that only four months after Randall was recaptured she gave birth. Her ability to refuse the sexual advances of Bolden (or any other guard in the camp) was profoundly foreclosed by his possession of two instruments of violent control: the whip and the gun, two instruments that would brutalize and scar her body during the course of her captivity in Georgia's convict

camps. Under conditions of profound coercion, Randall may have left
Bolton with Bolden, or he may have kidnapped her. Yet the dichotomy
between willingly leaving and being kidnapped is faulty, as it assumes
she had the freedom to make a willing choice; that she was a free actor
who wanted to run away with this particular man rather than a captive
person who had to negotiate between the proximity of violation or death
in both the camp and the rebellious guard's custody. She was caught in
an impossible bind where the certainty of violence and the strong possibility of death governed each calculation and negotiation that she was
forced to make. Indeed, when she was reimprisoned after the Bolden
escape, Randall was subject to the extreme but quotidian violence that
pervaded the convict lease system. She was whipped thirteen times for
cursing and fighting.[181] In 1893 she was shot in the shoulder during a gun-
fight between two guards and spent two months in the hospital.[182]

Eventually, at Camp Heardmont, authorities put Randall to work as a
mechanic, fixing and maintaining W. H. Maddox's mill machinery. Her
position as a mechanic was the feature of her complex life in Georgia's
penal regime that garnered the attention of the *Boston Globe*. In addition to her anomalous position as a female performing skilled manual
labor, the newspaper noted that she wore men's clothing in the camp,
although in this regard she was not unusual.[183]

In his *Some Notes on Negro Crime, Particularly in Georgia*, W. E. B. Du
Bois impugned the convict-lease system for its brutalization of black
women, writing "women were mingled indiscriminately with the men,
both in working and in sleeping, and dressed often in men's clothes."[184]
Du Bois was not alone; chapter 3 follows Selena Sloan Butler and Mary
Church Terrell of the NACW, who recognized that the regular practice
of forcing black women to wear male attire was a technique of gender violence under convict leasing that both constituted and enabled
it. According to the account of an anonymous black man who worked
alongside convict laborers in peonage in the late nineteenth century,
"within six months another stockade was built, and twenty or thirty
other convicts were brought to the plantation, among them six or eight
women!"[185] He described in further detail the predicament of black
women: "Most of the time the women who were peons or convicts were
compelled to wear men's clothes. Sometimes, when I have seen them
dressed like men, and plowing or hoeing or hauling logs or working at
the blacksmith's trade, just the same as men, my heart would bleed and
blood would boil, but I was powerless to raise a hand."[186] His recol-

lections attest to imprisoned men's deep knowledge of the humiliation that women experienced when forced to wear men's clothes and reflect feelings of responsibility for protecting women in their communities. The heartbreak produced by black men's inability to intervene, as any attempt to do so "would have meant death on the spot," was a profound form of violence that imbued the experience of imprisonment.[187] The ignominy of forced sartorial performances of masculinity was communal in character.

The forced imposition of male attire under conditions of profound violence marked the experience of another imprisoned black woman, a blacksmith, Mattie Crawford. Crawford earned a reputation as the only female blacksmith in America, although the above anonymous account suggests she was not the only woman to perform the trade in peon and convict camps. She did all of the blacksmithing for Milledgeville and was also leased out to area residents to do their blacksmithing.[188] In 1896 she, like Eliza Randall before her, was convicted of killing her abusive father. She, like Randall, was also subject to the terror of the lash. The *Atlanta Constitution* ran a large photo of her in men's clothes to contextualize the experience of Macon representative E. C. Bruffey, who visited Milledgeville and was confounded by Mattie Crawford when he saw her in the women's quarters. He remarked that upon seeing her it seemed "to the casual observer that one cardinal rule was being violated," the rule being the prohibition of male prisoners in the female quarters.[189]

Mattie Crawford's image exposes the convict labor system as a cultural institution that forced the performance of black female masculinity. Along with violence, field labor, mining, road construction, and quarrying, the imposition of male attire was a technique that distinguished black females from "women" whose bodies were associated with weakness.[190] To visitors she was indistinguishable as a "woman," and her masculinity was emblazoned for the Georgia public in its most important newspaper. Yet Crawford's drag was not merely a deviation from normative femininity, it was integral in its production.

Crawford's experience exemplifies the symbolic position of the black female subject in proximity to masculinity and in opposition to femininity. This positioning of the subject was accomplished in her case through extreme force and violation: "She was sentenced to serve a life term in the penitentiary and was sent to the Chattahoochee river brick works along with some other convicts. After being there a while her great strength and activity caused those in charge of her to plan heavy work

ONLY WOMAN BLACKSMITH
IN AMERICA IS A CONVICT

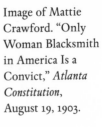

Image of Mattie Crawford. "Only Woman Blacksmith in America Is a Convict," *Atlanta Constitution*, August 19, 1903.

MATTIE CRAWFORD.
She Is a Blacksmith at the State Prison Farm and Wears Man's Clothing.

for her. She expressed a desire to become a blacksmith and she was taught the trade. *Her skirts being in the way, her guards forced her to put on trousers. Several whippings were necessary to make her consent to this. But after she had them on awhile she became so attached to them as to refuse absolutely to take them off.*[191] As this account from the *Atlanta Constitution* makes clear, Mattie Crawford held her own norms of womanhood, constituted through the sartorial presentation of femininity. A forced participant in the theater of black female abjection, she bravely contested white supremacist ideas about her body and her gendered subject position in the face of extreme violence. Already perceived as extraordinarily strong, she was whipped until she "consented" to perform masculinity by wearing male clothing. Female masculinity "actually affords us a glimpse of how masculinity is constructed as masculinity."[192] Crawford's forced performance also reveals the significance of race in constructing normative, white, femininity. Her presentation represents gender dissonance in late nineteenth- and early twentieth-century southern culture. While the performance of counternormative gender identities reveals the constructedness of gender, destabilizing the association between gender and biology, in Crawford's case the performance of masculinity reified biological racial difference; her forced performance of counternormativity stabilized and fortified normative gendered subject positions.

The *Atlanta Constitution* article states, "Mattie Crawford is the name of a woman who is a negro." Her experience reveals the incoherence of the concept "negro woman" in this historical moment. Even Frances Kellor, a leading northern liberal sociologist, remarked, "the stockade where she is incarcerated permits no men and a masculine style of dress was adopted because she is the blacksmith, mechanic, teamster, errand boy, etc." Kellor remarks upon the queerness of her femininity, noting "strangely enough she is not masculine, though she strikes a straight blow with her hammer . . . she has a soft, pleasant voice, adapts herself well to skirts and shows no tendency to even the small masculine details."[193] Kellor's assessment of Crawford is profound. Crawford is an ideal, her "movements" being "essentially feminine and she possesses more modesty than the average negress" who proved that "masculine labors do not necessarily induce masculine habits."[194] In this seeming celebration of Crawford's femininity there are myriad contradictions, qualifications, and dissonances. Because Kellor omitted the detail of Crawford's whipping, it is the *skirts* to which she became adapted not the pants. Her feminine voice and movements were, to Kellor, strange if admirable, and her modesty unique among black women assumed to be promiscuous and exhibitionist. The assumption of black female sexual immorality and propensity to vice as well as their aversion to hard work gained wide influence in northern Progressive circles; as Hazel Carby has argued, her "indictment of the sexual behavior of black migrant women registers the emergence of what would rapidly become a widely shared discourse of what was wrong with black urban life" and the basis for the intensified policing of black women in cities.[195] Kellor's liberal reverence for Crawford illuminates the entrenched expectations of black female queerness defined by promiscuity, aversion to hard work, and masculine comportment. That Crawford had learned the art of feminine performance and seemed comfortable in women's clothing made her a remarkable spectacle; that she embodied it through movements and voice made her all the more aberrant and extraordinary. Kellor seemed to be writing against a sartorial presumption, proving that Crawford was feminine despite her masculine sartorial presentation. Femininity was Crawford's extraordinary aberrance, the feature that justified her inclusion among a coterie of incarcerated black female freaks that Kellor had observed.

For Kellor, a leading proponent of cultural (rather than biological) inferiority arguments with respect to black criminality, it was Crawford's attachment to femininity and her sexual modesty that was curious, the latter trait remarkably distinguishing her among other black women. Kellor published what must have been Crawford's image in the *Chicago Tribune* in an article that concluded her series on the characteristics of Negro prisoners in the South with a focus on women.[196]

On this spectrum from masculine-presenting (Crawford's femaleness is indicated in the caption in case it was not self-evident) to "Indian" to "Congo" to infanticidal, black women and one black man are presented as spectacularly alien, bizarrely foreign, masculine, homicidal, and estranged from both cultural and political citizenship. Although Kellor stressed cultural over biological reasons for what she viewed as the problem of rampant black criminality, her presentation of a menagerie of criminal types associates physicality and criminality and black femaleness with oddness, especially because she did not reference any of the pictured prisoners or any of their alleged attributes in the actual article. Their images are meant to signify alone. Her description of Crawford appears in a separate book, *Experimental Sociology*, alongside another story on the "Cell of Infanticide" featured in the *Chicago Tribune*. According to Kellor, a woman had been convicted of infanticide and during her imprisonment a "strange desire for dolls possessed her."[197] In Kellor's narrative she spent all of her time playing with the dolls and making doll furniture in her cell instead of socializing with other women at the prison. While playing with dolls may have been normal girlhood behavior, in this case it was rendered as response to the ultimate maternal sin, situating motherhood for black women in the realm of fantasy

NEGRO FEMALE LABORER ON CONVICT FARM   INDIAN—NEGRO TYPE   CONGO TYPE OF NEGRO   CELL OF AN INFANTICIDE

"Social Conditions of Southern Negroes," *Chicago Tribune*, November 4, 1900.

rather than reality. Even in the most eminent northern liberal discourse black women were constituted through a narrative of freakish aberrance from normative gendered modes of morality and culture.

In the Jim Crow South, blackness did not merely modify womanness at the turn of the century. "Negro woman" was an empty signifier: the modifier "black" or "negro" repudiated the concept of womanness, and thus the label "woman" could be applied to Mattie Crawford despite the fact that by definition in the nineteenth-century South the term meant, in many respects, the opposite of Crawford. As it was invoked most commonly in white discourses, "woman" signified a subject who was vulnerable and must be protected from violence. It was possible to whip Mattie Crawford and dress her in men's clothing because the term "woman," although used to distinguish her from a biological man, lost its conventional meaning when accompanied by "Negro."

It may have been that Crawford derived some measure of dignity from her labor as a blacksmith.[198] Inasmuch as separate spheres of labor have historically served to subordinate women, the fact of performing male work or wearing men's clothing itself is, of course, not violent or oppressive. Yet the forced performance of masculine work and the forced imposition of masculine dress was, in this context, a violent reinforcement of the black female subject's position as an object of violence and beyond the boundaries of concern. The archive from which Crawford's story is drawn does not document her beliefs and desires and it is therefore impossible to recount her views about the labor she performed or the violence she faced. Yet even if she found blacksmithing meaningful, the

Convict Leasing and Gendered Racial Terror 99

pursuit of satisfaction from meaningful work in the context of captivity cannot redress her pained condition. Crawford assented to wearing men's clothes and performing blacksmithing under the terror of the whip. By performing masculinity and traditionally male work she forestalled some of the violence she might otherwise have endured (repeated whippings) if she had continued to refuse.

Mattie Crawford's predicament does not represent a departure from the common experiences of black women in Georgia's convict camps, who were forced to perform masculinity through acts of labor that demonstrated their strength. Inviolability also marked Crawford's estranged relationship to the category "woman," as her whipping was presented as profoundly ordinary, unremarkable even, especially when compared to the attention given to a white woman named Mamie De Cris. In fact, the article on Crawford begins by positioning her in the context of what was significant about Milledgeville at the time, since it was "now noted because of the whipping there of a white woman Mamie De Cris."[199]

Mamie De Cris may have been the only white woman whipped in Georgia's convict camps. Certainly it would have been the rarest of punishments, and such instances are not documented in whipping reports. The unfathomability of such a crime made Mamie De Cris's whipping the subject of a journalistic firestorm of outrage. De Cris was convicted of forgery in Chatham County in December 1902 and sentenced to two years at Milledgeville, where the superintendent was "expressly instructed not to put her to work in the field."[200] Instead De Cris was given limited housekeeping duties along with special privileges. Her clothes were washed with the warden's clothes, and she was given the same food to eat as prison staff. In June 1903, however, her life at Milledgeville changed; she was disciplined for what the warden, Captain Allagood, described vaguely as insubordination. Other prison officials described De Cris as a tricky prisoner who was ungrateful for her good treatment at Milledgeville.[201] Mrs. Allagood, the matron of the women's department, accused De Cris of complaining about her conditions and cursing at her.

Allagood's first mode of punishment was to put her to work in the fields, although he secretly told the overseer only to give her light fieldwork. When, in his account, she refused to behave, he consulted with the prison physician to determine whether her body could stand a whipping. With the doctor's permission, Allagood gave De Cris twenty lashes on her back. His consultation with the doctor reveals that even in the context of extreme violence white women's bodies were perceived to be more frail and more worthy of protection. The *Augusta Chronicle* printed a letter from the physician, Dr. I. H. Adams, to his reverend, proclaiming that he was against whipping in general; he "could not say that Miss De Cris was too weak to bear punishment: but did not thereby assent to the morality of it."[202]

What Allagood described as insubordination, De Cris alleged was retribution for refusing his sexual advances. Although she did not claim that he tried to use physical force, De Cris told the press that Allagood had made "improper proposals" to her and that when she turned him down she found her privileges withdrawn. Allagood, she said, had promised to "make it hot for her." De Cris had seen him kiss a white woman in the hospital ward and had also witnessed him "in the barn with a negro woman prisoner, she lying in hay and he standing by her."[203] She asked another white woman for advice about how to handle Allagood's advances, to which her confidant replied that if De Cris was "that kind of a woman" she should give in, but if she wasn't she should resist.[204] Almost immediately after Allagood discovered that De Cris had told of his harassment, he had whipped her.

When the press discovered De Cris's story on August 8, 1903, it was the subject of near daily coverage. Both local and national papers reported the details of her case. She was described as "young, pretty, and cultivated," and weak.[205] Although she had no diagnosed medical condition her perpetual nervousness was believed to be a symptom of her physical weakness. She described being forced, after the whipping, "to go out in the hot sun and work alongside healthy negro women who had never done anything but field work."[206] Her frailty sparked the ire of the public as well as politicians. One reporter observed that the "public mood" maintained that anyone who "would flog a delicate white woman" was "bad enough to be guilty of almost anything that could be charged against him."[207] Governor Terrell publicly declared, "it is almost impossible to conceive of circumstances . . . that would justify the whipping of a white female prisoner."[208] Georgia representative George H. Bell was outraged about the abuse of "a refined white woman" and in more than one account reporters alleged that De Cris received "three times as many licks as the average hardened negro woman criminal."[209] De Cris is positioned against black female subjects, and again violation of their criminalized bodies is considered profoundly ordinary while the enactment of such violence against white women's bodies is an unfathomable aberration. Bell and another member of the Georgia House of

Representatives sponsored legislation to investigate the entire penitentiary, with a specific focus on conditions for women. De Cris's position as a subject tethered to domesticity was represented through a photograph of her beside a sewing machine emblazoned in newspapers to incite the outrage of Georgia's public. The violation of this natural domestic location was a central concern for her advocates. Beyond the whipping she received, legislators wanted to investigate the fact "that she has been forced to do work in the fields and elsewhere out of all proportion to her physical condition."[210] Although they did not conduct such an investigation her case forced the superintendent of Milledgeville, Captain K. R. Foster, to resign on August 12, only a few days after the story broke.

Mamie De Cris's sexual harassment and physical assault is one of the many examples of violence and terror in Georgia's penal history. Yet hers stands out since most imprisoned white women were not subject to physical violence because such treatment was incompatible with the values of Jim Crow modernity. Captain Allagood's harassment of De Cris reveals that the iconography of white ladyhood did not provide absolute protection against the threat of sexual exploitation or rape. The outcry against her violation also reveals the public commitment to the image of virtuous white womanhood, and the extent to which it was positioned against black female lasciviousness. When her white female friend advised that she should resist Allagood's advances if she was not "that kind of woman," she took her advice.

While De Cris endured brutal physical violence as the price of her honor, she was positioned in stark contrast to the black woman with whom she found Allagood in the barn. Although De Cris reported witnessing Allagood kissing a white woman in the hospital ward, the woman's presumed incapacity and disability, and the relative innocence of the kiss, upheld the association between white women and virtue even in the face of limited sexual contact. Sex with Allagood was presented as a choice, suggesting that the black woman "in the hay" was a lascivious being. In De Cris's narrative, black women were seducers and accomplices in the creation of a licentious sexual culture at Milledgeville. Black women were the counterparts to her self-representation as an emblem of virtue. De Cris represented herself as triumphant in the face of moral adversity. She contrasted herself with the black woman in the hay in order to demonstrate the extremes to which a true woman would go in order to preserve her purity.

Mamie De Cris also alleged that black women were part of her torment. During her two weeks of fieldwork punishment, during which
she "nearly fainted," several of the black women reportedly "tantalized
her," calling her a "lazy, no good diamond queen, no better than we
are."[211] Whether black women actually expressed resentment or taunted
De Cris for her privileged position at the camp is unknowable. Yet they
were portrayed as ignorant and aggressive antagonists in a story of
white female subjectivity defined in part by forbearance in the face of
brutality. Along with the male guards, De Cris presented black women
in her narrative as accomplices to, or conspirators in, her assault by
men. This positioned black women symbolically closer to the masculinity that violated her than the femininity of which she was emblematic.

Virtue was the central issue at stake for De Cris and the influential
people who were concerned about her. Mrs. John E. Donaldson, cousin
to Governor Terrell, believed that "the whipping of Mamie De Cris was
a blot on the south . . . the white women of the south especially must be
protected."[212] In her opinion De Cris should have been sent to the state
sanitarium instead of a convict camp. Despite petitions from citizens of
two counties De Cris's first application for clemency was denied in October 1903. The Prison Commission refused to issue a reason for its decision. One year later members of the commission did pardon her, only
days before her sentence was to expire, in order to endorse the retriev-
ability of her character. Approximately two weeks before her sentence
expired she wrote a letter to the Prison Commission:

> I am going to ask a favor of you and sincerely hope you will grant
> it begging that you will please release me before my time expired
> if only one day it will be a great help to me in the future. I find
> that we is not looked down upon if they are pardoned as much
> as if they had served their full sentence. I know my character is
> ruin to a certain extent but I hope to retrieve it in the future. My
> desires are to prove myself if possible to the Georgia people and
> I feel with God's help I can. I hope you will decide in my favor.
> It will be appreciated more than I can express in words. Yours
> Gratefully, Mamie De Cris.[213]

Although she had received nothing but sympathy in the public arena
De Cris was concerned that her character was damaged by virtue of
her status as a prisoner. Prison officials pardoned her on November 14,
issuing a clemency order that expressed the hope that their decision

would assist her in leading a useful life in the future. More than a year had passed since the scandal broke and they could now maintain that De Cris's character was fully retrievable, thereby sparing Georgia's entire penal system from reproach.

Mamie De Cris's story of resistance to the sexual advances of Captain Allagood was unusual. It is perhaps the only narration of unwanted male sexual advances by a female prisoner in the late nineteenth and early twentieth centuries, making it a highly remarkable account of the violence of convict camp life. It is also the only evidence of any kind of the use of whipping as an instrument of punishment against white women. Despite the lack of women's firsthand accounts of sexual force, evidence exists that rape was an institutionalized feature of convict camp life, exacted disproportionately against black women. Rape and forced reproduction were techniques of racial terror that targeted black women's bodies. The main evidence revealing these techniques is passing references in penitentiary reports and hospital records that evidence childbirth.

Evidence of Things Not Seen

The incomplete accounting of pregnancy and childbirth in Georgia's convict camps is virtually the only archival trace of the systematic rape of imprisoned black women. Since hospital records only remain for a limited number of convict camps and for only a select few years, it is impossible to uncover with precision the number of imprisoned black women who were sexually assaulted. Moreover, the almost certain reprisals for reporting rape foreclosed black women's ability to expose the violence they suffered in the camps. Although many black women who gave birth in convict camps submitted clemency applications, none of them mentioned the children that had been conceived in the camps or revealed that they had been raped. This silence reflects the likely belief among black women that they had no claims to femininity that would legitimize assertions of rape. Virtually no archival evidence exists for black women who had been raped but had not become pregnant. Since not all black women who were raped would have become pregnant and not all records of black women's childbirth remain in the archive, it is clear that the magnitude of rape of imprisoned women is greater than that which can be proven by extant archival records.

The examples of rape that are included here are merely that; they are not an exhaustive account of all the black women who were sexually assaulted in Georgia's convict camps. The unrecorded rapes of black women by white men reflect the power of the archive in maintaining erasures and silences, functioning to compound the historical violence of sexual assault. Put another way, the magnitude of sexual terrorization inflicted upon black women is incalculable. In this case the archive allows us to compare the date of black women's sentencing and imprisonment with the birthdates of their children, revealing that many of the children who were born in Georgia's convict camps were born long after they had been imprisoned and that the children had been both conceived and born in the camps. Yet the archive does not enable us to document the full extent of rape as a tool of racial terror against black women. Moreover, documentation does not make these experiences legible—the terror, heartbreak, and love that must have defined the experience of birth and motherhood in a Georgia convict camp.

The archive presents an extreme challenge to analyses of rape because searching for rape in the archive means searching for an act that took place out of view of witnesses and an act that was unbelievable to the people whose documents comprise the historical archive. The archive also holds little that reflects imprisoned black women's interiority, aspirations, or theorizations of their present. This predicament, which reduces lives to numbers or objects, is best described by Saidiya Hartman's term "founding violence." Following Michel Foucault she argues that "violence determines, regulates, and organizes the kinds of statements that can be made about slavery and as well it creates subjects and objects of power."[214] In the process of using the archive to document black women's rape as well as their interior responses to violence we are searching for evidence of things not seen, not valued, and certainly not written.

Rape is revealed in records of human life. In one camp two of the six imprisoned women "gave birth to children after they had been there more than twelve months—and the babies had white men for their fathers!"[215] Sporadic medical records for the all-female Camp Heardmont exist for the years 1892, 1893, and 1895. They reveal the pervasiveness, indeed institutionalization, of rape as an instrument of violence in convict camps. The only men at Camp Heardmont were the white camp guards, so while there are no records of the paternity of the children born at Camp Heardmont, we can be certain that the children fathered at this camp were born to imprisoned black women and white guards. One woman at Camp Heardmont had become pregnant twice between 1892 and 1894 but had suffered a miscarriage during the first pregnancy.[216] Extant records reveal that during these years at least six black women gave birth, all more than one year after they arrived at the camp. Since some of the women who had been raped by guards would not have become pregnant, and some of the women would not have become pregnant the first time they were raped, pregnancies provide only a limited barometer of the extent of rape at the camp.

We must therefore assume that more women were raped at Camp Heardmont, or that the women who eventually did become pregnant were raped more than once. Despite the archival challenges of documenting every instance of rape, the evidence that is available demonstrates that rape was an inescapable, routine form of violence at Camp Heardmont. None of the guards there were ever prosecuted for rape, and the existence of force was never acknowledged in official statements regarding babies born to imprisoned women. The rape of black women by white men in convict camps, particularly at Camp Heardmont, was a source of outrage for black activists and intellectuals. As W. E. B. Du Bois reported, "A young girl at camp Hardmont [sic], Georgia, in 1895, was repeatedly outraged by several of her guards, and finally died in childbirth while in camp."[217]

Between 1888 and 1900 at least five black women at the Chattahoochee Brick Company's convict camp gave birth to children conceived at the site. As with all of the remaining camp medical records, Chattahoochee's ledgers for those who were sick only exist for a limited number of years, which means that the numbers of women who had children at that camp are undoubtedly far higher.[218] According to her clemency application Susannah Gilbert, who served at least some of her prison time at Chattahoochee, had six children during her twenty-year period of imprisonment, but she is not listed in any remaining convict camp medical records.[219] The medical records do indicate that by 1889 Sarah Autry had been transferred from George D. Harris's convict camp to Chattahoochee, where she gave birth. Like Eliza Cobb, white authorities described Sarah Autry as deviant and abject, but her production as beyond the bounds of recognizable humanity did not insulate her from gender-specific sexual violence.

Although there is no evidence that imprisoned black women negotiated sex for pleasure or reward, this of course remains a remote possibility. Imprisoned women's strategies of resistance to convict labor and its conditions is the subject of chapter 5, and the relationship between sexuality and resistance is discussed further there. Yet histories of rape necessarily raise questions about force and consent that must be considered. Historian Edward E. Baptist and feminist political theorist Carole Pateman provide analyses of rape that illuminate the dynamics of race, gender, and force under conditions of institutionalized violence and racial patriarchy. In his work on rape, sexual fetishism, and the domestic slave trade, Baptist charts a history of sexual commodification and trade in 1830s Louisiana. Although he primarily focuses on the cultural and commercial process of sexual fetishism and objectification of black women by white planters and traders, he adds an important analysis of the relationship between consent and force under racial domination. Regarding a letter from a planter proclaiming that his slave, Maria, enjoyed their sexual arrangement, Baptist argues, "while some enslaved women sold on the market for sexual purposes maneuvered to turn white male desires to their own or others' protection . . . the stark imbalance of power meant that women like Maria chose, at best, between negotiated surrender on the one hand and severe punishment and possible death on the other."[220] Enslaved or imprisoned black women's negotiation of sex under conditions of force can clearly only be defined as the most narrow, precarious form of acquired protection, where protection means the negotiation of sex with someone who would otherwise terrorize or kill you.

Pateman has critiqued democratic social contract theory premised upon the production of consent. Classical theorists including Locke, Hobbes, and Rousseau view consent as the foundation of democratic society because it is necessary for the maintenance of individual freedom and equality. At the core of consent theory is the idea that individual actors must voluntarily commit themselves to relationships and institutions in order to maintain a free society. Yet, as Pateman argues, the problem for theories in which consent produces freedom is that "individual freedom and democracy is also a precondition for the practice of consent."[221] Pateman applies her argument to a critique of rape law, which presumes consent unless force or resistance can be proven. She contends that consent theory fails to distinguish consent from "habitual acquiescence, assent, silent dissent, submission, or enforced submission."[222] These acts are agentive, situated alongside "negotiation, complicity, refusal, dissembling, mimicry, compromise, affiliation and revolt" in a continuum of practices that mediate dominance, and all occur in relation to the practice of rape.[223] In the context of imprisoned women's rape, assent may be the most significant practice. It is possible that imprisoned women assented to sex in some contexts, however assent is fundamentally different from consent under conditions of racial patriarchy, and especially in the context of the convict camp—a site of extreme, ubiquitous terror. While imprisoned black women certainly dissembled in the aftermath of rape and it is plausible to assume that they practiced assent or had moments of indecision about sexual relations in the camp, camp authorities had the resources and capacity to succeed in "settling matters of indecision with a violent excess of militarized masculinity."[224]

Principal keepers only rarely documented the sexual assault of black women, even under the euphemistic discourse of childbirth. In 1878 the principal keeper noted that there were twenty-two children born in the camps the year before. Since then there were three more births, and only one of those children was born to a woman who was pregnant at the time of her arrival in the camp. Between 1878 and 1890 there was no mention of children or childbirth in Georgia's convict camps in the reports. In the 1890 report the penitentiary physician, H. V. M. Miller, referenced childbirth in his report on disease in Georgia's penal system: "It is proper to explain that from this number of 1,198 cases of sickness reported should be deducted the number of accidental injuries occurring in various ways in the prosecution of their employment as convicts, which number is 177 and also the number of cases of epidemic contagious diseases and others not amenable to hygienic prevention or medical treatment, of which there were 22 cases of mumps, 34 cases of measles, 165 cases of la grippe and 9 cases of childbirth*, making a total of 407 cases."[225] Here childbirth is presented within the framework of unpreventable illness like the mumps, simultaneously recognizing and rejecting the distinction between childbirth (the result of sexual intercourse, not illness) and disease. Miller includes an asterisk footnote to diminish the culpability for childbirth that may reside with camp officers: "In justice to the officers of the camps, I desire to state that in several of these cases the mothers were in a state of pregnancy at the time of their reception in the Penitentiary."[226] Black women's injury was so far beyond the realm of popular concern that prison administrators rarely documented childbirth, even as a euphemism for rape. Moreover, when they did report childbirths, it was adequate to note that "several" of the women were pregnant before they were arrested, without providing exact numbers. The erratic and vague accounting for childbirth in the camps was an instrument through which to mask, and thereby enable, rape. Imprisoned black women were "living out the materialized affective relations of slavery within freedom, their wombs anything but free."[227]

Framing childbirth as illness helped to conceal the pandemic reality of sexual force in the lives of imprisoned women. Yet the impossibility of black women's rape was grounded in the production of black female subjects as "others" in the white imaginary. In the South a constituent feature of the normative subject position "woman" was vulnerability to rape by black men, and a fixture of white supremacist ideology was the protection of white women and womanhood from this threat. Black women's inviolability and perceived inability to be raped should not be viewed as a phenomenon distinct from white women's hyperviolability and the omnipresent threat that they would be raped. These binary social positionalities operated to reinforce the logic of white supremacist violence grounded in the exceptional status of white femininity and its constant threat. The inviolability of black women reinforced the exceptional status of white women and therefore the legitimacy of lynching black men.

Yet the rape and perceived inviolability of black women was not merely a historical phenomenon that enabled violence against black male lynching victims. In the South, and in Georgia specifically, black women were also lynched. In 1918 Mary Turner was pregnant when she and her husband were lynched in Valdosta, Georgia. According to Crystal Feimster at least 130 black women were lynched between 1880 and 1930. This number does not include black women who were tortured by lynch mobs but managed to survive their attack.[228] Black women were sexually assaulted and forced to bear children because they were not deemed to have the capacity for consent or dissent. Hartman has elaborated the "violence of the law" and its circumscription of slave agency, will, and capacity for consent or resistance in de jure legal statutes governing rape. The nonpersonhood of the female slave precluded her ability to exert sexual will, to refuse or consent to sex. Yet emancipation did not suddenly produce people perceived as fully human subjects by white society, and the formal codification of humanity was usurped by a host of cultural representations that enabled structures of violence and legal norms to continue to deny black personhood.

Rape was an assault upon territorialized "space between the legs," a place from which to normalize the logic of captivity and the penal regime.[229] Rape reduced black female bodies to objects of violation and therefore reinforced their social position as flesh, rather than persons, citizens, or social subjects whose freedom was presumed and therefore more difficult to efface. Black women's bodies and notions of black female sexuality have historically constituted the ground upon which racial ideologies have been developed in the white imaginary, "providing the moral and social distance from those they would enslave," and providing evidence of the "immutable difference between Africans and Europeans, a difference ultimately codified as race."[230] As early as the sixteenth century, white travelers circulated discourses about black female bodies that evidenced immutable racial difference, justifying the slave trade. Racial difference had everything to do with understandings of black women's bodies and their presumed status as reproducers of biologically different and inferior subjects. Hannah Rosen has revealed the frequency of white supremacist sexual assault during the post–Civil War years and provides a remarkable account of the testimonies of African American women about such violence, revealing that the denial of rape-victim status was part of the denial of citizenship during a period of marked uncertainty about the future of race relations and social and political organization. Importantly, Rosen also reveals that black women vociferously challenged this form of political subordination by claiming their rights and speaking out about their violation.[231]

In the aftermath of Reconstruction, the development of Jim Crow (like the trans-Atlantic slave trade) required the naturalization of racial difference, and black women's bodies would continue to serve an important role in this endeavor. Although black women were no longer enslaved and therefore no longer reproduced enslaved laborers, the black maternal remained politically fraught. The debt peonage and convict labor regimes created new, modern systems of captive labor and black women's roles as the reproducers of women and men who existed merely to work for the profit of white agricultural and industrial interests made the politics of their bodies and subject positions vitally important for the maintenance of Jim Crow/white supremacy.[232] Black women's rape, the violation of the geopolitical space between their legs, made possible other spaces of exploitation and violence by reinforcing the black female subject's position as dispossessed of rights, of economic entitlements, of bodily integrity, safety, and mobility. White male domination over the place between black women's legs was a strategy of control over the terrain of Jim Crow modernity, which was all about the taxonomy of place and the organization of bodies into appropriate places, one of which was the convict camp. The rape of black women did not warrant scrutiny or investigation precisely because it was part of the normalization, or naturalization, of Jim Crow modernity defined by white supremacist economic and social relations.

In 1887 a convict-leasing official boasted that he thought he had it "so arranged that such things will not occur heareafter. . . . The 'such things' which the officer indicated by a nod of the head were two scantily-clad pickaninnies of varying color and sizes playing about the door of the women's department."[233]

Accounts of the lives and futures of children born to women in southern convict camps are very scant because, as the article makes clear, children were considered mere objects that evidenced black female lasciviousness. Because they were "things" but not "convicts" they were only documented in relation to their mothers through the reports of childbirth, they do not even appear in reports of illness. Though thingified they are even less valuable than the inanimate objects contained within prison reports such as tools, bedding, or food. It was an absolute erasure, even from the voluminous inventory of property that constitutes the archive of American captivity, holding so many and shrouding so much and in so doing issuing what Hartman calls "a death sentence."[234] Their coughs and chills and deaths and injuries did not register in the registers of convict leasing's abuses, much less their hopes, wishes, and ideas. They were concealed through penal and journalistic discourses that thingified them or rendered them epidemiological phenomenon. The pickaninny, an icon invented in the antebellum period, would continue to be a "major figure in U.S. cultural history"; she was often portrayed as "insensate," and in the southern carceral lexicon this erasure of emotion was rendered visually through the "strange thing's" blank stare and through the absence of details and documentation about the social and emotional lives of young children in southern prison camps.[235] This "imagined, subhuman black juvenile" emerged in the seventeenth century, and its usage extended into the nineteenth century as a pejorative reference to black children in America and, at the turn of the

Black children described
as the worst features of the
convict labor system. "The
Georgia Prison Camp,"
St. Louis Globe-Democrat,
August 19, 1887.

The Worst Feature of the System.

century, to populations in the zone of overseas zones of U.S. overseas
imperialism.[236]

As the image caption makes clear, the children, not the sexual violence that produced them, were the "worst features" of convict leasing;
in this way, the southern convict labor system institutionalizes the long-
standing historical trend of discourses in which black reproduction is
mobilized to demonstrate that "racial inequality is perpetuated by Black
people themselves," and that reproductive control has been a "central aspect of racial oppression in America."[237] The 1887 report suggests that
at least some children remained in the convict camps and state farm for
some period of time, vulnerable to the heinous conditions, potentially
suffering from the violence that other imprisoned women and men

faced, and separated from their mothers by the grueling labor demands that so profoundly compromised parental bonds.

Pickaninnies of varying color and sizes playing about the door of the women's department: this depiction of black children invokes antebellum tropes and sanitizes the horror of childhood in a convict camp. *Scantily-clad and playing about the door*: these words are the ominous representations of toddlers deprived, cold, and wanting for emotional and material resources as they waited for their mothers to finish work. If the report is true, perhaps they spent days watching for mothers or adopted aunties to come back to their quarters; perhaps when they finally arrived they held arms outstretched for hugs and lips puckered for immediate kisses in the short time between supper and bed; perhaps they wandered into fields and laundry rooms and the guards allowed them to visit with their mothers at work; perhaps this was incentive for women's submission to authorities' orders and demands. Undoubtedly, imprisoned women were able to demonstrate love for their children in the midst of perennial violence and privation; however, the conditions of the camps leave many questions about how imprisoned children lived and the violence they endured.

Were their cheeks always wet from the tears of hunger or pain from the unattended cuts and scrapes and bruises from the falls they undoubtedly sustained in play? How did they play? Did older children, perhaps the youngest of those arrested for picking up coal or helping their mothers dump dirty water in the streets of Atlanta teach them hide and seek? Did they pretend they were hiding when they cowered behind walls to avoid seeing the lash hit the skin of their adopted aunties and uncles who kissed them when their mothers were busy? Were there dolls and if so did they fight over who would get to hold the doll babies? Did they hear stories of grandparents and aunties on the outside and what towns and cities looked like? Did they think that everyone in the world wore stripes? These are among the unanswerable questions in the context of lives figured through the lexicon of disease and things. Their lives erased and disregarded, the children of imprisoned women were spectral presences, making visible the social violence so consistently denied.

Despite the numerous instances of black women giving birth to children conceived during their periods of prolonged captivity there is not a single record of an investigation or prosecution for a guard's violation of black women in Georgia's convict camps. This follows the pattern of impunity with which black women were raped outside of prisons, which Ida B. Wells and the antilynching movement exposed during this period.[238] The willful denial of black women's rape despite its obviousness—literally borne out in human lives—and despite the fact that it was carried out by men charged with executing the will of the state, is significant. Here the state's crime of "omission and proaction," or lack of prosecution and tacit sanctioning of rape implies that the sexual assault of black women was part of the will of the state.[239] If, as Hartman argues, "sexuality formed the nexus in which black, female, and chattel were inextricably bound and acted to intensify the constraints of slave status by subjecting the body to another order of violations and whims" then the formal eradication of slavery did not obliterate the need for sexual force to serve as a technique to reinforce black subjection, to intensify the constraints on black freedom or economic advancement.[240]

Rape was a form of institutionalized white supremacist patriarchal violence. Rape in this context was a form of gendered racial terror (not just gender violence) that reinforced the subordination of the black subjects held captive in Georgia's convict camps. The rape of black women by white male guards reduced them to the level of female animal, property, or thing, a practice continuous with the rape of enslaved women by white men. Drawing from Simone de Beauvoir, Angela Y. Davis argues that the master, "aspiring with his sexual assaults to establish her as a female *animal*, he would be striving to destroy her proclivities toward resistance."[241] The institutionalized rape of black women in convict camps took them outside of the boundaries of the normative category "woman" that made personhood legible and that was defined in the late nineteenth-century South through domesticity, chastity, and the right to protection from sexual assault, and relegated them to animal and property status. While this status may have been "female," it was not "woman" and was therefore not legibly human. The routine sexual assault of black women helped to delineate the boundaries and degree of violation that was possible in the space of the convict camp. In a context in which labor extraction was the ultimate goal of the penal system, the tolerable degree of violation and injury became important considerations of everyday management.[242] The question for penal authorities was not how much labor is humane, or how much pain is humane, but rather how much pain can the laborer endure and continue to be a productive laborer? Or, how easily can we replace a laborer upon whom we inflict too much abuse?[243] The brutal and inhumane nature of the convict-lease system's labor demands required that those it ensnared be viewed as expendable, unworthy of concern. Rape, isolation, medical neglect, and whipping were all instruments in the management of a system of labor, the maintenance of which depended upon the expendability of black life and denial of black sentience. If we understand racial violence as a mechanism through which to exclude racialized subjects from the realm of human consideration, especially in order to maintain relations of economic and social domination, rape should be considered as central to a framework of gendered *and* racial terror. Yet as Hazel V. Carby has argued, "the institutionalized rape of black women has never been as powerful a symbol of black oppression as the spectacle of lynching . . . the links between black women and illicit sexuality consolidated during the antebellum years had powerful consequences for the next hundred and fifty years"[244] Lynching and rape are inextricable forms of gendered racial violence because the cultural constructions that justified them are mutually dependent and relational. The "passionless lady arose in symbiosis with the primitively sexual slave" and the popular justification for lynching; that is, the protection of white womanhood, rested upon the notion of *exceptionality*, that white women alone were in extreme need of protection because, as women, they were vulnerable to rape by black men.[245] Moreover, as the history of convict leasing reveals, the rape of black women was an institutionalized form of violence and oppression that pervaded black women's lives and subjected them to the violence of compulsory pregnancy, childbirth, and motherhood.

Sexual violence and judicial callousness about it did not end as a practice in the convict-leasing era. In 1923 a black woman named Bessie Lockhart gave birth at Milledgeville. Her rape was a contested issue in her clemency application, as evidenced in correspondence between her lawyer, Walter Steed, and Governor Clifford Walker. Steed wrote to Walker on July 7, 1923, informing him that the Prison Commission had recommended parole in Lockhart's case, and asked that Governor Walker approve the recommendation based upon the dubiousness of her guilt (Lockhart was convicted for murder, but he argued that the evidence actually revealed that she was acting in self-defense against an armed aggressor). In Steed's view an additional, but incidental, reason to grant clemency in Lockhart's case was that she had given birth while she was at Milledgeville. He argued that in having sex she was "acting most likely under threats or hope of reward."[246] In a shrewd move, her attorney told the governor he believed that Lockhart's case was an exceptional circumstance in a well-managed prison system, but that there were scandalmongers all over the state who would seize upon such an incident as an opportunity to besmirch "the fair name of the state."[247] Steed wrote that he was sure that it would not become necessary for him to resort to exposing her case as part of his advocacy on Lockhart's behalf. Although Steed's positing of two possibilities for Lockhart's impregnation—threat or enticement—disavows the extent and entrenchment of sexual violence in the space of the state farm, it remains one of the most explicit references to the possibility of sexual force against black women in extant penal and legal records. Steed's allusion to public sentiment was an activist approach to legal advocacy, yet this was a risky strategy since a black woman's rape in the state farm or convict camps was not a major area of public concern. It was especially risky because Clifford Walker was an unsympathetic audience. He won the governorship in part through an alliance with the Ku Klux Klan, which had a major southern resurgence in the 1920s. Walker remained loyal to the Klan and its white supremacist ideology throughout his administration.

Indeed the mention of Bessie Lockhart's possible rape became a sore spot and an obstacle to her release. A month after his initial letter Steed was forced to write to the governor for a third time, yet in this case the situation was more urgent. Between July and August Governor Walker had informed Steed that he planned to deny Lockhart's application for parole even though the Prison Commission had recommended clemency. Steed appealed to the governor to reconsider his decision. Although Governor Walker's letter to Steed is not part of the archival clemency record, Steed's response reveals much about the justification for Walker's decision. Steed assured the governor that Lockhart's status as a new mother was not the only ground for her parole case, and again urged him not to judge her negatively because she had become pregnant while she was in prison. Steed was clearly responding to Walker's reluctance to release Lockhart on the ground that she had been sexually assaulted, or because she was a mother, so he assured him that the facts surrounding her guilt were the primary reason she should be paroled. He reiterated his previous argument that Lockhart should not "be denied a parole for a condition which . . . she could not have reasonably prevented, acting most likely under threats, or hope of reward."[248] The exchange between Steed and Walker reveals the stubbornness and continuity of black women's popular representation as lascivious and unrapeable.

In the midst of her clemency case, Lockhart sent her own letter to the governor. She told him that she had tried hard to obey all of the rules while in prison and that she wanted to be released so that she could care for her mother and small children. Her letter began "I am writing a few lines in regard to my freedom" and continued "I pray you will please release me an let me go home to my old mother I sorry sorry in my heart that I had come to such places like this."[249] In her letter Lockhart did not tell Governor Walker that she had been raped. Instead, she alluded to the horribleness of prison and her terrorization in the phrase "such places like this." In her dissemblance Lockhart conveyed that the convict camp was a space of terror not because it imposed any one particular form of violence or deprivation. The confluence of isolation, familial estrangement, forced pregnancy and childbirth, medical neglect, arduous labor, and physical and sexual violence made the convict camp a space where violation and death were banal institutionalized practices. Disregarding Steed's appeal for leniency based upon sexual force, Walker denied Lockhart's parole because he could not accept her sexual or physical vulnerability or her status as a mother as an acceptable ground for leniency. He reproduced and reimposed the trauma and violence that led to the act for which she was arrested in the first place.

Black women who were raped and had children had to endure another form of gender-specific psychic violence: estrangement from their sons and daughters. Penal and clemency records include woefully little about the whereabouts of children born to imprisoned women, except to note that there were a few who remained with their mothers for brief periods of time in the camps. During her imprisonment Amanda Hill wrote a letter asking an unknown addressee, "have you heard anything from my folks or do you know them is they dead or living? . . . Please tell me how is my two children Freddy and my babe child I have forgot her name"[250] Although the first page of the letter is missing, Amanda's letter reflects the hardship of forced familial and maternal estrangement imposed by captivity. Although separation from family was an excruciating aspect of prison life for men and women, black women experienced the particular trauma of being forcibly separated from the newborn children who were born during their imprisonment.

There was no public narrative for the isolation and injury that black women endured. Indeed there remains almost no archival trace of the interior lives or sentiments of imprisoned black women during this era. By contrast, imprisoned white women's hardship was considered "tragic," and rendered in vivid detail. According to the reporter who interviewed Mamie De Cris her responses were "full of feeling. It was full of emotion. There was no stage play in any of it. The woman was in dead and hard earnest. She meant every word she said." Moreover, she was physically moved: "She did not tremble or quiver from fright because the warden was sitting near her. Her trembling came from the pent up feelings which were swaying her. She was wrought up. But in a second she calmed down and then as the tears began streaming down her cheeks, she sobbed out loud."[251] The richness of the discursive field for conveying white women's inner turmoil and angst is matched only by the intensity of black women's representation as subjects "of the lowest order of humanity" limited in sentience and associated with filth (Sarah Autry) and masculinity (Mattie Crawford). This predicament and its significance for the social position of black women was an issue of vital concern for black clubwomen. They would grapple with the available information about convict leasing's abuses as well as the absences in the documentary record in order to build a critique of state violence that placed black women at its center.

CHAPTER THREE

Race and the Sexual Politics of Prison Reform

We are waging a ceaseless war.

—MARY CHURCH TERRELL

At the time of the National Association of Colored Women (NACW)'s formation in July 1896, much was uncertain, including the organization's goals and agenda. Selena Sloan Butler came to the inaugural meeting prepared, armed with years worth of research on the violence imprisoned black women endured. She was exacting, dignified, and eloquent, as she had been taught to be at her alma mater, Spelman College. She had visited with dying women in Georgia's convict camps, and as she witnessed the formation of a historic movement she kept her memories of black women's terrorization, determined to mobilize the women around her in a moment of profound political urgency. Infuriated by governmental disregard for the women she had seen and met, she shared insights that would alter the trajectory of the most influential, if flawed, black women's organization in American history. If Selena Sloan Butler had anything to do with it, and she did, this new black women's formation would address convict leasing.

In 1895 Josephine St. Pierre Ruffin convened the first National Conference of Colored Women to argue for the formation of a permanent national organization of black women. This organization became a reality with the formation of the NACW in 1896. In her address to the conference Ruffin argued that black women faced a symbolic assault. She rallied the women to fight against the public defamation of black women's names, arguing that an essential reason for the formation of a national organization of black women was to break a silence that had been maintained too long in the face of "unjust and unholy charges; we cannot expect to have them removed until we disprove them through ourselves."[1] The goal was to organize collectively to shatter what Ruffin described as willful blindness to allegations against black women's character. Such charges were "of so humiliating and delicate a nature" that they "protect the accuser by driving the helpless accused into mortified silence."[2] Ruffin told her audience that "it is to break this silence, not by noisy protestations of what we are not, but by a dignified showing of what we are and hope to become that we are impelled to take this step, to make of this gathering an object lesson to the world."[3]

Ruffin's speech was inspired by specific charges leveled against black women in order to discredit Ida B. Wells's international antilynching campaign. To cast doubt upon Wells's arguments about the causes and extent of lynching, a Missouri journalist, John Jacks, alleged in March 1895 that black women were "prostitutes and all are natural liars and thieves."[4] Jacks's statement is a reflection of a generalized link between black women, criminality, and deviant sexuality. Lurid stories of black women's insanity and criminality were mainstays of the white press at the turn of the century, with headlines like "Crazier Than Carr: A Negro Woman Imagines She's a Horse and Eats Grass," "Old Woman Steals Dresses: Negress Sixty-Four Years Old Locked in Station House on Serious Charge," and "Fought the Officers: A Number of Negro Women Attack an Officer" abounding in the *Atlanta Constitution.*[5]

In order to change deleterious assumptions about black femininity black women would have to come together. They would fight "not by noisy protestations of what we are not, but by a dignified showing of what we are and hope to become."[6] This was a complex assertion about the black female subject position that often led reformers to adopt a maternalist stance toward working-class black women. Their programs included projects to remake black women's homes and train them to be better mothers. Yet through the campaign to end convict leasing, members of the NACW argued that the subjugation of women prisoners was integral to their fight for social equality. By attacking convict leasing the NACW made an assertion about who black women prisoners *were*—namely victims of state violence—and, by extension, who they were *not*—abject, malingering, criminal beings immune to pain and incapable of sexual consent or restraint.

It is important not to overstate the significance of the project of redeeming black women's reputations in the formation of the NACW or construe it as the sole reason for the existence of the organization since, as historian Stephanie Shaw argues, black women's mutual association long precedes the nadir of race relations that is commonly associated with the formation of the NACW.[7] While the NACW's work cannot be reduced to eradicating racist mythologies of black female deviance, it was an important goal. In the context of such pervasive representations of black women, Ruffin elaborated the problem of essentialism and gender incoherence that has been theorized as an American grammar.[8] Black women were the objects of multiple pervasive fictions explained through selective examples from the white supremacist imaginary. In this imaginary black female subjects were abject beings articulated through a series of nicknames, one being criminal. Black clubwomen knew that "this problematizing of gender places her [the black female subject] . . . outside of the traditional symbolics of female gender."[9] Ruffin and the founders of the NACW recognized white supremacy's totalizing narrative about gender and race. The construction of black female deviance was all-consuming, irrespective of class or social standing. With the assault on black womanhood as an overarching framework for considerations of the NACW's agenda, its members decided to undertake a campaign for the abolition of convict leasing.

Members of the NACW decided early on to fight against convict labor. This was not the only possible analysis for relatively elite and socially conservative black women concerned with their image in the white imaginary; nor was it necessarily the most obvious reaction to working-class black women's criminalization. In many ways this was a radical departure from the NACW's uplift work. The focus was not on individual responsibility and the uplift of African Americans, but on state violence. In light of the burden and mandate of redeeming black women's names, the leadership of the NACW had a difficult decision to make about how they would approach the issue of black women in convict camps. First they needed to decide whether they would touch the problem at all. They might have ignored the punishment regime that so abused women, disidentifying with them in order to proliferate a positive image of black femininity. Once they chose to tackle the problem they had to decide if they would emphasize uplift or moral regulation of women on the chain gang. Would they highlight the immorality of women who were convicted of crimes, emphasizing reform in order to draw a distinction between the real criminals and themselves? How, in short, would they craft a political position on black women prisoners, whose very existence threatened the cultural status of the most upstanding women of the race by serving in the popular imaginary as evidence of black women's symbolic deviance?

They chose to attack the problem directly, minimize discussions about the morality of the women in the camp, and frame convict leasing as an obstacle to the progress of black women. Such a critique of convict labor represents a nuanced and expansive vision of racial and social justice that broadened the bounds of community beyond those with literacy, property, or social status within black America to those who were denied all such cultural and material benefits. In exposing the conditions facing criminalized black women they took a risk by leaving themselves vulnerable to a widespread argument that all black women were merely criminals. Convict labor was an institutionalized form of violence that produced black women as subjects undeserving of protection and excluded from the traditional symbolics of gender. The women of the NACW realized that black women were bound up in a symbolic matrix of negative representation that linked the fates of black women regardless of geographical location, class, or social status. That one black woman could be subjected to convict leasing criminalized all black women. If one could be treated as an animal, none could achieve dignity or basic well-being. In waging a struggle against convict labor, Terrell, Butler, and others were in fact making a larger claim: that at its core the Jim Crow state used punishment as an instrument of white supremacist *patriarchal* terror.

Although the discourse on convict labor represents the radical end of a spectrum of black women's activism, it was by no means the NACW's only challenge to modern institutions of racist patriarchy. Along with mobilizations against the Jim Crow car and lynching, the anti–convict-leasing campaign represents an example of black clubwomen's opposition to institutionalized state violence in the era of Jim Crow. Leaders of the NACW reframed the issue of convict leasing, largely viewed as a system that ensnared black men, positioning black women at the center of discourses about the penal system. They used evidence they accumulated to confront and revise a dominant progressive narrative that focused on the abuses against men and the vulnerability of white women.

As Hazel Carby has demonstrated, black women intellectuals and activists during the "Woman's Era" of the late nineteenth century collectively produced knowledge about patriarchal power. Theorists of patriarchy and state violence brought their analyses to the NACW. Thus, "black women's clubs provided a support for, but were also influenced by, the work of their individual members."[10] These members included feminist anti-lynching activist Ida B. Wells, writer and temperance leader Frances E. W. Harper, and novelist Pauline Hopkins. Yet although the NACW incorporated radical critiques of patriarchy from leading black women intellectuals, its members also policed individual black women's behavior, hoping to remake women of the lower class who fell adrift, especially in rapidly industrializing cities.[11] Scholars including Carby, Kevin Gaines, Tera Hunter, Michelle Mitchell, Glenda Gilmore, Victoria Walcott, and Evelyn Brooks Higginbotham have argued convincingly that the performance, discourse, and politics of respectability as directed toward working-class women and men was simultaneously emancipatory and oppressive.[12] This analysis does not attempt to reconcile uplift's imbedded contradiction. Rather, it examines one important strand of black clubwomen's work, in this case, confronting state violence targeting poor black women who signified vice, moral deviance, and contagion in broader society.

Certainly the politics of respectability governed much of the work of Selena Sloan Butler, Mary Church Terrell, and other clubwomen. Yet in order to understand the political work of black clubwomen we must examine the full range of their activist projects. While they organized mothers' meetings to teach good morals, they also fought against institutionalized gender violence. If clubwomen were embroiled in a contested ideological battle with their working-class sisters in the city, they were also engaged in an intense confrontation with the state, whose violent oppression of poor black women they would not tolerate. The complexity and messiness of black women's institutional, intellectual, and political histories must be acknowledged. It is true that Terrell increasingly circulated narratives of moral uplift, to the chagrin of other activists, including Wells, who by some accounts was ousted from the NACW by Terrell, the beginning of bitterness between them.[13] While Terrell was not as strident or consistent in her critique of white supremacist violence as Wells, Terrell's politics cannot be neatly or simply summarized as conservative. In her race and gender politics she was a strident proponent of uplift as well as a zealous opponent of the state's high-intensity war.

Selena Sloan Butler and Mary Church Terrell were the most vocal critics of convict leasing within the ranks of the NACW. They had a strong ally in Lucy Thurman, founding member of the organization and the Woman's Christian Temperance Union (WCTU)'s superintendent of colored work, and the support of Margaret Murray Washington, the influential wife of Booker T. Washington. Margaret Murray Washington's opposition to convict leasing is significant because it departed from her husband's moderate stance that was informed by his broader ideology of racial betterment through the valorization of industrial labor. Although he opposed the convict lease system Washington also called for a decreased focus on its abuses. In a 1908 letter to educator and activist Hugh Mason Browne he equivocated, "It is the easiest thing in the world to set up a lot of discouraging figures showing the bad side of the Convict Lease System."[14] He advocated for a focus on the black man's economic contribution to the southern economy through convict labor before adopting a more vehement opposition to convict leasing in a speech on the topic in 1912. In a departure from her husband's view Margaret spearheaded efforts to spread a different analysis based on an argument developed by Selena Sloan Butler.

Born in 1872 in Thomasville, Georgia, Selena Sloan Butler is best known for establishing the first black parent-teacher association in Georgia, which would become the model for a national organization. For this work she was honored with a portrait in the Georgia State Capitol in 2000. Yet Butler was more than an advocate for maternalist reform. A proud graduate of Spelman College, she went on to become a kindergarten and night school teacher and editor of the *Woman's Advocate*, a monthly paper on social and political conditions pertaining to black women. She was a member of the Georgia Commission on Interracial Cooperation, and the first president of the Georgia Federation of Colored Women's Clubs. She was eventually elected president of the Atlanta Chautauqua Circle, an exclusive social, literary, and political club of black women, leading meetings on a wide range of philosophical, political, and social topics.[15] Butler's politics were as complex as the ideology and practice of racial uplift itself. She published conservative articles on "heredity and morals" in the *Spelman Messenger* that cautioned women against marrying a man who was not strong "physically, in morals, intellect, race-loyalty, and race-pride," positing a biological connection to character at the same time that she defended imprisoned black women against charges of innate inferiority and castigated state violence.[16] Certainly Butler's most renowned work as champion of the black parent-teacher association is also her least controversial. Despite conservative moral leanings, she pushed the boundaries of the organizations she led, challenging them to consider new ideas, unfamiliar kinds of work, and critiques of patriarchal violence. This is true of her work with the Chautauqua Circle, and is most evident in her participation in the NACW. Put differently, Butler had a complex politics that espoused uplift, but not to the exclusion of a powerful critique of state violence that stemmed from a determination to address white supremacist structures of gendered terror.

At the first national convention of the NACW in 1896 Butler "gave a full explanation of the Convict Lease System of Georgia" and explained the politics of prison reform in her home state, arguing that Governor William Y. Atkinson was making some progress toward eradicating the institution.[17] But it was not enough, and Butler was clear about the urgency of the problem. Her description of southern punishment inspired the other members to take several actions to fight convict leasing and its brutality. They planned to petition the WCTU to use its organizational influence to bring about the end of the convict lease system. Since Lucy Thurman was affiliated with both the NACW and the WCTU she was chosen as the liaison between the organizations. The membership of the NACW also resolved to send a delegation to the next annual meeting of the National Prison Association (NPA) to put convict leasing on the organization's agenda for penal reform policy in the United States. Finally, they formed a committee on convict leasing that would "interview representatives of the states where the system exists." In addition to raising questions they would exert pressure on politicians and "weary them, if needs be, concerning the atrocities which exist in their several states."[18]

Individual NACW chapters also conducted evangelical or rescue work at convict camps and prisons, in line with their uplift philosophy. In 1896 the Atlanta Women's Club, led by Butler, reported that they had distributed prayers and other biblical materials to prisoners at the local chain gang.[19] In 1897 the branch reported that they had rescued one little boy from the chain gang "and presented him to his mother as a Xmas gift."[20] In this story there is a subtle but important critique of the state. The convict camp is construed not only as a violent institution from which children should be rescued, but also an institution that estranged black mothers from their children. Black clubwomen's analysis of the state assault on maternal bonds is significant here because it conveys a contradiction imbedded in their analysis of poor black women and motherhood. While in other contexts they emphasized black women's negative mothering and unfit households, here they forcefully situated the state as the agent that precluded positive mothering and facilitated estrangement.[21]

At the second annual NACW convention in Nashville in 1897 Butler continued her efforts to make convict leasing a central issue for the organization. Although she was not able to be present she submitted a paper titled *The Chain-Gang System*, which Margaret Murray Washington presented to the membership. Butler argued that convict leasing challenged the very core of modernity, leaving her to wonder, "Are we living in a period of the 'dark ages'?"[22] Here Butler not only exposes the regime's abuse of women but counters mainstream understandings of Jim Crow modernity in which the convict lease system was a tool through which to advance the South, and especially Atlanta, toward the goal of industrial progress and modern social life. By highlighting the role of black women Butler repositions the convict lease system as a remnant of premodernity and the South as an antimodern state formation. After outlining the inhumane treatment of prisoners generally, she ends with a searing description of the terror women faced in convict camps:

> These are but mild illustrations of the torture that has been practiced in many of the private camps for years, not only upon men, but women, who have committed some small offense. In some camps men and women are worked indiscriminately, the latter being dressed in men's clothes. No provision is made for the separation of the sexes in the sleeping quarters. A young girl was sent to chain-gang camp in Wilkes county, where she was made to put on men's clothes and dig ditches, just as the men did. For any small offense the white "boss" would beat her on her bare back before the male convicts. Her pleadings would have no effect on the white "boss." The governor pardoned this unfortunate girl that she might be relieved of her sufferings.[23]

Butler described the plight of a black woman named Lizzie Boatwright, and although she did not mention her name or race, Boatwright's race would have been taken for granted by the listeners, and was ultimately reinforced by Butler's use of the term "white boss." This case was highlighted in Phillip Byrd's 1897 investigation of Georgia's misdemeanor camps, which the state's most influential black newspaper, the *Savannah Tribune*, published in its entirety. The *Tribune* did not often publish reports about the arrest or imprisonment of black women, but when such articles did appear, they focused on the differential treatment that black and white women faced. In 1905, three years before convict leasing was abolished, the newspaper published a brief report about two women, one white and one black, who were apprehended for shoplifting. The white woman received a sentence of $30 or four months in jail, while the black woman was given a larger fine or a "long sentence on the chain gang."[24] The *Tribune* bemoaned the unfairness of the judge's ruling, reporting that the "colored woman [was] to be further degraded by a long term on the chain gang and the white woman for the same offense is given a jail sentence of only four months." Although vague, the language of degradation is significant. Stories of men ensnared in the brutal convict labor system tended to focus on the physical abuse and brutal conditions of the camp; here the language of degradation is gendered, suggesting a recognition that for black women punishment in the chain gang was colored by humiliation, was a commentary on their deviant morality and social position, and implied sexual violation and the ruination of their honor. According to the report, the black woman was not only given a heftier fine, which the court rightly assumed she could not pay, but also a sentence of convict labor rather than jail. The report maintained that such contrasting punishment was an affront to the entire black community, "and yet it is boasted that the colored people are being treated justly in this section."[25]

Like Byrd's report, numerous articles on convict labor in the *Tribune*, the *Atlanta Independent* (another black newspaper), and the *Atlanta Constitution* focused on abuses against male convicts. Amidst dozens of cases of brutality targeting male convicts was the story of Lizzie Boatwright, the lone example of violence against a black woman. Aside from his mention of the Boatwright case, Phillip Byrd was optimistic about the plight of women in Georgia's camps. In his observation, "the sexes are effectually separated at night, and no female convict has become pregnant during detention in the camps for the past two years."[26] Apparently ignorant of or unfazed by the high rates of childbirth at Atlanta's Camp Bolton, he described this women's camp as a model.[27] Butler rejected Byrd's rather optimistic picture of convict life for women and contradicted it with her own observations and supplementary research. Byrd's report presented Lizzie Boatwright as an anomaly by describing her case but emphasizing the positive conditions for women, especially in gender-segregated camps. Butler presented the everydayness of torture against black women in the camps. According to her, women were not separated from men, and Boatwright exemplified the situation of "women in some camps" or a broader pattern in which black women were forced to perform the same labor as men.

If part of the NACW's mission was to alter the black woman's image in the white imaginary, the forced performance of masculinity in Lizzie Boatwright's case was a violation, a symbol of black women's gender inferiority. The histories of Mattie Crawford and Lizzie Boatwright, which were told in chapter 2, reveal that masculine dress was not just an incidence of extreme physical brutality; rather it was evidence that gendered racial terror positioned black female subjects at the "locus of confounded identities."[28] If the *Savannah Tribune* described imprisoned black women's plight as degradation, Boatwright's case provides yet another historical example to support Nell Painter's analysis that "whether on a mundane or catastrophic level, the essence of pornographic power is degradation."[29] Lizzie Boatwright's story is a prime example of the violent reification of the category "other" through an extreme spectacle of humiliation. Her brutalization constituted a symbolic rape, or a ritual of power and degradation meant to control the black female subject through physical violence accompanied by a humiliating performance of sexual subjection or masculinity.[30] For Butler the symbolic significance of Boatwright's case gave it the power to generalize, making it the only evidence she needed to support her claim that black women were worked indiscriminately with men.

In the context of this symbolic rape Butler went on to narrate the literal rape of black women by white male guards:

> One of the most touching cases that has come before the public,
> is that of a young girl at Camp Hardmont [*sic*], a camp for women.
> The guards became so infatuated with her, that peace did not always
> reign within the camp among the guards. One day an offspring
> came; both mother and child died. The matter was kept quiet for
> some time.... These two cases will give you an idea of the life of
> a woman committed to the chain-gang camps. Women, though
> already steeped in sin, find these chain-gang camps and "bosses,"
> already repulsive to their polluted lives. I have given you but a brief
> talk on the "Convict Lease System" as it really is. There is much
> more to be said, but too awful to relate to such a gathering as this.[31]

Although she maintained delicacy by omitting details and engaged in moral policing by referencing the perceived preexisting immorality of women prisoners, this move was likely a preemptive strategy to counter the inevitable charges that black women were so lecherous that any sex in the camps must have been instigated by imprisoned women. Through the filter of Victorian prose used to describe the guard's "infatuation," Butler emphasizes sexual force and violence by using the language of repulsion; in her analysis criminality does not instantiate consent or preclude force—quite the opposite. The terror of rape was far from an aberration and instead defined "the life of a woman" in convict camps. Butler's interpretation of examples from the archive of convict-leasing reports revealed the brutal conditions for imprisoned women and reflected their construction in the broader popular imagination as criminals without claims to their own bodies. Butler extricated black women from the margins of the discourse on criminal punishment and recast them as subjects who deserved protection and, more than that, freedom.

Butler's analysis of convict leasing was a catalyst to further action. Her *Chain-Gang System* paper was particularly inspirational because she presented her own model of activism. She included a description of her work to investigate the conditions for women in Georgia's convict camps. She had visited a convict camp and sat with a young woman who had contracted a terminal disease during her imprisonment.[32] Butler also observed the notorious 1896 trial of Georgia's convict lessees over which Governor Atkinson presided. There she gathered some of the information for her paper. She remarked upon the lack of oversight, pandemic violence in the camps, and the limitations of court testimony. She "saw, as did everyone in the room, the shyness with which the convicts would answer questions put to them by the State, that would expose the treatment they received. They knew that on their return to the camps they would be at the mercy of their 'bosses.'"[33] Butler's reflection upon retribution and the forced silence of prisoners in convict camps served as a reminder to the members of the NACW of their mandate to speak the unspeakable, to break the silence that circumscribed the lives of the vulnerable.

The NACW planned to distribute Butler's paper "all over the country to our members that they might know of the terrible crimes committed when this system was in vogue."[34] The use of the past tense in this declaration makes clear that the women of the NACW believed that the terrible crimes would soon be history. Their triumph against convict leasing was inevitable; yet they had to attend to another urgent matter. They needed to create an archive so that the irrefutable evidence of black women's extreme brutalization at the hands of the state would be preserved. They did not know all of the facts. They did not know, for instance, about Mollie White, who received ten lashes for allegedly failing to work in the Old Town Camp in 1885, or Leila Burgess who received thirteen lashes for idleness. They did not know about Rose Henderson who was wounded by a falling tree in a women's convict camp in 1896. Yet they had the stories that Butler had excavated from newspapers and special investigations. Those examples, Butler's analysis, and the knowledge that black women were in general positioned as others, convinced them that the imprisonment of women in convict camps was an exigent matter.

AFTER SOME BUSINESS and the reading of a letter condemning lynching from Frances Willard, president of the WCTU, the subject returned to Butler's paper. Lucy Thurman advocated for the circulation of the paper as a pamphlet.[35] As she was charged with appealing to the WCTU for support, Butler's paper would serve as a powerful organizing tool. Thurman's suggestion was remarkable as it was the only paper delivered at the NACW's early conventions that was circulated for wide distribution. Although a few unnamed members objected to the distribution of the pamphlets at the WCTU meeting, the motion passed. Thurman was again chosen to represent the NACW, this time at the World's WCTU Conference to be held the following month. The women voted to designate funds to rush the printing of the pamphlets so that they would be ready for circulation at the conference.[36]

Butler's work did not end with her visit to Camp Heardmont or her advocacy within the ranks of the NACW. In 1900 she and her husband Dr. Henry R. Butler embarked on a systematic study of the criminal process in Atlanta. They visited Atlanta's criminal courts with a focus on its lowest court, the recorder's court. Their attention to the recorder's court is significant because it was the jurisdiction in which most women were convicted, primarily for "quality of life" crimes including disorderly conduct, operating a house of ill-repute, quarreling, and cursing.[37] Dr. Butler wrote in the *Spelman Messenger*,

> Just here we would say that those who study the statistics of the races make a fearful mistake by going to the prisons to gather material or by taking it from the printed records of the various prisons for the following reasons: five of the cases against white defendants were dismissed. White defendants, as a rule, pay their fines, or their friends do so for them. Hence, only a few of the poorest or worst cases find their way into prison. Two of the cases against colored defendants were dismissed. Colored defendants as a rule do not pay their fines. Unless some old mother or father comes forward and pays the fine of some wayward boy or girl, to the stockade he or she goes to return in a few days worse by far than when sent in, by reason of contact with older more desperate criminals.[38]

The Butlers argued that the sentencing process was a crucial window onto the injustices of the prison system, offering a nuanced critique of social science methodology and economic and racial bias. The Butlers attempted to leave a more complete archival trail by publishing their findings about municipal sentencing patterns. They were outraged by the triviality of the crimes for which most black people were convicted in Georgia. Dr. Butler wrote, "The following is a partial list of the crimes committed by these people: swearing, disorderly conduct, fights, drunks, careless driving, females out after hours, attempts to rob, carrying concealed weapons, stealing old sacks, selling without licenses, etc."[39] The Butlers recognized that the local court was primarily charged with prosecuting poor people's crimes. Black women, of course, were more likely to be poor, more likely to be working for low wages, and therefore more likely to be in public and subject to arrest. Although the number of white wage-earning women was growing significantly, by 1900 only 42.5 percent of white households in Atlanta included a working woman, compared with 62.5 percent of black households.[40] Dr. Butler also focused on the problem of legislation, arguing that people could scarcely avoid the legal system in Georgia, with its excessive mess of laws. Dr. Butler's article is not devoid of the classist elements of uplift ideology, as he argued for the establishment of a juvenile reformatory to make young women and men into proper members of society. Yet the focus of the article is a critique of racist criminal justice: it was not the criminal life that degraded black youth, but discriminatory sentencing and awful conditions in Atlanta's stockade and convict camps.

If part of Jim Crow's legacy was the invisibility of black women's experiences of rape, Selena Sloan Butler's paper on the convict lease system attacked rape and gendered violence as one of the system's consistent features. She compiled data from firsthand observations and highlighted evidence from Phillip Byrd's special report while changing his narrative about the model conditions in women's camps. Butler was centrally involved in a long-term fight that connected the plight of women prisoners to a broader movement to improve conditions facing black communities in Georgia. Long after convict leasing ended, as late as 1926, she and other black women continued to investigate and advocate for systemic change in the conditions imprisoned women faced, particularly those who suffered so brutally in the Fulton County women's stockade.[41] Mary Church Terrell used examples from Butler's early archive, building upon it in her work to identify and eradicate the obstacles to black women's political and social progress.

Mary Church Terrell's Ceaseless War

In 1905 Selena Sloan Butler convinced the distinguished Mary Church Terrell to speak at Spelman College.[42] Born to an affluent Memphis family in 1863 and educated at Oberlin College, Terrell would teach at Wilberforce University before traveling to Europe for two years, returning to the United States, serving on the Board of Education in Washington, D.C., and embarking on a path to become one of her era's most influential activists.[43] She was a founding member of the NACW and the National Association for the Advancement of Colored People, and would lead fights for woman's suffrage and against segregation. She served as the NACW's first president in 1896 and held the position until 1901. In 1953, at age ninety, she successfully fought to desegregate Washington, D.C.'s public facilities. Importantly, that year she also led the Georgia delegation of the Women's Committee for Equal Justice, demanding justice for Rosa Lee Ingram, an African American woman from Americus, Georgia. Ingram had been convicted of murder in 1948 for the killing of John Ethron Stratford, a white sharecropper who had, by most accounts, come on to her property with a gun and tried to assault her. Two of Rosa's teenage sons intervened to protect her, and all three were sentenced to death by electrocution. Terrell was at the center of the campaign to free Ingram, serving as chairman of the National Committee to Free the Ingram Family beginning in 1949. According to historian Dayo F. Gore, Ingram's was "one of the most significant civil rights cases of the decade."[44] Although Rosa and her sons were sentenced to death, Rosa served as the symbolic figure of the campaign. According to Gore, Rosa's centrality reframed traditional civil rights messages, making clear that the racism of the criminal legal system was linked to black women's vulnerability to sexualized racial terror and their blanket denial of the right to protection.

Terrell ended her career by leading a campaign against African American women's persecution in Georgia's criminal legal system, marking the final phase of her ceaseless battle to expose the harms facing women in Georgia's prisons. Indeed, Terrell was a true ally for Butler in her fight to abolish convict leasing. She did not merely condemn the system for its endemic brutality but went further to cite it as an obstacle to the progress of colored women. When she opened the 1897 annual meeting of the NACW she touched on the issue, insisting, "In public questions affecting our legal status, let us engage intelligently and continuously, whenever and wherever it is possible to strike a blow for equality and right. Against atrocities like the Convict Lease System whose barbarity no tongue can utter, whose brutality no pen can portray, let us wage a ceaseless war."[45]

The atrocity of convict leasing existed across the South—in Alabama, Arkansas, Mississippi, Louisiana, Tennessee, Texas, Florida, and the Carolinas. Yet a few months after Butler's paper was presented at the NACW national convention Terrell began to refer to the convict lease system as "the convict lease system of Georgia." She would not conduct her own extensive research on convict labor until 1907, so it is likely that she acquired much of her information from Butler's speech and advocacy.[46] Like Butler, she did not highlight problems of crime or immorality that were assumed by others to lead to women's convictions. Rather, she focused on the barbarity of southern punishment. This was a complicated political framework; in some ways the association between convict leasing and barbarism, or premodernity, implies that an "enlightened" system of punishment was possible and, perhaps, desirable, if only the terms and edifice were changed. Such an implication represents an important pitfall of the NACW's approach. Yet Butler and Terrell were critiquing the system in place, and did so with carefully chosen language that challenged white supremacist logic by positioning carceral agents as brutes, destabilizing the association between blackness and inherent criminality and savagery, the discursive and ideological underpinnings of carceral white supremacy. Butler's and Terrell's activism therefore represents a pivotal moment in the history of black social movements to end white supremacy. Their decisions to center gender anticipate and challenge the erasure of black women in struggles against imprisonment and racial violence that marked the century that followed.

In 1898 Terrell addressed the National American Woman's Suffrage Association. Titled "The Progress of Colored Women," her speech delineated the accomplishments and obstacles facing the women of her race. Charles R. Douglass, son of Frederick Douglass, was in attendance and remarked upon Terrell's ability to cover massive ground, detailing a litany of "obnoxious systems" that degrade black women, including the convict lease system.[47] After describing the repugnant Jim Crow laws, she declared: "Against the barbarous Convict Lease System of Georgia, of which negroes, especially the female prisoners, are the principal victims, colored women are waging a ceaseless war."[48]

Terrell's belief that the convict lease system was an obstacle to the progress of black women motivated her to incorporate the issue into her speaking tour. In 1900 she spoke at the annual convention of the National Council of Women. In this speech Terrell used the anti-convict-leasing campaign as an example of both the obstacles and accomplishments of her organization. Terrell boasted that the NACW had taken on institutions of discrimination, including the "obnoxious Jim Crow laws." She then repeated what was now her stock phrase: "against the convict lease system of Georgia, of which Negroes, and especially female prisoners, are the principal victims, we are waging a ceaseless war."[49]

Terrell's unfailing assertion that women were the "principal victims" placed them at the center of the discourse about southern punishment and the Jim Crow state, despite mainstream representations of the system as predominantly, or solely, male. Terrell's hometown paper, the *Washington Post*, implied that Georgia's lease system was entirely male, noting in 1897 that "no plan has been agreed upon for the employment of 2,500 men whom the expiration of the lease will relegate to idleness."[50] For leaders of an organization that sought to redeem black women's names, black women's representation in southern convict camps was significant. Despite their relatively small numbers in comparison with black men, their vastly disproportionate imprisonment as compared with white women was a reminder of black women's deviant subject position. In 1897, at the time of Byrd's report, there were ninety-five black women and only four white women in Georgia's state convict camps.[51] Black women's dramatic overrepresentation in convict camps revealed their position as white women's symbolic alter egos. They were not sent to convict camps merely because they were black, but precisely because they were not white and thus could not embody womanhood. For this reason, they were also subject to rape and forced to perform men's work, wear men's clothes, and undress in front of men. The logic of gender deviance that justified this forced drag was circular and was mutually constitutive.[52] If black women were able to do the work that they were forced to do, they were gender-deviant. If they were gender-deviant, they deserved to be subjected to traditionally male forms of violence: whipping, brutality, and more forced labor, which in turn reinforced that deviance.

Terrell often emphasized the particularities of women's experiences while at other times she recognized their similarity in treatment with black men. After serving as the NACW's president for five years she offered an assessment of the organization's unfinished work to its members. Terrell argued that opposing convict leasing was part of this work, because "as long as there is a system in this country for a trivial offense that drags men and women of our race into cells, whose air space is less than the cubic contents of a good size grave, there is something for thoughtful charitable colored women to do."[53] She implied that black women received no protection from the abuses that men endured. And they were subject to the terror of rape. She immediately followed her call for action against convict leasing with demand for an end to the silence "which seals the lips of colored women, about the rape of black girls."[54]

In 1907 Mary Church Terrell penned her most famous and thorough critique of convict leasing. Her "Peonage in the United States: The Convict Lease System and Chain Gangs" was published in the popular journal *Nineteenth Century*. Terrell repeatedly emphasized that black men, women, and children alike were subject to a regime "in some respects more cruel and more crushing than that from which their parents were emancipated forty years ago."[55] She also paid special attention to the plight of women, both white and black, who were brutalized and "outraged" in convict camps. Terrell theorized the chain gang system as a form of debt peonage that resembled slavery and subjected its victims to atrocities, many of which were too horrible to name. She illuminated the deep relationship between convict labor and economic oppression by examining the system of petty offenses and fines that relegated the poor to labor in convict camps. She exposed the fetters of freedom by analyzing instances in which planters paid the criminal fines for poor whites and blacks in order to ensure a constant, enslaved labor force on their farms.

Terrell came to write the article after an experience she had during a lecture at the Baptist Women's Home Missionary Society in Massachusetts. The members of the Baptist Missionary Society were shocked by Terrell's assertion that "women have often been placed in dark, damp, disease-breeding cells whose cubic contents were less than a good-sized grave."[56] They offered to extend her speaking time so that she could explain the convict lease system in more depth. Afterward she decided to scour the archives for ammunition for an extensive article on convict leasing. She researched at the Congressional Library and "spent six weeks looking over old files of the *Atlanta Constitution* and other newspapers."[57] Terrell uncovered information about state and federal case law on convict labor, Georgia Prison Commission reports, and governors' speeches, all of which she included in her essay. Although the NPA records do not include NACW members in their listing of convention participants, it is clear that if she was not physically present, Terrell closely followed the work of the organization. In her essays she cites recent speeches delivered at the National Prison Association's annual meetings. All this Terrell culled and transformed into a sophisticated critique of white supremacy, patriarchy, and economic oppression in the south. Amidst unsparing examples of the brutality facing men in convict camps, she exposed the unique oppression of women in the southern legal system.

Terrell also detailed the abuses against women in Georgia's convict camps. Like Butler she used the case of Lizzie Boatwright not as an exception to an otherwise pristine picture but as an example of the general conditions facing black women. She included a more explicit account of Boatwright's torture that revealed that "this girl and another woman were stripped and beaten unmercifully in plain view of the men convicts because they stopped on the side of the road to bind a rag about their sore feet."[58] Terrell's essay included a succinct summary of wrongs that were discovered through an investigation of Georgia's camps, which included "outraging the women."[59] Terrell also discussed the plight of white women in the camps, arguing that in Florida and elsewhere white girls were held in a state of peonage. She claimed that in 1906 "came the startling announcement that one thousand white girls . . . wear men's clothing and work side by side with coloured men who are held in slavery as well as the girls."[60] Terrell invoked the racist rhetoric of white slavery that abounded during the Progressive Era, which she might have anticipated would overshadow her account of black women.

As Angela Davis has argued, her decision to incorporate this narrative without documentation may have been a strategy to raise awareness about the broader predicament of peonage and convict leasing. Davis has critiqued Terrell and the broader anti–convict-leasing movement for its failure to confront broader presumptions of black criminality and to "openly examine the structural role of the expanding network of penitentiaries and convict labor camps in constructing and affirming these ideologies" of black criminalization.[61] As Davis compellingly argues, the movement to end convict leasing was limited by its failure to fully elaborate the relationship between punishment and the structures of precarity and premature death that marked the turn of the century.[62] This shortcoming is critical because, as Davis's scholarship has demonstrated, criminalization was and continues to be a central mechanism of anti-black economic, political, and social control; moreover, as Davis has argued, the role of incarceration cannot be understood without an engagement of the failure of Reconstruction to establish rich structures of material well-being and social life. Despite their critical limitations, black women reformers did offer a powerful critique of black female criminalization that challenged black women's pervasive violation; this was fundamental to undermining white supremacist ideology that was premised upon the disposability of black female bodies, the ubiquitous rape of black women a sign of white power and superiority. By highlighting black women's brutalization and by contesting their imprisonment in convict camps *without* relying upon claims that they were innocent of the crimes for which they were imprisoned, Terrell, Butler, and others did make transformative if not comprehensive critiques of the carceral system. The significance of Terrell's decision to address black women is illustrated in the letters she received about the *Nineteenth Century* article. Most expressed disbelief about her claims about white girls. But not one letter expressed concern about Lizzie Boatwright or other black women in the convict lease system. At least two letters warned her that she best have proof of her claims about white women because they were unbelievable. The chairman of the Republican Club of New York City wrote that he was upset when an intelligent white man charged that her claims about white women could not be verified. If after years of advocating for black women in convict camps, Terrell incorporated the stories of white women as a tactic to increase concern for black women as well, her efforts had failed. However, the letters responding to her article reveal how entrenched the disregard for black women's injury was, making the importance of Terrell's sustained work to raise awareness to imprisoned black women all the more significant.[63]

Terrell's concern for black women mired in the ferocious trenches of the southern legal system emerged in an unexpected realm in 1907, the same year that she published "Peonage in the United States." That year she wrote to the editors of the *Atlanta Independent* asking for detailed information about the public legal woes of Miss Lucy Laney.[64] Lucy Laney, a prominent activist, member of the NACW, and a trailblazer in black education, was arrested on November 30, 1907, in what would come to be known as the "Madame Laney Episode." She was the founder and principal of the Haines Normal and Industrial Institute in Georgia. When she returned from a sick day in 1907 she found two public health physicians there to vaccinate the children. Laney argued that the pupils were "panic stricken" in fear of the doctors and she tried to intervene in the process to calm them. In her early fifties, Laney was sentenced to a $25 fine or fifty days of jail or street work for violating the vaccination ordinance. Another teacher, May D. Belcher, was charged with disorderly conduct.[65] Laney's court hearing exploded into conflict when her attorney referred to her as Miss Laney and got a swift reminder from the recorder's court judge that "it was not in accordance with southern view that negroes were so addressed."[66] Lucy Laney's immediate reaction to the judge's reprimand remains a mystery. Although she was likely furious about the judge's degrading treatment, she would not have been shocked. Back in 1896 Laney had been a part of the NACW Committee on Resolutions that condemned "the omission of titles by the Southern Press when referring to our women."[67] Ten years later the significance of the NACW's work to change the discursive landscape of southern culture would hit home, as the limitations on black women's claims to femininity nearly cost Laney fifty days of freedom.

Opinions in the male-dominated black press were harsh toward both Laney's conduct and the judge's bias. The *Independent* opined, "The conduct of both the judge and Miss Laney deserves condemnation in this case. Miss Laney ought to be reproved by public opinion for her refusal to respect the constituted authorities, and Judge Picquet for his attempt to prejudice the interest of a client at bar before him by reminding her that she could not expect the treatment of a lady in his court."[68] Mary Church Terrell likely followed the case because a fellow member of the NACW was in trouble and her plight was splashed across the pages of several newspapers. Yet the specifics of the case also likely piqued Terrell's interest. Laney's attempt to assert her right as an educator and stand up against potential abuses of her students by the state had landed her in a position similar to that of women who were arrested every day in the South. She was confronted with the demand to pay or work the streets. Laney could afford to pay the fine and so was spared the harsher punishment.[69] Yet her status as an elite black woman only barely saved her. As a black woman, her alleged insolence in the face of white authority caused her arrest in the first place. Moreover, the ambiguity of the justification for her sentence—whether it was Laney's actual conduct or her lawyer's insistence that she be referred to as "Miss"—revealed the extent to which the racial construction of gender in the South left black women vulnerable to state penal violence. In this case economic standing clearly saved Laney from the convict labor system; however, the discrimination she faced and her narrow escape from punishment resonated within black clubwomen's circles.

While Terrell's letter requesting information from the *Atlanta Constitution* reveals that she was clearly concerned about Lucy Laney's arrest, it was not the only incident that may have forced her to consider her own subject position (or that of elite black women) in relation to prisoners. During a major lecture tour Terrell rode in a segregated train car on her way to her next engagement. As always, she had to endure the degrading conditions of the Jim Crow car. Yet while she would normally have to pay to ride in inferior conditions, on this day a group of convicts and a racist conductor secured her a free ticket to ride. As Terrell described it, "A sheriff had brought a group of prisoners into this car and gave a bunch of tickets to the conductor."[70] Although it is unclear why, she sat near the prisoners when she boarded the train. When the conductor looked at her he "evidently took it for granted that I belonged to the crowd in charge of the sheriff and passed by without asking me for my railroad ticket. For a long time I preserved that ticket as a rare souvenir of an experience which is guaranteed to give a thrill that comes only once in a lifetime."[71]

While on her way to give a speech that likely included condemnations of both the Jim Crow car and convict leasing, the two issues merged as she was momentarily able to beat the system and fool the conductor by passing for a convict. Terrell's description of the scene emphasized the thrill of everyday resistance—her deception enabled her to avoid paying a fare that supported segregation. Yet equally important is the behavior and assumptions of the conductor. Despite all of the markers of Victorian middle-class femininity, he took it for granted that she was a convict. In doing so he evidenced an absolute association between race and criminality. Any black person was a criminal, despite other markers of class. Just as Lucy Laney only narrowly escaped a convict labor sentence despite her class status, the conductor's actions reveal that in the white imagination the association between blackness and criminality was absolute and transcended gender distinction. Terrell could hardly overlook the political weight of being mistaken for a convict, an experience that reinforced her political and social proximity to her sisters in the prison camp.

The NACW addressed convict labor consistently through the first decade of the twentieth century. The issue was discussed at each national conference until 1906. Yet the organization's efforts to extricate black women from convict camps would be tragically undermined in Georgia by a pervasive political discourse that ignored black women's pain and emphasized white women's suffering and vulnerability. This rhetoric was espoused by an ostensible ally in the anti–convict-leasing movement, who was also a formidable foe in the fight to end white supremacy: Rebecca Latimer Felton. Georgia's most influential white WCTU member would proliferate a discourse that demonized black women even as she exposed them as victims of the injustice of southern punishment.

In her essay "Peonage in the United States," Mary Church Terrell had reflected upon how "even intelligent people" knew very little about the convict lease system.[72] While the ignorance of elite white women in the North perplexed Terrell, their southern counterparts were no strangers to the issue of convict labor. By the time "Peonage in the United States" was published the WCTU had been fighting against convict labor for over twenty years. Rebecca Latimer Felton brought the issue to the organization in 1881, which began her long career in penal reform. Felton's campaign to abolish the convict lease system exposes the racial logic of gender ideology in the late nineteenth-century South, which drew much of its ideological sustenance from antebellum thought. She would become one of the most prominent and powerful women in Georgia, serving momentarily as the first female U.S. senator in 1922.[73] An advocate of lynching and ardent opponent of convict leasing, Felton's stance reveals the intimate connection between black women's invisibility as targets of rape and the dominant mythology of the black male rapist.

Rape, both actual and symbolic, had an elusive archive in turn-of-the-century Georgia. Although rape was only tangentially reported in state investigative and newspaper reports about convict leasing, black and white female activists expanded the available archive of mainstream convict leasing accounts through both reinterpretation and independent investigation. Selena Sloan Butler and Mary Church Terrell, leaders of the NACW, and Rebecca Latimer Felton, a leader of the WCTU, all mobilized the record of convict leasing's abuses toward broader claims about gender ideology in the South. At the turn of the twentieth century African American activists including Butler and Terrell needed an archive in order to convince a hostile world that black women were the victims of gendered violence and deserved safety from terror. They worked diligently toward this goal from the last decade of the nineteenth century through the first decade of the twentieth. During roughly the same period, Felton, Georgia's most prominent white female reformer, conducted extensive research on convict leasing to attack the system as an institution that promoted unholy miscegenation. She mobilized the large membership of the WCTU to support her goal.

While black and white women reformers had the same ostensible aim—the abolition of the convict lease system in Georgia—their divergent approaches provide a window into broader ideologies of race, gender, and class in the white and black clubwomen's movements. Felton's rhetoric in particular reveals that white supremacy was imbedded in the anti–convict-leasing movement. In addition to illuminating gender ideology at the turn of the century, white and black women's contested interpretations of the convict-leasing archive help contextualize the shift in penal policy, or "reform," that took place in 1908, and which established separate systems of punishment for black and white women in Georgia.

Rebecca Latimer Felton's Strange Career

Rebecca Latimer Felton held a deep belief in black women's natural proclivity for sexual deviance and white women's vulnerability to rape by black men, and this belief guided her discourse on gender segregation in southern convict camps. For Felton the convict lease system was cruel, violent, and barbaric. In one speech about convict leasing she vowed, "I will apologize to the law and to you if I don't prove it to be an epitomized hell."[74] But she and her husband believed that convict leasing truly "epitomized hell" because it propagated the vice of miscegenation. The campaign to abolish convict leasing was consistent with temperance because both liquor and convict camps were viewed as forces that corrupted good morals. To Felton, convict camps represented a training ground for already corrupted black women, which ensured that they would be further inculcated into a salacious lifestyle. They would pull white men down with them. Felton's reform platform was driven by her overriding fear of the generations of criminals she believed black female convicts produced.

A turning point in Felton's political life was 1881, when Frances Willard, president of the WCTU, made her first national tour. That was also the year Felton learned about the case of Adaline Maddox, a fifteen-year-old black girl who was sentenced to five years on the convict lease for stealing fifty cents from another child.[75] Felton had been politically active as the campaign manager for her husband, politician William H. Felton, but she joined the WCTU in 1887 to persuade them to mobilize against convict leasing. Like the NACW, the WCTU took up the issue of convict labor through the influence of individual leaders who demanded that the issue be placed on the organization's agenda. Through the WCTU Felton was able to deploy a statewide network of white women to exert political pressure and bring public scrutiny to the issue of convict leasing. Although the first Georgia WCTU chapter was formed in 1874, it would take nine years before there were enough chapters to form a statewide organization. Felton capitalized upon the growth of the WCTU; shortly after the state organization's founding in 1886 she identified it as the vehicle through which she would wage her campaign against leasing. Her conviction about the evils of convict labor was unyielding and prompted her to introduce a resolution pledging the WCTU to advocate for a reformatory for youthful criminals and a separate prison for women.[76]

Much of the WCTU's prison reform work consisted of visits to jails and convict camps where they distributed literature about temperance and observed prisoners' living conditions. The WCTU's first major action on the issue of convict labor was its 1886 petition to the Georgia state legislature, which demanded a separate reformatory for women and children. Although Felton credited the petition for getting "the ball rolling" on separate prison camps for men and women, separate quarters for women in the state prison farm at Milledgeville were not established until 1899.[77] It was not until 1905 that the Georgia state legislature provided for the creation of a state juvenile reformatory, which opened at Milledgeville two years later.[78] Despite limited gains, the WCTU consistently fought for a reformatory and oversight of prison conditions in Georgia. Indeed, the state branch maintained a Prison Committee from 1886 to 1932. Their work situates the WCTU within a broader, national progressive prison reform movement that intersected with the aims and strategies of the temperance movement.[79]

The WCTU's penal reform work was fundamentally evangelistic. The "prison and jail work" committees of local branches distributed

Bibles and temperance literature to male and female prisoners. In some branches these visits were quite frequent. The Savannah WCTU, for example, paid forty-six visits to the local jail between 1889 and 1890. They petitioned the prisoners to sign temperance or "abstinence" pledges and followed up on their progress in maintaining a liquor-free lifestyle.[80] The WCTU advocated a measure of compassion, preventive punishment, and containment. At one annual convention Mrs. Webb, superintendent of prison and jail work, described the case of a fairly educated woman with training in domestic science who had spent thirty-three of the last thirty-six months in the Chatham County Jail. Mrs. Webb reported this story at the state convention, remarking, "It seems to my weak woman's judgment that it might be a better plan . . . if, after the third offense, the offender could be sentenced for two years to some institution where they could be made to earn their bread by the sweat of their brow."[81] Although Mrs. Webb did not suggest that criminals should be sent to the chain gang, part of the work of the WCTU was to establish an inebriate asylum.[82] Inebriate asylums, women's reformatories, juvenile reformatories, and industrial training schools were among the extensive array of penal alternatives that the women of the WCTU imagined to be necessary to transform distinct deviant populations into better reformed citizens, or to separate them from the general population.

The Savannah WCTU was not exceptional in its prison, jail, and almshouse work. In 1890 the South Atlanta WCTU's superintendent visited the jail each week and the chapter held "forty-six services, ten special services, visited the camp ten times, wrote 28 letters, distributed 3,574 papers, 125 books, 12 catechisms, 27 testaments, 9 bibles, and 45 hymn books."[83] The Georgia WCTU also regularly passed resolutions calling for a separate prison for women and children. The next year the WCTU made headlines with a visit to the Chattahoochee Brick Company convict camp. Governor William Northen accompanied the group of white women to the men's camp where they distributed flowers and evangelical reading materials. Although women in the WCTU were no strangers to jail and convict camp visits, Northen made much of the novelty of the scene, remarking: "This is an unusual sight . . . to see ladies here who come to pray for you. They came to you with tender hearts and warm sympathy."[84] The Georgia WCTU sporadically gathered local jail and prison statistics, and even corresponded with women prisoners about the conditions at the state prison.[85]

The WCTU continued its tradition of penal reform into the early twentieth century. Among its progressive activities, the organization's leaders viewed prison reform as a shining accomplishment. In 1900 Rebecca Latimer Felton and Jane Elizabeth Sibley, the first president of the Georgia WCTU, wrote to the *Atlanta Constitution* demanding recognition of the WCTU's role in the juvenile reformatory movement. Responding to a letter that discussed the reformatory movement but failed to reference the WCTU, Felton was adamant that her organization be credited for "what justly and properly belongs to the temperance women of Georgia on these and other lines of reform and public benefit" and continued on to say that she was gratified "to know that the Woman's Christian Temperance Union's faithful work is being accepted in quarters where indifference long prevailed but the truth of history should be vindicated."[86] For Felton and Sibley prison reform exemplified the great need for women to enter politics to compensate for male lethargy on important social issues. One important motivation for Felton's political activism and support for suffrage emerged from her frustration with male politicians' undervaluation of women's roles on farms and the need for women's protection in an urban sphere that was transforming with rapid industrialization.[87]

Indeed the WCTU's prison work epitomized white women's entrance into the male-dominated public spheres, perhaps most powerfully exemplified in the political career of Felton herself.[88] A 1913 special edition of the *Atlanta Constitution* commissioned by the WCTU reveals that the organization sent two white members on assignment as police reporters covering the Fulton County jail. This entrance into an incontrovertibly public domain helped its WCTU members subtly raise the question of women's rights. As the headline suggests, police chief Beavers broke his "long silence" about women's roles in politics and policing. The article depicts the women luring Beavers into a comfortable relationship with them, allowing him to open up about women's roles. They questioned him about whether there was a place for women in political life and on the police force; the chief replied by asserting that women should guide their husbands on moral issues related to politics and suggested that women occupy positions as probation officers, but not police.[89] The huge spread of photographs depicting the WCTU reporters at the police station and jail proclaimed women's entrance into spaces that were traditionally male-dominated. There was also a feature on Mary Bohnefeld, the city's first female prison matron, who empha-

At the top, left, the woman's edition police reporters, Misses Passie May Ottley and Marjorie Brown, are seen interviewing Newport Lanford, Chief of Detectives; at right they are showing their notes to Britt Craig, their guide; at the bottom, Judge Broyles is giving them an exclusive story; next, they are talking to a prisoner; last, Mrs. Bohnefeld is telling them what a "bad boy" Mr. Craig is.

"Confronted by Woman's Edition Reporters, Police Chief Beavers Breaks Long Silence," *Atlanta Constitution* (Special Women's Edition), June 4, 1913.

sized the care that the women prisoners received. The picture of life in the courtroom and jail was generally a rosy one, filled with amusing stories and reports of conditions so sanitary that "Dickens even would have sniffed in vain for any odor but carbolic acid. It was a comfort to know that this dreadful place is one of the lightest, cleanest, airiest and best in the whole country."[90]

In the WCTU's article, prisoners were represented as drunk, comical, disillusioned, and generally pathetic. Amidst references to Sunday drunks there was the description of a black mother who was present in city court to pay the fine for her son's release. She was described as a "good old mammy" who proclaimed to the judge, "Yessir, Boss, I sho is claimin' dis here boy. He's all I'se got ter claim." There were also two black male prisoners who were condemned to death and broke into a rendition of the song "Whiter Than Snow" upon seeing the women visitors. These stories are emblematic of the WCTU's representation of their evangelical work. There were similar narratives by white WCTU members in North Carolina. One visit to a North Carolina jail was an "emotional turning point" during which WCTU members enjoyed a lunch consisting of ham biscuits and led prisoners in song.[91] In the Georgia WCTU members' apocryphal account, the poignant song "Whiter Than Snow" drove the prisoners, women visitors, and chaperones alike to tears.

Within the context of a project of conversion and discipline, the WCTU's participation in an amusement or song was also a process of cultivating black contentedness and subjection.[92] The prison was depicted as a familiar antebellum scene, replete with the recognizable tropes of plantation life: the pitiful mammy, complete with dialectal dialogue, and a sorrow song, which both invokes and inures the reader to the pain of the black subject. The song is derived from the psalm "Wash Me and I Shall Be Whiter Than Snow." If it was sung at all it may be read as a hidden critique of white supremacist terror and the power of white privilege. Yet the WCTU presented the singing as a poignant expression of grief and an appeal for redemption that so epitomized the black male prisoner's subjection. Shortly after they were serenaded the women left the stockade, breathing a sigh of relief "as the last doors clanged behind them."[93] The WCTU's brief encounter with adventure and misery and ultimate escape into the sunshine reinforced one of the symbolic vestiges of slavery and abolition: the profound permanence and spectacularity of black suffering, dramatically counterposed by the brevity of white women's exposure to it.

Although white women in the WCTU regularly visited convict camps and jails, the experience was difficult for them. As Mrs. E. E. Harper explained to the National Prison Association in 1886, "I have to be locked up with the prisoners until I am ready to go out—just like a prisoner would be; and that is not pleasant for a woman."[94] Harper was superintendent of prison and jail work for the Atlanta chapter of the WCTU, a position she had sought immediately upon arriving in the city in 1882. During at least one meeting she "gave a thrilling report of her work in the jails and convict camps of Atlanta."[95] Harper was an influential leader, especially with respect to the organization's penal reform work. Moreover, her position in the Atlanta chapter, where one of the female convict camps was located, made her opinion on issues of criminal punishment especially valuable.

Harper's comments at the 1886 NPA annual meeting reveal the commingling of concern and derision within the WCTU. After describing her visits to the men's department of the Atlanta jail where prisoners sang old-fashioned hymns with her, she went on to tell the story of her first interaction with a black woman in a county convict camp. The imprisoned woman waved to her, yelling, "How d'y do!" and asked whether she remembered her. She told Harper that she used to belong to someone in Louisiana, to which Harper replied that she was sorry to see her in the convict camp. Harper described her dismay when the woman replied, "Oh! I don't mind it, I have been here three times."[96] For Harper this was evidence of the impossibility of attempts to change the character of black convicts. She was perplexed and wondered how to make black women "feel" the shame and hardship of imprisonment when "ninety-nine out of a hundred do not mind it, or feel it."[97] Her claims about the unpleasantness of prison for herself lie in sharp contrast with the black female subject's contentedness, representing yet another example of the limitation of the imagination of WCTU members with regard to black pain and sentience.

The women of the WCTU believed that they were engaged in a progressive outreach campaign to reach black women who did not recognize the immorality of their actions or feel shame at their imprisonment. White women reformers' temporary exposure to convicts and penal institutions represented sacrifice because it forced them to experience discomfort and emotional distress, conditions that were "not pleasant for a woman." Their very concern exposed them to physical and emotional distress. A singular account of black women's comfort in convict camp captivity was mobilized by the WCTU to underscore black women's general incommensurability with and deviation from gender normativity.

Like the WCTU's article, Rebecca Latimer Felton's writings on convict labor obfuscate black pain and racial terror and are thereby rooted in antebellum mythologies of race and gender. She highlights the injustices and hardships confronting black women in the convict lease system while tacitly enforcing assumptions about black female hypersexuality. Felton was a tireless advocate for separate reformatories for women, yet she held a profound belief in black sexual deviance and white feminine vulnerability. It was this set of beliefs that eventually shaped penal policy. After 1908, black women would continue to be sentenced to the mixed-sex chain gang after the abolition of the convict lease system, while white women would be diverted from the misdemeanor convict camp to the all-women's section of the state farm at Milledgeville.

Felton left no stone unturned in her efforts to abolish convict labor. She collected special legislative reports and scoured Georgia newspapers.[98] She also investigated Georgia state legislative history. In a mammoth, vigorously researched speech on convict leasing she offered a litany of cases that she believed revealed the injustices of the system: a black man sentenced to life for stealing a mackerel from a grocery store; a black woman sentenced to three years for stealing eggs from her boss, and so on and so on. Her rhetorical flourish was no less impressive than her research. In the same speech she incorporated theatrical techniques. She reenacted her own confrontation with a man who sought to convince her of the barbarity of convict leasing. She recalled telling her informant, "You go too fast my dear Sir—show me your proof that I may tell all my people of these things and give the proper credit where they can verify such statements." He answered her by telling her the story of the aforementioned Adaline Maddox, "a colored girl [who] was convicted of robbing a negro child of fifty cents and was sentenced to five years in the penitentiary.... Is that explicit enough? Here read it yourself." In her speech Felton recounted her own disbelief, wondering if there was some mistake, declaring, "How in the name of common justice could such sentences be reconciled with the law and the evidence? What sort of people are your judges?"[99] As Felton narrated the story of herself as an everywoman who stumbled upon urgent information from an informed man, she illuminated the intense injustice of southern punishment, which oppressed black men and women for the most trivial offenses. After listening to the informant describe the details of the case, including the judge's decision to prosecute the defendant for robbery even though the only witness was a child, Felton again described her astonishment: "My God, Cried I, Can these things be—and can the state of Georgia tamely submit to them?"[100]

Felton has the informant go on to elaborate upon the prevalence of children born to guards in the convict camps—he told her that there were twenty-five children born in the camps, and at least one of them was found to be fathered by a guard. He demanded to know, "what do you think of that?" For Felton "that" fact of sex, pregnancy, and childbirth in the camps was the system's most detestable feature. As LeeAnn Whites has argued, interracial sex and mulatto children ignited in her the deepest moral outrage over slavery and convict leasing: mixed-race children born to criminal black mothers and morally adrift white fathers.[101] Felton reasoned that it was deplorable for the state to allow a system to exist that would endanger the moral fabric of Georgia society and allow a population of mulatto criminals to burgeon. This was the same state that did far too little to protect true womanhood, leaving white women vulnerable to rape. Lynching, then, became the main recourse to protect and redress this grave problem, but abolishing convict labor might spare Georgia another generation of mulatto rapists.

Felton left a powerful archival condemnation of convict leasing in which gender was at the forefront of her concerns. Her sympathy was directed toward both white and black women, as stories of black women sentenced to reprehensively long sentences permeate her notes and speeches. Yet concern and sympathy may be misleading here, as they tend to obscure as much as they reveal. Felton's tireless opposition to convict leasing must be considered in the context of her radical feminist politics, which ultimately critiqued inequalities between farm wives and husbands, inserted women into the public, political arena, and agitated for the primacy of white motherhood and white femininity while simultaneously construing black women as abject hypersexual beings who both give birth to and serve as symbolic counterparts for black male rapists. Black women's immorality and hypersexuality was the cornerstone of a social and political order that nurtured black male rapists.

To be clear, Felton was one of the few voices that raised concern for black women in convict camps. She was one of the anti–convict-leasing movement's loudest proponents. She was also more easily heard than black clubwomen. Her archive reveals a wrenching, carefully constructed appeal for a spotlight that would expose injustice callously meted out against both black and white women. Felton's inclusion of black women within the group that belonged in reformatories, not convict camps, might be read as a call for their protection under the banner of true womanhood, but it was not. Felton's archival trail of concern and determination belies her overriding belief that black women, though unjustly sentenced, were not primarily victims of rape, but bearers of bad morals. They spread the diseases of hypersexuality and criminality. There was an undeniable dark side to Felton's sympathy. Her appeal for the reformatory was ultimately a demand for quarantine.

The Black Hole of Calcutta

Rebecca Latimer Felton's feminist political analysis begins not with the convict lease, but with slavery. As Leann Whites has argued, her most searing critique of slavery rested on the prevalence of interracial sex and mixed-race children. Much like her critique of the convict camp, she daringly framed the problem within a language of abuse, the ultimate target of which was white women: "There were abuses, many of them. I do not pretend to defend these abuses. There were kind masters and cruel masters. There were violations of the moral law that made mulattoes as common as blackberries. In this one particular slavery doomed itself."[102] Felton's critique of slavery parallels her position on convict labor. She does not mince words in declaring the cruelty of the master or the guard. She does not hesitate to describe the degradation and physical harshness of either institution. Yet the violation she describes is of that of the moral prohibition against miscegenation. Here, black women are erased as victims of violence:

> Men and women were worked together during the day and were chained in the same sleeping bunks at night. In November 1878, a short time before this report was read to the legislature—many of the convict women were reported to be pregnant—soon to become mothers—while 25 children were then in the penitentiary under three years—and one convict female ascribed the paternity of three to the brutal lessee!—The chain gang was merely *droves of Negro slaves.*[103]

As LeeAnn Whites argues, Felton's core concern was miscegenation, and because of her vehement opposition to interracial sex she is perceived to have been "more than capable of naming the 'nameless crime,'" in other words, to name the rape of black women, because it exposed the way that sexual abuse "undercut the position of white women as their wives."[104]

But while Felton did indeed rail against miscegenation, and certainly criticized white men for their immoral interracial sexual behavior, this did not amount to a political recognition of the rape of black women. This distinction is important in understanding gender ideology in an apex moment of white supremacy, since sexual vulnerability was such a constituent feature of normative womanhood. The obfuscation of violence as a part of interracial sex between black women and white men was part of Felton's generalized belief in the preeminent association be-tween blackness and sexual danger. Just as the rape of white women by black men constituted a threat to the household, so did white men's sexual relations with black women. Yet the act of sex between black women and white men was construed as neither rape nor intimacy. Rather, it was a result of immoral and exploitative behavior by white men and the inherent sexual lasciviousness of black women. For this reason black women were not "ruined" by sex with white men but rather in-cited to sexual fiendishness. Rape and lynching discourse relied upon the spectacle of "the quintessential white woman" ravished, "polluted, 'ru-ined for life,' the object of fantasy and secret contempt. Humiliation, however, mingled with heightened worth as she played for a moment the role of the Fair Maiden violated and avenged. For this privilege—if the alleged assault had in fact taken place—she might pay with suffer-ing in the extreme."[105] On the contrary, black women's character was already abject. Sexual relations in the convict camp were construed as a process through which black women's preexisting immorality was unleashed. Unless contained, this unleashing would become an all-consuming threat to the white supremacist moral fabric of southern life, including white femininity and womanhood.

Rarely in her prolific writing does Felton reference force in acts of sex between women prisoners and guards. She includes a quote from a private letter between penitentiary officials, which notes that four women had complained that the overseer had threatened to whip women pris-oners if they did not comply with "his carnal desires," the language she also uses to describe forced interracial sex in *My Country Life in Geor-gia*.[106] After reporting this atrocity, Felton describes the true danger of such a situation, arguing that "women are placed in normal schools of degradation and will necessarily become fiends in these compulsory dens of vice."[107] In this instance in which the use of force was described in explicit terms, it is employed as evidence of the dangers of bringing out black women's sexual libido. While black women were subjects in a larger story of moral degradation, in accounts that emphasized experi-ences of pain, Felton specified that her primary subjects were white. She called for the protection of a "white woman from a brute who laid 110 lashes on her back and whose wailing—aye her curses were almost loud enough to be heard in the State Capitol," yet her writings conspicuously omit specific references to black women's sentience and experiences of pain.[108] In Felton's view, white women were being injured and pained, with absolute indifference from white men. While black women's abuse provoked them to become dangerously immoral subjects, she argued that the tortured white woman should "have been a martyr" and railed against white male penitentiary officials who "actually patted [the whipping boss] on the back after he had put 100 lashes on that miserable white woman's back in an Atlanta prison camp!"[109]

Although concern is omnipresent in Felton's writing, it is primarily a concern for the production of deviant motherhood and the reproduction of bastard mulatto children. Here the camp is brutal, abusive, but not the site of the rape of black women. The brutality, then, lies in the perverse act of interracial sex between imprisoned women and lessees and the generalized immorality of convict guards who worked prisoners to the bone, not in the violent act of rape. As Saidiya Hartman asks, "If subjectivity is calculated in accordance with degrees of injury and sexual violation is not within the scope of offenses that affected slave existence, what are the consequences of this repression and disavowal in regard to gender and sexuality?"[110] Felton's propensity to call attention to the rape of white women in her appeals for lynching, her description of white women's shrieks which could be heard in the halls of the state capitol, and her simultaneous emphasis on black women's deviance over their injury amount to a methodical delineation of the boundaries of "woman" as a social category that extends from slavery to the convict leasing era.

When she presented an appeal for a reformatory to the Georgia state legislature in 1887 Felton argued that the convict camp was a "black hole of Calcutta . . . where virtue had no ray of hope, and sickening filth lay deep on dead and dying humanity."[111] She elaborated this concern in a speech to the Georgia Sociological Society several years later in 1902:

> The negro's education in books has been largely unproductive of good results, because it antedated the proper training of the mothers in their lewd homes. This land is burdened with convicts and ex-convicts, the latter without character or credit, after they are turned loose on the community. These lewd homes are continual crime-promoters. They pull down faster than book education can build up. If I could only whisper a word in Mr. Carnegie's willing ear, I'd say spend some of your money on reformatories for ignorant women and girls, who should never be permitted to marry or propagate their kind until good character shall have been established.[112]

To Felton, black mothers were to blame for surging crime; lewd black women and black women criminals should be prevented from bearing children. The convict camp was the most extreme extension of the bad home. The convict camps where children were born each day needed to be abolished in favor of reformatories where society could "shut the door of the species that continues to fill the chain-gangs."[113] By diverting resources from schools to reformatories, "society" could create a system where deviants "do not marry and are not given in marriage until they can present a clean bill of moral health, at least."[114] Felton's anguished dedication to penal reform derived from a profound vision of eugenic social control.

Felton's political formulation regarded black women as sexual threats to the white supremacist social order. When they had sex with white men they were not "ruined" victims like the farmwomen whom Felton defended in her call for lynching. Rather, they were always already depraved and therefore needed the most severe form of sexual control: sterilization. Though they sometimes failed at their duties, white men were still protectors, not insatiable beasts. White women had the exclusive property rights in sanctity, and its protection, along with a profound disappointment in white male democratic politics and efforts to protect white women, motivated Felton's most infamous invective: "If it takes lynching to protect woman's dearest possession from ravening human beasts, then I say lynch a thousand a week if necessary."[115] Innocence and purity are necessary constituents for the symbolic production of a true rape victim. For that reason white women required from their men the "sheltering arm about innocence and virtue."[116] Felton's true white women were robbed of their virtue by the black male rapist, which resulted in their humiliation, injury, and degradation. Felton's black female prisoners who had sex with the guards were exploited and sometimes abused, but since they were never fully innocent or pure to begin with, the result was the production of a beastly sexual fiend. Black women had no "dearest possession" that could be robbed through the act of rape. Lynching was reserved for black men because only white women could be raped. Although black women may have received unjustly long sentences, they were ultimately threats to society because their unruly carnal impulses and perverse mothering reproduced a class of black and mulatto male criminals that threatened the sanctity of the household and the safety of white women, especially in industrializing cities.[117] White men, thought flawed, were called upon to better fill their

Cend w

patriarchal political roles as protectors; the protector could not also be the criminal.

In her groundbreaking book on the gendered politics of rape and lynching, Crystal Feimster argues compellingly that by 1898 Rebecca Latimer Felton had experienced an important political shift. After disappointment with democratic resistance to rape-preventive and protective measures for black and white women in the 1880s and early 1890s, Felton capitulated to the virulent southern democratic politics in which the rape/lynch myth was white women's only source of protection against rape.[118] As Feimster shows, Felton's vitriolic language and calls for lynching had escalated by the late 1890s. Yet this bargain for white women's protection is dramatic not only because it represented the abandonment of a previous campaign against convict leasing, the campaign upon which she entered political life, but also because in some ways it reflects the implicit boundaries of her conception of gender normativity all along. Felton succumbed to such vehement racism, abandoned a precious fight against convict leasing, and regarded black women as vile criminals who should be sterilized rather than educated because such ideas exalted the singular status of white femininity, a powerful political tool. For Felton, black women's plight under convict leasing was pitiable and included exploitation, and she endeavored to ameliorate their condition within a maternalist discourse that alternated between concern and pathologization. However, poor white women were the objects of her primary concern from the beginning. It was poor white women, along with their elite white counterparts, who belonged to the normative gender family. The transition from arguing that the age of sexual consent should be reduced to calling for lynching represents more of a tactical shift than a core value change.[119] Interracial sex was the vice that mattered so dearly to Felton, and if black women were exploited, they were not its ultimate victims. Both white men's failure to protect white women and their engagement in sex with black women ultimately meant sexual and cultural violence against white women. Black women's fight against gender violence could be marginalized, indeed erased, in Felton's political trajectory because it meant something altogether different; it was not essential to the fight for true womanhood or to upholding chivalry and masculine protection because black female subjects were excised from the category of true woman.

The anti–convict-leasing campaign tested the racial-sexual ideology of the South because it provided clear evidence of white men's sexual violation of black women. Yet the discourse on southern punishment became an opportunity to convey, through sentimentalism, both sympathy and contempt for black women, as they were configured in Felton's imagination as both victims of state corruption and perpetrators of societal disaster. The WCTU became increasingly concerned with the extraction of women from Georgia's chain gangs. Between 1906 and 1908 the issue reemerged as a focus of conversation at the organization's annual conventions. In 1907 Mrs. Charles Morris, state superintendent of prison and jail work, encouraged her fellow sisters to "use all your influence to get women sent to the state farm and not worked in chain gangs." In 1908 she repeated this request, urging her comrades to "work and pray for women to be sent to farms and *not* to chain gangs." When the 1908 parole law was passed, the WCTU hailed it for providing conditions conducive to restoring "good citizenship" and preventing prisoners from being the "object of charity." The WCTU maintained a campaign for separate gendered spheres of incarceration after 1908, while also lauding the parole law that subordinated black women to white domestic managerial control and providing white women with free or nearly free black female labor.[120]

By the time convict labor changed from private to public hands in 1908, the logic that guided Felton's position on convict labor would change the course of women prisoners' experiences in Georgia. As with other reforms in the Progressive Era South, penal reform would be envisioned through the language of segregation, and Jim Crow punishment would be codified through a discourse about white women's bodies. Gendered subject positions, defined by race, were recodified and enforced by county judges. The principal victims of patriarchal violence under the carceral state remained the same.

CHAPTER FOUR

Engendering the Chain Gang Economy and the Domestic Carceral Sphere

Sofia on parole, she say. Got to act nice.

—ALICE WALKER

Subject position is everything in my analysis of the law.

—PATRICIA J. WILLIAMS

Fifteen years after Selena Sloan Butler described the plight of a "young girl sent to a chain-gang camp in Wilkes county, where she was made to put on men's clothes and dig ditches, just as the men did," a woman imprisoned in that very same camp would face the very same conditions and scorn.[1] The judge of the city court of Washington County called Hattie Johnson an "incorrigible thief" and a "notorious strumpet" even declaring that any sympathy would be wasted on her. Although she could not escape the carceral logics of antiblackness and patriarchy that ensnared her, she adamantly refused to accept them. Convicted of larceny and sentenced to twelve months on the Wilkes County chain gang in 1912, Hattie Johnson's imprisonment did not serve its intended purpose; she was of very little use to the road-building project because she took a debilitating fall almost immediately after she arrived on the chain gang; she explained as much in a letter to the Prison Commission that was both desperate and decisive: "I am in Know shape to be out here I am in a family way . . . three months gone." She argued, "It is a shame for me to be out here with all of These mens it is 26 mens and if I get sick know one know what to do for me nothing But all mens and me one woman and they carriage me on the Road every day like I was a man."[2]

In resolutely asserting her difference from men, Hattie Johnson did not elaborate upon the meaning of this distinction. In other words, her letter does not necessarily affirm traditional notions of womanhood or the politics of respectability; in that sense it is ambiguous. The limited available facts about her—that she was unmarried and pregnant when she was arrested—suggest that she defied at least some of the conventions of respectability. She persistently and decisively asserted that her subjection to the brutal conditions of convict labor, the disregard for her pregnancy, and the particular angst that resulted from her predicament as the only woman on a chain gang were gendered injustices that should not be ignored. The erasure of black women's specific needs and experiences was a form of terrifying carceral violence, and Johnson's vehement objection to being positioned on the road like a man illuminates black women's objection to southern carcerality as a critical terrain of gender ideology and a vital technology within the broader apparatus of white supremacy that "engendered black femaleness as a condition of unredressed injury."[3] Johnson's torment was distinct from, but not worse than, the anguish suffered by women in gender-segregated camps; her despair was part of the landscape of terror in which all women and men captive in southern convict camps were entangled. She was granted clemency in November 1912, after she had served three months of crushing labor on the chain gang. Her letter is particularly significant because it comes just a few years after racial gender ideology was entrenched through legislative "reforms" to the convict labor system.

In a September 1908 special session of the Georgia General Assembly, legislators passed two major penal reform laws, ostensibly creating a more enlightened system of punishment. Yet the laws did not reduce the number of black women imprisoned in Georgia, nor did they alleviate the harm of imprisonment. Instead, this legislative package initiated new forms of subjection for imprisoned black women and created a penal regime more compatible with the gendered logic of southern economic development. To reduce competition between free labor and convict labor, the legislature eliminated the convict lease system, replacing it with the chain gang. Imprisoned women and men would no longer be forced to work for private companies in various modernization industries, including railroad construction, the lumber industry, mining, and brickmaking. Now they would be forced to work on roads while living in camps managed by state governmental authorities. Yet this reform, deceptively hailed as abolition, replicated the same egregious problems of the system that came before.[4] The deadly conditions that plagued convict lease camps persisted under chain gangs. Moreover, prison labor continued to be integral to the state's modernization project as captive, unpaid labor would now be used to expand and surface municipal and county roads—the infrastructure necessary for intrastate transport of goods and people and the ground upon which one of the most important symbols of American modernity—the automobile—would travel.

The 1908 chain gang law's descriptive title began, "Act to Provide for the Future Employment of Felony and Misdemeanor Male Convicts upon the Public Roads of the Several Counties of the State . . . to Amend Section 1039 of the Code So Far as the Same Relates to Females." The exclusion of women/females from the chain gang is elaborated in the law's first paragraph:

> State authorities may employ the chaingang, not to exceed twelve months, any one or more of these punishments in the discretion of the judge; provided that nothing herein contained shall authorize the giving the control to private persons . . . in such mechanical pursuits as will bring the products of their labor into competition with the products of free labor. *If the convict be a female the judge may, in his discretion, sentence her to labor and confinement in the woman's prison on the State farm, in lieu of a chaingang sentence, not to exceed twelve months.*[5]

To Georgia's judges, the racial specificity of the gendered directive was obvious, and they consistently enforced it in their rulings. Between 1908 and 1936, only four white women were sent to Georgia's misdemeanor chain gangs compared with nearly two thousand black women.[6]

The legislature also passed a law establishing parole, essentially negating the logic of chain gang reform, which ostensibly ended private punishment. The Georgia Prison Commission was now empowered to conscript prisoners to work for private individuals or businesses for at least one year instead of simply releasing them after they had served their minimum sentence. Paroled prisoners remained "within the legal custody and under the control of said prison commission and subject at any time to be taken into custody on order of said commission."[7] Under parole, black women were forced to labor as domestic workers for white families, giving new meaning to the concept of the prison of the home. They were subject to constant surveillance and the threat of return to the prison camp for any transgression; private individuals, many of whom were now white women, continued to serve as police and warders.[8]

While historians have analyzed the relationship between slavery and the white supremacist logic of postbellum convict labor regimes, the violent reproduction of racially specific gender categories represents another continuity. The chain gang replicated the particular dialectics of black women's oppression under slavery. As Angela Y. Davis has argued of the black woman: "she was a victim of the myth that only the woman ... should do degrading household work. Yet, the alleged benefits of the ideology of femininity did not accrue to her. She was not sheltered or protected; she would not remain oblivious to the desperate struggle for existence unfolding outside the 'home.' She was also there in the fields, alongside the man, toiling under the lash from sun-up to sun-down."[9] Daina Berry's research on gender and plantation labor in Georgia is particularly critical. "Because many of the required tasks on a plantation were performed by either sex," writes Berry, "it is no surprise that enslaved women often boasted about being able to work hard " 'jus like a man.' "[10] She continues: "Lowcountry bondswomen represented the majority of the agricultural workers and contributed substantially to the plantation economy. They labored alongside bondmen at similar tasks and completed traditionally gender-specific jobs at night."[11] These gendered continuities between antebellum plantation labor and convict labor are critical to understanding the southern carceral regime as a form of neoslavery, with "gender neutrality," the employment of black women in hard labor alongside men, being one of its critical features. While the quote above reveals that some enslaved women bragged about their abilities as agricultural laborers, Berry also emphasizes the prevalence of complaints about the grueling nature of the work. Whether in the years preceding or following 1865, women in bondage commented upon the ways that labor extraction positioned them in close relation to masculinity.

Evelyn Nakano Glenn has convincingly argued that "an integral aspect of systems of labor coercion, whether formal slavery, indenture, debt bondage, [or] convict leasing, ... was an appropriation of not only men's and women's productive labor but also women's reproductive labor—that is, caring labor. Whereas men in subordinated groups were commonly compelled to perform hard physical labor on agriculture, construction, and mining, women and girls were directed into domestic service, where they performed caring labor for their social superiors."[12] Black women's labor was profoundly flexible, the absence of a normative gendered subject position making it possible for authorities to force them to labor on both sides of the gender divide. The Jim Crow carceral regime replicated slavery's gendered economic logic. As Kathleen Brown argues, "rooted in planters' assumptions about English and African women's proper roles in the tobacco economy, early definitions of racial difference and the accompanying discriminatory practices resulted ultimately in a race-specific concept of womanhood."[13] This forced double labor burden was unbearably violent. Rather than being released after they had served their minimum sentence under conditions of such extreme violence, black women were thrust into the domestic carceral regime of parole. The domestic carceral sphere expanded the purview of the prison regime. By forcing imprisoned black women to work as servants in private white homes, domestic service parole and chain gang punishment isolated them from their communities and left them vulnerable to moral and physical control by prison authorities and white masters and mistresses.

Although in practice the chain gang law only extended the disparate treatment that black women had received in the convict leasing era, its language is significant: "If the convict be a female the judge may, in his discretion, sentence her to labor and confinement in the woman's prison on the State farm, in lieu of a chaingang sentence, not to exceed twelve months."[14] Black women continued to be sent to the chain gang under this very law, reflecting their exclusion from not just the category "woman" but also the category "female." They occupied a position "out of the traditional symbolics of female gender," a "paradox of nonbeing" reflecting, through their gendered and racialized difference, "what a human being was *not*."[15] This unbearable flexibility of nonbeing was constituted through the double burden of road labor and domestic labor in Georgia's penal regime.

Georgia's Jim Crow carceral regime produced women every day, and all of the women were white. That is, Georgia's 1908 law established chain gangs under the condition that white women could constitute a separate and unique class of persons, defined as female, who would be protected from its brutal throes. Black feminist scholars have produced invaluable analyses of the racial construction of womanhood in the U.S. South.[16] In describing the legal regime that rendered black women as absent/present paradoxes in gender discourse I do not want to reify the racial construction of gender that was proliferated through penal legislation. I also do not want to reinforce ideals of normative femininity by emphasizing black women's perceived deviation from it. Instead, I wish to highlight tensions and contradictions within white supremacist gender ideology that meaningfully contributed to the production of black dehumanization. Black women's incorporation within a convict class that was explicitly gendered masculine under the law and their simultaneous subjection to distinct regimes of labor exploitation through the domestic carceral sphere reveal that gender ambiguity was necessary to produce black abjection. As Hattie Johnson's letter indicates, black women exposed and rejected the paradoxes and violence of this gendered racial order. Employed as a critical institution for the maintenance of white supremacy, this gendered racial order had to be reasserted through legislation and carceral practice precisely because of black women's challenges from within and beyond the prison boundaries.

Through Georgia's carceral system the market for chain gang road labor and the market for domestic labor merged in the body of the black woman. By 1915 Georgia had "13,000 miles of rural surfaced roads," more than any other southern state and fifth in the United States overall, most of which was constructed through chain gang labor.[17] Southern infrastructure development "was symbolized by the pickax of the convict laborer, and middle-class prosperity heightened the demand for black women domestic servants."[18] Widespread understanding of racialized gender roles set the terms for acceptable and unacceptable imprisonment, yet prisons were not merely outgrowths of such ideas. The prison functioned as a productive regime, the "localization and a constitutive logic of the state's juridical, spatial, and militarized dominion" rather than a discrete institution, building, or peripheral manifestation of domination.[19] The turn-of-the-century southern carceral regime generated and consolidated logics of racial and gender subordination conducive to southern industrial capitalism. The exploitation of labor under the chain gang system was materially useful for building roads and maintaining the racial domestic order through carceral domestic servitude; it also served the interests of capitalist social organization, producing knowledge about the proper role of gendered and racialized laboring bodies, upholding gendered spheres of labor, and reinforcing the sanctity of the prominent symbolic rationale for Jim Crow: protection for white women's bodies.

At the turn of the twentieth century white women entered the paid labor force in record numbers in the urban South. They began to obtain positions as sales clerks, telephone and telegraph operators, and textile, hosiery, and candy factory workers.[20] The white female workforce in Atlanta nearly quadrupled between 1890 and 1910, when over 18 percent of white women performed paid work. Between 1900 and 1920 the percentage of wage-earning women who were white grew dramatically from 28 percent to 48 percent.[21] Young unmarried white women were popularly represented as dainty, attractive, docile workers whose paid employment in limited economic sectors conformed to traditional attributes of white womanhood—purity, submissiveness, and fragility.[22] Yet the growth of the female workforce was also perceived as a significant threat, since middle-class white Georgians "assumed that black women should work and would probably be sexually active" but feared independent white working women as "a new and frightening phenomenon."[23]

This was Rebecca Latimer Felton's Progressive Era, but it was also, as Jacquelyn Dowd Hall has famously revealed, Ola Delight Smith's Progressive Era. Smith exemplified a burgeoning class of white women in the urban South who challenged conventional sexual norms, entering the workforce, labor movement, and public life in novel ways. In 1907 she left her job as a telegrapher and moved to Atlanta, where she worked a variety of jobs before becoming president of the ladies auxiliary of the Commercial Telegraphers Union of America. Smith wrote an essay titled "The Penalty of Being a Woman" and championed working-class feminism, challenging clubwomen's domestication of politics and the idealization of "married bliss."[24] While her stature in the labor movement may have been extraordinary, Smith represented a growing class of white women in various industries.

In addition to women's paid labor, new forms of leisure threatened traditional gender roles. By World War I Atlanta's downtown was filled with cheap theaters and dance halls catering to wage-earning women. White women's newfound independence and participation in heterosocial leisure spheres was a threat to the existing social order, including segregation, prohibitions against interracial sex, and arrangements of patriarchal dependency. Religious reformers increasingly associated labor, sex work, and sexual exploitation. Some Atlantans even argued for "an end to women's wage work as the only means by which women could be safe from sexual exploitation of employers."[25] Since white women's paid labor was tolerable only insofar as it was a temporary stop on the path to married domesticity, the increasing number of married white women in the labor force was viewed as a particularly significant threat to white male authority. The percentage of working white women who were married grew from 12.6 percent to 21.3 percent between 1900 and 1910, threatening the sexual contract that governed capitalist society and proletarian social positions.[26] As Carole Pateman argues, the very "construction of the 'worker' presupposes that he is a man who has a woman, a (house)wife, to take care of his daily needs."[27]

In Georgia, the housewives who helped constitute the social position of the white proletarian man also hired black female employees. At the turn of the century most black women in Atlanta were employed in domestic service, but they were slowly entering other occupations as well. The "proportion of black women in domestic work dropped from 92 to 84 percent between 1900 and 1910," and more black women found employment as "seamstresses, dressmakers, tailoresses, and milliners."[28] Between 1910 and 1920 the percentage of black women employed in domestic work in Georgia dropped to 75 percent.[29] This slow but significant shift in black women's work produced a reactionary backlash that manifested as early as 1897, when white women employed at the Fulton Bag and Cotton Mill engaged in a strike to protest the hiring of black women at the mill.[30] As Tera Hunter argues, the "strike reinforced the pervasive association among black women, degradation, and domestic work just when more employers were in search of women workers."[31] In the first two decades of the twentieth century black women used myriad forms of resistance to combat their social and economic subordination. They continued to refuse to live in the homes of their employers, they engaged in collective work stoppages, and they strategically negotiated the terms of their labor. They left the South and migrated north for new employment opportunities in numbers that outpaced their male counterparts.

As black women resisted the exploitation of their labor and as white women both undermined gendered divisions of labor and reinforced black women's subordination through domestic service work, the carceral regime was violently employed to reinforce capitalist labor organization and white supremacist patriarchy. Manliness was seen as bedrock for building fortunes in the midst of fluctuations in the market economy.[32] Characterized by white women's labor competition, capitalist shifts in labor organization that diminished opportunities for self-employment and promotion, the growth of a national movement for suffrage, and black resistance to economic subordination, the turn of the century marked a significant threat to the white patriarchal order of things and required a serious state response.

Had "women" been forced to perform manual labor on the chain gang, notions of vulnerability, purity, and domesticity would have been radically undermined, and the idea that they could enter male domains of labor and politics would have been reinforced. Yet black female bodies were put to work on chain gangs, where all of the other laboring bodies were male. The watershed 1908 law providing judicial discretion for sentencing females reasserted the racial definition of femaleness and womanhood that had operated under convict leasing precisely because it did not specify that it was only applicable to white women. The very lack of a racial modifier meant that the law was intended to exclude females/women generally—not specific types of women. All those recognized under the law to be normative females were to be sent to the appropriate site for the imprisonment of women: not the chain gang but the women's section of the Milledgeville State Prison Farm.

Jim Crow Modernity and the Alchemy of Race and Riots

While 1908 was the year that Georgia, the symbolic capital of the New South, formally defined "woman" as a category constituted by whiteness, white women's protection from the worst features of the penal regime represented continuity from the convict lease era. Before 1908 they were excluded from difficult labor in convict camps and Milledgeville, where they were given light work such as mending uniforms instead of fieldwork. During the same period, black women had been forced to perform hard domestic work such as cooking and cleaning for the entire convict camp, as well as all other forms of labor such as brickmaking, mining, and farming. The formal codification of "female" as a category defined by whiteness in 1908 reflects the gendered logic of Jim Crow modernity, making de jure what had been de facto differences.

The prison regime was part of the development of the Jim Crow segregation laws that were implemented in Georgia throughout the first decade of the twentieth century. In 1900, black residents lived throughout Augusta, but that would change in the first years of the century as white city officials razed mixed neighborhoods, forcing occupants out. Although white and black opposition had defeated Atlanta's Jim Crow streetcar ordinance in 1902, the law passed in 1906.[33] Atlanta's residential segregation law, which formally established black and white neighborhoods, was enacted in 1913, and by the 1920s nearly all of Georgia's major cities had passed laws segregating or excluding black people from public spaces.[34] Segregation and antiblack terror responded to challenges to the economic and social status quo. Perceived threats to the white masculine hold over good jobs exploded in Georgia in 1909, drawing "the widest national press attention of any labor based conflict before the 1917 East St. Louis riot."[35] White railroad firemen struck in protest against black men's acquisition of seniority in railroad firemen positions—seniority that had only been achieved through their exclusion from other railroad positions. White workers waged a three-week strike that was thwarted by railroad managers; however, efforts to preclude black railroad employment and seniority would become more successful in the years to follow.[36]

Yet under white supremacy, "fundamental social hierarchies . . . depended nearly as much upon fixed gender roles as they did on the privileges of whiteness."[37] White women's vulnerability and dependency was reasserted through extreme violence, justified through a discourse about the threat of black male rape. Atlanta's white newspapers had circulated stories about black male assaults on white women for years, but the rhetoric and threats of violent white retribution escalated after Annie Laurie Poole charged a black man with rape on July 31, 1906. Following her charge, a group of white men went to the home of her alleged attacker, Frank Carmichael, and killed him. Over the next two months the press published stories about several other white women who had accused black men of rape and attempted assault, with scandalous titles such as "The Reign of Terror for Southern Women." Popular calls for the lynching of black men escalated; at least one reporter also called for the sterilization of black girls.[38] On September 22, 1906, white Georgians began a collective attack on black women and men in Atlanta that lasted four days. The worst white mob violence since Reconstruction, this assault left at least twenty-five black people dead and sixty injured.[39] The Atlanta race riot must be understood as a pursuit of urban order communicating that segregation was paramount in the context of rapid industrial growth.[40] As a growing population of white and black women became increasingly public through wage work and new commercial amusements, reassertions of control over the social location and hierarchal status of female bodies became increasingly necessary. As David Godshalk notes, one of the remarkable features of the "antiblack crusade . . . was the wide range of whites . . . who deliberately deployed provocative racist images in pursuit of their own narrow political and economic goals."[41]

Joseph Turner, Georgia's prison commissioner at the time, certainly did not escape the 1906 panic. In a report issued that year he bemoaned the fact that there was no separation of the sexes in misdemeanor convict camps: "Two instances within the past twelve months have especially attracted the attention of the Commission, in each of which a white woman had been convicted of selling whiskey illegally and confined in a chain gang in which all of the other inmates were negro men. . . . The close daily contact of males and females, especially of white women and negro men, is shocking to the moral sensibility, and demands a change."[42] Turner's incendiary complaint was issued despite the fact that (according to his own report) there was only one white woman in Georgia's misdemeanor convict camp system at the time, in contrast to 165 black women.[43] Turner reiterated his appeal for the separation of imprisoned white women from black men in a section of his 1907–8 report titled "Women in Chain Gangs."[44] He repeated his observation about the problem that white women convicted of selling whiskey were being confined in a convict camp with black men and claimed that two more had been subjected to that fate since his previous report. According to official reports there was still only one white woman confined in the misdemeanor convict camps; however, proposals for legislative action were still necessary to provide judicial discretion and "remedy this evil."[45] His attention to the problem of proximity between white female and black male bodies was grounded in the possible threat to even one white woman's body.

Following Turner's 1907–8 report, the state legislature passed its penal reform act. The state's assumption of authority over convict labor depended on the protection of white womanhood through exempting them from the chain gang: the provision that "nothing herein contained shall authorize . . . giving the control to private persons" was linked to the mandate that "the judge may, in his discretion, sentence her to labor and confinement in the woman's prison on the State farm, in lieu of a chaingang sentence."[46] Since only four white women were sentenced to the chain gang from 1908 to 1936, as compared with nearly two thousand black women, exposure to the brutal conditions of the chain gang was not a matter of racial disproportionality in female imprisonment; the new system of punishment rested upon the prohibition of white women's imprisonment on the chain gang entirely, a ban that was only violated in a rare few instances over the course of thirty years.

According to its title, the goal of the 1908 chain gang legislation was to "provide for the future employment of felony and misdemeanor male convicts upon the public roads." The case of prison reform in Georgia is particularly significant because it privileged gendered subjectivities within a broader taxonomy of beings; women, who were legally construed (through legislation and its juridical interpretation) to be white, were to be segregated within a separate apparatus of punishment from black women, black men, and white men. Only two weeks after the passage of the 1908 act, the ordinary of Habersham County wrote to Commissioner Turner for legal guidance: "We have two misdemeanor convicts in the County Jail, they are both females. What disposition shall we make of them?" The very next day he received a reply from the secretary of the Prison Commission: "Are the female misdemeanor convicts, white, or black? We do not yet know what to do about these prisoners. Are trying to get the new law properly interpreted, and will later be in position to let you know what is to be done with them."[47]

Official interpretation of the new law came swiftly once Habersham authorities informed the Prison Commission that both women who were being held in jail were white. The women, Vona Addis and Jane Hunter, had been convicted of keeping a lewd house. Hunter had previously been convicted of adultery and selling liquor. The judge had sentenced them to pay fines of $25 and $50, respectively, and ordered them to leave the state or be rearrested and sent to the chain gang. At least one community member described Addis and Hunter as "disolute women" who threatened the moral fabric of the entire town.[48] A few weeks later authorities arrested both women for failing to leave the state. Both women denied that they intended to defy their sentence. Addis believed she was only ordered to leave the county, not the state, while Hunter maintained that she was in the process of relocating when she was arrested. Although Addis and Hunter were Habersham County's most licentious residents, they received significant support for their clemency appeal. The mayor and forty other residents signed a petition asking the court for sympathy. They argued that Addis was an orphan "who was absolutely a stranger to the love and protection of a Guardian" and "very, very poor."[49] The prison commissioner opined that Addis was "a young white woman capable of reform," and since the 1908 chain gang law mandated that "women who have committed offenses should be sent to the Woman's Department State Farm," he ordered that she and Hunter be transferred from the county jail to Milledgeville.[50] Although poor and dissolute, their status as women precluded punishment on the chain gang.

Kate O'Dwyer was sent to a Clarke County chain gang for keeping a lewd house in 1908, although the underlying act for which she was prosecuted seemed to be an affair with a married man. The victim of moral policing, she received a harsh sentence of six months in jail and twelve months on the chain gang, although by some accounts the sentence was entered incorrectly and the judge had actually sentenced her to serve less than a year. Early on, a court ruled that she could be sent to the chain gang but could not be shackled with black prisoners, which in effect meant that she could not be shackled at all.[51] A member of the Board of Aldermen supported on her clemency case, stating that in his recollection Kate O'Dwyer was the only white woman to have been sentenced to the chain gang and therefore deserved clemency.[52] Solicitor General S. J. Tribble also wrote a letter advocating for O'Dwyer's release. It was quite brief, consisting of only three sentences: the first verified his identity as solicitor at the time of her sentencing; the second verified that she was the only white woman who had been sentenced to the chain gang in Clarke County; and the third offered his opinion that the ends of justice had been served by the time she had already spent on the chain gang, which was nearly six months.[53] O'Dwyer submitted a brief stating that she was "thoroughly crushed in body and spirit," that her health was failing and wanted to be "relieved from the odium of further service in the chain-gang."[54] When the prison commissioner commuted O'Dwyer's sentence after she had served half of her term, he cited three reasons: the public sentiment supporting her release; the fact that the man with whom O'Dwyer had had an affair had not been punished; and Tribble's endorsement, the sole substance of which was that she was a white woman. The exceptional and insufferable nature of white female chain gang punishment was, in O'Dwyer's case, grounds enough for her freedom.

Maude Davis was only sixteen years old in 1910 when she was convicted of larceny and sentenced to six months at the Fulton County convict camp adjacent to its pauper farm. Davis was the only white woman at the camp.[55] Like Addis, Hunter, and O'Dwyer, Davis received support from many local residents who used her as an example of the need for a home for wayward girls in the city. When the press uncovered that her conviction was for stealing a shirt from a black woman and that she was working at the camp alongside "negro women who are foul with crime and disease," they were infuriated.[56] Prison Commissioner R. H. Davison granted her a commutation after three months, reciting the narrative from the *Constitution*'s editorial: "her present surroundings where she has only negroes and criminals for associates she deserves the sympathy and care of good society."[57] While proximity to black men constituted a sexual threat, black women represented the potential for transmogrification—the possibility that black female grotesqueness and foulness would infect white womanhood.[58]

Although white women were routinely sent to Milledgeville rather than the convict camp, their rates of imprisonment there were also very low. The number of white women in the lease system (including Milledgeville) in any given year between 1909 and 1936 ranged from 4 to 29, while the number of black women ranged from 61 to 197.[59] "Maude Davis, White girl," as she was listed on her clemency form, did not merit chain gang punishment or domestic service captivity. Hazel Carby has argued that black women migrants to the urban North were the targets of "moral panics" and that their behavior was characterized as "a social and political problem that had to be rectified in order to restore a moral social order."[60] Indeed, this panic led prison administrators in New York to institute a southern parole program, forcing black women who had been imprisoned after migrating north to return to the South for domestic service parole.[61] As northern prison authorities were sending criminalized black women South, some of Davis's advocates sought a reverse migration, arguing that sending the "white girl" North to the Good Shepherd home would lead to her "ultimate salvation."[62] However, the judge did not impose this as a condition of Davis's commutation; instead, according to the prison commissioner, her case should garner the "sympathy and care of good society," and she was allowed to return to her family in Athens.[63] The judge commuted her sentence and released her from the chain gang four months early.

Eleven years after Davis's commutation, in 1921, juridical concern for white female vulnerability to carceral surroundings remained strong; in July of that year Margaret Harris was sentenced to nine months for petty larceny, and a petition from over twenty-five members of the Senate Chamber of Atlanta supported her application for clemency. The petition described her as a "17 year old white girl serving a sentence . . . for a minor offense of larceny, and now amidst surroundings and conditions that will totally wreck and destroy her physically and morally."[64] The petition asserted that her pardon would "save her from total ruin." Her clemency application was approved and she was released on August 1 that year.[65]

Chain gang legislation created a class of hard-laboring prisoners, all of whom represented the "other" to normative womanhood. Other Jim

Crow codes subjected all black women and men to one set of facilities and all white women and men to another. The chain gang protected white women only, as a separate legal class and category of human being. This legislation exemplified the character of juridical power that seemed to operate only negatively through limitations, restrictions, or prohibitions but was also productive since "the subjects regulated by such structures are, by virtue of being subjected to them, formed, defined, and reproduced in accordance with the requirements of those structures."[66]

During this period trade and development in Georgia depended on chain gangs. By 1910 chain gangs had been established in 106 of Georgia's approximately 150 counties; by 1920 the number had been expanded to 135. With Georgia using chain gangs to execute its "Good Roads" construction project, the sight of cages and prisoners became even more common than under the convict leasing era. "Good Roads," as Alex Lichtenstein argues, blended "agrarian discontent with urban Progressivism" to bring the South's agricultural goods into the hands of southern and northern merchants.[67] Georgia prided itself on being a leader in road construction, and in the first two decades of the twentieth century, the movement to industrialize the South by improving its roads converged with a progressive penal reform ideology that criticized the abuses exposed under convict leasing but idealized fresh air and robust labor as conditions for rehabilitation. Imprisoned women and men would construct and maintain the roads that would carry automobiles and carry Georgia into the modern, industrialized twentieth century.

In stripes and chains, imprisoned women and men were visible constructing county roads and other public works. One black journalist wrote that blacks could be seen near Atlanta University "during any week day digging away ... in chains and stripes."[68] Atlanta was the "Gate City," with a newly built comprehensive railroad system making it an epicenter of commerce. It was home to a burgeoning population, mushrooming bank earnings, growing manufacture production, and a vibrant tourist industry.[69] Jim Crow enforced white male access to the jobs and profits in modern Atlanta. Anxiety over white women's use of public space and attempts to confine the degree and type of white female wage labor was important as Atlanta and Georgia's other major cities flourished. White supremacist standards of normative masculinity and femininity mandated that white female bodies could not be a laboring spectacle on the Georgia chain gang. The exclusion of white women from the chain gang also veiled white women's unruliness in the form of their newfound propensity for alcohol, public amusements, and sexual experimentation. When it came to white women, it was the stripes and the shovel that had to be removed from view, but it was the property interest in whiteness that made such opacity and protection possible and necessary. This gendered deployment of whiteness protected white male authority over paid labor and Georgia's industrial capital growth.

Chain gang legislation codified into law the "the defeminizing mythology of monstrous black womanhood [that] had taken hold of the southern imagination by the end of the nineteenth century," producing a subject position that vexed traditional gender categorization.[70] Regardless of their age, black women were sent to the chain gang for minor offenses, especially larceny and possessing or selling whiskey. Statewide prohibition was passed in Georgia in 1907 and lasted until 1935, expanding the number of arrests and convictions in the state. The ban on liquor created a new category of crime for which women and men could be arrested throughout the state, although 125 counties had already passed antiliquor laws by 1907.[71] The length of their sentences varied by county and by judge, but prohibition exposed black women in particular to the brutality of the chain gang. After being convicted of selling whiskey, Annie Tucker received a twelve-month chain gang sentence. Lizzie Curry was sent to the chain gang for six months for the same crime. Stella Kemp and Lucy Jackson were teenagers when they were sentenced for possessing whiskey, while Lizzie McConnell was sixty-four when she was sent to the chain gang for running a lewd house for the purposes of providing abortions.[72] In 1910 Minnie Smith was sent to the Cobb County chain gang at age sixty-one for selling whiskey. Proclaiming her innocence, she declared at trial, "If I am to go in stripes and chains, let me go for what I have done."[73] She requested clemency on the basis of her age and the fact that she had dropsy; in the words of her attorney, she was "about worn out."[74] After being denied clemency on her first try, she submitted a second application several months later that was approved.

As Smith likely feared, to "go in stripes and chains" meant subjection to torture. Chain gang conditions included whipping, overwork, medical neglect, being housed in cages that were nine-by-nine-feet wide, being hit with rifles, consuming rotten food, and bug infestation.[75] In 1920 "prisoners complained of indiscriminate beatings, being worked in the rain . . . and drunken guards."[76] The brutal conditions on Georgia's chain gangs inspired two popular novels, John Burns's *I Am a Fugitive from a Georgia Chain Gang!* and John Spivak's *Georgia Nigger*, both published in 1932. Spivak, a radical journalist, reported the horrors of the Georgia chain gang and published photos of conditions and the whipping reports he had discovered, which garnered widespread mainstream attention. Burns's novel told his autobiographical story of escaping the brutal Georgia chain gang from his own perspective as a white man. A film version quickly followed, drawing large audiences and earning Academy Award nominations, including Best Picture. As late as 1943, when Governor Ellis Arnall investigated chain gang conditions, imprisoned women and men reported being forced to work from sunup to sundown and being given brutal whippings by guards, including being beaten with hoses. That year two imprisoned men cut their heel strings to protest conditions at Cartersville work camp.[77]

In 1909 Essie Coleman and Hazel Lewis, both black women, received six lashes each for disobedience at the Southern Lumber Company chain gang in Tifton County.[78] In the same year, at the Atlanta stockade a "13 year-old black girl wearing only two thin undergarments was whipped in the bucking machine by assistant superintendent R.M. Clay."[79] The infamous bucking machine was a contraption that looked like a pillory and was used to constrain and exacerbate the pain of imprisoned women and men while they were whipped. After she was released, "the girl became hysterical . . . and said something unintelligible to the superintendent. He ordered her back into the chair, where Clay beat her again. Clay said he whipped her because she was 'mean and fussing with the other prisoners.'"[80] In 1910 Annie Tucker's lawyer argued that she should be released early because she was pregnant and there were "already two [sic] many babies in the penitentiary."[81] Although both official and popular accounts of pregnancy and childbirth in convict camps diminished with convict leasing as officials stopped keeping statistics on deaths, childbirth, and illness in the camps, the chain gang continued to be a space of antiblack terror.

Although Milledgeville State Prison Farm was comparatively less brutal than the chain gang camps that littered Georgia's county roads, women imprisoned there also faced overcrowding, harsh labor conditions, and fatal threats to their health. Black women convicted of felonies were confined in rooms adjacent to white women convicted of either misdemeanors or felonies. In 1915 there were several reports of deplorable conditions at Milledgeville. Typhoid was rampant, caused by wells, buckets of still water, and filthy facilities. Women who were healthy and women who were sick with contagious diseases were confined in rooms together, and for years overcrowding was consistently reported.[82] In 1911 the *Atlanta Constitution* reported that, in contrast to Milledgeville, where "old human hulks are beyond repair," in the reformatory three miles away there "was hope for every prisoner," including the small boys and a single white woman who were confined there.[83] In 1917, appropriations were made for new prison facilities at Milledgeville: a new stockade for black prisoners, a new building for white female inmates, an enlargement of the reformatory for white boys, and the installation of a modern sewer system.[84] While at first glance it appeared that white women and all black prisoners would be housed in new facilities, the report went on to specify that "the new buildings for the white women, and the negro men are new throughout, and are fire-proof."[85] Black women remained in the old quarters, ignored and denied even the slightest improvements in the generally deplorable space of the state farm.

In 1908 a black woman named Helen Drew was convicted of carrying a concealed weapon and using opprobrious language in the presence of a female. She received chain gang sentences of eight months for the concealed weapon charge and twelve months for obscene language, to be served consecutively. She served part of her time on the Mitchell County chain gang and finished her sentence at Milledgeville. There is limited available information about her case. However, a friend who wrote to the Prison Commission on Drew's behalf suggested that she was innocent and that some of the state's witnesses were retaliating against her because she had refused their sexual advances. Drew requested clemency on the grounds that her sentence was excessive and that she was very sick with a pelvic hernia and tuberculosis. Her continued imprisonment was a threat to her own health and the health of the "75 or 80 female convicts at this institution, all of them except the whites sleep in the same room, the room is about 120 feet long by 40 feet wide." Drew faced the threat of violence by at least one of the guards at Milledgeville, who said he would "have the damn bitch spaid, and she would not get to write to anyone soon."[86] The threat to her safety was of extreme concern to her friend, who had overheard the guard's statement in court, and had not received any word from Drew since she was imprisoned at Milledgeville. In fact, after recounting the story of the guard's threat, he wrote that he wondered if Drew was "sick or dead."[87]

In addition to abominable health conditions, the labor demands at Milledgeville were strenuous and there is evidence to suggest that women on the farm were worked harder than their imprisoned male counterparts. In 1910 the prison commissioner outlined Milledgeville's agricultural production goals for the following year by race and gender. That year there were 64 black women at Milledgeville and 4 white women, compared with 2,236 black men and 244 white men. Although women comprised less than 3 percent of the state farm's imprisoned population, they were expected to cultivate 44 percent of the corn, 40 percent of the cotton, 38 percent of the oats, and 49 percent of the wheat produced on the farm that year. In total, they were expected to farm more than 41 percent of Milledgeville's overall acreage and produce 41 percent of its overall yield.[88] If we assume that farming assignments were apportioned equally among all female prisoners, black women performed 94 percent of that work. However, work assignments were probably not equal, as there was precedent in previous years for white women to be sheltered from the most strenuous field labor at Milledgeville. Many of the men at Milledgeville were sick and feeble, and it is clear that black women were perceived to be the superior laborers and expected to carry a tremendous proportion of the workload at the farm; the logic of black female indomitability likely guided the management of work at the farm. Their work was not done upon their release from hard labor on the chain gang or state farm, however. Many black women released from Milledgeville after serving long felony sentences were not sent into the free world; instead, they were paroled and forced to serve an additional year or more as servants in white homes. Parole established a newly institutionalized space of carceral domestic servitude.

Domestic Carcerality

In September 1908 the Georgia General Assembly passed the Act to Create a System of Parole or Conditional Pardons of Prisoners Convicted of Crime and for Other Purposes. This legislation allowed the Prison Commission to grant parole to any prisoner (usually those convicted of felonies) who had served the minimum sentence fixed by law, or a minimum of ten years for those serving life sentences. Instead of being released after their minimum time was up, imprisoned women and men would serve additional time outside of the penitentiary, but they would "remain within the legal custody and under the control of said prison commission and subject at any time to be taken into custody on order of said commission."[89] In rare cases black women on parole worked on white-owned farms, but the majority were paroled into domestic servitude. Although the Prison Commission would consider their pardon case after one year, the law did not guarantee that parolees would be pardoned or that their sentences would be commuted after one year on parole.

Between 1913 and 1919 two additional pieces of legislation were passed, enabling imprisoned women and men to leave the chain gang or penitentiary before their sentences were completed. The 1913 Probation Act authorized judges and the Prison Commission to reduce felonies to misdemeanors, making imprisoned women and men eligible for probation. They would need to report to a probation officer, and ordinary citizens could volunteer as probation officers. While on probation, imprisoned women and men needed to "observe all rules prescribed for [their] conduct by the court, report to the probation officer as directed, and maintain a correct life," but unlike parole they were not mandated to maintain employment or live and work in the home of their employer.[90] Failure to comply with probation reporting and regulation rules meant rearrest and reimprisonment. Additionally, in 1919 the Georgia legislature modified the 1908 Parole Act so that women and men sentenced to life imprisonment would no longer need to serve the minimum sentence required by law to receive parole, but instead could be eligible after three years in prison.

White and black women received markedly differential treatment under the parole and probation acts. White women were more likely to receive the benefit of prosecutorial discretion and therefore were more likely to be charged with misdemeanors rather than felonies. After the passage of the Probation Act in 1913, this meant that they received probation more often than parole. For women, whether white or black, parole invariably meant relegation to the domestic sphere since parole was contingent upon a guarantee that prisoners "will be given honest employment with a good home."[91] Black women were nearly seven times more likely than white women to be released on parole rather than commutation, probation (which did not mandate work), or full pardon. In 1921 a white woman named Mary Moore had been given a two-to-four-year sentence for forgery. She was not forced to remain in prison or to complete her sentence on parole; instead her sentence was commuted to present service (time served) after one year; she was released into the free world before serving her minimum sentence.[92]

By contrast, imprisoned black women were generally released into domestic service captivity. Paroled black women who performed domestic service for white employers were always under the threat of being sent back to the chain gang or state farm if they broke a rule or failed to work up to their employers' standard. Employers had to ensure that the paroled prisoner sent monthly reports to the Prison Commission and had to read and endorse these reports. It was the responsibility of each employer to "see that she forwards monthly reports on the first of each month."[93] If they did not submit these reports it was the paroled women who often received letters threatening the cancellation of their parole.[94] Employers also had to sign a pledge to "take a friendly interest in said person, to counsel and direct her in that which is good, and to promptly report to the Prison Board any unnecessary absence from work, and tendency to low and evil associations."[95] White women and men wrote letters to the Prison Commission asking for female prisoners. Employers sometimes wrote asking that their former servants be released so that they could resume work for them, promising to report on their behavior and work performance monthly.[96]

The 1908 Parole Act brought convict labor for private profit into the territory of the white home. Black women's disproportionate presence in the sphere of domestic carceral servitude differentiated them from men but did not place them closer to normative femininity, since the relation of servant to employer also served to expose black women's difference from the white women for whom they worked. Black women who were exclusively forced to perform hard labor at Milledgeville were then made to perform hard domestic labor so that white women would not have to.[97] This double labor burden, a vestige of slavery and a historical reality for much of the twentieth century, was significant for the development of gender ideology in the South. Just as the ability to perform domestic labor under slavery in proximity to white women did not make enslaved female subjects more human or recognizable as women, imprisoned black women's labor in the home reinforced their subordinate status but did not grant them claims to femininity or womanhood. Black women were made to perform convict labor on the chain gang, hard agricultural work at Milledgeville, and domestic labor in the home on parole, and the flexibility and magnitude of their perceived labor capacity was part of their ungendering. Real working-class, wage-earning white women threatened the iconic image of southern womanhood, defined by domesticity but also fragility and control over a subservient black female domestic workforce that would fulfill the most difficult labor demands of the home. The commonly held view that black women could perform any kind of work made them distinct from both men and white women, positioning them as confounding subjects who existed in a liminal sphere of hyperexploitability and gender unintelligibility.

When imprisoned women asked for an end to their parole servitude they wrote letters as if from the inside, from the position of prisoners in a private domestic sphere whose location outside of the physical boundaries of the camp did not make them free. They imagined themselves as prisoners who had been transferred to a different carceral terrain. It was from the entire penal complex that they wanted to be "liberated." This place was a new site in the prison regime that reasserted a disciplinary project aimed at enforcing black female docility and black women's proper role as domestic workers. Black women on the outside struggled over the terms of domestic labor, and white women endeavored to enter wage work, ending their relegation to the home. These struggles over gender roles, domesticity, and labor exploitation provided the context in which the new institutionalized domestic prison sphere emerged, with unique forms of subjugation. Imprisoned black women were forced to fulfill the every need of their bosses and were often represented as contented servants despite their exploitative conditions of labor and captive condition.

Parole fixed black women in Georgia in domestic positions in white homes from 1908 through the 1930s, during a period when they were leaving the rural and urban South en masse for the urban North. By 1910 black Americans in Atlanta were leaving the South for Ohio and Pennsylvania. After 1920 women comprised the majority of black migrants to the urban North, as jobs for black women in industry became a possibility.[98] The Great Migration gave rise to fears of a labor shortage, and parole stalled black female mobility, confining black women to domestic service work and reasserting white control over their movement and possible migration North. With disproportionate arrest and imprisonment and gender-specific terror, the establishment of a domestic labor sphere was a late feature in the development of a penal regime that threatened black women's physical, economic, and personal lives, and indeed reified the contingency of their position as fully human subjects.

As an institution, parole buoyed the gender logic of white supremacy to police black women's bodies in the aftermath of the Atlanta racial massacre, during the historical transformations of Jim Crow and the Great Migration. It was a Progressive reform, part of a network of disciplinary reform practices including prohibition, vice legislation, and homes for wayward women, directed at black women's migrating bodies in the urban South and North. While some of these institutions were also directed at the emergent class of white women wage earners and leisure consumers, the apparatus of domestic service imprisonment was almost exclusively reserved for black women.[99] Parole law produced racialized gendered subjects fit for domestic servitude and control because whites were only included in the system insofar as they were employers.

The domestic carceral regime served the interest of middling and wealthy whites who could afford to pay for the services of a domestic worker but instead enjoyed the benefits of unfree labor. While paroled women might get a pardon after a year, there was no guarantee of that outcome, and they were under complete control of private masters and mistresses. Tera Hunter's influential scholarship on black domestic workers in Georgia has uncovered a hidden history of collective and individual resistance. After emancipation, black domestic workers fought to improve their labor conditions by organizing strikes and negotiating between employers to undercut the egregious southern domestic wage system. They left their residences in white homes, feigned illness, and stole breaks in order to exert autonomy over their work and home lives. They created spheres of entertainment and leisure, thereby defying the scrutiny of white southerners and exerting control over their bodies and movement.[100] Parole undermined black women's economic and social advances, creating a carceral world outside of the state farm and chain gang in an attempt to guarantee white satisfaction with their domestic servants.

The representation of satisfaction was central to the parole system. In order for a black woman to gain parole, the judge, as in Florence Grimes's case, had to be convinced that release was in the interest of justice. In 1926 he offered a statement endorsing her release from the chain gang, indicating that he would be "perfectly satisfied for her to be paroled for the balance of her term."[101] The Prison Commission wanted paroled workers to fulfill their employers' every need while employers wanted to portray the contentment of their paroled workers to the prison administration. J. E. Smith, then warden of Milledgeville, wrote to Doyle Campbell in 1923 expressing his confidence in Sallie Washington, who would soon be paroled to Campbell. Smith was certain that Washington "would make a splendid servant" since she was "a good all around negro." Based upon her good conduct in prison he pledged to Doyle that "she will I am sure give you perfect satisfaction."[102]

When Carrie Scott was paroled there was a contest for her labor between J. F. Gunn and J. E. Holliman, mediated by her lawyer, Marion Felts. Scott had Felts submit a petition requesting a transfer from Holliman (an automobile merchandiser to whom she initially was paroled) to Gunn, who owned the plantation on which her family lived.[103] Her petition asserted that she wanted to live with Gunn and her family in Warrenton rather than with Holliman, who resided fifty miles away, and where she was "completely among strangers."[104] The request was granted during an in-person conversation between Felts and one of the prison commissioners. After moving, Scott asked her lawyer to obtain a written order documenting the transfer, presumably because she did not want to risk erroneous accusations that she had escaped.[105] Yet before the transfer order could be executed in writing, Holliman intervened by sending a letter to the prison commission; he argued that his own family was very happy with Scott and that she seemed like "a mighty good darkie." Scott was, in his opinion, well cared for and "perfectly satisfied."[106] After initially endorsing Scott's request that she be transferred to him, Gunn changed his account, contending that Scott told him she wanted to stay with Holliman. The confusion sent Scott's lawyer into a fury, and he wrote to the prison commission, calling his own client "one of the most notorious liers [sic] I know anything about" and requesting that the prison commission ignore his previous request for transfer.[107] Since there are no firsthand letters from Scott, what emerges in the contest is the entanglement of status, reputation, and labor among three well-established white men in the New South. The abundance of evidence suggests that Scott indeed wanted to serve the remainder of her sentence with her family, since she went to great lengths to secure the transfer through her lawyer. However, it is possible that she could have changed her mind; perhaps she decided the Holliman home was a better work environment after all. Perhaps Holliman threatened her and coerced her into changing her story. Perhaps she had a fight with her family and, after being in prison for more than ten years, realized she couldn't go home again. Her true intentions may never be known, but it is clear the three men's concerns about reputation and status were played out over Scott's future, and that their various positions mattered more than her preference. Felts prized his reputation with the prison board over client advocacy. There was no attempt to thoroughly ascertain Scott's own preference, only an extended exchange of supposition and inference that centered on the good standing of Scott's lawyer and potential employers.

Parole warders enjoyed carceral enforcement of their rules and authority. They "promptly report[ed] to the Prison Board any unnecessary absence from work, and tendency to low and evil associations."[108] Parolees were required to send monthly reports to the Prison Commission, reports that had to be verified by the master or mistress. If they did not submit these reports, they sometimes received letters threatening the cancellation of their parole and return to the state farm. Mattie Jane (sometimes called Honey Ann) Price received such a letter. Her name and the date appeared at the top of the page, followed by "Dear Sir: This is to notify you that we have received no monthly report from you as a condition of your parole.... Further delinquencies in forwarding your monthly reports will result in the cancellation of your parole."[109] Although it may have been a stock template, it was a typewritten letter rather than a form and was personalized enough to include her name. Yet such a letter reflects, through the masculine salutation, black women's paradoxical gendered subject position.

While their sameness in relation to men often defined formal communication with prison authorities, difference from both men and white women also marked black women's positioning. White middle-class men and women vied for the labor of imprisoned black women specifically. Most of these applications came from widows or well-to-do married couples requesting assistance for housewives. Having a live-in black domestic worker reasserted the connection between marriage and domesticity in a southern society increasingly hostile to the notion that married white women might work for wages. As Jacqueline Jones argues, "domestic service recapitulated the mistress-slave relationship in the midst of industrializing America."[110] The domestic carceral sphere restored white women's historical role as domestic managers with full control over black female workers.[111] As Elsa Barkley Brown argues with respect to the workings of "difference," "White women and women of color not only live different lives but white women live the lives they do in large part because women of color live the ones they do."[112]

Domestic carceral servitude reinforced patriarchal notions of white women's dependency and white supremacist structures of racial subordination in a historical context riddled with challenges to those relations. White women and men vied for the labor of specific women who they knew were serving prison sentences. Sometimes they were merely familiar with these women's cases, while at other times the imprisoned women had been working as laundresses, cooks, or housekeepers for them before they were convicted.[113]

In 1910 Alicia Mosley considered requesting that a woman named Queen Kelly be paroled to her. First, however, she wrote to two of Kelly's previous employers asking for a report about her prior service to them. She received letters indicating that Queen Kelly was "good and faithful," and Mosley proceeded to draft a letter to the Prison Commission with details about her situation.[114] Mosley described herself as "one of the frailest of her sex" and "woefully in need of a servant to help with the drudgery."[115] She requested that Queen Kelly be paroled to her for this purpose. Mosley's letter was not enough to garner Kelly's release, however; the Prison Commission denied the parole application because she had only served three years of her ten-year sentence for voluntary manslaughter. In 1925 a white man named E. M. Williams expressed interest in having a woman paroled to him, and believed that he was to receive the services of Bertha Simmons. To the dismay of Williams, the Prison Commission decided to parole Simmons to G. F. Battles, who had obtained the services of an attorney to assist with his request to have her as his parolee. The Prison Commission nevertheless pledged to "keep on the lookout" for a female prisoner for Williams. At "the first opportunity we have, where there is a woman eligible for parole, we will take pleasure in paroling her to you to take this woman's place."[116]

In 1921 Mrs. J. H. Taylor wrote to the warden at Milledgeville requesting that "Aunt" Emma Wimms be paroled to her. Taylor would "see to her having a good home with some white people if she likes."[117] Taylor recognized that Wimms had a daughter in their community whom she might want to go to, but argued that her daughter "can't do anything for her any way."[118] Contrary to this assertion, other community residents signed a petition that verified her daughter's willingness to care for her mother, stating that she was "able and anxious to provide" for Wimms.[119] Following up on Taylor's letter, the warden wrote to the Prison Commission to endorse Wimms's application for parole. Unbeknownst to her, Taylor was competing for Wimms's parole with Samuel B. Jordan, the student secretary of the Georgia Baptist Mission Board, who wrote that "the old negress" Emma Wimms should be paroled to him. They would both be disappointed. Wimms was not released on parole until 1923, and she was not paroled to Taylor or Jordan, but rather to the "prominent family of Hon. Emmett Barnes."[120] Barnes's success likely rested on his local prominence, since his application was quite brief. His short letter to the Prison Commission explained, "I would like to have this old woman."[121]

Wimms had been convicted of killing Raymond High, her daughter's significant other, who had "beaten her daughter severely." In her statement to the court Wimms said that she shot High after they had an argument about his abuse of her daughter and he came at her with a razor.[122] Although Wimms had been imprisoned for thirteen years after defending her daughter, she would not soon see her because she was paroled to Barnes in Macon, fifty-seven miles from her daughter's home in McDonough County. The trade in imprisoned women's domestic labor, disavowal of their kinship networks, and erasure of their physical, personal, and moral autonomy reflect the elision of a "definitive marker between slavery and its aftermath."[123] Under the domestic carceral sphere, gendered forms of subjection, compulsion, obligation, and proprietorial entitlement persisted, and neoslavery was an indelible feature of twentieth-century notions and practices of freedom. White middle-class women and men wrote to prison authorities asserting their right to "have" black women's domestic labor and bodies but framed their requests as liberal efforts to liberate them from prison and to care for them.

White domestic managers were not required to provide wages, and most black women on parole were paid only once in a while. In one of her monthly reports, Mrs. E. J. Barnes confirmed with the Prison Commission that she was "not required to pay" Eliza Martin, who was paroled to her, "a fixed salary, only give her what she needs and wants, which we have done."[124] She went on to explain that Martin always had money to "buy insignificant things," although she did not keep an account of her wage payments. Barnes estimated that she may give Eliza as much as $4 a month, although this remuneration was sporadic. In 1911 Julia Anderson was paroled after serving ten years for shooting another woman whom she said attempted to stab her; in the monthly reports she submitted to the prison commission she revealed that she did both farm and domestic work, "doing Everything come to hand" for E. E. Chance, and was paid an irregular salary that ranged between

$3 and $15 per month.[125] However, there were months when Chance deducted money for essentials and debts. She reported that she worked between twenty-seven and thirty-one days out of the month, depending on whether rain inhibited agricultural labor.[126] Economic deprivation was not the only violent feature of the domestic carceral sphere that resembled the plantation household. The carceral regime's infrastructure of force re-created conditions of struggle and operations of power that had defined black women's domestic labor under slavery. In the antebellum era, violence carried out by white slaveholding women was not random, infrequent, or spontaneous but endemic to the plantation regime, where "peace accords" between mistresses and enslaved women "were as fragile as the last dish broken."[127] Black women's ability to resist violence and control in the domestic carceral sphere was significantly thwarted but not destroyed by the Prison Commission's regulatory structure and the threat of reimprisonment. Many black women on parole chose not to take any risks; they did not disclose experiences of violence or economic or sexual exploitation during parole and performed model behavior for their employers. For some women this strategy proved beneficial, and bosses wrote glowing letters in support of the commutation of their sentences. Others chose to defy white authority.

Mattie Reid cried every day she was interned in domestic servitude. Mrs. J. L. Archer did not pay her a salary but gave her money to spend and boasted that she treated Reid "just like a member of the family."[128] Reid's tears attest to the gulf between her feelings and Archer's representation. If Reid's consistent crying was not plain enough, her actions revealed her sadness and discontentment. In late April 1923, she asked for permission to go to the train station to meet a friend who had just been paroled from Milledgeville. She never returned to Archer's custody. After boasting about Reid's exemplary treatment, Archer wrote to the Prison Commission saying that Reid "has *grossly violated* her parole and in justice to other *paroled prisoners* I think she should be returned to the state farm."[129] Archer's sense of justice was perverse, as if Reid's freedom infringed upon that of other prisoners, as if justice for anyone meant injustice for everyone.

Mattie Reid contested the terms of her captivity and, like many black women in her position on the "outside," she bravely fought for her survival and asserted her perspective in her own letter to the Prison Commission:

I am writing you in reference to myself. I get dissatisfied with
Mrs. Archer and I don't want to stay with her. I went to the office
Monday morning to report to you Gentlemen, but on my arrival I
did not find either one of you there and for fear I would be locked
up I came to Macon and reported to Captain Ethereidge and asked
him to report to you all for me. I did not intend to run away at
all whatever, as I know I am in the hands of the Prison Commissioners and I hope you won't consider me a runaway and I did not
intend to do same. I want to ask you Gentlemen to please transfer
me to Mrs. E.A. Barker, 145 Charles St., Macon, Ga., as I feel like
I have a good home with her. I am well satisfied here and hope you
gentlemen will let me remain here as I want to make my paroled
time according to law.[130]

Reid appealed to the commission's own discursive and coercive logic
in a letter that is both ominous and powerful. Her strong assertion of
her own right to perfect satisfaction complicated the narrative of white
gratification. She expropriated authority, attempting to report on her
own boss, refusing the terms of subjection that employer reporting inflicted on black women's lives. Using a strategy that black women had
been crafting for decades, she attempted to wield one white employer
against another, positioning Barker's interests against Archer's. Barker
then wrote to the Prison Commission asking to "have this woman" for
Barker was "a poor widow woman with two children and no one to help
me but myself."[131] While Reid presented an alternative in which she could
be satisfied under white carceral authority, her language also implicates
the predicament of neoslavery: "I am writing you in reference to myself"
employs self-referentiality and speech markers through which she refused her designation as captive object. Yet even the hope that she would
not be considered "a runaway" signified the afterlife of slavery, illuminating the stubbornness of both the association with property and the
expectation that she display contentment with forced labor. Despite her
appeal, the Prison Commission issued an arrest order for her capture four
days after Reid wrote her letter. Had she not left Archer's house to com-
plain about her treatment she would have had six more months to serve
on parole before she was eligible for commutation. She was returned to
the state farm on May 8, 1923, to serve the remaining six months there
before her sentence was commuted in December. Milledgeville was a
nightmarish institution, but Reid was clearly in despair under Archer's

authority in the domestic carceral sphere. Her return was an indisputable form of punishment, but for Reid it remains unclear whether it was the lesser dungeon in which to serve out her time.

Reid was far from the only woman to protest the brutality of domestic carceral servitude. Mattie Price had to deal with a host of discursive indignities. In addition to being referred to as "Sir" in her official communication from the Prison Commission, her warder, Mrs. Smith, expressed her utter dismay at Price's behavior. Smith alleged that after Price "became pregnant she displayed the most violent temper and not only mistreated my children but showed her temper in every other way."[132] Price defied every parole rule and regulation, choosing instead to "carouse" "until two or three o'clock in the morning" and refuse the authority of the carceral state. She had violated the moral tenets of respectability and the dictates of prisoner conduct by having sex, and her new status as a mother was perceived to be incompatible with her care for Smith's children. She defied the expectations of docile servant and mammy, refusing to privilege her mistress's children to the detriment of her own.[133] Smith was "disgusted with her immorality" and "after her baby came" was "too glad to get rid of her." Smith speculated that Price's behavior indicated that she was more suited to fieldwork, leading her to doubt whether "she had ever worked in a white person's house before."[134] Rather than returning Price to the state farm, the Prison Commission gave Smith permission to trade her to a Mr. Simmons, for whom she began parole servitude with her two-week-old baby.[135] The trafficking of Mattie Price, an agreement between private white domestic managers enforced by the state, is the last record of her whereabouts.

Isabelle Elders's experience of parole was harrowing, marked by radical precariousness. Before she began parole, Elders received several laudatory letters from prison officials, including one from the chaplain. She was paroled to T. A. McCord and was paid $2 per week for child care and farm work, far below the $1.50 per day or $9.00 per week that African American domestic workers demanded when they collectively organized in the 1870s and 1880s.[136] After several months, McCord reported that Elders was insolent toward his wife, that she drank, and that she left his child unattended. Since she was, in McCord's opinion, "everything but what she should have been," he had her reimprisoned at the state farm.[137] After more than a year at Milledgeville, Elders was given a second chance at parole and was released to H. G. Robinson in September 1925. Yet Robinson was also dissatisfied with Elders and had her returned to bondage at Milledgeville in June of 1926 for refusing to work. She was then sent to work for J. F. Monk. He and his family were happy with her work, and she remained with them until Monk died. Elders's life under parole was violently circumscribed by the moral authority and judgment of her white civilian warders and the perennial threat of life in a cage at Milledgeville. McCord's and Robinson's opinions about her behavior in one carceral sphere determined whether she would be doomed to another.

Women who wrote requests for pardons or commutations clearly envisioned parole as captivity; they were writing from the inside, from the position of prisoners in a domestic carceral sphere whose location in a space outside of traditional camp boundaries did not at all represent liberty. Although Mrs. E. J. Barnes had boasted to prison authorities about the good environment she provided for Eliza Martin, Martin herself was clear that she wanted freedom from domestic servitude. She wrote to the Prison Commission explaining that while on parole she "never lost a day [of work]" and did not drink liquor. She "meant to make good so when the time came for the real Hon. Discharge papers there would be nothing to keep me from getting them."[138] While on parole, Sylla Stinson wrote letters wanting to know when she would get her "free pardon." She had completed one year on parole and wanted to know "if there is anything else for me to do now. . . . Will I get any more papers or not, *please let me know just what to do and whether I am free or not.*"[139] The request for free papers resembles the struggles of enslaved women and men attempting to secure their manumission documents. Even when manumission was ordered by slave owners, the elusive free papers were often secured only through a protracted process involving numerous requests, making the period between when manumission was granted and the procurement of papers a liminal space of unfreedom.[140] Sylla Stinson was equally determined, vowing to the Prison Commission that "I won't be content until I get the last hearing from you."

The archive leaves little record of the complexity of black women's views of their incarceration, yet available records do reveal ideas about their strategies of resistance and positioning within a racialized and gendered economy of bodies. Perhaps the least successful resistance strategy was that of the aforementioned Emma Wimms. Before she was paroled she wrote a letter to the Prison Commission proclaiming that she "was an old woman" and wanted to be released in order to live the rest of her life as a "True Woman."[141] Although Wimms asserted a claim to normative womanhood, the carceral system that institutionally entrenched the ideology of black female deviance made this appeal unwise, and she could not persuade prison officials to allow her to live with her daughter. Isabelle Elders and Mattie Reid used escape to negotiate for the best possible labor conditions within a context of extreme violence. Mattie Price refused to conform to expectations that she be a docile worker, to fit within the stereotype of the mammy, or to abstain from sex. As we saw at the start of this chapter, Hattie Johnson asserted the gender specificity of her body when she told prison authorities that it was a shame for them to force her to work "like I was a man." She emphasized her femininity by making the point that she was not receiving medical care for her pregnancy. Johnson identified her forced positioning outside of the boundaries of womanhood as a moral outrage and a form of physical violence. She does not offer remorse for her alleged crime nor does she pledge to lead a different life. In Johnson's theorization of her predicament she offers a complex understanding of gender categories and respectability. She does not subscribe to uplift ideology nor does she situate herself within the politics of black middle-class respectability. Her analysis is important because she asserts her identity as a woman but directs her moral outrage at the state rather than internalizing it through an assertion of innocence or a repudiation of her status as criminal.

Western legal doctrine, premised upon the "drawing of bright lines and clear taxonomies" and dichotomies including "rights/needs, moral/immoral, public/private, white/black," produces and reproduces oppositional subject positions.[142] Chain gang legislation and its application by judges and prison authorities made woman/nonwoman a key dichotomy in sentencing and clemency decisions. The difference here was not woman/man, but woman and all other subjects who did not fit that category. For black subjects, differential gendering meant that they were largely deprived of the "sympathy and care of good society" that would merit their freedom. When they were released early, it was usually through parole rather than commutation and generally only after they had served years and years of hard labor rather than a few months. Moreover, the discourses that justified such clemency decisions were about black women's ignorance and abjection rather than their vulnerability, innocence, youth, or emotional anguish—the features that defined normative femininity.

White womanhood was also constituted as a property right, one that meant protection from extreme labor, disease, and whipping. As critical race scholar Cheryl Harris notes, "according whiteness actual legal status converted an aspect of identity into an external object of property, moving whiteness from privileged identity to a vested interest."[143] Normative femininity, defined through whiteness, was vested under the 1908 chain gang law and was enshrined through judicial interpretation that maintained it as an "'object' over which continued control was—and is—expected."[144] That whiteness had the qualities of property through the "exclusive rights of use, disposition and possession, with possession embracing the absolute right to exclude," reveals the gendered character of Georgia's carceral regime.[145] Whiteness "is something that can be both experienced and deployed as a resource ... thus a white person used and enjoyed whiteness whenever she took advantage of the privileges accorded white people simply by virtue of their whiteness."[146] Property rights in whiteness were constituted through expectation, and the domestic carceral sphere protected white expectations of perfect satisfaction and property rights in black female bodies. The fact that it was an inalienable right, not one easily disavowed or rejected, does not diminish its definition as property, for, as Harris notes, classic property law recognizes that there is limited alienability of certain forms of property. It is worth noting that the benefit of this property interest was not absolute. Although white women garnered significant protection from harm, this reform initiative also made their imprisonment tolerable. By outlining the reform conditions for their imprisonment, they were not shielded from the penal apparatus altogether. Nevertheless, the penal reform law codified a property in white womanhood in particular within a broader framework of material interest in whiteness.

Femaleness/womanhood operated at once as a subject position and a usable social, material, and physical asset. This property right in womanhood maintained order in a moment when black domestic workers in Atlanta migrated North to escape rape and economic subordination; those who remained contested their economic exploitation and advocated for improvements in the conditions of their labor in dynamic and powerful ways.[147] Widespread fears of a labor shortage made parole a necessary technology to maintain control over black women's domestic labor, sabotaging their economic and social advances and leaving them vulnerable to the forms of violence from which many were fleeing.[148] The relation of servant to employer served to expose black women's differ-

ence from the white women for whom they worked, with white femaleness defined through the perceived absence of work and black bodies
defined as gender-nonconforming by the ability to endure and carry out
multiple forms of hard labor.[149]

Black women were caught in a violent abyss where gender differentiation was constructed for white women through the language of exceptionality and the practice of protection. Yet it was black female otherness
that made "white woman" possible as a subject position. Such discursive and symbolic positioning was a material resource for the progress
of the Jim Crow modernity project. Jim Crow modernity required the
restoration of southern white women's traditional association with domesticity and with the management of domestic servants in the home,
since "making . . . women the servants of the male work-force . . . was a
major aspect of capitalist development."[150] It also required the circumscription of black women and men within segregated spheres marked
by docility and subservience. The violent imposition of black female
labor flexibility—work on the road alongside men and in the home in
service of white female domesticity—was the formal institutionalization
of black women's "absence from a subject position."[151]

Murdered Down

The domestic carceral sphere of parole demonstrates that southern punishment was not located in the periphery of society but rather at its
center. After 1908 imprisonment in Georgia continued to be a hybrid
public/private regime; it was intimately connected to another institution principally responsible for southern "progress" but historically un-
seen as part of the public, political sphere: the home. The white home,
which had since slavery existed as a site of regulation, policing, discipline, and punishment for black women who worked as domestics, was
formally incorporated into the penal sphere through the establishment
of domestic carceral servitude.

By the time black women arrived at Milledgeville, where they were
expected to carry a huge portion of the load of field labor, or the chain
gang, or the domestic carceral sphere, many were already bruised and exhausted both psychically and physically. Many had been criminalized,
convicted, and imprisoned for self-defense against domestic or sexual
violence. Imprisoned women's lives reflect the extreme brutality of
familial, intraracial, intracommunal violence. The explicit, wrenching

testimonies of black women regarding the patriarchal violence they endured in their homes and communities reveal that they were not only dehumanized and treated as animals on the chain gang. The home was sometimes a site of black female abjection, and self-defense against domestic violence meant internment in carceral dungeons that they could not shake.

Between 1909 and 1936, approximately sixty-seven women convicted of murder, attempted murder, or manslaughter in Georgia filed petitions for clemency. Forty percent of those applicants claimed to be defending themselves against abusive husbands or sexual assaults.[152] The percentage of women arrested and convicted for crimes stemming from domestic abuse or rape may have been substantially higher, since many of the clemency petitions filed did not include specific accounts of the alleged crimes. Only two of these women, Edna Godbee and Stella Abbott, were white. Since it is certain that black and white women faced gender violence, two possible reasons for this disparity in criminalization exist: that white women were less likely to defend themselves against abuse or that they were less likely to be arrested and convicted for crimes of self-defense against abusive men. Given the overall disproportionality between black women's and white women's arrests and convictions, it is more plausible that police and prosecutors exerted greater discretion in shielding white women from criminal charges in self-defense cases.

In 1909 a black woman named Ella Pride tried to avoid sexual harassment and the threat of rape by a man named Swanie Cook. She told Cook that she would go to the police to file charges against him, but he did not stop pursuing her. He had, according to other black community residents, attempted "to become intimate with her." Cook made statements that he was going to "get a baby with Ella Pride . . . and that he would either force her to do what he wanted or kill her."[153] Pride was on her way to the police station to file a warrant against Cook when he stopped her on the street and threatened her with a knife. She shot him and was convicted of murder despite two witnesses who corroborated the fact that Cook had a knife when she shot him. She was sentenced to life imprisonment and served two years before her sentence was commuted. While it is possible to view Pride's punishment as lenient because she served only two years of her sentence, this view is belied by the white supremacist legal context that denied her right to protect her own life and to be free from sexual violence. Moreover, her release was not justified by sympathy for the circumstances of her crime, but by her medical condition. She was subjected to the possibility of premature death and psychic trauma at Milledgeville, where she spent two of the last years of her life caged and away from her six children.[154] Pride was fifty years old when she was released. According to her clemency petition she was ill, her years were "fast drawing to a close," and she had "the expectancy of only a few more years of life."[155]

If Ella Pride had not been released in August 1911, she would have served time with two other black women whose stories of being convicted of murder for defending themselves against rape are part of the legal record. Charlotte Walker was convicted for killing her stepfather, Anderson Harper, in 1915. On the night of the alleged murder Walker was brought to the Bibb County jail where she told police that Harper had been following her that night on the street. He would not stop following her and threatened to kill her if she did not go with him. When he stooped down to light a match with his shoe, she hit him with a hammer, fatally wounding him. She told police that she had been "continually and habitually" sexually harassed by Harper and had "moved three times to avoid him."[156] Eventually, Walker was released on the grounds that she was mentally impaired, not that she had acted in self-defense.

The white community residents who wrote in support of Dora Holly's application for parole described her as an "unusually good negro." According to them she was "always respectful, faithful and an humble negro." They felt that she "deserves all that is due a negro for good conduct."[157] Although whites in her community considered Holly a "good negro," this did not translate into belief about her virtue when she was found guilty of murder at trial. Holly was convicted despite her claim that a stranger named Charley Moore came into her house in 1911, threatened her with a gun, and said "he was going to stay with her, meaning have sexual relations with her, or he would kill her."[158] According to Holly, she ran throughout the house to get away from him and "she fought him as furiously as she could to protect her virtue." He hit her in the face with the gun, broke one of her teeth, and then hit her again on the side and hip. As she was crawling around beside the bed, he shot at her but missed. She reached under the mattress for a gun that she kept there and shot him. There was no evidence presented at trial to dispute her claims, as the state's witnesses only testified that they heard gunshots coming from the house, not that they knew anything else about the alleged crime. Still, Holly was convicted and sentenced to life at Milledgeville.

Feminist legal theorists have rightly identified a long history of juridical imperviousness to women's claims of rape in court, citing the
production of a male legal standard of reasonableness and burdens
of proof that render women's allegations of rape illegitimate.[159] Yet the
political economy of the Jim Crow South in this moment was organized around the legitimacy of the threat of black male rape. It was
black women's legal claims to self-defense against rape in particular
that were disavowed. Their resistance to sexual assault meant that they
would be forced to endure carceral violence at the hands of the state.
This double bind of intraracial intimate violence and disproportionate
imprisonment for self-defense meant that many black women were en-
trapped in a circle of unyielding assault. The history of black women's
imprisonment in the South illuminates the pervasiveness of gendered
violence within their communities and families, a history that is clear
and blistering in the record of criminal punishment, but that cannot be
fully explored through these records and deserves its own full consideration in future research.

In 1911 Carrie Scott, whose parole case is covered above, was charged
with murdering her husband, Henry Scott. According to a friend, her
husband's treatment had "through a period of years so injured her
physical condition until it had completely unnerved her and lead her
to look upon him as absolutely unsafe for her to be around."[160] Carrie's
daughter Bessie testified at the murder trial, making conflicting statements about whether she believed her father was a mortal danger to the
family. Bessie had become pregnant out of wedlock and testified that her
father did not threaten to kill her but that she thought he might anyway
because "I never had done such a thing as that before."[161] Bessie testified
that her mother and father had been arguing about his supper "because
she had corn for his supper and he told her didn't she know he didn't
love corn and she told him she was trying to make the rations last as long
as she could . . . she was crying because she did not have sufficient supper
for him." According to Bessie's testimony, while her father did not say
when or why he would kill her mother, he did make general threats to
kill her. "It is true," Bessie also stated, "that he would beat her." Implying
that Carrie's abuse was deserved, the prosecution asked Bessie further
questions about why her father was abusive, to which Bessie replied,
"I can't tell what it was about. . . . I would not try to protect my mother
because I was afraid he would do me worse if I did, than he did her."
Bessie revealed that she herself sometimes received beatings from her

father. She also stated that she did not hear him threaten her mother with a gun. She had only seen him "beat my mother with a stick, . . . I have never seen my mother fight back at Henry when he would beat her; she would just take it."

Bessie's trial statement is contradictory, but it is from the perspective of a young woman in an impossible situation, balancing concern for her entire family and trying to make sense of the violence she and her mother endured in the face of a legal system that regarded their injury as irrelevant if not deserved. She was repeatedly asked to measure her degree of fear and the degree of abuse she and her mother experienced. She mediated the severity of her claim about her father's threats by stating that they were vague rather than specific about when and where he would kill Carrie. She repeated that she did not know why they fought, or what he was beating her about, but that Henry did jump on Carrie. Bessie stated at first that she did not witness her father threaten Carrie with a pistol and that she had not defended her mother. Yet upon questioning by a different lawyer Bessie admitted that she "caught hold of his hand to keep him from shooting her [Carrie] with a pistol." Carrie's own court statement graphically described both verbal and physical abuse. After being beaten she would "run off from my house and went to the white people for protection, and then he beat like a dog because I went to the white people." Carrie described being *"tied up like a dog"* and *"murdered down."*[162]

Carrie was convicted and then paroled in 1921 after her first clemency petition was denied in 1917. But while she was at Milledgeville she was imprisoned alongside at least ten other women who were convicted of crimes of self-defense against domestic violence. The pervasiveness of gendered violence is an underexplored aspect of black women's experiences that merits further exploration if their historical lives are to be fully uncovered. Carceral history provides a glimpse into this important history. Most women prosecuted after resisting intimate violence testified in court to treacherous abuse. Victoria Clowden, for example, explained that her husband "beat me and dogged me around as if I was a dog . . . he dugged me in the stomach and caused me to have a miscarriage."[163]

Some women who had white neighbors nearby suffered from the mythologies of black female indomitability and aggressiveness. Lena Bell Warren was convicted of killing her husband Eugene in 1913, although there were no witnesses to the alleged murder. She claimed that she shot him accidentally "by me and him tussling over the gun and I having on a ragged sleeve I think my sleeve must have got caught—I don't know how it was done myself." But Mr. Blount, Lena Bell Warren's landlord, testified at her trial. When asked if she and her husband got along Blount stated that they "didn't get along so well." One of the lawyers then followed up, asking, "These were not the first negroes you ever had with you that quarreled occasionally?" Blount responded, "It is common for them to quarrel."[164] Ideas about the natural propensity of black women and men for violence and unruliness helped seal black women's legal fate, ensuring that they would be viewed as equal participants in violent altercations with their husbands rather than victims of aggression and assault.

Black women who sought to protect themselves from domestic violence and exploitation faced the disavowal of their experiences as legal actors and prison authorities reinscribed violation as a normative part of the black female condition. Criminalized women would continue to defend themselves against violence and struggle for bodily autonomy in prison, sabotaging carceral logic and structures. The next chapter traces the range of black women's strategies to resist state violence and achieve freedom from captivity. As important, black women forged alternative community networks within the carceral regime and developed radical epistemologies of love, life, labor, and freedom. Violent state force was a response to the consistency, complexity, and dynamism of black women's challenges to carceral authority and repression.

CHAPTER FIVE

Sabotage and Black Radical Feminist Refusal

> Their transgressions are best understood as an elaborate ethos
> that informed the ambitions, daily struggles, and consciousness
> of the black majority—a blues aesthetic.
>
> —TERA HUNTER

> Poetry, therefore, is not what we simply recognize as the formal
> "poem," but a revolt: a scream in the night, an emancipation of
> language and old ways of thinking.
>
> —ROBIN D. G. KELLEY

> Wake up, Rosie, tell your midnight dream.
>
> —FROM "GO WAY DEVIL, LEAVE ME ALONE"

The details of what transpired on November 27, 1918, remain a mystery. It seems that flowers were debased in a section of Albany, Georgia, that represented the complex landscape of Jim Crow modernity. Three black girls were held responsible. Two of the girls were neighbors: Carrie Williams, age sixteen, lived in the shadow of modernization at 616 Standard Oil Alley, where the view from her front window was the grandeur of gas gauges and tanks.[1] To help her family pay for the small home with the blighted view she worked as a laundress.[2] Hattie Bishop lived around the corner from Williams and two doors down from Standard Oil; she worked as a home nurse at the young age of eleven.[3] Along with Gladis Trumbick, age twelve, Williams and Bishop were charged with malicious mischief, two crimes floral in nature: destroying the flowerpots of Mrs. G. R. Baker, who lived on an adjacent white block, and throwing a flowerpot into a plate glass window of the home belonging to Mrs. Wooten, located eight blocks away from Mrs. Baker, just south of Society Avenue.[4]

According to the court the actions that took place in this landscape of Jim Crow modernity where Standard Oil Alley met Society Avenue were "willful, premeditated, and without excuse, justification or cause."[5] To make matters worse, the "negro women" were said to have visited "a number of houses in the City of Albany" belonging to white people, destroying the flowers in their path. The judge for the city court of Albany described the crime as simply "a case of racial antipathy."[6] The girls had exceeded the sullied alley of southern industrialization where they lived, walking the short distance to the winsome white blocks not for the acceptable task of work but for the dastardly objective of aesthetic political sabotage. Indeed, instead of delivering laundry or nursing white children, that day they tarnished the pristine adorned homes of housewives, upsetting the domestic tranquility of domiciles that represented the zenith of white femininity. For this most unforgivable act they each received a sentence of one year on the Dougherty County chain gang, provoking the anguish of their neighbors at the thought of girls so young at hard labor under unfathomable conditions.

Perhaps the destruction of flowers was the "mischievous playfulness of children" as their lawyers contended.[7] Perhaps the girls were indeed criminals, insofar as challenging white supremacy was a most grave juridical transgression. Perhaps the mischievous playfulness of black girls under Jim Crow was a criminal positionality and a subversive fugitive endeavor of material and political theft. Perhaps they were loud, raucous, and messy, exuberant in their conspiratorial intentions. Perhaps they were stealth, quiet, and deliberate in their debasement. Perhaps they recognized the power imbued in the flowers, conspicuous symbols of the structures of racial capitalism that governed their daily lives: the base landscape of industrialization that claimed their front and back yards, and the daily labors of lifting and scrubbing and folding that structured Hattie Bishop's life. Perhaps in addition to discussing friends and games and their "too heavy a load," they complained about the unfairness of it all: that Stella, Mrs. Wooten's sixteen-year-old daughter, did not have to work at all.[8] Perhaps they thought it only fair that they get to pluck a few flowers for their own hair. Perhaps the girls wondered as they wandered, in their own youthful way, about the patterns of segregation that made it so that black blocks were ornamented with gas pumps and white blocks were decorated with roses. Perhaps the iniquity of property rights in whiteness was on their mind.

Perhaps, as Fred Moten poetically suggests, fugitivity "is immanent to the thing but is manifest transversally":

1.

between the object and the floor
the couch is a pedestal and a shawl

and just woke up her hair. she never

ever leaves the floating other house

but through some stories they call.

later that was her name the collaborator

of things shine in the picture. hand

flew off her early hair though held

by flowers. later her name was grete.

her hair feels angles by flowers that

before her name was shori the
penetrator in the history of no décor.

the station agent intimate with tight
spaces refuse to hit back or be carried.

later her name was danielle goldman

and his serene highness thierry henry.

her head is cut off by a shadow of primary

folded streets she harrass with enjoyment.
later her name is piet. she come from cubie.

with the whole club economy in her hand.

when she reclines her head is lifted

by a turn, someone's arm they left there.
later her name was elouise. watch her

move into the story she still move.

2.

and tear shit up. always a pleasure the banned
deep brown of faces in the otherwise
whack. the cruel disposed won't stand

still. apparatus tear shit up and

always. you see they can't get off when

they get off. some stateless folks
spurn the pleasure they are driven

to be and strive against. man, hit me again.[9]

Did the girls' hair feel (t)angles created by the contraband flowers they
may have placed there, the perfect barrettes constructed from fugitive
material? Yes they moved *transversally*, cutting through and across white
blocks, unabashedly, leaving a trail of translucent shards behind them. It
was, in a certain sense, a *history of no décor*; a spatial and temporal shock
to the residents of Society Avenue produced by the denial and destruction of both décor and decorum. No longer lingering in a political geography delineated by stepping aside or averting one's eyes or perfectly
pitched greetings; for a moment these were their streets to penetrate and
harass with enjoyment. Watch them move into the story they still move.

It could be that they threw the flowerpot through the window and
giggled or shrieked with joy at the sound of broken glass, smashing sounds
splintering pain and generating joy that, perhaps, fortified their friendship.
Glass, as "an enclosure" signifying immobility and "located in the slippages
of contradiction," "both brittle—breaking readily—and malleable—having
the capacity for adaptive change," was an important site of contestation;
the breaking of such material was a challenge to the political economy of
racial visibility and exclusion constituted through its aesthetic and infrastructural dynamics, a manifestation of the fragility and power of racial
capital.[10] This destruction was meaningful, part of a broader practice of
smashing, fracturing, and "slanging rocks," the deployment of weapons of
the weak for social change.[11] Their wandering and breaking of glass was
a traversal of "the micropenality of everyday life" toward the creation
of a black girl commons that obliterated existing relations of household
and property; that is to say, the enclosures of white supremacy.[12] The
abolition of the entanglements of economic and sexual subordina-

tion as structured through domestic wage labor, carceral violation, and rape might represent the "meaning of emancipation according to black women" as theorized by Angela Y. Davis;[13] perhaps, then, the breaking of the edifice of racial domesticity constituted an intersectional fugitive practice rupturing the power of white supremacist regimes.[14]

Certainly, on that fall day the girls refused the structures that thwarted dreams of a more meaningful life and in response they chose mischief over respectability. And as fall turned to winter the girls found themselves not in their small homes in the vicinity of Standard Oil Alley, but in a Dougherty County chain gang stockade where they again refused their conscription to hard labor in the service of Jim Crow modernity. The imaginary that contested white supremacy through the shattering of a window pane and the appropriation of beauty fostered a rebellious friendship that was deep and grew more criminal with the slamming of cage doors.

Watch them move into the story, they still move. Fugitivity was immanent, freedom ingrained in their interior lives even as the external world indicated they were trapped. Depth, of both friendship and earth, was marshaled as a natural anticarceral resource. In prison they dug and dug and dug, deep into the terra firma in order to create a hole just big enough to loosen the stockade bars and wiggle their small bodies through. They were caught "just before the escape was perfected."[15] An escape plan carried out by girls whose trust, connection, and capacity to sabotage had been strengthened by prior political mischief: the quotidian, deviant, and gendered fugitive practice of floral theft and redistribution, the inspired collective imaginary.

Flowers were replanted and the girls remained in captivity. But their plans represented a sabotage of the built landscape of white supremacist capitalist patriarchy. Splendor did not naturally exist as the sole province of white society, but was instead transferable. They disrupted, if temporarily, property rights in whiteness and produced significant angst about the presence of "racial antipathy" in black girls. In this sense they move into the history as "troublemakers, wretches, strangers, dissenters, killers of joy," destroying the aesthetic pleasures of white property rights and in so doing creating a history of no décor.[16] And for this they were punished, receiving no mercy despite their neighbors "begging the parole of" the young girls from the chain gang and requesting that they be released "as a xmas gift to the colored people of Albany"; a most mollifying appeal by communities in pain, most certainly designed to counter the girls' ostentatious rejection of white authority.[17] But no presents were to be had, only subjection to the red hot coal of white supremacist anger; the girls served their entire sentence, serving southern industrial capitalism by building the roads of Dougherty County under conditions of starvation and disease before returning home to Standard Oil Alley.

Sabotage is not about success or triumph against systematic violence and dispossession. Instead it is about the practice of life, living, disruption, rupture, and imagined futures; it is about the development of epistemologies of justice and collectivity, contestations of the binaries produced through Western juridical doctrine and the individualizing ethos of criminal punishment. Many, though not all, of the ruptures recounted below challenged the politics of respectability and sought to break rather than reform the carceral system. It is for this reason—the will to break and transform rather than to tweak—that they are conceptualized as sabotage. Black girls' criminal practices of breaking windows and stealing flowers are part of the black radical tradition. The rupture and negation of Western epistemologies of law and order, racial hierarchy, and gendered racial difference and docility, and the power of coerced black female subservience is solidly within a black radical tradition of gendered fugitive practice. Inside southern prisons, jails, and convict camps women incorporated expressive tools to critique liberal legal constructs, challenge the legitimacy of punishment, and diminish its capacity. The overlooked black radical tradition of criminalized black women responded to "an oppression emergent from the immediate determinants of European development in the modern era and framed by orders of human exploitation woven into the interstices of European social life from the inception of Western civilization."[18] Imprisoned women, and those who created expressive cultures centering their plight, produced epistemologies that refused and destabilized Western juridical logics, individually and collectively upset carceral temporalities and spatiality, and reimagined spaces of dispossession in ways that fundamentally challenged Jim Crow modernity by making its gendered carceral logic visible. It was a negation of Western modernity sewn from forms of sociality that were uniquely black women's.

Hattie Bishop, Carrie Williams, and Gladis Trumbick cultivated an affinity that defied policing, born of flowers plucked and placed furtively in dress pockets, enriched in the ease with which blooms could be uprooted from the dirt of white supremacy, and impervious to the fragile white temperament. Theirs was not an exceptional sabotage sisterhood; flight, frustration, feigning, freedom imaginaries, and fire comprise criminalized black women's collective and individual sabotage practices. Sabotage was ideological, the contestation of "high crimes against the flesh" and spirit; it manifested in the circulation of dreams, dreams of meaningful life so vivid that they transcended bars and borders, altered lifescapes, and created relationships and realities.[19] Theirs were "stayed woke dreams" desirous of the dismantling of captivity and the production of new ways of knowing, and as such constituted part of a black radical tradition's blueprint.

The term "sabotage" refers to "the malicious damaging or destruction of an employer's property by workmen during the strike or the like."[20] Since the imprisoned women under consideration here did stop work but did not collectively organize strikes, this chapter examines "the like," the myriad forms of disruption that imprisoned women caused in the carceral regime. But sabotage also has an expanded meaning that includes ruining, destroying, and disabling intentionally, though often through indirect means; the disruption of the military and economic resources of an enemy; the wanton destruction of property in order to humiliate or injure an enemy.[21] Both the narrow and expansive meanings of sabotage describe the actions of imprisoned women and black female artists' depictions of imprisonment and the law: the resources that they disrupted were material and ideological.

The Industrial Workers of the World's (IWW) advocacy of sabotage was a source of great controversy beginning in the 1910s. The idea of sabotage ranged from the normal slowing down practiced by most workers to what Mike Davis has called the "inflammatory connotation" of the "destruction of capitalist property and occasionally persons."[22] For proponents in the IWW, sabotage was a mass tactic "requiring some form of continuing, although clandestine, mass organization ... a flexible family of different tactics which effectively reduce output and efficiency."[23] As Rebecca Hill notes, the "Wobblies," as IWW members were commonly known, could circulate imagery of their members that positioned them as ferocious, masculine, and exceedingly strong without actually terrifying the American public. Yet, "the most striking images of working-class Blacks that appeared in the socialist press were of brutalized, mutilated, burning bodies ... photographed to shock and horrify."[24] Such portrayals carefully avoided the associations between blackness, threat, and criminality that were so pervasive. Elizabeth Gurley Flynn was one of the IWW's most visible sabotage proponents. According to Rosalyn Baxandall her lawyers described her as "the coming Socialist woman orator of America."[25] Radicalized in her youth, she began giving political speeches at the age of fifteen and spent a significant part of her political career defending women political prisoners; she was herself imprisoned in Alderson in the 1950s where she developed a close relationship with black women prisoners.[26]

But this chapter does not situate black women prisoners as victims, as in the images of mutilation that the IWW strategically circulated. Instead this chapter includes imprisoned black female workers in the illustrious tradition of militant industrial labor sabotage. It also challenges the parameters of the definition of sabotage to include the unique conditions of black women's death and dehumanization that characterized the convict camp as well as black feminist epistemology that produced new understandings of justice and community.[27] In this sense it situates imprisoned women within two traditions that historian Robin D. G. Kelley has powerfully elucidated: the first is the tradition of the creators of freedom dreams. Although the women in this chapter were not part of an organized movement, they nevertheless envisioned an emancipatory future and, in radical black feminist tradition, interrogated normativity and constructed "a politics rooted in desire."[28] The second is the tradition of working-class saboteurs that both Kelley and Tera Hunter explore. Kelley's now classic analysis of black infrapolitics illuminated "how power operates and how seemingly innocuous, individual acts of survival and resistance shape politics, workplace struggles, and the social order generally."[29]

Gendered practices of carceral sabotage signal the ways that the carceral imposition of extreme violence was a form of gendered warfare, and uncover the means through which black women were involved in undermining and neutralizing the physical and epistemological weaponry of captivity. In this sense, the tradition of which they were a part stretches back to the antebellum era, to the modes of eroding slavery that W. E. B. Du Bois, Angela Y. Davis, and Thavolia Glymph have analyzed variously as abolition democracy and slave women's war for freedom.[30] But black feminist blues also prefigure the ideological and epistemological challenges to legal and political structures of white supremacist patriarchy that would, much later, be termed "critical race feminism."

Flight, Frustration, Feigning

Since convict labor was an essential resource in industrial development, running away was at once life preservation and resource appropriation.

According to Colonel Maddox, the overseer of the all-female Camp Heardmont, women were always looking for ways to escape. For this reason he housed a pack of hounds at the camp to catch fugitive women.[31] Later, blues legend Victoria Spivey would lament, "Bloodhounds, bloodhounds, bloodhounds are on my trail," circulating to all that heard her record a sonic acknowledgment, despair, warning, and excoriation of the threat that imprisoned black women faced, of being torn limb from limb. Dogs that would "tear a man or woman to pieces in a little while," whips, and guns were all employed to keep women prisoners in the camps.[32]

Lula Brooks, Lucy Howard, Martha Turner, Annie Summerlain, Lizzie Williams, Mollie Walker, Sarah James, Laura Harris, Louisa Jarbon, Ella Hudson, Eliza Lynn, Lizzie Cleveland, and Ella Wood all successfully escaped.[33] Many more women were unsuccessful in their attempt to escape Georgia's carceral dungeon. Pearl Williams fled Milledgeville State Prison Farm on August 30, 1905, and was recaptured the same day.[34] Sylla Stinson, on the other hand, remained at liberty for a year after she escaped in 1912. According to Colonel Maddox, the average length of an escape from Camp Heardmont was two to three weeks.[35] Lula Brooks, who had a child in a Georgia railroad camp sometime between 1872 and 1873, escaped twice. She was remanded in October 1876, six months after her first escape. She fled the camp again two years later, perhaps forever, as there is no record indicating whether she was ever caught.[36] In 1875 Rachel Crowder tried to assist her cousin Albert in his plan to escape with other imprisoned men from the Terrell County jail by bringing him a stolen auger, which they used to cut holes in the cell walls. Although she managed to hide the tools during a search that prison guard L. M. Roberts conducted by "feeling her person all over," he soon discovered the plot.[37] He then became "vexed with the prisoner" and "whipped her." A witness at Crowder's trial observed that the guard "struck her about thirty licks he made considerable noise seemed like he was doing his best."[38]

In 1893 five women escaped from Camp Heardmont, perhaps to evade the ubiquitous threat of rape there. According to one sensational article, even though Colonel Maddox had "tried to be considerate of his prisoners, and was as easy on them as he could afford to be . . . all the remaining sixty are watching their chance to get away."[39] Alice White, a white woman who was seventeen when she was arrested for kidnapping, and Annie Wooten, a black woman who was also seventeen when she was convicted of murder, planned an escape together in 1893. In recounting what was perhaps an apocryphal story, Colonel Maddox expressed reverence for White's cunning. Over a long period of time she had become like an owner to the hounds that were supposed to follow the scent of any escaped woman, playing with them and feeding them often. During her escape with Wooten she apparently ran into the woods with the guards and dogs behind her on her trail. At some point the dogs were running ahead of the guards and, as the story goes, White promptly fed them and they turned around, stopped the pursuit, and returned to the guards wagging their tails. She and Annie were caught after a couple of weeks.[40] While the guards were looking for them, three other women seized the opportunity to make an escape. Nora Lea and Susie Mitchell fled with Fred Simpson, a woman who was reputedly "one of the worst to manage in the camp," and were free for a couple of weeks before they were caught and reimprisoned.[41] Many imprisoned women who escaped did so collectively, planning and making their run together.

Imprisoned women practiced a range of sabotage techniques, both quotidian and extraordinary, frustrating the order of the convict camp. In convict camps men transgressed the disciplinary sexual norms of the day by engaging in sex with each other while in prison. Punishment records from E. H. Jackson's camp from 1906 to 1908 reveal that prison guards whipped twenty male prisoners a total of 443 times for sodomy.[42] Women's sexual practices seem not to have been policed in the same way; sex between women was not explicitly listed among the camp violations.[43] It is difficult to know the reason for this discrepancy. Perhaps they were better at hiding sexual relationships. Or perhaps the systematic rape of black women and their subjection to pornographic torture rituals was the method through which sexual-racial control was imposed, making submission rather than conformity and abstinence the means of behavioral control and discipline. What is clear is that black women were punished for other daily practices of insubordination—severely.

In 1886, Norah Daniel was whipped seventy-three times. Her alleged transgressions included fighting, idleness, impudence, burning clothes, swearing, and disobedience, reflecting the range of actions that imprisoned women undertook to rebel against the conditions of their captivity.[44] Women were brutally beaten for frustrating the camp's disciplinary order and labor efficiency. Idleness, failing to work, and bad work were among the gravest offenses. Outright insubordination including disobedience, cursing, and fighting were also punishable by the lash.

Such everyday forms of resistance bear out "the prosaic but constant struggle between the peasantry and those who seek to extract labor ... from them."[45] They reflect continuities with plantation resistance such as "theft, foot dragging, short-term flight, and feigning illness [which] were commonplace acts in the Old South and are widely understood to be everyday forms of resistance."[46]

It was February and Norah Daniel and Mollie White were both starving and cold. To combat the cold they burned their soiled and tattered clothes, choosing warmth over compliance with the camp disciplinary order that imposed upon them the stripes as final marker of prisoner status and object status. Daniel and White were not attempting to assert their humanity to the guards, to the outside world, to white authorities; this was instead a refusal to accept the conditions that made them vulnerable to death, and the collective creation of alternative, if fleeting, life-sustaining conditions.[47]

Black women's bodily strength was a site of contestation. Prison authorities believed that Mamie Haygood's body was strong and healthy enough, so when she complained of illness to the camp doctor she was punished with ten lashes. In addition to sickness, slowness was an offense that resulted in swift and sure torture. Florence Eli was one of many imprisoned women who were whipped for "idling." The demands of convict labor were extraordinary, and neither illness nor fatigue nor foul conditions were acceptable excuses; women were routinely whipped for "bad plowing," "failing to work," and being "filthy about cooking." The subjective evaluation of "bad work" rested solely with the guard, who may have found any excuse to exercise terroristic authority on a whim or as retribution for other behaviors that provoked his rage. As with arrest records it would be a mistake to assume that all of the women who were beaten unmercifully by guards were actually dallying or performing work poorly; however, the extent to which women were punished reveals a likelihood that at least some resisted the extreme work demands, unhealthy conditions of their captivity, and medical neglect by resting or slowing down, sabotaging work from which they were profoundly alienated. Black women's refusal of the carceral timetable thwarted carceral productivity and also undermined the notion that their bodies were state property and resources for southern modernization.

These refusals were accompanied by the rejection of psychic and social domination; imprisoned women were insubordinate, and disobeying rules and impudence were frequent charges leveled against black women in Georgia's camps.[48] Everyday rebellion or defiance must be understood within the overall context of domination; such practices of resistance "have neither the means to secure the territory outside the space of domination nor the power to keep or maintain what is won in fleeting, surreptitious, and necessarily incomplete victories."[49] By refusing orders or violating rules, imprisoned women fought the terms of their domination and exerted their will, but they were not able to achieve lasting change or dismantle carceral domination. With only logs of violation or whippings imposed during the course of a few years instead of an archival trail of personal papers left by imprisoned women, it is difficult to detail the specificity of their beliefs and politics. Many of the women who were punished for idleness or bad work were the same women who were whipped for outright insubordination. Kate Clark, Mollie White, and Leila Burgess were all whipped for both idleness and disobedience. Laura Heard was beaten for both impudence to a guard and bad work.[50] She may not have acted in either of these ways. The guard may have simply needed a reason to cite on his ledger for exacting physical punishment against a woman in his camp. She may have been whipped for poor work because she was impudent to the guard or she may have developed a sabotage praxis that consisted of multiple forms of defiance—some passive and some aggressive.

While guards regularly leveled the dubious charge of feigning illness, feigning obsequity was a strategy that imprisoned women seeking parole, pardon, or commutation used when they wrote for their freedom, limited as it may have been. As I argued in chapter 4, the domestic carceral sphere of parole often circumscribed this freedom. Nevertheless, clemency applications reveal that women employed a variety of discursive strategies of self-representation in order to secure their release. Silence was one tactic. Only approximately 11 percent of black women who submitted clemency applications wrote a personal letter to bolster their case.[51] Although constraints on literacy certainly account for some of this silence, at least 44 percent of black Americans were literate by 1900, and between 50 percent and 60 percent were literate by 1910.[52] With literacy rates outpacing the number of letters written by women seeking clemency, the politics of silence was likely a deliberate strategy to ensure that they would not disclose something that would be off-putting to the governor or hurtful to their case; they were anxious not to exacerbate their already abject position within the juridical sphere.

As it was, women who did submit letters were very careful. They wore the mask, dissembled, and contorted themselves into the servile subjects idealized in the white imagination. The crafted statements meant to convey docility, humility, and subservience. In 1913 Lena Bell was only seventeen years old when she was charged with murder for killing her abusive husband. Although she maintained it was an accident, she was convicted and sentenced to a life prison term. In December 1918 she enlisted attorney Robert H. Lewis for assistance with her clemency case, asking that he apply for clemency on her behalf. Her request was denied because she had not served her minimum time to be eligible for parole and Lewis had not presented any new evidence of her innocence to warrant a commutation or pardon.[53] Warren did not give up. Two months later she appealed to her lawyer again because things were so bad that she wondered if there was "any way in the world to get out" and "what can be done for me."[54] Labor at Milledgeville was grueling and was increasingly taking its toll on her body. Warren had her "feet cut in 1914 . . . and I got cut last year in Sept. I got my hand cut into . . . and I was cutting wood. Both times I was at work and if you can get me out please let me know."[55]

The demand to produce new evidence was capriciously invoked; a few years earlier, Dolly Pritchett had been pardoned despite a life sentence for infanticide and without new evidence to prove her innocence. Like Pritchett, Warren had support from the original jurors in her case, who confirmed that she probably killed her husband by accident. Despite the denial, Warren remained determined. She kept apprising her attorney of her distress and resolve to get out, writing in August that she was "verry [sic] sick" and "would be very glad to get back home once more in life to live with my mother and my child" as "prison life" was "a very hard life to live."[56] There was no progress in Warren's case until 1920, when she had served her minimum seven-year sentence. Lewis wrote to the governor stating that he was "just in receipt of a most pathetic letter" from his client requesting parole.[57] The warden also wrote on behalf of Warren, invoking southern white aptitude in assessing black perjury: "Now, Gentlemen there is one thing about a negro, anyone who has had to handle many of them, can always tell when they are telling the truth, and I beg to submit, that she convinced me, that she was absolutely innocent of this intentional killing."[58] The obsequious tone of Warren's letters was thorough and convincing to white supremacists who believed that they had developed expertise in Negro manners and character. She was paroled on February 12, 1920, but remained deter-mined in her plight to achieve a fuller freedom, persistently writing for discharge papers after she was paroled to Mr. Underwood and had been working for him for a year;[59] her sentence was finally commuted in February 1921.[60] Only one year earlier, in 1919, Lethia Higdon wrote to prison authorities that "she had lots of white friends" who were "in-terested in her case," and she managed to get the sheriff to advocate on her behalf; he argued that Higdon "had a character above the average negro."[61] Release from captivity was frequently accomplished through commentary from white potential parole employers, wardens, or guards that a given applicant was "above the average negro," an exemplary ex-ception to generalized black maleficence.[62]

Emma Wimms, whose case was discussed in chapter 4, made what turned out to be a grave mistake when she wrote to the governor explain-ing that she was "a old woman and have been in prison for over twelve years and I would like to spend the rest of my life as a True Woman so I could be happy the rest of my life."[63] Her invocation of the language of "True Woman(hood)," a category that bore no application to black women, did not sway the governor, and her request for parole was de-nied. She would not be released until two years later, after she had sub-mitted several letters from white supporters attesting to her qualities as a good worker.

The records of the whippings women were forced to endure also re-veal feigning as a strategy to obtain release from captivity. Ella Gamble and Janie Mays practiced both defiance and dissimulation in order to ameliorate the conditions of bondage and escape captivity. When Gamble wrote to Joseph Turner of the Prison Commission in 1908, she repre-sented the picture of a humble and docile prisoner. Writing in pain, she told Turner that she was suffering in prison, and appealed to him to "have mercy judge I humbly beg you to have mercy."[64] She signed her letter "yours humbly servant, Ella Gamble."[65] Janie Mays also wrote a letter, to Mr. Hertwig, asking him to help secure her release from Milledgeville, after which she would serve as his domestic servant under parole. Mays knew of Hertwig because her cousin, whom he described as "an old darky," worked for him and lived on his property. Mays wrote simply, "I am charge of murder in the year 1885 . . . I will stay with you until you are satisfied. I have been here 24 years and do want to be free one more time in my life."[66] Ella Gamble and Janie Mays knew the obvious, that letters representing their docility would be more effective than ones that reflected the range of their tactics for ameliorating the conditions of their servitude and captivity. The women would have known each other for about twenty years, as they were both imprisoned at Chattahoochee convict camp in the late 1880s, and both were eventually transferred to the women's farm at Milledgeville. On several occasions at Chattahoochee they were both punished by whipping for breaking the rules, insubordination, and cursing.[67] These records reveal refusals of carceral dominion over their speech, labor, bodies, and movement, which they concealed from governors and prison commissioners in their clemency applications.[68] Although Gamble and Mays consistently resisted the terms of their captivity, they re-created their image through clemency files constructed by white voices, who often disparaged them, but compared them favorably with others of their race. In an appeal for support of Mays's clemency, her former neighbor wrote of her abusive childhood, describing her adoptive mother in racist terms as a "Hottentot." Although Mays was "good as any of them," he described her as an "errant little thief, pick up anything that she saw lying around that she wanted."[69] Caught in a representational bind and in confrontation with the state, women like Mays presented themselves narrowly and allowed their cases to be bolstered by white voices, the only recourse for achieving freedom from prison. For her part Mays only asked her interlocutors on the outside to put together a petition on her behalf and send it to Milledgeville "and everything will be alright." To her lawyer she wrote only that she had been convicted of murder and that she had "been here 24 years and do want to be free one more time in life."[70] Her neighbor's letter bolstered her case; a self-professed expert in Negro character, he portrayed her as a relatively docile "and capable washerwoman" by positioning her in contrast to her husband and his family. In her neighbor's estimation, "a more heathenish den of negroes never lived out of the jungle of Africa."[71] His white supremacist language and anthropological tone was persuasive, and the Prison Commission granted her a pardon.

Like Gamble and Mays, Amanda Hill, who had been whipped twenty-eight times for neglecting work, disobeying rules, and cursing when she was at Old Town Camp in the 1880s, submitted a clemency application emphasizing her status as a mother.[72] In 1903, after serving twenty-four years in Georgia's camps, she wrote to a man named Mr. Massengale, who was likely a potential parole employer, "in the regards of getting me out of prison."[73] She told Massengale that she "had been no trouble" while at Milledgeville and asked if he knew whether her folks were "dead or living" and if he could find out about her two children, "Freddy and my Babe child I have forgot her name."[74] She was granted a pardon in August 1904.

While imprisoned women veiled their history of insubordination, they also remained silent about their experiences of rape inside Georgia's convict camps when filing for clemency. None of the women who experienced rape inside the convict camps or sexual violence before they were imprisoned discussed sexual violation in their clemency petitions. Eliza Cobb, Lizzie Boatwright, Bessie Lockhart, Leila Burgess, Susannah Gilbert, and Sarah Autry all stood silent on the subject of their sexual abuse. Ella Pride, Charlotte Walker, and Dora Holly likely learned that making statements about their sexual abuse and describing their psychic pain at trial had backfired, as they were still convicted. They did not submit letters along with their applications for parole. Black clubwomen discussed the rape of imprisoned women, but imprisoned women themselves were all too aware that they were vulnerable to charges of licentiousness and that a strategy of openness about matters of sex, sexual abuse, and exploitation could close the door to their potential freedom rather than sway the men who held their futures in their hands. It is important to note that dissemblance was not a universal strategy employed by black women as the songs of blues women attest, but rather a specific strategy employed by imprisoned women appealing for mercy in the context of a high-stakes attempt to escape captivity and torture. Mercy, as they knew well, could not be conceived as a response to black female violation but instead had to be delivered through the fashioning of obligation, accountability, and blameworthiness—an "appeal to the only form of agency exercised by the enslaved—that is, criminal liability."[75] They attempted to prove their fitness for the white supremacist economic order by conveying unfettered industriousness and docility in sharp contrast with the dangerous, idle, or vagrant; the letters reflect a tactical craft developed in the dungeon of captivity, a literary performance of dutiful selfhood made for a political economy in which white authority prized contented black servitude and eternal laboring, an economy of "indebted servitude" that defined emancipation as both a "breach with slavery and a reproduction or reorganization of the plantation system."[76]

The men to whom they were writing—penitentiary keepers, parole managers, and governors—had legitimated the convict lease and chain gang systems in reports and legislative decisions; there is no record that they ever fired or arrested a guard for rape. As Darlene Clark Hine argues, the veil of secrecy with which black women shrouded themselves was not merely reactive but a deliberate tactic to maintain personal autonomy and, in this case, escape imprisonment. Silence was the most common exit strategy.[77] Women employed tactics that rested on a continuum of silence (from partial to complete) in order to weaken authorities' stranglehold on their freedom. In addition to slowing down, burning clothing, insubordination, and "wearing the mask" of docility, imprisoned black women "stole" autonomy over their bodies and emotional lives by inventing a representational and artistic sphere inside the prison.

The overwhelming majority of successful clemency applications contained authenticating narratives from prison officials or private white citizens who verified the veracity of women's claims to innocence, moral suasion, or character as workers, which usually meant their ability to perform domestic service. Given the prominence of "authenticating machinery" in slave narratives, these requests for release from captivity legitimized by documentary accounts from white neighbors, prison authorities, or former employers represent neoslave narratives.[78] The genre of neoslave narratives, originally characterized by works of fiction as well as other cultural products such as work songs that depict escape from bondage to freedom, has been expanded to include a body of literature that is set during enslavement or depicts enslaved subjects as central protagonists; it has most recently been applied to contemporary writings from imprisoned women and men.[79] Yet while the necessity of authentication links imprisoned black women with the subject position of the slave, whose veracity and ability to craft a narrative was in perpetual question, these letters from prison also depart from the literary tradition of both slave narratives and neoslave narratives written by imprisoned radicals in the twentieth century. If "the strident, moral voice of the former slave recounting, exposing, appealing, apostrophizing, and above all *remembering* his ordeal in bondage is the single most impressive feature of the slave narrative," black women's clemency letters lack this voice; instead, their radical, strident voices would emerge through the blues songs that are considered in the pages that follow.[80]

What does it mean to examine black radical political imaginaries in the geography of cages from which no memoirs and books would be published? This black radical political imaginary would circulate primarily within a gendered world of captivity, only sometimes exceeding the prison to reach family, friends, and lovers, the stage, and the published page—a gendered black political imaginary of prisoners that is rarely even acknowledged as part of the sonic radical blues tradition. Such a black radical imaginary might offer tropes of "black political modernity" beyond "black charismatic authority" and the "reinscription of gender and sexual normativities," beyond charismatic structures of authority and storytelling regimes.[81] Following Erica Edwards and Robin D. G. Kelley, the blues of black feminist sabotage might be understood as a political mode "beyond heroic models or romantic stories of triumph," as a site for "chronicling and rethinking black working-class politics, culture, and resistance."[82] Like dance, song has the potential to "resist containment but hold history."[83] The blues of black feminist sabotage presented an interstitial historical embrace in which political recognition and critique encompassed criminal practice, sexual controversy, intimacy between women, and an epistemology of collective rebuke of structures of authority, disavowing a politics of ascendance even as it proliferated the allure of rebellion. The blues of black feminist sabotage emerged in recordings, hastily written or whispered lyrics, revised performances, in the glances that signaled distinction between what would be written and what would be sung, what would be shared and what would remain (and still remains) secret.

The Blues of Black Feminist Sabotage

If remorse and obsequiousness is what the court wanted of black women, blues artist Bessie Smith practiced a politics of ostentatious refusal. She had several prison-themed songs, including "Jail-House Blues" and "Send Me to the 'Lectric Chair," which had lives beyond her career through covers by Ella Fitzgerald and Dinah Washington, respectively. In "Sing Sing Blues," Smith performs a rejection of the mandate to display remorse, and to provide a narrative of obligation and supplication in the legal sphere:

> All the judge tryin' to tell me, my lawyer pleadin' self-defense.
>
> The judge said, "Listen Bessie, tell my why you killed your man."
> The judge said, "Listen, Bessie, tell me why you killed your man."
> I said, "Judge you ain't no woman, and you can't understand."[84]

Smith illuminated and rejected the mandate to offer narrative in the service of maintaining structures of legal authority and power, arguing that legal objectivity is a violent ruse. In asserting the judge's inability to understand her actions, experience, and state of mind, she emphasizes the gulf between herself and him, which would manifest in the imposition of his reasonableness over hers. Given this gulf, the outcome of such a proceeding would be foregone; self-defense was a presumptively false and therefore failed option. Instead, the song's protagonist refuses to provide the court with the one thing in her possession that would legitimize juridical persecution and cruelty: her motive. Her refusal sabotages the means through which the court derives its power, breaking the discursive tools for black subjection. The blues "confront raw emotional and sexual matters associated with a very specific reality."[85] Smith's complex confrontation with the law at once invokes and withholds emotion in a subtly layered critique of testimony that simultaneously asserts the legitimacy of black women's interior lives without offering them to the court as material for prosecution, destabilizing legal categories of objectivity, neutrality, and universality.

In refusing the judge's persistent questioning and responding by acknowledging the gulf between her experience and his, Smith's song illuminates a central element of modern juridical culture in which "it is the criminal, not the crime, that is needed for determining the sentence."[86] Smith's lyrical persona recognizes that her positionality will not garner her leniency or understanding from legal authority and she resists the demand from the judge that she be complicit in her prosecution. The lyrics illuminate the futility and disingenuousness in his question, for she is always already constructed through her position as a black woman. Michel Foucault argues that this dynamic is central to modern juridical logic and procedure, as "the magistrates and the jurors, the lawyers too, and the department of the public prosecutor cannot really play their roles unless they are provided with another type of discourse, the one given by the accused about himself."[87] Smith recognizes the problem that her refusal induces in lyrics that respond to judicial frustration and delineate her own fate:

> You can send me up the river or send me to that mean old jail
> You can send me up the river or send me to that mean old jail
> I killed my man and I don't need no bail.[88]

"Sing Sing Prison Blues" anticipates Foucault's assertion that the absence of a discourse about one's self throws the court into flux: prosecutors "urge, they push the accused, he does not play the game. He is not unlike those condemned to the guillotine or the electric chair because they drag their feet. They really ought to walk a little by themselves, if indeed they want to be executed. They really ought to speak a little about themselves, if they want to be judged."[89]

Bessie Smith's acoustic challenge to a core legal deceit—that a universal standard of reasonableness could be deployed to offer justice for the marginalized if only they would disclose—was just one instance of epistemological sabotage developed and circulated through early twentieth-century blues recordings. In fact, one of the defining characteristics of women's blues narratives is a critique of legal moralism, incarceration, and physical and psychic violence in the legal sphere. In her representation of the courtroom Smith creates a black female blues figure who refuses to participate in the legal mandate that she offer a piece of herself in order to be imprisoned or executed. By highlighting this dynamic Smith illuminates the role of requisite testimony in maintaining racial and gendered regimes of persecution and constructing a subject fit for discipline. In this way she extended nineteenth-century traditions of performance in which black women "used their bodies in dissent of the social, political, and juridical categories assigned to them."[90]

The point is not to attest to the authenticity of experiences rendered in the blues, although the representation of buried and disregarded histories is important. Rather, blues creations render an imaginative world of carceral dismantling, not by merely recounting the terror of gendered regimes of imprisonment but by challenging the very foundations of ideologies justifying carceral control. While the experiences named in the imaginative and ideological blues realm often bore a stark resemblance to the material lives black women led inside convict camps, the depictions are resemblances rather than reports, a reflection of a range of critiques of gendered forms of punishment rather than an iconic or monolithic black female blues perspective. Imprisoned women's ideas and feelings, which have been largely hidden from view in prison records, emerge in the blues but cannot fill this glaring lacuna. The expressive realm offers commentary on the law and penal state, a sabotage soundscape, and a critical black radical catalogue—a glimpse of the interior that complicates the legal archive.

The blues challenged carceral terror and produced a terrain of art and knowledge that provided alternative visions of community and freedom. This blues tradition consists of legends whose records altered the musical landscape as well as unknown artists imprisoned at Parchman Penitentiary in the 1930s. Four women performed particularly poignant and complex black feminist carceral critiques, shattering the logics of incarceration: Gertrude "Ma" Rainey, Sara Martin, Bessie Smith, and Victoria Spivey. Ma Rainey, born in 1886, was one of the pioneers of the classical blues era, recording at least ninety songs during the 1920s, about thirty of which she wrote herself. Known for her blend of folk and commercial blues, melancholy and hokum, an emotional range influenced by minstrelsy and vaudeville, Rainey was among the most dynamic performers of her day. And she was linked, in both music history and popular lore, to Bessie Smith. Rumors circulated that Rainey had not only discovered Smith, but had in fact kidnapped her to take her on tour, during which she and Smith became lovers. Although unsubstantiated, the rumor reflects their rebellious reputation and their connectedness in the public's imagination. During the 1920s Smith earned more money than any other black entertainer, selling over four million records between 1924 and 1929.[91] The immensity of her life and career stands in sharp contrast to its brevity. Her career was slowing by the mid-1930s and was never to return to its previous high; her life was cut short by a car accident in September 1937.[92]

Born in Houston, Texas, in 1906, Victoria Spivey was known for her bleak and sarcastic recordings, and for the moans and shrieks associated with the Texas blues sound.[93] She outpaced most other female blues icons of her generation, consistently recording through the 1930s and staying musically active, singing and scouting talent, through the blues revival of the 1960s until her death in 1976. In addition to her distinct recording style she is known for her talent as a composer and for influencing other important artists, including Dinah Washington, Esther Phillips, Patti LaBelle, Alberta Hunter, and Bob Dylan, whom she allowed to play harmonica on an early Spivey Records recording.[94] Vaudeville veteran Sara Martin was born in 1888 in Louisville, Kentucky, and retired from blues singing in the early 1930s. Although she was not as famous as Rainey, Smith, or Spivey, she made her mark as a glamorous and cosmopolitan icon who was known for dramatic presentation, rich voice, and lively sound.

Scholars have analyzed the gendered and working-class politics of the blues, producing influential and illuminating analyses of blues women, their performances, and the cultural politics of recreational leisure in which they were central. Blues women's specific renderings of legal machinery provide insight about the logics and dynamics of criminal punishment, and in so doing provide an anticarceral conception of social life. Alongside Rainey, Smith, Spivey, and Martin are the blues songs of Mattie Mae Thomas, Hattie Goff, Eva White, Edna Taylor, and unnamed collectives of women imprisoned at Mississippi's Parchman Penitentiary. Although famed folklorists John A. Lomax and Herbert Halpert were overwhelmed by the musical richness at Parchman and made many trips there over the course of twenty-five years, most of the songs referenced in this chapter were collected in a single visit by Herbert Halpert in 1939 and rereleased by Rosetta Records in 1987 on the album *Jailhouse Blues: Women's A Capella Songs from the Parchman Penitentiary*.[95] David Cohn, another folklorist, visited Parchman and asked some of the women to transcribe their songs. The transcriptions and recordings are indelible portraits of women's experiences and imaginaries before and during imprisonment. They alternate between dissemblance and candor and, like the famed aesthetic theorizations of Smith and Rainey, they link gender oppression at home and in the prison. Finally, they reveal a quotidian feminist ideology, theorizing sexual autonomy and emancipation from captivity, labor exploitation, and patriarchal violence. In total, thirteen women appeared as soloists on Halpert's 1939 recording, which also included several group songs. Their songs blended the sacred and secular, and ranged in tempo from upbeat group songs to solo blues ballads. The male prisoners were Lomax and Halpert's top priority, and the "women were recorded as an afterthought, more for their spirituals than anything else."[96] The songs were recorded in the fields; in the women's sewing room at Parchman where they made prisoners' uniforms, mattresses, and bedding for three thousand prison beds; and in the canning room where they canned fifteen thousand cans of produce from the prison gardens and performed field labor.[97] Dr. Bernice Johnson Reagon wrote the liner notes of *Jailhouse Blues*; the extraordinary SNCC activist, scholar, and freedom singer called the songs "the best singing lesson I have ever had in Black American vocal songstyle."[98]

Women's blues was sonic sabotage; fundamentally a revelation and rejection of the logics undergirding American punishment, with an emphasis on its southern form and function. It was a part of what Clyde

Woods has theorized as "the blues epistemology" that "emerged in spite of, and in opposition to, plantation powers," elaborating and altering black realities and reestablishing "collective sensibility in the face of constant attacks."[99] This manifestation of sabotage included the disruption of enemy resources; in this case that disruption was epistemological rather than economic or military. The blues epistemology robbed white supremacist ideology of the power it derived from common sense—the purported natural hierarchies, the association between criminality and moral and political inferiority, the legitimacy of carceral damnation. The blues threatened such discursive and institutionalized principles, ingrained through repetition so as to be unassailable, producing a counterpopular. The blues also profoundly challenged legal reasoning by contesting expertise and revealing such reasoning as fundamentally opinion. Blues women accomplished this by deconstructing the logics of the law and by excavating, sometimes in wrenching detail, the role of race and gender in shaping experience, understanding, and dispossession. By elucidating in beautiful poetic form *particular* experience and asserting their own ethics and judgments, they challenged a principal claim of Western juridical doctrine: the ability to govern through universal tenets of reasonability and the legitimacy of legal actors' decisions and actions.

Bessie Smith's rejection of the court's demand for a narrative through which to justify legal decisions that ultimately erased, even as they requested stories about, black women's lives is merely one example of this challenge to legal reasoning. Morality was a terrain in which blues women lingered, undermining the very validity of the law to govern action and revealing the paradoxes of laws that governed behavior.

With her penchant for combining the tragic and comedic in one song, Ma Rainey offered a commentary on drink and prohibition that represents a major challenge to early twentieth-century carceral logic and practice. Liquor and the blues created about it provided a platform upon which Rainey could comment upon everyday life and ethics. In Georgia, Prohibition lasted from 1907 to 1935. In 1921 violating Prohibition was the second most common crime in Georgia after gaming; between 1920 and 1928 arrests for drunkenness more than doubled from 4,214 to 9,910.[100] The increased policing in the Prohibition era hit African Americans hardest because of their inability to pay fines. Writing and performing during the era in which women and men were increasingly arrested for drinking and possessing whiskey, Ma Rainey boasted about booze, with imprisonment serving as a harsh and inconvenient barrier to indulgence. There are no lessons learned, there is no remorse, not even the remotest possibility of tempered behavior or moral uncertainty. There is only the question of when she will be able to drink again, and the pain of imprisonment, where she is both lonely and parched. In "Booze and Blues" she wakes up in the morning, after "being in" her "tea," to the police shaking her. After receiving sixty days in jail because "money couldn't pay my fine," she proclaims:

> Sixty days ain't long when you can spend them as you choose
> Sixty days ain't long when you can spend them as you choose
> But they seem like years in a cell where there ain't no booze
>
> My life is all misery when I cannot get my booze
> My life is all misery when I cannot get my booze
> I can't live without my liquor, got to have the booze to cure
>   those blues.[101]

In Rainey's booze oeuvre, the jail, the courts, and the law have no authority, but simply exist as an obstacle to her ability to flagrantly enjoy the stuff. Legal force operates paradoxically to disrupt the mechanism for coping with the blues conditions that produced her imprisonment—poverty and the inability to pay the fine. Rainey's "Blues the World Forgot," a two-part song recorded between 1925 and 1926, represents an even more defiant Ma, hell-bent on drinking no matter what. Rainey plays with erasure, contradiction, tragedy, and frivolity in a song that declares, "I feel like going to jail!"

When Part I begins, Rainey has a blues so bad it is the "the blues that the world forgot," a blues so bad that she doesn't care that the sergeant is standing on the corner ready to take her to jail. Instead, she declares, "Tell the sergeant I said come in and bring all the corn mash he have with him!" In the song, everybody, including the sergeant, is drunk or at least in possession of whiskey, but as Part I ends and Part II begins Rainey is declaring she knows nothing about "it"—"it" meaning getting drunk or the actions of Tack Annie, who has cut her old man's head (again). The song blends the mournful and playful, the protagonist declaring her innocence and asking for help for "poor little bitty old me" on the one hand and drinking whiskey in the jail and announcing she is drunk on the other. The song complicates the categories of guilty and innocent—one can simultaneously be both, thereby rendering them nearly irrelevant. Hypocrisy is the more salient issue, conveyed through the sergeant's own participation in the crime he is policing. By troubling guilt and innocence and implicating the sergeant, Rainey destabilizes the category of "crime" altogether, exposing it as a constructed category.

As Rainey suggests, sixty days wasn't long—at least it was not the longest sentence one could receive for whiskey-related offenses. Possessing, making, or selling liquor in Prohibition Georgia carried sentences ranging from sixty days to a year on the chain gang or at the state farm, as Stella Kemp discovered in the same year that Rainey recorded "Blues the World Forgot." Kemp got married when she was fourteen years old; one year later, in 1925, police found whiskey in her home on Decatur Street in Atlanta. At age fifteen she was arrested along with brothers-in-law Newt and Joe Kemp. She was issued a $100 fine and was sentenced to twelve months on the Fulton County women's chain gang. Stella alleged that her older brother-in-law told her to claim responsibility for the whiskey, figuring that she would not be prosecuted because of her age. By April 1926 her mother, Dora, had saved $93 in order to pay the bulk of her fine, and asked that she be released from the chain gang. She was eventually released after serving five months.[102] By 1930, she had left her husband. She was working as a laundress and was living alone in a new home a few miles away from Decatur Street.[103]

The modern southern city was an ambiguous space, a site of leisure and danger, both of which were given voice through the blues. Black women's experiences of punishment, hidden from most popular discourse, were articulated through the blues as an impingement upon pleasure, challenging Progressive Era discourses about the dangers of drinking. Criminalization and incarceration, not liquor, were the causes of harm.[104] The blues was one of the only popular representations that framed the loneliness of imprisonment as a source of black women's depression. An untitled song Birtha Riley wrote at Parchman Farm that was transcribed for David Cohn contains the lines "When I was free I had friends from miles around / No I ant got no money my friends cannot be found."[105] Perhaps Riley knew and was borrowing from Bessie Smith's "Woman's Trouble Blues" recorded in December 1924, which links imprisonment with loneliness and lost love, community abandonment converging with judicial tyranny and cruelty:

When a woman gets in trouble, everybody throws her down
When a woman gets in trouble, everybody throws her down
She'll look for her friends, and none can be found

I got to go to jail innocent, I got to do my time
I got to go to jail innocent, I got to do my time
Because the judge is so cruel, he won't take no fine.[106]

Smith's meditation exposes the patriarchal character of judicial cruelty. "Woman's Trouble Blues" is not a song about a particular crime, or a song about the prison. Rather, in its generality it makes the claim that black women were targets of a regime of judicial terror not easily evaded. The vagueness of "trouble" centers black female criminalization, indeed the targeting of black women as a class, as a categorical imperative of the law. While stories of imprisoned white women's emotional hardship consumed media accounts, effectively erasing black women's torment, Smith foisted a parallel narrative about black women's isolation and interiority into the public discourse about race, gender, and punishment. She posits leaving as a solution, albeit a limited one, to her trouble:

When I get out I'm going to leave this town
When I get out I'm going to leave this town
Everybody'll miss me when they don't see me around[107]

"Woman's Trouble Blues" is credited to Jack Gee, but according to Edward Brooks, may have been written by Smith herself. An important commentary on black women's interior lives and community, it is a theorization of the necessity of collectivity in the face of carceral terror and the recognition of black women's vulnerability to state violence.[108] Linking the emotional and material, it suggests that collective critique of carceral terror is a form of black radical sociality that might produce new communities and societies. The song links abandonment, judicial terror, and migration in an account of black women's troubled condition, theorizing the everydayness of all three and giving voice to the predicament of black women in Georgia's prison camps in the face of dominant narratives of pathologization and an erasure of their experiences as targets of legal violence. Smith's poignant rendering of black women's isolation in the face of impending captivity as a "push" factor for migration is not the only representation of the intertwined nature of imprisonment and loneliness in the blues.[109]

Smith's poetic performance elucidates the entanglements of judicial and social relations, the "complicity of the public with the actions of the courts, the consent of the governed and the discontent of the governed," by registering her own despair and by depicting the compounding of her violation by the courts in her community: everybody throws her down.[110] Like "Woman's Trouble Blues," "Jail-House Blues," credited to Clarence Williams and Bessie Smith, also renders the forlorn predicament of incarceration:

> Thirty days in jail with my back turned to the wall, turned
>   to the wall
> Thirty days in jail with my back turned to the wall
> Look here, Mr. Jail Keeper, put another girl in my stall
>
> I don't mind being in jail but I got to stay there so long, so long
> I don't mind being in jail but I got to stay there so long, so long
> When every friend I had is done shook hands and gone[111]

Through the scene of the prison cell, "Jail-House Blues" offers an alternative construction of community, using the interminable temporality of imprisonment to assert the primacy of relationships between women in a way that is deftly suggestive of same-sex desire. Desire, fulfilled by another woman, is the only punctuation on her long sentence.

These songs, especially "Blues the World Forgot" and "Woman's Trouble Blues," seek to transform the forgotten plight of imprisoned women into rememories, recollections that exceed the memories of the individuals who experienced a particular event, loss, or violence, and exist in the terrain of popular awareness as encounters with the forgotten that confront listeners and shape the contours of communities;[112] sonic carceral rememories offer alternative temporalities where time is measured based on desire (for drink) and relationships (to friends and other imprisoned women) rather than the linear progression of months, days, and years. This sabotage emphasized black feminist sociality and critiqued legal knowledge and structures, troubling the category of crime itself and envisioning lives shaped by reflection, pleasure, loyalty, and autonomy. Through the blues, women artists articulated the general harm of captivity as well as the horrific conditions of southern punishment, the possibility of escape, and the pervasiveness of gendered racial terror, both within and beyond the prison.

This commentary was not limited to the realm of race records, which sold millions of copies. The a capella recordings from Parchman Farm also challenged prohibition and legal authority. Like Ma Rainey, Hattie Goff was playful in her embrace of illicit drink in a song titled "Mr. Dooley Don 'Rest Me," repeating "Oh Mr. Dooley, don' 'rest me / For I'm just as drunk as a man can be."[113] "No Mo Freedom" was sung in two parts, the first featuring Eva White and the second Mattie Mae Thomas. Part I includes the lines "I was standing, standing on the corner of North Farish and Church Street / When that old big bad policeman came up and 'rested me."[114] Just *why* she was standing on the corner, whether as a vendor, sex worker, mother waiting for her child, or waiting to cross the street, is left unspoken, troubling the listener's ability to judge her innocence or guilt. This song conveys another commentary on the arbitrariness of the law, the micropenality of everyday life, and the pandemic criminalization of black womanhood. The everydayness of the scene gives the song an everywoman/everygirl quality. The protagonist could have been Eva White, Mattie Mae Thomas, or eleven-year-old Hattie Bishop in an encounter with the "old big bad policeman." Regardless of the person or the crime, the certainty of the punishment is stark. She goes on to sing, "When those jurors found me guilty that old mean clerk he wrote it down / I could tell by that paper I was Parchman bound." The force and staccato with which White sings "When those jurors" reflects her judgment of *them* as well as their alienation from her in a powerful critique of racial and gendered discrimination, and the court's erasure of the subjectivity she establishes in the beginning of the song. It is the same force and staccato that she uses in her delivery of the lines that follow: "No more freedom, no more good times in this whole wide world for me," sung with a combination of force and melancholy.[115] "No more freedom, no more good times" seems definitive in the moment, but in quick succession illuminates another possibility: "But someday, yes, someday, someday I will go free / I'm gon' treat all you people just like you treated me."

If Eva White's Part I critiques the injustice of her arrest and imprisonment, Mattie Mae Thomas's much shorter Part II expounds upon the impact of captivity, the absence of love and family, of lovers who never received her letters, the hope of reunion. Thomas sings, "Did you get that letter, that I throwed in your back door / Says I would come to see you but that old bad man has got me barred."[116]

"No Mo Freedom's" consistent challenge to legal objectivity is more than a sentiment of anger toward agents of white supremacy. By highlighting the subjectivity of the legal personality (the old big bad policeman, the mean clerk, the contemptuous and contemptible jurors, the old bad man), blues feminists anticipate the concern of critical race feminists and feminist legal theorists. As Angela P. Harris explains, "legal thinkers have veered . . . toward a voice, which speaks from the position of 'objectivity' rather than 'subjectivity,' 'neutrality' rather than 'bias.' This voice is ultimately authoritarian and coercive in its attempt to speak for everyone."[117] Blues feminists' proclamation that the law did not speak for them and their representations of juridical meanness rather than objectivity or objectivity *as* meanness are part of an epistemology that demystifies the law and its actors as unmediated voices and reasonable entities. They anticipate the radical paradigm shift of legal theorist Patricia J. Williams's 1991 text *Alchemy of Race and Rights*, which opens with the assertion, "Subject position is everything in my analysis of the law."[118] The blues compositions and performances of Rainey, Smith, White, and Thomas provide a longer genealogy for Williams's influential analysis of Western law defined by dichotomy, the simplification of complication, transcendent or universal truths, and "the existence of objective, 'unmediated' voices by which those transcendent, universal truths find their expression."[119] In this way blues feminists destabilize all three features of Western law critiqued by Williams by rejecting the binary of innocence/guilt, troubling legal authority, and contextualizing their actions with poignant revelations about their experiences and conditions.

In addition to expressing the complexity of social conditions on the outside, the blues provided piercing reflections about the agony of prison conditions and vivid dreams of escape. In this way they were, as Caleb Smith argues, "aesthetic instruments of endurance that imagine the possibility of liberation."[120] "Penitentiary Blues," as sung by Mattie Mae Thomas and a collective of women at Parchman, laments, "Sergeant, sergeant, sergeant can't you see / Can't you see that these peas and cornbread, Lord, is killing me."[121] The brutality of imprisonment was rendered through consumption, not just production. In another representation of food to signify the harshness of prison life, "Big Man from Macamere," Thomas sings, "Oh, me in trouble eatin' cornbread 'n' molasses too."[122]

"Penitentiary Blues" reiterates the critique of a social presumption of guilt and absolute criminalization with the lines "Well I asked the sergeant what was my crime, my crime / Well I asked the sergeant what might be my crime." The response to this query is a silence pregnant with black women's subjection. In the song's next line they merely receive a rejoinder in the form of an order: "Well, a pick and a shovel, dig it deep down in the mines." This is not the only assertion that economic exploitation (rather than crime) is the reason for women's imprisonment and the core function of the Parchman regime. The persistent chant of the unknown singer of "Go Way Devil, Leave Me Alone" is "Leave me alone, good Lordy, leave me alone ... I come to Parchman just to pull these hoes."[123] Birtha Riley lamented the interminability of prison labor alongside the persistence of her freedom dreams: "I can't roal from sun until sun / I woke up this morning with freedom on my mind."[124]

The *Jailhouse Blues* recordings "Big Man from Macamere," "Go Way Devil, Leave Me Alone," and "Penitentiary Blues" protest the harshness of prison life, as do Ma Rainey's "Chain Gang Blues" and Sara Martin's "Georgia Stockade Blues." "Chain Gang Blues" and "Georgia Stockade Blues" are significant because they directly employ images of convict labor. Other punishment-themed songs in women's blues employ hybrid imagery, combining the image of chains with that of the cell in order to evoke both the harshness of punishment and the isolation and loneliness of imprisonment. Eva White or Mattie Mae Thomas may have heard Rainey's "Chain Gang Blues" because there is overlap between that song's lyrics and those of "No Mo Freedom." The latter's lines "When those jurors found me guilty that old mean clerk he wrote it down / I could tell by that paper that I was Parchman bound" overlap with the beginning of "Chain Gang Blues":

> The judge found me guilty, the clerk he wrote it down
> The judge found me guilty, the clerk he wrote it down
> Just a poor gal in trouble, I know I'm county road bound
>
> Many days of sorrow, many nights of woe
> Many days of sorrow, many nights of woe
> And a ball and chain, everywhere I go
>
> Chains on my feet, padlock on my hand
> Chains on my feet, padlock on my hand
> It's all on account of stealing a woman's man
>
> It was early this mornin' that I had my trial
> It was early this mornin' that I had my trial
> Ninety days on the county road and the judge didn't even smile.[125]

In a steady melodic lament, Rainey renders the "sorrow" and "woe" of imprisonment, its shackles, and, once again, the brutal legal personalities. But Sara Martin's "Georgia Stockade Blues" may be the definitive popular expression of the brutality of southern women's imprisonment:

Days are dreary, nights seem long
Down in Georgia on a stockade farm
Doing time for a crime
They found me guilty without one dime

Guards all around me with their guns
Shoot me down like a rabbit if I start to run
Five long years, Lord, in a state stockade
Working from sun to sun

Evening goes, morning comes
My daily task is never done
Chippin' boxes, Lord, on a turpentine farm
At night, can't raise my arms

Both legs shackled to a ball and chain
Pleading for mercy but it's all in vain
Ankles all swollen, can't wear no shoes
I've got the meanest kind of Georgia stockade blues

Five long years, Lord, in a state stockade
Working from sun to sun

Evening goes, morning comes
My daily task is never done
Chippin' boxes, Lord, on a turpentine farm
At night, can't raise my arms

Both legs shackled to a ball and chain
Pleading for mercy but it's all in vain
Ankles all swollen, can't wear no shoes
I've got the meanest kind of Georgia stockade blues.[126]

Martin incorporates the familiar tropes of the women's prison blues composition: the ambiguity of guilt or innocence; the crime is relatively unimportant and the details are omitted; the protagonist had no money to pay fines and, next thing she knows, guards are all around her. But Martin's song is more explicit than any of Smith's or Rainey's about the horrors of imprisonment, the treachery of escape, the specificity of turpentine labor, the agony of that work, the sunup-to-sundown hours. The meanness of chain gang labor is rendered here with unique intensity. Composed and first recorded by noted songwriter Tom Delaney, the lack of gender references in the song is also notable. Martin's performance exposes black queer positionality, as gender distinctions are not made to modify prison conditions or work demands. The lack of gender differentiation revises the male prison blues narrative to illuminate white supremacist patriarchy.

One of the most trenchant and direct condemnations of the legal system among the Parchman Farm recordings comes from "Penitentiary Blues":

> Well the judge that sentenced me ought to be here his self, his self
> 'Cause I'd rather be dead, Lord, than to be in this lowdown place.[127]

Mattie Mae Thomas and the women who sang "Penitentiary Blues" with her positioned the judge as a criminal, deserving of a fate worse than death. If Parchman was a place that made life not worth living (and in so doing constructed the black female subject as less than human), Thomas and her fellow singers argued that it was the judge who was subhuman, who deserved to survive on peas and cornbread, who deserved to pull the hoes, who deserved to be subjected to the alienation, captivity, and loneliness.

Thomas's analysis of punishment is woven through the Parchman Farm recordings and figures the prison as the bottom, as a deep marked by deprivation, alienation, and violence. Her narrative of being confined to a place of rape and labor extraction theorizes Parchman as a place worse than death, constructed through sexual, psychic, and material terror, a place where race and gender determine who gets to live and who gets to die. The lowdown exists alongside the hobbled-down and the murdered-down as frameworks through which to understand the particular ways in which black women's bodies were rendered flesh and psyches battered. The flesh, the "zero degree of social conceptualization" as theorized by Hortense Spillers, is prior to the body, which is never constituted for black female subjects. The "materialized scene of unprotected female flesh—of female flesh ungendered" is spatially rendered through the descriptions of the down—low, hobbled, and murdered—that constitute the violent terrain of black female life in carceral and domestic violence captivity. In Thomas's reading of Parchman as a space of constant siege, race and gender merge and determine the boundaries of humanity, the degrees of injury, and the magnitude of disposability.

Indeed the prison was consistently rendered a space of black women's death, as revealed in a song called "Long Line" by Alma Hicks, also imprisoned at Parchman.

> This long line is killing me
> He wakes me up in the morning by that old iron
> Hitting dang dang dang
> And roll from sun to sun
> Oh this long line is killing me
> I wrote to the Governor and asked him to
> Please turn me loose
> He wrote and told me
> Girl, I will look over your case
> Let me tell you girls it aint no mercy here
> Lord catching this long line is killing me
> It's so many women
> Here and so many different kind
> Some high yellows but I'm a chocolate Brown
> This long line is killing me[128]

Hicks's poetic complication of black female subjectivity illuminates difference as well as the spatiotemporal production of terror: the long line. As in Smith's "Jail-House Blues," other women enter the narrative of carceral temporality in "Long Line." For Smith the prospect of another woman presents the possibility of rupture, but in Hicks's song the sheer number of women only serves to reinforce the magnitude of prison violence. Whereas Smith calls for another woman, Hicks laments the pervasiveness of gendered racial terror. There is no solace and there is no solstice, with carcerality overshadowing the variation that the sun's movement provides. But other songs, such as "Go Way Devil, Leave Me Alone," reveal possibility in opaque dreams through which black women who were rendered flesh might also render liberation.[129]

> Go way, devil, devil leave me alone
> Go way, devil, devil leave me alone
>
> Leave me alone, good Lordy, leave me alone
> Leave me alone, good Lordy, leave me alone

Some folks come to Parchman just to show they're grown
I come to Parchman just to pull these hoes
Pull these hoes, good Lordy, pull these hoes
I come to Parchman just to pull these hoes

Wake up, Rosie, tell your midnight dream
Wake up, Rosie, tell your midnight dream
Midnight dream, good Lordy, midnight dream
Wake up Rosie, tell your midnight dream

My brother Willie keep on writing me
My brother Willie keep on writing me
Ain't gon' marry 'til you go free
Ain't gon' marry 'til you go free

You go free, good Lordy, you go free
You go free, good Lordy, you go free

I find the devil round the head of my bed
I find the devil round the head of my bed
Head of my bed, good Lordy, head of my bed
I find the devil round the head of my bed.[130]

"Go Way Devil" incorporates and alters aspects of the song "Rosie," one of the most ubiquitous texts in the men's prison blues tradition included in the Library of Congress's Lomax Family Iconic Song List. The song issues a plea to Rosie, waiting on the outside: "Stick to the promise, gal, 'at you made me / Wasn't gonna marry 'til-ah I go free / I go free, Lordy, I go free." "Rosie" is referenced and reimagined in the line from "Go Way Devil," "My brother Willie keep on writing me / Ain't gon' marry 'til you go free." Regardless of the version, in "Rosie" black women exist on the outside of the borders of the cage and prison plantation, embodying both the hopes and anxieties of imprisoned men who seeking to reunite with their beloved. "Go Way Devil" explores Rosie's material and interior life in captivity, rendering her own carceral nightmare of backbreaking convict labor. Other songs were more explicit about freedom dreams: "I dream last night that I was free / when I wake up this morning I find out it was all a dream."[131] "Go Way Devil" urges, seemingly for everyone's sake, that Rosie tell something of her dream life—her hopes, fears, possibly her desires for a romantic reunion of her own. It recasts Rosie by treading in the demonic.

Following Sylvia Wynter and drawing from theories of the demonic in physics and computer science, Katherine McKittrick has conceptualized the demonic as a conceptual pathway outside of determinism, linearity, certainty, and knowability. The demonic has held multiple meanings in physics and philosophy. In the early nineteenth century, physicist Pierre LaPlace asserted the possibility of a demon or being who possessed epistemic omniscience: precise knowledge of the state of the universe at a particular moment. With this knowledge the demon could predict future outcomes and events. This was an early (if not the first) articulation of scientific or causal determinism. Yet the more influential reference to the demonic in physics is that which likely influences Wynter's conception of the potential of demonic observation,

> posited by physicists who seek to conceive of a vantage point outside the space-time orientation of the humuncular observer. . . . The possibility of such a vantage point, we argue, towards which the diacritical term "womanist" (i.e. these readings as both gender, and not-gender readings, as both Caribbean/Black nationalist and not-Caribbean/Black nationalist, Marxian and not-Marxian readings) point can only be projected from a "demonic model" generated, parallely to the vantage point/demonic model with which the laity intelligentsia of Western Europe effected the first rupture of humans with their/our supernaturally guaranteed narrative schemas of origin, from the situational "ground" or slot of Caliban's woman, and therefore of her systematic behavior regulatory role or function as the ontological "native/nigger," within the motivational apparatus by means of which our present model of being/definition-of-the-human is given dynamic "material" existence, rather than from merely the vantage point of her/our gender, racial, class or cultural being.[132]

The demon to which Wynter might refer appears in a mid-nineteenth-century thought experiment pertaining to thermodynamics and could, without expending excess energy, violate the laws of thermodynamics by altering the velocity of molecules, but only from its position on the outside, observing molecular movement and speed and channeling it in different directions. This demonic challenge to the second law of thermodynamics is significant because it asserts the possibility of disrupting the ostensibly "natural" or inevitable progression of energy.

Examples of the demonic potential typically include the challenge to such presumptions that an ice cube at room temperature will melt or a rock lifted and let go will fall downward; in the carceral context the demonic challenge to entropy presents the potential that a cage door swung shut might reverse and swing open. The demonic confronts thermodynamic inevitability and irreversibility, undermining temporal, spatial, and indeed historical inexorability by manipulating the order of things from the periphery. This is the demonic potential of Wynter's and McKittrick's subaltern absented/presented black female subjects, who contribute to a "re-presentation of human geography."[133]

"Go Way Devil" banishes particular configurations of the demonic—both its metaphysical and sacred powers of evil making (the devil) and its association with scientific determinism—and replacing it with a demonic vision that disrupts the past and current predicament of forced labor (pulling these hoes), with a dreamscape produced outside or perhaps parallel to the known world, nebulous and distinct from but nevertheless related to the material reality of imprisonment. This site from which the seemingly impossible might be materialized is invoked but never explained or detailed, constituting a rupture rather than a roadmap, the predicate rather than the plan for "going free." In this demonic soundscape the still indiscernible rather than the knowable constitutes the terrain of futurities of freedom and a rejection of the ideologies of modernity that conscripted specific racialized and gendered bodies for the pulling of hoes—a rejection of the human categories upon which convict labor is premised. Between pulling hoes and enjoying reunion is the dream, the vehicle that changes history toward the direction of seemingly impossible justice.

In unison the singers linger on the words "dream" and "free" for three beats, the same length of time that they lingered on "hoes," countering injury and deprivation with imagination, desire, and possibility. The sonic articulation of dreams represents the manipulation of matter to unravel the evil and deterministic world of carceral violence, captivity, and punishing physical exertion. Like demonic reordering in physics, demonic sonic imaginaries do not always require excess physical energy that bodies fatigued from pulling hoes may lack; they reconstitute the human through the imagined future of a social world free of sexual violence and bodily exhaustion. Freedom in this instance is not contained in the physical labor of sabotage or escape; instead the expressive and epistemic fields of dreams offer the potential to disrupt the structures of seemingly irrevocable harm. The vantage point of imprisoned black women and their blues extricates Rosie from the margin, or absented present, of a traditional blues canon and cultural history of southern punishment in which they exist as a referent for the desires and experiences of imprisoned men. Alan Lomax recorded at least six versions of "Rosie" during his visit to the men's section of Parchman, more than any other song in the Mississippi Prison Recordings collection, reflecting its centrality to the prison's cultural and social world and revealing both longing and ambivalence in the lyrical adaptations and improvisations. Walter Jackson's version departs from the others, suggesting that Rosie "go 'head and marry, don't you wait on me / Might not want you when I go free."[134]

"Rosie" is buried in "Go Way Devil," subtly sonically traversing carceral divisions that separated the men's and women's prison quarters as a rejoinder to Rosie's place. Rosie in "Go Way Devil" is at once related to and utterly distinct from "Rosie," the girl who might break her promise to wait for her detained man. In addition to traversing the male and female camp quarters through the adaptation of Rosie in both camps, "Go Way Devil" reconstitutes space by representing the bed as a geographic site of encounter between Rosie's dream and the devil. In Georgia some imprisoned women brought their work tools (including axes and hoes), hidden in buckets of water, into to their sleeping quarters for protection.[135] "Go Way Devil" renders the bed as a site of political contest and Rosie's body is territorialized as a terrain of confrontation with gendered racial terror, labor exploitation, and captivity. "Go Way Devil" centers on Rosie, a buried and often disregarded black female subjectivity in both the corpus of male prison blues that Alan Lomax made famous and in the history of southern punishment. Popular cultural representations of the chain gang, such as Sterling Brown's "Cabaret" (which one scholar calls the single most important New Negro Movement poem dealing with black performers' exploitation), juxtaposed black male suffering in the muddy-watered southern chain gang with urban, commercialized lust and sex symbolized by the black chorus-line girl, erasing black women's sexual and labor exploitation and black female performers' contestations of power.[136] "Go Way Devil" shatters such masculinist depictions by invoking and repositioning Rosie's interior life. A southern chorus of collective black female suffering and dreams asserts that black women's experiences and expressive cultures are the ground upon which both carcerality and freedom should be understood and rendered through a modern blues aesthetic.

The elusive but integral dream was not the only evasive response to suffering in black women's blues. Victoria Spivey's masterful "Blood Hound Blues" is a unique portrait of escape from domestic violence and imprisonment, situating them as inextricable sources of black female violation and thereby disrupting public/private binaries and elucidating the role of the state in enforcing black women's patriarchal subordination. Although she is less renowned than Smith or Rainey, Spivey gained influence with her Texas blues sound over her fifty-year career. She begins "Blood Hound Blues" with the following lines:

> Well I poisoned my man, I put it in his drinking
> Now I'm in jail and I can't keep from thinking
> I poisoned my man, I put it in his drinking cup[137]

She proceeds to describe the scene that Alice White and Annie Wooten encountered during their escape:

> Well I broke out of my cell when the jailer turned his back
> I broke out of my cell when the jailer turned his back
> But now I'm so sorry, blood hounds are on my track[138]

By the end the listener comes to understand that she has been caught between two fatal scenarios: her man's violence, which instigated her action—"Well I know I done wrong but he kicked me and blacked my eye"; and the inevitable result if she is recaptured—"But if the blood hounds ever catch me, in the 'lectric chair I'll die."[139] "Blood Hound Blues" conveys regret—the protagonist knows the crime was wrong, and only did it "in a passion." Still, she reiterates the reason: "I know I done wrong but he kicked me and blacked my eye."[140] Importantly Spivey does not portray this experience as an extraordinary response to domestic violence, reflecting: "I did it in a passion / I thought it was a fashion."[141] The double entendre is important, encompassing both a style or trend, representing black women's prevalent need for self-defense against domestic violence, and a manner or behavior, crafting self-defense as a legitimate way of behaving in the world. The lines assert both the legitimacy and frequency of self-defense as a means of asserting bodily protection and autonomy, as sartorial political armor worn in the midst of pervasive domestic assault.

If self-defense was a fashion it was because gender violence was pervasive, a reality that the Parchman recordings convey. Mattie Mae Thomas's "Dangerous Blues" begins:

You keep on talking 'bout the dangerous blues
If I had me a pistol I'd be dangerous too
You may be a bully but I don't know
But I'll fix you so you won't gimme no more trouble
   in the world I know[142]

"Dangerous Blues" stands alone in this collection with such an account of domestic abuse, and this may explain why historian David Oshinsky has also noted its significance. Thomas sings the first verse as a warning or reprimand: "I'll fix you so . . ." The song begins by boasting her own propensity for dangerousness, and the mood is definitive and assertive. The most profound, wrenching, and revelatory parts of Thomas's song follow the first verse. First she embodies the male voice, in sullen complaint:

"She won't cook no breakfast, she won't wash no clothes.
   Said that woman don't do nothing but walk that road."[143]

Then in the last two verses she returns to the position of protagonist, less determined and more tired:

My knee bone hurt me and my ankles swell
Said I may get better but I won't get well

There Mattie had a baby and he got blue eyes
Said must be the Captain, he keep on hanging around
Said it must be the Captain, keep on hanging around,
   keep on hanging around.[144]

As she recounts her rape by the warden her voice is haunting and resigned, and there is audible muttering by other women in the background of the recording after she sings the line, "Said must be the Captain, he keep on hanging around." The reiteration of the phrase "keep on hanging around" conveys the inescapability of rape, perhaps its rampancy. She exposes the prison farm as a site of terror defined by constant surveillance, authorities' unfettered access to imprisoned women, and sexual violence. It was a site of depression, where physical recovery did not constitute wellness. But Thomas was not the only one whose baby had blue eyes; Birtha Riley's "Peas and Bread," as transcribed for David Cohn, includes the line "Coreana's got a baby and he's got blue eyes, it must be the Captain's he ant none of mine."[145] Rape was pandemic, and the repeated refrain of blue-eyed babies was both its representation and refusal. The blue-eyed baby haunted Parchman, sonically spectral, physically absent, but making sexual violence known.[146]

Led by Edna Taylor, the up-tempo group song "Susie Gal" also suggests ubiquitous sexual harassment and possibly sexual assault. Taylor's lead call assumes the position of the male aggressor while the women's collective response evokes the perspective of a female counselor or protector:

> I'm a-peepin', Susie (Susie Gal)
> Better look out Susie (Susie Gal)
> I'll catch you directly (Susie Gal)[147]

According to Lewis Jenkins's interview with the Works Progress Administration, "Susie Gal" is a revision of a song sung by black children in the antebellum period; the lyrics ended with the line, "Just peep through the window, Susie gal."[148] The Parchman version may describe escape from pursuit that may have taken place inside or outside the penitentiary. "Ricketiest Superintendent" also tells the story of a young girl's rape outside of the camp, also sung in a collective voice by a group. "Evil Superintendent" and "Ricketiest Superintendent" are two versions of the same song. "Evil Superintendent" was transcribed for David Cohn, while "Ricketiest Superintendent" was performed for Lomax and Halpert at Parchman several years later. Neither song was sung in the presence of camp authorities.[149]

Evil Superintendent

> We've got a evil superintendent and the worst sergeant on the
>   farm (*repeat*)
> If I make it to the bushes, the sergeant can't do me no harm
>
> The sun is too hot and seven years is too long (*repeat*)
> The first chance I get I'm gonna make a start for home
>
> Captain, Captain please don't drive my man so hard (*repeat*)
> He ain't nothing but a hustler and never had a job
>
> When I leave this place I will sure have something to tell (*repeat*)
> I can tell the world just what is meant by hell.[150]

Ricketiest Superintendent

> Got the ricketiest superintendent, got the worst sergeant
>   on the farm (*repeat*)
> And if I make it to the bushes, my sergeant can't do me no harm

It was early one morning, I was on my way to school (*repeat*)
Some grey-headed man and he broke my mama's rule

What you gon' do babe when they tear your jailhouse down (*repeat*)
Go get me a wick and a blanket and jailhouse on the ground

Got the ricketiest superintendent, got the worst sergeant
   on the farm (*repeat*)
And if I make it to the bushes, my sergeant can't do me no harm
[male voice asks for another verse]

What you gon' do babe when they send your man to war (*repeat*)
I'm gonna drink muddy water, sleep in a hollow log.[151]

"Ricketiest Superintendent" conveys the message that this story of a young girl's rape is not detached from the singers' site of imprisonment; the song links misogynist violence in the outside world to the threat of violence by authorities inside Parchman, blurring the line between patriarchal violence as it is constituted under captivity and in the so-called free world. The sergeant and the grey-headed man are both potential dangers, and the inclusion of the story of rape leads to a more radical act of sabotage—the destruction of the camp replaces the decision to "make a start for home." The song depicts home not in idealized terms, but as a profoundly troubled location. At home, or at least nearby, there existed the omnipresent threat of assault, represented as a collective threat by the group of women singing and through the location of the event: on an everyday walk from home to school. This revision of "Evil Superintendent" reveals far more about the feminist consciousness of the women imprisoned at Parchman, their experiences, and their creation of a vision of emancipation.

The replacement of "evil" with "ricketiest" infuses the song with a more sardonic quality, yet it also changes the song's theme from one of total domination to satirical derision. In addition to its common usage to signify unsteadiness or dilapidation, rickets was also the name for a disease believed to be caused by a lack of sunlight, vitamin D, and exercise.[152] The song's change in theme situates the women, who came to Parchman "to pull these hoes," as "Go Way Devil, Leave Me Alone" has it, in stark dichotomy to the sergeant, whose limited outdoor labor left him diseased. Whether diseased, shaky, or unsound, in this version the sergeant and the prison system more broadly are repellent but also perhaps vulnerable and capable of being broken. Hence the unambiguous lines "What you gon' do babe when they tear your jailhouse down" and "If I make it to the bushes, my sergeant can't do me no harm." In "Ricketiest Superintendent" individual escape is linked with the destruction of systems and structures of power and collective freedom, revealing multiple visions of emancipation and sabotage while also reflecting the abolitionist character of women's critique of the punishment regime. Its injustice was not linked to a prisoner's individual case or morality, but rather to the inherent tyranny of southern penality that needed to be destroyed. The inextricability of dismantling the prison and the production of new social and political relations is rendered powerfully in "Ricketiest Superintendent," a vision of the possibility of abolitionist transformation premised not merely upon the negation of regimes of captivity, but also upon the elimination of systemic violation of the black female body as a condition of possibility for the creation of antisexist structures of life and affinities.[153]

Together "Dangerous Blues," "Susie Gal," and "Ricketiest Superintendent" reveal the pervasiveness of force and sexual violence in the lives of imprisoned women in the U.S. South, and offer a rejoinder to the dominant mythology of black women as licentious beings, incapable of experiencing rape. Collectively the songs link women's experiences of rape inside and outside the prison, blurring the boundary between the two worlds and exposing the inescapability of the threat of rape in women's lives. The performances of these songs are also—and perhaps most importantly—political events. By naming rape, a technology of violence that is sustained through silence and whose existence is so often denied, Mattie Mae Thomas, Edna Taylor, and the unnamed singers on the recording waged an attack against it. If "syncopation, performance, and the anarchic organization of phonic substance delineate an ontological field wherein black radicalism is set to work," the blues produced by black women in southern prisons represents a particular tradition of black feminist fugitive work that produced an ontological field in which a rejection of rape and black sexual objecthood was constitutive of black radicalism.[154]

Sex was not merely theorized through narratives of violence, but also through a discourse of autonomy. The Parchman recording "Anybody Here Wants to Buy Some Cabbage?" is an upbeat sardonic group song about sex work that begins:

If there's anybody here wants to buy some cabbage just holler hey!
If there's anybody here wants some brown-skinned cabbage, right
    down this way[155]

In the landscape of ubiquitous sexual terror, the humor illuminates both a challenge to respectability and a complex relationship to sex. The song's verve disrupts the shame and silence associated with sex, while also illuminating it as labor, as black women's labor, as value. This presentation of black labor among women whose bodies were among the most exploited, abused, and vulnerable illuminates the workings of power; the demand for sex routinely fulfilled through brutal force as well as the black female subject's relegation to sexual object is rendered visible in the interpellation of sexual consumers. Beatrice Perry, Leana Johnson, and Mary Parks powerfully satirized perceptions of the black female body in their song "Where Have You Been John Billy?" The chorus sweetly renders expectations of black womanhood, domesticity, and beauty: "Can she cook a pone-bread Billy Boy, Billy Boy, can she cook a pone-bread John Billy?" To which a single sarcastic and more staccato voice responds, "Yes she'n cook good bread and she'll crack a nigga's head." The chorus then chimes in: "She's a young girl cannot leave her mother."[156] They sound most conspiratorial in the final verse, the sound of collective smiles audible as they begin:

> "Has she got good hair Billy boy, Billy boy, Has she got good hair John Billy?"
> "Yeah she's got good hair don't you comb it don't you try, she'll break every comb you can buy"
> "She's a young thing cannot leave her mother."[157]

Unabashed, black feminist blues variously embraced and mocked both interracial and intraracial expectations imposed upon the black female body, flaunting and flouting norms of respectability laden in violent sexual exploitation, domestic drudgery, and standards of beauty, recasting them through conspiratorial sonic gestures and the assertion of sexual control in the realm of cultural production.

"How'm I Doin It," which after a brief pause leads into "I Got a Man in New Orleans" on *Jailhouse Blues*, radically reconfigures conventions of leisure, relations of dominance, and gendered divisions of labor. Both are sung by Josephine Parker, and although they are listed separately in the liner notes, they have the same track number.

How'm I Doin It

I pulled my dress above my knees
I give myself to who I please

Now, how'm I doin it, hey hey
How'm I doin it hey hey
Now, how'm I doin it, hey hey
Do wee do wee do wa do wa do wa

Me and my baby don't fuss and fight
Gets into bed and shakes a thing all right

Now, how'm I doin it, hey hey
How'm I doin it, hey hey
do wee do wee do wa do wa do wa[158]

I Got a Man in New Orleans

I got a gal, I got a man in New Orleans
I got a man in New Orleans
He don't do nothin' with the money I give him
He buys cold ice cream

Hey buys cold ice cream
Hey buys cold ice cream
He don't do *nothing* with the money I give him
He buys cold ice cream

I'm gonna walk your log
I'm gonna walk your log
If I ever get back to New Orleans,
I'm gonna walk your log

I remember one night
Between three and four
That's the last word I told my lovin' baby
Turn your lights down low

Turn your light down low
Turn your light down low
That's the last word I told my lovin' man
Turn your lights down low.[159]

"How'm I Doin It" is a revision of the 1932 Don Redman Orchestra song "How'm I Doin'?" featured in Ginger Rogers's first film, *Twenty Million Sweethearts*.

I know a gal named Sadie Green
Hottest gal in New Orlean,
She loves to dance, she loves to sing,
Say, she'll take a chance on any old thing!

The other night down at the hall
When the band would play,
You know, Miss Sadie'd get on that floor,
Boy, and this is what she'd say
(What'd she say, Don?)

How'm I doin'? (Hey, hey!)
Twee-twee-twee-twa-twa!
Oh, how'm I doin'? (Hey, hey!)
Oh, gee, baby, oh sure!

Say, I'll admit I'm not the best in town,
But I'll be best until the best come 'round.
How'm I doin'? (Hey, hey!)
Twee-twee-twee-twa-twa!

I'm asking you
How'm I doin' (Hey, hey)
Twee-twee-twee-twee-twa-twa!

Oh, how'm I doin'? (Hey, hey!)
Oh, gee, baby, oh sure!
I'm not bragging but it's understood
That everything I do I sure do good
How'm I doin'? (Hey, hey!)
Hmmmmmm

Oh, how'm I doin'? (Hey, hey!)
Twee-twee-twee-nya-nya-nya-nya!
Oh, how'm I doin'? (Hey, hey!)
Oh, gee, baby, oh sure!

Now I only meant to do a little bit
You done made me like it and I just can't quit
How'm I doin'? (Hey, hey!)
Twee-twee-twee-twee-twa-twa![160]

Josephine Parker's "How'm I Doin It" unabashedly recasts leisure, replacing Sadie Green's love of dancing and singing in "How'm I Doin'?" with the lifting of skirts and shaking in bed as her chosen pleasure. The convergence of "How'm I Doin It" with "I Got a Man in New Orleans" provides a narrative that challenges the politics of respectability and shatters carceral and moral regulation through the reversal of gender roles and the threat of violence.

"I Got a Man in New Orleans" is sung to the tune of "Another Man Done Gone" and was recorded by John A. Lomax four years before he recorded Vera Hall's masterful 1940 performance of the latter song and introduced it to the world. "Another Man Done Gone" has since been covered by some of the most celebrated artists of the twentieth century, including Odetta, Johnny Cash, and Bob Dylan. The song, which Lomax described as "an Alabama chain gang chant," is widely credited to Hall, as Lomax's recording of her launched it into popularity.[161]

Another Man Done Gone

Another man done gone
From the county farm
Another man done gone

I didn't know his name
I didn't know his name
I didn't know his name
I didn't know his name

He had a long chain on
He had a long chain on
He had a long chain on
He had a long chain on

He killed another man
He killed another man
He killed another man
He killed another man
He killed another man

I don't know where he's gone
I don't know where he's gone
I don't know where he's gone

I'm gonna walk your log
I'm gonna walk your log
I'm gonna walk your log
I'm gonna walk your log[162]

Hall's masterful interpretation is the most widely known and studied version of the song, but as Lomax scholar Stephen Wade reveals, the tune can be traced to other songs including Joe Williams's "Baby Please Don't Go" (1935) and Leonard Caston's "I'm Gonna Walk Your Log" (1940). The scholarship on "Another Man Done Gone" traces the song's deep southern roots and routes, including performances by possibly another woman in a Livingston, Alabama, prison in 1950. Yet Josephine Parker's "I Got a Man in New Orleans" remains significant and unexamined despite her connection to the Lomaxes. Certainly, it would have been one of the first versions that the folklorists heard since it was recorded earlier than the other songs on the *Jailhouse Blues* collection, which were collected by Halpert in 1939. Parker, Hall, and Odetta share a sonic imaginary of southern punishment, women lamenting the terror of the chain gang. All three produce haunting, gorgeous, and distinctive versions. Like "Rosie," Hall's version of "Another Man Done Gone" is part of the Lomax Family Iconic Song List, and it was also included as part of the Library of Congress's exhibition celebrating the seventy-fifth anniversary of the ratification of the Thirteenth Amendment.[163]

The popular celebrations of the song are tied to its masculine prisoner subject. In Hall's version the violence of the protagonist's incarceration and death is rendered through black female witness and testimony; her experience of carceral terror was through observation and mourning rather than imprisonment. It was a sonic protest against southern punishment and political violence, but it may also have been influenced by her experience of domestic abuse. Hall claimed to have learned the song from her husband who, according to Ruby Pickens Tartt, the educator, folklorist, and benefactor who introduced Hall to Lomax, was frequently jailed for beating her.[164] What is striking about this history is that Hall's pivotal cultural and political contribution to the world was a critique of southern punishment, the loneliness it wrought compounding the experience of emotional and physical violation she may have experienced in her home. But the song's meaning is multifold, bound up in the ambiguous signification of the line "I'm gonna walk your log." Vera Hall told Lomax that it meant that the escaped prisoner would kill his lover if she did not meet him after he escaped. In later performances she clarified its meaning in a lyrical revision: "I'm gonna walk your log / You don't meet me at the waterfall / I'm gonna walk your log."[165] Other performers have argued that the line referred to a man who would do anything for his woman. Controversial folklorist Harold Courlander echoes Hall's explanation in his study of the circulation of "Baby Please Don't Go" in southern prisons.[166] Hall's version appears to blend, disconcertingly, the torment of incarceration and gender violence, a testimony to the entanglement of the two.

Parker's "I Got a Man in New Orleans" also attests to this complex entanglement, but not through sonic witness. She instead assumes the position of antagonist, reversing both economic and domestic roles in an audacious, unsettling, and unapologetic portrait of gendered life. In Parker's middle two verses she assumes economic, emotional, and physical control, upsetting the dominant relations of power that structured most imprisoned women's lives and revealing the complexity of gender roles in black communities. Her performance begins, "I got a gal," before she corrects herself, continuing, "I got a man," revealing clearly that her performance is a destabilization of traditional gender roles and, perhaps, heterosexual norms. She gives him money, which he squanders on cold ice cream; she is not a man complaining about feminine consumption but rather a woman whose disdain is captured in the lyric "He don't do *nothing* with the money," which is the song's hardest, most jarring lyric, an unmistakable complaint. Parker continues with the controversial and contested line "I'm gonna walk your log." If "the body is continually a contested field and an instrument of contestation and question," Parker's performance explores these questions by flagrantly rebuking conventions of respectability through a mimetic interpretation in which gendered violence resonates powerfully, expanding the discourse of such violence beyond victimization toward ridicule, a vivid if uneasy representation of gender roles and violence.[167] In this practice she was not alone, and Bessie Smith's "Mistreating Daddy" does similar work:

Mistreating daddy, mistreating mama all the time
Just because she wouldn't let you
Mistreating daddy, mama's drawed the danger line
Yes, you cross it, I'll get you

If you see me setting on another daddy's knee
Don't bother me I'm as mean as can be

I'm like the butcher right down the street

I can cut you all to pieces like I would a piece of meat[168]

As the album *Jailhouse Blues* is arranged, Parker's song follows "Mr. Dooley Don 'Rest Me," the sass of Hattie Goff's drunken taunt of the police ("I'm just as drunk as a man can be") segueing into the lifting of skirts to whomever Josephine Parker pleases, a playful challenge to respectability politics. Both Parker and Goff embody and articulate an abolitionist rupture in the black feminist tradition of challenging racial, sexual, and gendered normativity, demonstrating the range of possibilities, both dangerous and liberatory, in black feminist criminal stridency. In the context of southern punishment, which exhausted the bodies of poor women through hard labor, enforced captivity through the imposition of fines, policed public behavior, and punished those who defended themselves against intimate intraracial violence, Parker's performance refuses patriarchal structures of violence and authority through an inversion of roles in which she articulates and enacts control over the terms of sexual economy, economic dispensation, even life and death.

Jailhouse Blues moves from the secular "How'm I Doin It/I Got a Man in New Orleans" to a popular song in the sacred tradition: "The Last Month of the Year." The quick succession of songs about arrest, sexual agency, authority in relationships, sexual pleasure, and murder followed by a spiritual ("What month was my Jesus born in? / The last month of the year") reveals the fluidity of working-class black women's political, spiritual, and sexual ethics. Explicit narratives of sex, sexual labor, and Jesus offered a working-class feminist rejoinder to the religious and moral ethos of middle-class uplift ideology and a conception of spirituality that encompassed sexual desire, pleasure, messiness, criminality, and gender transgression. The politics of respectability and the cultural practice of dissemblance were interwoven strategies of protection from the political violence wrought by negative stereotypes of black female sexuality. The blues epistemology conveyed through the Parchman Farm recordings reflects a different culture through which black women protected themselves from negative perceptions by constructing and disseminating a nuanced image of themselves as simultaneously sexual and spiritual, dangerous and vulnerable, heartbroken and strong. Imprisoned women at Parchman often rejected respectability and the authority of legal and carceral actors and refused innocence as a means of subjectification, often choosing disobedience, sexual rebellion, and guilt, as revealed in the Parchman song "Ham Bone Boiled," transcribed for David Cohn:

> I'm going to the free world to get my ham bone boiled
> Cause these Parchman men done let my ham bone spoil
> I sware to god I sure ain't lieing to you
>
> The Sup't. don't like it
> Seargeant aint gonne have it here
> These convict women making and drinking this beer
> I sware to god I sure ain't lieing to you
>
> Let me tell you what the Supt has done
> He took off my man's blue suit
> And put him on a striped one
> When I leave this place
> I will sure have something to tell
> I can tell the world just what is meant by hell[169]

Desire, defiance, a rebuke of punishment, and the characterization of Parchman as hell converge in a "system of explanation" that named and critiqued structures of power that dehumanized both black women and men.[170] The blues system of explanation was a lyrical and narrative critique and lament about who imprisoned women were on their own terms, outside of the discourses of the state or the middle class, an assertion of control over self-fashioning in a context of violent subordination.

Artists at Parchman conveyed complex gendered and sexual subjectivities in which deviance was potentially resistance, destabilizing modern conservative sexual regimes; this places them within the queer theoretical and historical frameworks that scholars Cathy Cohen and Regina Kunzel have delineated.[171] Songs were sung and heard in succession by women whose lengthy sentences meant familiarity and intimacy with each other and with messages over time. The closeness and deep knowledge of the songs can be heard through the moments of laughter, verbal exchanges about the correct lyrics, and the unison that marks these recordings. The recordings are imbricated with the power relations between performer, recorder, and audience, as were the interview performances of formerly enslaved women and men for field interviewers. These recordings are, therefore, undoubtedly starkly different from the hums, whispers, and songs sung in snatches of privacy in the highly surveilled environs of the Parchman women's camp, Camp Thirteen. Thus they must be understood as firmly bounded by relations of coercion and pleasure that delineated white male freedom and black female captivity and rendered performances of both joy and sorrow pleasurable for field interviewers, field recorders, and the audiences that would have heard Parchman recordings when they were released by Rosetta Records on the 1987 album *Jailhouse Blues*. The black feminist criminal dreams represented therein both reflect and exceed those relations of power. Over time and through repetition, the power of these lyrics and their cumulative warnings, explications, and affirmations were magnified, whether through shout or whisper, the convergence of songs they sang and heard over the years.

> Make it to the bushes / You go free / The Sergeant can't do me no harm / You go free / Just to pull these hoes / Peas and cornbread, lord is killing me / A wick and a blanket / Coreana's got a baby and he's got blue eyes / Said Mattie had a baby and he got blue eyes / No more good times / Let me tell you what the Supt has done / You go free / Wake up, Rosie, tell your midnight dream / What you gon' do babe when they tear your jailhouse down / You go free / I'm gonna treat all you people like you treated me / And jailhouse on the ground . . .

The Parchman songs worked together and circulated through the course of the day and night, as the songs we can't get out of our head tend to do. The women who created them were part of a broader women's blues repertoire that included works by Bessie Smith, Ma Rainey, Sara Martin, Victoria Spivey, and other famous blues artists on the outside. Black women's blues was an aesthetic of embodied justice, and as Ruth Wilson Gilmore argues, "if justice is embodied, it is then therefore always spatial, which is to say, part of a process of making a place."[172] Detailing the harms of policing, the unfairness of the juridical field, the gendered cruelties of incarceration, and the terror of intimate violence was central to blues culture's world creation. The black feminist blues culture of abolition often embraced criminality while simultaneously refusing abjection and moral judgment; it "embodied the social relations and contradictions of black displacement" and the nexus of racial-sexual torment that carceral displacement wrought.[173] Black women's blues situated punishment as a system of harm that only caused and exacerbated the interlocking structures of violence that they named.

They sarcastically asked their captors, "What you gon' do, babe, when they tear your jailhouse down?" Music, as Shana L. Redmond argues, is "a method" that "allows us to do and imagine things that may otherwise be unimaginable or seem impossible."[174] In this instance, black women's blues articulated an abolition democracy consciousness invested in the relationship between dismantling and building; the question "What you gon' do . . . ?" suggests the necessity for the creation of new political visions and life-sustaining structures from and through the rubble of the prison. Imaginaries of worlds without prisons or jails imbued the black feminist blues tradition, and the possibility imbedded in the question was a world not governed by gendered racial terror. This question, far from abstract, was both urgent and concrete. Where there was smoke there was fire.

Fire

About five hundred miles and almost forty years separated Eva White, Mattie Mae Thomas, Josephine Parker, Birtha Riley, Edna Taylor, and Hattie Goff from four women at Milledgeville State Prison Farm who were also engaged meaningfully with the same question of the possibility created from the embers of the prison. "Just at dark this afternoon a telephone message from the state farm told the people of this place that the woman's building of the state farm was rapidly burning, to the ground."[175] That was how the Atlanta Constitution described the rebellion that four women at Milledgeville executed. In 1900, Emma Yates, Roxie Collier, and Lethie Beech, who were black, conspired with Mary Traylor, one of the few white women prisoners at Milledgeville, to destroy the female prison camp quarters. Yates and Beech served as lookouts while Traylor set the fire. There were conflicting reports about whether Collier helped Traylor or whether she was also in charge of looking out. The four saboteurs did not manage to escape, although there were reports that other unnamed prisoners did flee the camp during the fire.[176] They were all charged with arson, including "maliciously burning the occupied dwelling house of F. M. Allagood."[177] Warden Allagood lived in a house located in the women's camp. Conveniently, this location allowed him the greatest sexual access to imprisoned women whom he was reputed to have coerced and harassed.[178] The fire took place only three years before his highly publicized harassment and whipping of Mamie De Cris described in chapter 2.

The specific motive for the extraordinary act of sabotage is uncertain. Mary Traylor said she had no intention of escaping, although this claim may have been part of her defense strategy. The archive is mum about the motives, beliefs, and life histories of Roxie Collier, Lethie Beech, and Emma Yates since they were barely mentioned in reports about the arson. The destruction cost the state $4,500 in losses and prompted the completion of a waterworks system. The Prison Commission adopted a gradual plan to rebuild all of the prisoners' quarters with stone instead of wood, which would create a "practically fireproof prison."[179]

It is unclear whether the women believed that Allagood was inside his quarters at the time they burned it down, but the destruction of his house and possibly the man inside represents resistance to sexual terror; the burning of the prison itself was a historically significant effort to interfere with production and resist the brutal conditions of labor and captivity. At trial, the prosecution bussed in "two wagonloads of female convicts" to testify against the four women.[180] Warden Allagood and Superintendent Foster also testified for the prosecution. Attorneys for the defense cleverly decided to call Mary Traylor as their only witness. The public view of the black women on trial was predictably negative: they were perceived as callous and indifferent, and according to one report, "the three negroes on trial to all appearances took absolutely no interest in the progress of the case."[181] By contrast, "the white woman, Mary Traylor . . . gave it from start to finish an uneasy attention that showed she was greatly affected by the procedure. Her face wore a drawn, uneasy expression."[182]

The jurors may have been familiar with Mary Traylor, since three years before she was tried for the Milledgeville arson she had been the subject of a highly publicized arson case. Traylor was then employed as a domestic worker, living in the home of a prominent white Atlanta couple. She was charged with arson and larceny in 1897 when her employers returned from a trip to Nashville to find Traylor gone, their house damaged by fire, and articles of clothing and jewelry missing. The jewelry and clothes were later found in Traylor's possession and she confessed to being drunk, having company, and accidentally setting the house on fire. The case of a poor white woman under the influence of intoxicating drink drew significant publicity. Traylor herself attributed "her downfall to whisky and declared that she was under its influence on the night she became a firebug."[183]

Despite popular sympathy, she was given a ten-year sentence, which reflects only a modicum of leniency for charges that could have carried a life sentence. Reports that she would be given domestic work rather than hard prison labor did not ameliorate Traylor's depression; she was prescribed medicine for anxiety and depression, and the day after her sentencing she tried to commit suicide.[184] Only two days after her sentencing, Atlanta sheriff John Nelms visited Georgia's prison commissioners with a special petition to reduce Traylor's sentence from ten years to one. His plea was denied and, one year later, her clemency application was also denied.[185] Four months later, after being frustrated by official channels, Traylor participated in the Milledgeville arson conspiracy.

The Milledgeville arson trial reflected a classic legal struggle over witness testimony, filtered through the lens of race, gender, and class. The prosecution's strategy of marching dozens of imprisoned black women in the court to counter Mary Traylor's word backfired. Despite the testimony of the warden and superintendent, who stated that all of the women had confessed, the jurors apparently sympathized with Traylor and were reluctant to prosecute her based primarily on the word of black female convicts who had all been convicted of murder.[186] They acquitted all four women.

Conclusion

> The present is mostly illegible to me without rooting myself in
> the past. History is my vernacular; it's the language that allows
> me to express my thoughts and feelings about my life and
> experiences. The past bleeds into the present.
>
> —MARIAME KABA

> We cannot hope to reconstitute ourselves in all our absences, or
> to rectify the ill-concealed presences that invade herstory from
> *his*tory, but we do wish to bear witness to our own herstories.
>
> —HAZEL V. CARBY

The bars that held imprisoned black women in the first two decades of
the twentieth century remain; despite deep and expansive transformations the bars endure for a regime that is past but not ended. The barred
windows of a small back room in the Chastain Arts Center that used to
hold imprisoned black women who cooked and cleaned for residents
of the county's segregated poorhouse and farmed the surrounding land
still exist. Now the city's landmark arts center, the website for Chastain
Arts Center used to acknowledge the imprisoned women and men who
labored on the grounds for the segregated poorhouses with a paragraph
detailing its history:

> Female African-Americans from the Fulton County prison system
> cooked and cleaned for both almshouses. The smaller building of
> the Black almshouse, presently City Gallery at Chastain, housed
> a caretaker and his family as well as the female prisoners. Male
> Fulton County prisoners, who were kept in a prison building lo-
> cated on the current site of the baseball fields, raised livestock and
> vegetables to provide food for the almshouse residents. Known as
> the Fulton County Farm, these gardens were located on the site of
> what is now Chastain Park Golf Course.[1]

The website has since been redesigned, and the above statement omitted, along with the "History of the Center" section. The history of prison
labor and segregation has been erased from the center's website, removed

A barred window in a former women's convict camp quarters, now the site of the Chastain Arts Center Gallery, Atlanta, Georgia (photograph by the author).

sometime in 2010 during the long moment of American postracial celebration that accompanied the election of the first black president. Although they have been attacked as fraudulent and burdensome on the state welfare apparatus, black women built and maintained the infrastructure of care for Georgia's poor. They made the brick for the state's poorhouses, farmed its almshouse land, and daily ensured the welfare of the state's poorest elderly daughters and sons.

Shortly after the Chastain Arts Center website was revamped came the dead, or the revelation of the dead: in 2014 surveyors realized that more than eighty unmarked graves were located on the adjacent North Fulton Golf Course, behind the fifth green. Commenters remarked that three black almshouse residents' bodies had been "donated to science," but information concerning the cause of death and burial locations of most of the other almshouse residents remained elusive.[2] None of the reports mentioned the prisoners who labored at the almshouse or the possibility that they, too, might now lay in the potter's field of scattered graves that bordered this site of play, delineating a terrain of poverty, exclusion, and violence bordering wealth, stability, and amusement.

Researchers and activists are increasingly highlighting black women's violation at the hands of police and prison authorities, though there is much work to do in this respect given the magnitude of their historical erasure. Families have disclosed stories and protesters have bared their bodies in opposition to the carceral brutalization of black women and girls.[3] Black women's imprisonment, abuse, and murder at the hands of police and prison guards is increasingly being seen as central to contemporary processes of wealth stratification and neoliberal regimes of precariousness that define contemporary economic and social life.

In a prior moment of industrial development, gender ideology was critical to the carceral production of Jim Crow modernity. Southern punishment was a technology of gender construction, reconstituting and reinforcing ideologies of absolute racial difference through black female abjection. Through the promulgation of discourses of black female deviance, disparate policing and prosecution, injurious labor exploitation, regimes of gendered racial terror, theatrical rituals of black female violation, and legislative entrenchment of black female subordination, carcerality constructed and reconstructed a racially specific gendered order. This carceral project was part of a process of consolidating Jim Crow modernity as the social and political fabric of southern development. Gender regulation was necessary for the development of racial regimes of carceral capitalist development.

By examining the gendered complexities of the carceral state, new continuities with slavery emerge. Although black women's reproduction was not directly responsible for the reproduction of prisoners, the rape of black women was crucial to the establishment of white superiority and black women's representation as subjects who reproduced black criminality was critical to black criminalization. Reproduction, both social and biological, remained an important feature of black captivity in the aftermath of 1865. The lens of southern punishment provides new insight into traditional categories of inquiry such as criminal punishment, southern race relations, African American and gender history, and gender theory by illuminating the technologies of racial and gendered subordination. As scholars have long argued, race and gender are mutually constitutive categories; southern punishment provides one glimpse into how they have been structurally mutually constituted over time. A gendered history of southern convict labor also adds nuance to discussions of the character and meaning of southern racial violence, illuminating a theater of black female violation that included rape and pornographic performative rituals of violence and humiliation.

The representation of black female subjects in the white imaginary reveals that they were not merely different sorts of women but rather that they occupied a position wholly at odds with normative femininity, a category that was always already defined by whiteness. Black women maintained varying understandings of gender, femininity, and womanhood and contested their representation and violation. But in the domain of southern punishment, black female bodies were productive, flexible resources that could be contorted and circulated in the representational realm in the service of southern development and black political subordination. While black women were unable to inhabit the category "woman" in the nineteenth century, by 1908 this logic shifted in form from de facto to de jure, as womanhood was codified through whiteness in major penal reform law. Combined, policing, surveillance, the convict camp, the chain gang, and the privately owned houses transformed into carceral sites for paroled women should be understood to comprise a regime that consolidates broader structures of power.

White womanhood was a patriarchal cultural production based upon chastity, frailty, graciousness, and ladyhood. It was a performance that required repetition and reiteration through physical and discursive acts that took place in literary, interpersonal, and institutional realms. A lady was, as Jacquelyn Dowd Hall puts it, "always in a state of becoming."[4] Black womanhood was, in distinction, always in a state of unbecoming, requiring relentless cultural and political arresting. By this I do not mean to imply that black womanhood was any less constructed than white womanhood but rather that the very possibility of black subjects' claim to womanhood was a perceived threat to white supremacy and the carceral state was a key mechanism to crush such a possibility. This was the dialectic of becoming and unbecoming that vitally contributed to the consolidation of Jim Crow modernity as an economic and political system grounded in notions of absolute difference that was consistently challenged by black political action and that reconstituted itself through technologies of violence that included gendered carceral terror toward the end of racial capitalist development. Of course Jim Crow modernity was not an abstraction. It was a political and social order that was produced through the actions of specific historical actors. This study has adopted gender as a framework of analysis through which to understand the historical actions of carceral actors and the lives of imprisoned women.

No Mercy Here reveals that imprisoned black women subscribed to some traditional notions of gender, but it is not apparent that they consumed, internalized, and adopted normative gender constructs in the throes of displacement from gender normativity. Instead they resisted their association with masculinity for the havoc it wreaked on their bodies and the pain that captivity imposed upon their lives, producing a range of ideas about their place in the world and identity. Explicit in the archive is resistance to the violence of being battered and tortured; however, the refusal to be treated like a man does not necessarily also suggest the goal of being treated like a traditional woman. That is to say, the nebulosity of gender is clearly and consistently articulated by imprisoned women as a form of violence but only sometimes is this accompanied by an embrace of modes of self-fashioning and self-awareness that subscribe to traditional womanhood. Imprisoned black women's critique of forced proximity to masculinity does not mean a simultaneous investment in gender binaries.

The violence of convict labor was utterly inescapable and the toll in physical death and psychic and spiritual anguish is irrefutable. And while this history evidences a relentless continuity in gendered racial terror and ideologies and technologies of racial terror in the aftermath of emancipation and Reconstruction, the very force of this terror reveals white supremacy's imperfection. Because they were so challenged, the ideologies and structures of racial inferiority that constituted Jim Crow had to be reinforced through gendered technologies of violence and the reproduction and continued dissemination of knowledge about black female aberrance. The ferocity of black resistance is borne out in the ferocity of white supremacist terror.

Black women resisted Jim Crow modernity in myriad ways, from collectively opposing state violence, to developing modes of sabotage that interfered with the carceral state and creating social life connected to shared experiences of loss, love, and violation. Members of the National Association of Colored Women, so invested in the strategy of respectability, suspended it in their opposition to black women's incarceration on the convict lease, knowing that poor black women required concerted defense rather than defense comingled with training or judgment or reform. This approach reveals that while respectability was certainly a belief system it was also, profoundly, a strategy to evade and eliminate violence that was sometimes dispensed with when it did not further that goal.

Imprisoned women developed epistemologies of refusal that both countered and transcended respectability and Jim Crow juridical doctrine and violence. Their expressive culture combined both sociality and theory, and presaged later black feminist critiques of the law by mobilizing powerful resources of "parody, parable, and poetry" in a system of blues explanation that cohered community and challenged the theoretical and moral tenets of Western juridical doctrine.[5] They critiqued the legal personality, abstract, binaristic, and universalizing constructs of personhood and reasonability, and consistently illuminated the constructedness of crime. Moreover, their songs reflect a refusal of innocence as a means of subjectification or freedom, choosing instead guilt or ambiguity and privileging questions of social structure, political conditions, and human relationships in a vision of community and justice that was transgressive, transformative, and abolitionist in character.

Convict labor in Georgia did not die in the embers of the fire that Mary Traylor, Emma Yates, Roxie Collier, and Lethie Beech set. Its demise began in the late 1930s and continued into the 1940s as the Cold War intensified international scrutiny on race relations in the U.S. South.[6] In 1946 the "whipping of inmates and all forms of corporal punishment" including "shackles, manacles, picks, leg-irons, and chains" were barred from correctional institutions under the authority of the State Board of Corrections, effectively eliminating the chain gang from state and county penal institutions.[7] Still, the chain gang was kept on life support for far longer than historians have heretofore imagined. While the chain gang era is generally periodized roughly from 1900 to the 1940s, it remained an on-the-books method of punishment for far longer in Georgia municipalities.[8] Instead of being removed, chain gangs were moved, used after the 1940s in order to meet local demands for punishment and labor that exceeded the capacity of local jails. Examining county and state penal institutions under the auspices of the State Board of Corrections is misleading because chain gangs remained legal in the charters of cities and towns from the 1940s to the 1980s. The last trace of the chain gang appears in an act to modify the City of Homerville's charter in 1991:

> Said police court shall have power and authority to impose finds [sic] and to inflict punishments, after convictions, upon all violators of the laws, resolutions, and ordinances of said city, by fines

not exceeding $200.00 *and by compulsory labor in the chaingang upon the streets or public works of said city* under the control and direction of proper officers, not to exceed 50 days . . . and all sentences may be in the alternative and fines may be imposed with the alternative of other punishment in the event the fines are not paid.[9]

As local governments in Georgia drafted and revised their charters from the 1950s through the 1980s they continued to codify and recodify the chain gang as punishment for violations of municipal law, sometimes amending the stipulations under which the chain gang was to be imposed as punishment. In the 1950s the towns of Colbert, Ivey, College Park, Ila, Blairsville, East Point, Lincolnton, Turner, Avondale, Baconton, Chatsworth, Elijah, Hazelhurst, Tazewell, Woodbine, Wrightsville, Carlton, McDuffie, Lula, East Dublin, and Eastman all recodified the chain gang as punishment for violations of city law. From the 1960s through the 1980s, Chattahoochee Plantation, Claxton, Rochelle, Cuthbert, Dallas, Aragon, Avon, Albany, Fannin, Elberton, Decatur, Jesup, Oconee, Wadley, Omaha, Esphesus, Elizabeth, Franklin, Rome, Long, Ambrose, Newton, Lula, Hart, and Thomaston all did the same.[10] In Griffin, Georgia, where the sight of a white woman on the chain gang had so outraged the community in 1883, the laws regarding chain gangs were modified several times between 1957 and 1973. In 1957 a person could be convicted of a city crime and sentenced to either a fine of up to $400 or six months on the chain gang; in 1960 the charter was amended so that the maximum fine was $750 and the maximum chain gang sentence was ten months. Finally, in 1973, the charter was revised again, this time mandating that all references to the chain gang be deleted and replaced with the phrase "prisoner work detail."[11] The City of Moultrie was a similar case. In 1964 violations of city law carried a maximum penalty of $300 or 100 days on the chain gang. In 1968 the charter was revised so that all references to the chain gang or guardhouse were to be struck and replaced with "different words" that are not specified in the act. In 1980, however, the chain gang crept back into the new city charter, as punishment for evasion of taxes.[12] The difficulty of eliminating the chain gang as a penal concept reveals its cultural significance, including the deep connections between capitalism and carcerality and the limitations on freedom in the long civil rights movement era in the South. As evidenced by the Moultrie charter, words that would reconceptualize the chain gang were not readily accessible, since the link between convict labor and punishment was so entrenched in officials' understandings of criminal punishment; the lack of words to replace "chain gang" reflects the limitation of an alternative penal praxis in the 1960s and beyond.

Finding these charters was accidental and was precipitated by an unsuccessful search for changes in the law with respect to women on chain gangs. While there were no such specifications for women to be found, searching locally and searching for women exposed new paths for the historiography of convict labor in the South, demonstrating its stubborn persistence in the lexicon of criminal punishment in Georgia. Black women's imprisonment on chain gangs, in convict camps, in private homes, and at Milledgeville State Prison Farm illuminates the nuances of gender ideology, the complexity and violence of the archive, the cultural development of modernity as constituted by and through Jim Crow, the strategies and ideologies of women's reform, the role of the domestic sphere in public institutions, and the gendered nature of racial violence in the nineteenth- and twentieth-century South. The discovery of the persistence of laws authorizing the chain gang was an outgrowth of these abiding concerns— the result of looking for women, and for gender(ed) ideology. Whether and how these municipalities used chain gang labor in their daily punishment is beyond the scope of this study, however charters delineate the rules, responsibilities, and parameters of local governments and the nagging persistence of the chain gang as part of the *purpose* of local government is revealing.

The widespread contemporary practice of shackling imprisoned women during childbirth is one example of the difficulty in demarcating where southern historical penal logic ends and contemporary penal logic begins, but an analysis of the current configuration of Georgia's penal system is beyond the scope of this account.[13] Convict labor was a system of gendered racial terror that maintained and propagated race/gender logics in the face of economic and social shifts including industrialization, urbanization, explosions in white women's wage work, and black migration. The contemporary prison regime enforces very different capitalist structures and geographies; although private profit in punishment persists, representing a system of gross hyperexploitation, convict labor no longer structures the carceral regime to the degree it did in the late nineteenth and early twentieth centuries. The past lends clarity to the present, however. By drawing attention to continuity or the persistence of gendered regimes of racial terror I do not mean to suggest that the current regime is the same as the previous one—the economic structures of late capitalist precarity that mass incarceration sediments are dramatically different, though no less grave, in the twentieth century and need to be understood in their totality in order to be eliminated.

Extraordinary as it was, the arson carried out by the Milledgeville Four would not be enough to obliterate gendered racial terror or alter the logics of white supremacist patriarchy generated through Georgia's penal regime. That project relies upon a future collectivity mobilized and committed to challenging the afterlife of slavery and fundamental incompleteness of abolition's first act and envisioning new strategies and possibilities in the face of shifting capitalist arrangements and persisting regimes of racial and gendered dispossession and captivity, an abolitionist collectivity perhaps constituted in the tradition of black feminist blues incendiarism, determined to shake, if not torch, entire dungeons, to "change, destroy, and rebuild."[14]

Notes

Abbreviations

AC   Applications for Clemency 1858–1942, Convict and Fugitive Papers, Record Group 1-4-42, Georgia Archives, Morrow, Georgia

AHC   Atlanta History Center, Atlanta, Georgia

AR   Annual Reports of the Georgia Prison Commission, 1897–1936, State Prison Commission, Record Group 21-1-40, Georgia Archives, Morrow, Georgia

AUC   Robert W. Woodruff Library, Archives/Special Collections, Atlanta University Center, Atlanta, Georgia

Butler Papers   Selena Sloan Butler Papers, Auburn Avenue Research Library on African Culture and History, Atlanta, Georgia

DCC   David L. Cohn Collection, Parchman Folder, Box 4, University of Mississippi Archives and Collections, MUM00079, Jackson, Mississippi

DRRBML   Rosetta Reitz Papers, David M. Rubenstein Rare Book & Manuscript Library, Duke University, Durham, North Carolina

Felton Papers   Rebecca Latimer Felton Papers, Hargrett Rare Book and Manuscript Library, University of Georgia, Athens, Georgia

GAA   Georgia Archives, Morrow, Georgia

Georgia WCTU Records   Georgia Women's Christian Temperance Union Records, 1888–1982, MSS 647, Emory University, Atlanta, Georgia

NACW Records   Records of the National Association of Colored Women's Clubs, 1895–1992, Part 1 [Microfilm], edited by Lillian Serece Williams (Bethesda, Md.: University Publications of America)

PK   Principal Keeper's Annual Reports 1852–97, State Prison Commission, Record Group 21-1-1, Georgia Archives, Morrow, Georgia

Police Reports   Atlanta Police Department, Annual Reports of the Chief of Police of the City of Atlanta, Georgia, James G. Kenan Research Center, Atlanta History Center, Atlanta, Georgia

Proceedings   Georgia General Assembly, *Proceedings of the Joint Committee Appointed to Investigate the Condition of the Georgia Penitentiary*. 1870; reprint, New York: Arno Press, 1974

Punishment Reports   Corporal Punishment Monthly Reports (Whipping Reports), 1884–89, Record Group 21-1-11, Georgia Archives, Morrow, Georgia

RG   Record Group (GAA)

Terrell Papers   Mary Church Terrell Papers 1851–1962, MSS42549, Manuscript Division, Library of Congress, Washington, D.C.

UGA   University of Georgia, Athens, Georgia

Introduction

1. Lula Walker to Prison Commission, September 16, 1909, Emma Johnson file, AC. Several chapter titles and subtitles in this book are inspired by thinkers who have influenced this work including Patricia J. Williams (*Alchemy of Race and Rights*) and James Baldwin (*The Evidence of Things Not Seen*). I am very grateful to these intellectual interventions.

2. Lula Walker to Prison Commission, September 16, 1909, Emma Johnson file, AC. Spelling and grammar in original.

3. Ibid.; "Rome's Excitement Is Intense over the Sanford Tragedy," *Atlanta Constitution*, July 30, 1905.

4. Lula Walker to Prison Commission, September 16, 1909, Emma Johnson file, AC. Emphasis in original.

5. Ibid.

6. Ibid.

7. W. M. Henry to T. W. Rucker, Esq., February 13, 1915, Emma Johnson file, AC.

8. The aggregate number of women imprisoned on misdemeanor chain gangs is drawn from AR 1909–36 and AC.

9. See Duggan, *Sapphic Slashers*; Somerville, *Queering the Color Line*; Jacquelyn Dowd Hall, "'Mind That Burns in Each Body'"; Carby, "'On the Threshold of Woman's Era'"; and Hine, "Rape and the Inner Lives of Black Women."

10. "A Queer Colony of Female Convicts in Georgia," *Weekly News and Courier*, November 17, 1897.

11. Spillers, *Black, White, and in Color*, 155.

12. See Somerville, *Queering the Color Line*, esp. chap. 1.

13. On carcerality and inversion, see Kunzel, *Criminal Intimacy*. See also Spillers's theorization of the distinction between the body and flesh, "that zero degree of social conceptualization that does not escape concealment under the brush of discourse, or the reflexes of iconography" ("Mama's Baby, Papa's Maybe," 67).

14. Influential histories of the relational production of gendered and sexual positionalities include Najmabadi, *Women without Mustaches*, and Higginbotham, "African American Women's History."

15. Hartman, "Seduction and the Ruses of Power," 538. I am grateful for critical exchanges with C. Riley Snorton on ungendering and differential gendering.

16. Spillers, "Mama's Baby, Papa's Maybe," 66.

17. Cheryl I. Harris, "Finding Sojourner's Truth," 312.

18. Carby, *Reconstructing Womanhood*, 39. Racial violence, or white supremacist terror, has largely been symbolized through white mob violence and lynching. Influential texts on white race riots and lynching include Williamson, *Crucible of Race*; Markovitz, *Legacies of Lynching*; McGovern, *Anatomy of a Lynching*; Brundage, *Under Sentence of Death*, and his *Lynching in the New South*.

19. Influential analyses of black women and racial terror include Giddings, *When and Where I Enter*, which illuminates the pervasiveness of sexual exploitation of

black female domestic workers. Giddings also argues that the perception of black female lasciviousness not only made black women vulnerable to rape, but also constructed the mythology of the black male rapist, for "the stereotype of the sexually potent Black male was largely based on that of the promiscuous Black female" (31). According to Giddings, there was an assumption that black men had to be hyperaggressive sexually to satisfy libidinous black women (86–87). See also White, *Ar'n't I a Woman?*, for an examination of black women's sexual violation by both black and white men. Importantly, James argues in *Shadowboxing* that lynching, draped in the cloak of antirape rhetoric, enabled the sexual assault of black women (48). Other crucial theoretical works on black women and sexual violence include Spillers, "Mama's Baby, Papa's Maybe"; Angela Y. Davis, "Reflections on the Black Woman's Role"; hooks, *Feminist Theory*; Collins, "Pornography and Black Women's Bodies"; Hartman, *Scenes of Subjection*; Carby, *Reconstructing Womanhood*; Jacqueline Dowd Hall, "'Mind That Burns in Each Body'"; Carby, "'On the Threshold of Woman's Era'"; and Hine, "Rape and the Inner Lives of Black Women." Recent historical works by Lee, *For Freedom's Sake*; Glymph, *Out of the House of Bondage*; Feimster, *Southern Horrors*; Williams, *They Left Great Marks on Me*; Rosen, *Terror in the Heart of Freedom*; and McGuire, *At the Dark End of the Street* place gender and black women's experiences at the center of the history of southern racial terror.

20. Rodriguez, *Forced Passages*, 40.

21. Ibid.

22. Ibid., 47. Later chapters engage with southern punishment as neoslavery. Joy James's work on both neoslavery and carceral modernity challenges Foucauldian historiographies of modern punishment. For James the history of antiblack punishment and violence belies the Foucauldian historical penal trajectory from public torture spectacle to discipline and surveillance. Foucault miscalculates the demise of the public torture spectacle in the U.S. context by omitting an account of antiblack terror. For James's critique of Foucault's universalizing narrative of punishment see her *Resisting State Violence*, 25.

23. Joan W. Scott, "Gender."

24. McMillen, *Dark Journey*; Rabinowitz, *Southern Black Leaders*, and his *Race Relations*; Glenda Elizabeth Gilmore, *Gender and Jim Crow*.

25. Delanty, *Social Theory*, 2; see also Stuart Hall et al., *Modernity*; Gilroy, *Black Atlantic*; Frisby, *Fragments of Modernity*; Goldsby, *Spectacular Secret*. For an important account of modernity that reveals the convergence of ideas about sexual and racial difference see Somerville, *Queering the Color Line*. On the role of gender ideology in the establishment of new world slavery see Morgan's groundbreaking *Laboring Women*.

26. Jacquelyn Dowd Hall, "Private Eyes, Public Women," 261. On white women and wage labor in the industrializing South see Hall's "Ola Delight Smith's Progressive Era" and her "Disorderly Women." In addition to the scholarship of Hall, Hickey's thorough study *Hope and Danger in the New South City* has been particularly important for this study. Machlachlan's "Women's Work" has also provided foundational information and analysis.

27. The central role of gender in constructing ideologies of race that were central to the establishment of economic, political, and social orders is explored in Morgan, *Laboring Women*.

28. David Scott, *Conscripts of Modernity*. Quotes from pages 106 and 9, respectively.

29. This book focuses on the cultural and social histories of convict leasing in Georgia, however economic and political histories of convict leasing and chain gangs have provided a foundation for my analysis and interrogation of convict labor and gendered racial capitalism. Alex Lichtenstein's political and economic history *Twice the Work of Free Labor* is an invaluable text for understanding the centrality of convict labor to southern economic development. This pathbreaking work vexes the association between modernization and progress, revealing that convict leasing was profoundly modern, representing the relics of slavery grafted onto new industrial relations. In *Race, Labor, and Punishment*, Martha Meyers offers a quantitative sociological account of punishment in Georgia from 1870 to 1940 that stresses the role of political economy while rejecting the causality between bad economies and increased punishment. She focuses on crime and prison sentencing. See also Blackmon, *Slavery by Another Name*; Walker, *Penology for Profit*; Fierce, *Slavery Revisited*; Oshinsky, *Worse Than Slavery*; Mancini, *One Dies, Get Another*; Shapiro, *New South Rebellion*; Curtin, *Black Prisoners*; Taylor, *Brokered Justice*; and Perkinson, *Texas Tough*. Classic works on peonage, convict labor, and coerced labor in the South after slavery include Pete Daniel, *Shadow of Slavery*; Novack *Wheel of Servitude*; Ayers, *Vengeance and Justice*; Ward and Rogers, *Convicts, Coal, and the Banner Mine Tragedy*; Cohen, "Negro Involuntary Servitude in the South"; Adamson, "Punishment after Slavery"; and David Charles Berry, "Free Labor He Found Unsatisfactory."

30. Lichtenstein, *Twice the Work of Free Labor*, 177.

31. For an excellent analysis of the significance of New Deal on southern economic development see Wright, "New Deal."

32. For foundational earlier histories of women and punishment see Anne M. Butler, *Gendered Justice*, and Freedman, *Their Sisters' Keepers*. Oshinsky, *Worse Than Slavery*, and Curtin, *Black Prisoners*, incorporate important analyses of women in their works on convict labor in Mississippi and Alabama respectively.

33. Gross, *Colored Amazons*.

34. Hicks, *Talk With You Like a Woman*.

35. As this book was going to press Talitha LeFlouria's *Chained in Silence* was published, representing a critical contribution to the historiography of black women and punishment.

36. Booker T. Washington, "The Manuscript Version of the Atlanta Exposition Address," 580.

37. Du Bois, *Souls of Black Folk*, 70.

38. Hunter, "Domination and Resistance," 207.

39. Hickey, *Hope and Danger in the New South City*, 26. On women, gender, paid labor and industrialization in the urban North and Midwest, Joanne Meyerowitz, Kathy Peiss, and Elizabeth Ewen have independently demonstrated that

urban public space and wage work were important features of women's lives at the turn of the twentieth century. They agree that the urban sphere was neither entirely liberating nor oppressive for women, and challenge earlier claims that urban women were victims of capitalism and false consciousness. Rather, they argue that working women in cities used public space in innovative and creative ways to achieve new forms of independence and to adopt anti-Victorian sexual identities. Gendered industrial logic often foreclosed economic independence, and through leisure and consumer activities women sometimes reinscribed female sexual objectification. Meyerowitz argues that new "women adrift" in cities helped forge modern sexual expression, and became cultural icons by the 1920s. Mary Odem argues that as this idea of the new woman was emerging in popular culture, women's sexuality became increasingly vilified. See Meyerowitz, *Women Adrift*; Peiss, *Cheap Amusements*; Ewen, *Immigrant Women*; Odem, *Delinquent Daughters*. For the false-consciousness thesis see Tentler, *Wage-Earning Women*. Enstad, *Ladies of Labor*, examines women's consumer culture in the context of labor activism. For a cultural analysis of gendered ideologies of public and private spaces in this era see Rabinovitz, *For the Love of Pleasure*; Alexander, *"Girl Problem,"* also represents important work in this area.

40. Lichtenstein, *Twice the Work of Free Labor*, 11.

41. Hartman, *Lose Your Mother*, 17.

Chapter One

1. Undated motion from attorneys for petitioner to Prison Commission, Eliza Cobb file, AC.

2. Prison Commission Recommendation, Eliza Cobb file, AC.

3. On black lumber workers in the Jim Crow South see Jones, *Tribe of Black Ulysses*, 17.

4. According to the 1900 census of Milledgeville State Prison Farm, the ages of imprisoned black women ranged from 14 to 58. Twelfth Census of the United States, Milledgeville State Prison Farm, Baldwin County, Georgia, 1900. Roll: 178; Page: 3A; Enumeration District: 0106; FHL microfilm: 1240178. *1900 United States Federal Census* [database on-line] (Provo, Utah: Ancestry.com Operations Inc, 2004).

5. Undated motion from attorneys for petitioner to Prison Commission, Eliza Cobb file, AC.

6. Ibid.

7. Coroner affidavit, Eliza Cobb file, AC.

8. J. Matthews to Prison Commission, undated, Eliza Cobb file, AC.

9. S. N. Dawson to Prison Commission, undated, Eliza Cobb file, AC.

10. On what constitutes personhood I am drawing from Judith Butler's analysis in *Gender Trouble*.

11. See Butler's discussion of juridical power in *Gender Trouble*, drawing from Michel Foucault's argument that juridical power is deceptive in its ability to represent what it actually produces (3).

12. Jno S. Wood to Georgia Prison Commission, July 3, 1924, Martha Gault file, AC.

13. Ibid.

14. On the centrality and acceptability of white women's loving friendships in eighteenth- and nineteenth-century American culture see Smith-Rosenberg, "Female World of Love and Ritual." Smith-Rosenberg argues that "rigid gender-role differentiation within the family and within society" created a gendered emotional world in which women's loving friendships was considered part of the cultural landscape of normative womanhood (9).

15. Jno S. Wood to Georgia Prison Commission, July 3, 1924, Martha Gault file, AC.

16. Ibid.

17. J. E. Smith to Governor Clifford Walker, May 29, 1924, Martha Gault file, AC.

18. Letter from Milledgeville Matron, Mrs. J. E. Smith, to Georgia Prison Commission and the Governor, undated, Martha Gault file, AC.

19. Jno S. Wood to Governor and Prison Commission, July 3, 1924, Martha Gault file, AC.

20. As Jessica Evans argues in "Feeble Monsters," in the nineteenth century "the photograph was seen as slave to the visible fact" (278).

21. J. C. Jones to the Prison Commission, June 10, 1924, Martha Gault file, AC.

22. J. Matthews to Georgia Prison Commission, undated, Eliza Cobb file, AC.

23. Prison Camp Hospital Weekly Registers 1899, RG 21-1-9, GAA.

24. As Hortense Spillers notes in "Mama's Baby, Papa's Maybe," black women are "a locus of confounded identities, a meeting ground of investments and privations in the national treasury of rhetorical wealth. My country needs me, and if I were not here, I would have to be invented" (65).

25. Halberstam, *Skin Shows*, 3.

26. For an analysis of the unrealized potential for transformations in gender roles during and after the Civil War see Whites, *Civil War*.

27. Lichtenstein, *Twice the Work of Free Labor*, 23.

28. The phrase "chain gang" was used to refer to the institution of convict labor during its early period, between 1868 and 1908. Despite the term's early popularity, the official shift from convict leasing to chain gang labor did not occur until 1908, which is the subject of chapter 4.

29. Foucault, *Discipline and Punish*, 257.

30. Although this study focuses on the particular arrangements of gendered carceral power in the South the brutality of the violence is not recounted herein to reinforce notions of southern exceptionalism or to suggest that extreme violence and labor exploitation occurred solely there, since these were core features of punishment in the urban North as well. This account details the particular working of imprisonment as a technology of southern racial modernity, distinct from northern penitentiary models in character but not necessarily in scale. For an important critique of notions of southern exceptionalism in carceral state history see Thompson, "Blinded by a 'Barbaric' South."

31. Dr. R. L. Hope, "A Glimpse into the Life of Fulton County's Poor," *Atlanta Constitution*, January 6, 1895, 11.

32. *Proceedings*, 62–66.

33. For a critical analysis of the relationship between convict leasing, race, and capitalist modernization see Lichtenstein, *Twice the Work of Free Labor*. Lichtenstein argues that convict leasing was a driving institution of southern modernity in which resistance to black freedom and the drive to modernize converged. For Lichtenstein the binary between premodern slavery and modern wage labor is false, as the racial logic of U.S. modernity was born out through the imposition of antebellum techniques of captivity in the southern modernization industries.

34. Mollie Kinsey Interview with Debra Crosby, Federal Writers Project, 1939. Reprinted in Waters, *On Jordan's Stormy Banks*, 21–22.

35. Ibid.

36. Ibid.

37. Police Report 1866.

38. Women in Atlanta made up between 17 percent and 20 percent of the arrests from 1866 to 1900. In 1888 7,817 people were arrested in Atlanta. Of that number 3,164 were white men, 3,228 were black men, 1,218 were black women, and 207 were white women. Police Reports 1866, 1888, 1894, 1896, 1897, 1898, 1899, 1900.

39. Hunter, *To 'Joy My Freedom*, 52–53.

40. Fulton County Recorder's Court Docket, June–July 1886, AHC. The docket from 1886 is the sole existing local docket from Atlanta in which the race of the defendant is consistently recorded, and therefore provides a basis for comparing data on white and black women's arrests, convictions, and punishment.

41. Ibid.

42. "The Courts," *Atlanta Constitution*, August 22, 1873, 3.

43. C. Vann. Woodward argues that the 1890s were defined by the South's "capitulation to racism" in the form of new disfranchisement and other Jim Crow legislation across southern states, as well as negrophobic journalistic campaigns. See Woodward, *Strange Career of Jim Crow*, esp. chap. 3.

44. Police Reports 1893–1900.

45. Police Reports 1888, 238; Police Report 1893.

46. 1,248 black male and ninety-six black female minors were arrested in 1893. Police Report 1893.

47. Fulton County Recorder's Court Dockets, 1871, 1872, 1878, 1879, 1885, 1886, AHC.

48. Petition to Governor William Y. Atkinson, March 11, 1895, Lucinda Stevens file, AC.

49. PK 1870, 7.

50. John Darnell statement in *Proceedings*, 4.

51. Hubbard Cureton statement in ibid., 122.

52. PK 1870–79.

53. PK 1888, 4.

54. "The Female Convicts Have Increased Twenty Percent in Two Years," *Atlanta Constitution*, October 17, 1888, 8.

55. AR 1898–1909.

56. See coverage in the *Atlanta Constitution* including "Her New Year's Gift: The Only White Woman in Penitentiary Pardoned Out. She is Pardoned," December 31, 1875; "Court and Capitol," June 26, 1887; "Free at Last," November 24, 1887; "Death Pardoned Her," July 19, 1890; "Women in Stripes," July 22, 1893; "With Closed Doors," January 18, 1896; and "Georgia Female Convicts," *Washington Post*, July 30, 1890; "The Only White Female Convict," *St. Louis Globe-Democrat* reprinted from *Macon Telegraph*, May 24, 1887.

57. "The Female Moonshiner," *Atlanta Constitution*, December 29, 1889, 8.

58. See the following articles in the *Atlanta Constitution*: "Free at Last," November 24, 1887; "Court and Capitol," June 26, 1887; "Pardon for a Woman," July 29, 1896; "The Female Moonshiner," December 29, 1889; "Girl Refuses Pardon to Stay with a Friend Who Is Slowly Dying," July 29, 1907; Untitled, September 25, 1888; "White Woman May Be Freed," October 3, 1912.

59. Wagner, *Disturbing the Peace*, 126.

60. "The Recorder and His Victims," *Atlanta Constitution*, August 19, 1876, 4.

61. Ibid.

62. Ibid.

63. Maclachlan, "Women's Work," 48. Emphasis added.

64. Hunter, *To 'Joy My Freedom*, esp. chaps. 3 and 4.

65. Fulton County Recorder's Court Dockets, 1871, 1872, 1878, 1879, 1885, 1886, AHC.

66. Southern, *Progressive Era and Race*, 88.

67. The term "negress" was in common usage during the late nineteenth century, often modified by other deleterious labels. For examples of these references see articles in the *Atlanta Constitution* including "Georgia Glimpses," January 21, 1885, 2; "Two Lunatics (A Crazy Negress)," March 14, 1885, 7; "Mixed Matters: What Happened with the Police Last Night," June 23, 1886, 5; and "Atlanta Negress," March 30, 1889, 3. "A Terrible Charge" details the case of two black women charged with "enticing and attempting to entice young white girls away from home for immoral purposes" (May 7, 1887, 5); "A Blue-Eyed Babe" provides an example of sensational reporting during this period, recounting allegations against a black woman for stealing a white child and mercilessly beating him with a broomstick (January 25, 1887, 7). Black women were also accused of beating or poisoning white men and women; see "Police Pointers," June 20, 1888, 5; "An Exciting Case in Danielsville," May 9, 1882, 2; and "Calhoun, Georgia: Prisoners in Jail," September 27, 1883, 2.

68. "Lively Scenes at Police Matinee as Depicted by Gordon Noel Hurtel," *Atlanta Constitution*, October 29, 1900, 5.

69. Ibid.

70. Ibid.

71. Ibid.

72. Two groundbreaking examples of scholarship on the pathologization of black female bodies, the regulation of reproduction, and historical regimes of

captivity and subordination include Morgan, *Laboring Women*, and Roberts, *Killing the Black Body*.

73. "A Queer Colony of Female Convicts in Georgia," *Weekly News and Courier*, November 17, 1897.

74. Ibid.

75. Ibid.

76. Ibid.

77. Santiago-Valles, "'Still Longing,'" 30. Emphasis in original.

78. Santiago-Valles makes this insightful argument in ibid., 22.

79. McClintock, "'No Longer in a Future Heaven,'" 92–93. Emphasis in original.

80. Ibid., 89.

81. "A Queer Colony of Female Convicts in Georgia," *Weekly News and Courier*, November 17, 1897.

82. On the development of "queer" as label and self-identification among men in the urban North see Chauncey, *Gay New York*.

83. These are merely a few examples from the *Atlanta Constitution*: "Lively Police Items: Queer Prisoners Fight," May 9, 1897, 13; "At Judge Andy's Matinee: Queer Characters Were before the Recorder for Petty Offenses," December 29, 1897, 10; "Must Get a Shirt: Recorder Makes a Queer Demand of a Prisoner," September 20, 1897, 10; "Queer Police Court Terms: Used by Negroes Who Frequent Police Circles," September 20, 1897, 5; "He Declined to Dress," June 14, 1897, 3.

84. "Patterson's Poison," *Atlanta Constitution*, July 17, 1883, 7.

85. "The Haunted Stockade," *Atlanta Constitution*, July 20, 1883, 7.

86. Ibid.

87. Ibid.

88. Statistics compiled from all recorded ages for women in the following record collections: PK; Individual Camp Registers, RG 21-1-6, GAA; AC; and Central Register of Convicts, RG 21-3-27, GAA.

89. On the policing of black girls under New York's wayward minor laws see Hicks, *Talk with You*.

90. Police Report 1893.

91. On the creation of a reformatory see AR 1905, 6; AR 1908–9, 10; AR 1910, 6. On the black-child–saving movement see Ward, *Black Child-Savers*.

92. "Save the Girls, Too!," *Atlanta Constitution*, March 23, 1912, B4.

93. "County to Close Home for Girls," *Atlanta Constitution*, April 17, 1919, 4.

94. Clark Foreman to Selena Sloan Butler, July 15, 1925, Butler Papers, Box 1, Folder 9.

95. Statistics compiled from all recorded ages for women in the following record collections: PK; Individual Convict Camp Registers, RG 21-1-6, GAA; AC; Central Register of Convicts, RG 21-3-27, GAA.

96. Florida Thomas file, AC.

97. Pleasant Morgan file, AC.

98. Sophia Baker file, AC.

99. PK 1897–98.

100. Ibid.

101. Statistical analysis of criminal convictions compiled from recorded crimes in the following record collections: PK; Individual Camp Registers, RG 21-1-6, GAA; AC; Central Register of Convicts, RG 21-3-27, GAA.

102. Rabinowitz, *Race Relations*, 74.

103. See clemency files of Mary Campbell, Della Cole, Rosa Thomas, Nancy Smith, and Hattie Trawick, AC.

104. Judge Davis Freeman to Prison Commission, June 28, 1909, Susan Morgan file, AC.

105. Numerical data for women convicted of infanticide is culled from records where the offense is listed in the following record collections: PK; Individual Camp Registers, RG 21-1-6, GAA; AC; Central Register of Convicts, RG 21-3-27, GAA.

106. For news stories about suspected infanticides of white babies see the following articles in the *Atlanta Constitution*: "A Dead Baby," June 1, 1883; "A Horrible Crime," April 2, 1890; and "Baby Found among Leaves," November 22, 1900.

107. "A Queer Verdict," *Atlanta Constitution*, October 28, 1895.

108. "Charged with Infanticide," *Atlanta Constitution*, February 7, 1899.

109. See the following articles in the *Atlanta Constitution*: "Charged with Infanticide," August 26, 1900; "Want Pardon for Dolly Pritchard," January 5, 1901; "Pitiable Story of Dolly Pritchett; Flimsy Evidence That Convicted Her," January 6, 1901; "Justice First for Dolly Pritchett and Then, if Need Be, a Modicum of Mercy," January 9, 1901; "Carroll Refused a Pardon," January 18, 1901; "Pardon for Dolly Pritchett Urged," March 9, 1901; "Strong Petition May Bring Pardon," July 25, 1901; "Dolly's Mother Must Consent," August 3, 1901; "Legacy Precludes Pardon," August 16, 1901; "Dolly Pritchett to Stay in Penitentiary," September 25, 1901; "He Pleaded for the Girl's Pardon," May 16, 1902; "Mountain Girl Gets a Pardon," December 4, 1902.

110. E. W. Coleman, "Pitiable Story of Dolly Pritchett; Flimsy Evidence That Convicted Her," *Atlanta Constitution*, January 6, 1901, 3.

111. Unidentified newspaper article clipping, Dolly Pritchard file, AC. Note: there was some confusion over Dolly Pritchett's name. Penal and newspaper references vacillated between Pritchett and Pritchard.

112. Coleman, "Pitiable Story."

113. Ibid.

114. "Justice First for Dolly Pritchett."

115. Ibid.

116. Ibid.

117. Dolly Pritchett file, AC; "Mountain Girl Gets a Pardon."

118. "Dolly's Mother Must Consent."

119. Ibid.

120. Glenda Elizabeth Gilmore, *Gender and Jim Crow*, 72.

121. Feimster, *Southern Horrors*, 32–33.

122. Anna Brock file, AC.

123. Annie Darcy file, AC.

124. These figures are based upon indications of sentence lengths in the following record collections: PK; AR; Central Register of Convicts, RG 21-3-27, GAA; AC; and newspaper accounts.

125. "A Terrible Charge: Attempts to Entrap Children for Lives of Sin," *Atlanta Constitution*, May 7, 1887, 5.

126. Flora Richardson and Louisa Lindsay files, AC.

127. Hal Johnson letter to Prison Commission, Flora Richardson file, AC.

128. Flora Richardson file, AC.

129. Julia Whitfield file, AC.

130. Jones, *Labor of Love, Labor of Sorrow.*

131. Ibid., 8, 123.

132. Sharon M. Harris, *Executing Race.*

133. "Article 8—No Title," *Atlanta Constitution*, November 16, 1886.

134. Amanda Hill file, AC.

135. Rose Henderson file, AC.

136. "An Infanticide Case," *Atlanta Constitution*, July 13, 1883.

137. "Pardon Granted to Louisa Lindsay," *Atlanta Constitution*, August 29, 1909.

138. Susannah Gilbert file, AC.

139. Elizabeth Pitts file, AC.

140. Sarah Robinson file, AC.

141. See especially files of Bertha Cox, Rose Henderson, Mattie Jones, Martha Link, E. Pitts, Martha Reynolds, and Queen Kelly, AC.

142. Martha Link file, AC.

143. Hartman, *Scenes of Subjection*, 94.

144. Ibid.

145. For an analysis of the ideology of manhood in late nineteenth-century context see Bederman, *Manliness and Civilization.*

146. Ibid., 7.

Chapter Two

1. According to the Central Register of Convicts (RG 21-3-27, GAA), Nancy Morris arrived at Dade in October 1884 while Adeline Henderson arrived there in January 1885. Both women were in their early 1920s. The following is a speculative account of the experiences of Nancy Morris and Adeline Henderson who served time together at the Dade and Heardmont convict camps for approximately thirteen years. Since no records exist documenting the character of imprisoned women's relationships, this account of the relationship between two young girls who traveled from brutal camp to brutal camp is meant to be suggestive although it is based upon a constellation of archival records including Morris's and Henderson's clemency files, camp reports, hospital ledgers, and newspaper reports. Archival gaps have been filled with speculative narratives about their feelings, desires, and development of their relationship.

2. Description of Conditions from PK October 1884–1886, 110. "The usual abundant supply of vegetables from the vegetable farm . . . was very

greatly lessened. . . . Succulent vegetables were scarce and scantily issued to the convicts. . . . Fresh meat was also scantily issued."

3. See the account in the pages that follow on imprisoned women's double labor burden.

4. Filthy bedding is reported in the March 2, 1888, Grand Jury Report on conditions at the Dade County/Rising Fawn camp. Individual Convict Camp Reports, Miscellaneous Records, RG 21-1-19, GAA.

5. Letter from Moses Hollinshead to Governor Gordon, January 6, 1890, Adeline Henderson file, AC.

6. On diseases at the camp, the principal keeper noted that "incipient scurvy" (a symptom of which is severe gum bleeding) had caused eight deaths at Dade. Other common diseases including pneumonia, typhoid, and consumption at Dade are documented in "Table of Sickness and Mortality." PK October 1884–October 1886, 110–16.

7. The principal keeper cited as one reason for the poor conditions inadequate food preparation, noting "I was impressed with the idea that the food issued was not prepared as well as formerly and sometimes not in quantities sufficient" (ibid., x).

8. According to her clemency records Adeline Henderson had four children and a mother in ill health. Adeline Henderson file, AC.

9. Adeline Henderson was convicted of infanticide in sometime between late 1884 and January 1885 (ibid.). Quotations reference Morrison, *Beloved*.

10. Morrison, *Beloved*, 324.

11. Prisoners waged a two-day general strike at Dade Coal Mines in 1886 while Adeline Henderson and Nancy Morris were imprisoned there. Details about the demands, guard response, shackling, and leadership appear in "All Quiet in Dade: The Full Story of the Insurrection," *Atlanta Constitution*, July 15, 1886, 1. See also "Georgia Convicts Revolt," *St. Louis Globe-Democrat*, July 13, 1886, 2. One account indicates that prisoners had stored extra food in their bunks in the event that they were deprived of food in order to quash the strike.

12. Whipping of insurgency leaders reported in "All Quiet in Dade," 1.

13. "The Convict Camps: Report of the Joint Committee on Their Condition," *Atlanta Constitution*, December 12, 1886, 6, details the new strap.

14. Petitions for the pardon of Adeline Henderson from white and black residents to Governor John B. Gordon, Adeline Henderson file, AC.

15. Letter from Moses Hollinshead to John B. Gordon, January 6, 1890, Adeline Henderson file, AC.

16. Ibid.

17. On nineteenth-century menstruation see Phillips and Phillips, "History from Below," 139.

18. Nancy Morris was diagnosed with hysterical neuralgia on March 1, 1892, and "all overs" and general debility on April 2, 1892. Camp Heardmont Hospital Weekly Registers 1892, RG 21-1-9, GAA.

19. Nancy Morris was hospitalized for rheumatism on May 10, 1896. Ibid., 1896.

20. Ibid., April–May 1897, RG 21-1-9, GAA.

21. Adeline Henderson's age ascertained from PK 1890–92, which indicates that she was twenty-six years old that year.

22. Adeline Henderson's death from "fecal impaction" is recorded in Camp Heardmont Hospital Weekly Registers May–June 1897, RG 21-1-9, GAA.

23. Nancy Morris was granted clemency in 1909. Nancy Morris file, AC.

24. The introduction to this chapter is a speculative, subjunctive offering of *what might have been*. I draw from a wide array of archival sources but the account also lingers where the archive is brutally silent, in the realm of Nancy and Adeline's relationship with each other. The narrative is informed by critical fabulation, the writing practice brilliantly proposed by Saidiya Hartman in "Venus in Two Acts," offering a narrative "at the intersection of the fictive and the historical" (12). Yet this narrative also differs in some important respects. In conversation with cultural theorist Lisa Lowe, Hartman argues for the rearrangement of elements of the story, the presentation of multiple competing accounts, and explicit references to the subjunctive in the narrative. Although this introductory account does not necessarily throw the archive into crisis in these explicit ways as Hartman suggests, it does contest archival authority by shrouding the archival-historical in the speculative-fictive, "straining against the limits of the archive," in an attempt to raise rather than resolve questions regarding captive black women's lives.

25. "Is It a Dead Woman," *Atlanta Constitution*, March 8, 1884.

26. PK 1875, 8.

27. George D. Harris, sworn affidavit, March 31, 1875, Miscellaneous Records, RG 21-1-19, GAA.

28. Ibid.

29. PK 1875.

30. Ibid.

31. Zachariah Penn, sworn affidavit, March 31, 1875, Miscellaneous Records, RG 21-1-19, GAA.

32. On disidentification see Muñoz, *Disidentifications*.

33. Weinstein, "The Significance of the Armagh Dirty Protest."

34. PK 1875, 8.

35. John Towers, Principal Keeper, *Orders and Instructions to Lessees of the Georgia Penitentiary*, 1885, RG 21-1-19, GAA; PK 1878.

36. PK 1870.

37. Hubbard Cureton testimony in *Proceedings*, 119–20.

38. Ibid.

39. James Maxwell testimony in ibid., 144.

40. PK 1886; "The Official Inquiry," *Atlanta Constitution*, September 9, 1887.

41. Polk County Grand Jury Report 1887, Individual Convict Camp Reports, Miscellaneous Records, RG 21-1-19, GAA.

42. Dade County Grand Jury Report, 1888, ibid.

43. Fulton County Grand Jury Report, 1889, ibid.

44. Joseph Turner, Principal Keeper, Letter to Governor William Y. Atkinson, October 22, 1895; Executive Department Correspondence of William Y. Atkinson, July–November 1895, RG 1-1-5, GAA.

45. Several key histories document the deplorable condition and lack of oversight of convict camps in Georgia and elsewhere throughout the South including Lichtenstein, *Twice the Work*; Meyers, *Race, Labor, and Punishment*; Blackmon, *Slavery by Another Name*; Walker, *Penology for Profit*; Fierce, *Slavery Revisited*; Oshinsky, *Worse Than Slavery*; Mancini, *One Dies, Get Another*; Shapiro, *New South Rebellion*; Curtin, *Black Prisoners*; and Perkinson, *Texas Tough*.

46. Wright, *Special Report*, 5.

47. Byrd, *Report of Special Inspector*, 7.

48. Ayers, *Vengeance and Justice*. Ayers encapsulates the relationship between convict leasing and the South's transition to industrial capitalism in the following passage: "The convict lease system, along with the other variations of forced labor, bridged the chasm between an agricultural slave economy and a society in the earliest states of capitalist industrial development. On railroads and then in mines, the convict lease system served as the entering wedge, as the only labor force capitalists investing in the South knew they could count on to penetrate dangerous swamps and to work in deadly primitive mines" (192).

49. For a thorough and convincing analysis of the relationship between lynching and modernity see Goldsby, *Spectacular Secret*, esp. chap. 1. By saying this I do not mean to suggest that it is the only institution that made modernity, but rather that it was one of the central institutions in its development.

50. Affidavit of John G. Johnson, camp guard, Bartow Iron Camp, March 31, 1875, Miscellaneous Records, 1816–19, RG 21-1-19, GAA.

51. PK 1875, 12.

52. On labor and the plantation household see Glymph, *Out of the House of Bondage*.

53. PK 1871, 9.

54. Ibid., 6–7; PK 1873, 4, 22.

55. Lichtenstein, *Twice the Work*, 46.

56. Ibid.

57. Blackmon, *Slavery by Another Name*, 1152.

58. PK 1875, 12.

59. Ibid.

60. Perkinson, *Texas Tough*, 114.

61. PK 1870, 9.

62. William D. Grant testimony in *Proceedings*, 79.

63. Thornton Hightower testimony in ibid., 137.

64. Vaughn Clayton testimony in ibid., 39.

65. Lichtenstein, *Twice the Work*, 53–56.

66. Wright, *Special Report*, 8.

67. PK 1874, 9–10. On "promiscuous" in penology discourse, see Kunzel, *Criminal Intimacy*, 25–26.

68. Thomas Alexander testimony in *Proceedings*, 176.

69. George D. Harris, sworn affidavit, March 31, 1875, Miscellaneous Records, 1816–19, RG 21-1-19, GAA.

70. PK 1873, 4.

71. Ibid.

72. Ibid., 21, 13.

73. Pearl Black file, AC.

74. Hunter, *To 'Joy My Freedom*, 12.

75. "Patterson's Poison," *Atlanta Constitution*, July 17, 1883.

76. Susan Conyers file, AC.

77. Prison Camp Hospital Weekly Registers 1891 and 1888–1907, RG 21-1-9, GAA.

78. Lizzie Boatwright file, AC.

79. "The Convicts: A Visit to the Georgia Camps," *Atlanta Constitution*, July 16, 1881.

80. See clemency files of Mamie Cubbo, Lula Johnson, Hattie Johnson, and Annie Lucas. AC.

81. Susan Gardner file, AC.

82. "Local Tin-Types," *Atlanta Constitution*, September 14, 1881.

83. Camp location reported in Central Register of Convicts, 1869–1923, A-Z, RG 21-03-27, GAA.

84. Pregnancy reported in Camp No. 3, 1884, Individual Convict Camp Registers, RG 21-1-6, GAA.

85. Ella Gamble file, AC.

86. Letter from Ella Gamble to Judge Turner, July 31, 1904. Ella Gamble file, AC.

87. Ella Gamble Clemency file, AC.

88. Petition to the Prison Commission of Georgia, Nellie Carpenter file, AC.

89. Ibid.

90. Ibid.

91. Joseph Turner, Clemency Application Form, Leila Blackman file, AC.

92. Julia Morton file, AC.

93. Ibid.

94. See especially the clemency files of Minnie Black, Josephine Pittman, Sarah E. Dixon, Mrs. R. B. Hill, Jennie Pope, Narcissa Reynolds, Cornelia Rake, and Belle Russell, AC.

95. Carby, *Reconstructing Womanhood*, 25.

96. Letter from W. M. Gammon to Prison Board, Mrs. R. B. Hill file, AC.

97. Kali Gross's study of black women and crime in Philadelphia corroborates this conclusion; she argues that popular discourses about black female criminality emphasized their "brute strength, excessive violence, hypersexuality, and utter lack of remorse" (*Colored Amazons*, 115).

98. Wright, *Special Report*; Byrd, *Report of Special Inspector*; *Proceedings*, 138.

99. Mattie Black file, AC.

100. Sarah Mayes file, AC; Anna Hendley file, AC.

101. Prison Camp Hospital Weekly Registers 1892–96, RG 21-1-9, GAA.

102. Ibid., 1895 and 1897.

103. Mary Boy file, AC.

104. Sarah Dixon file, AC.

105. Prison Camp Hospital Weekly Registers 1890, RG 21-1-9, GAA; "Death Pardoned Her," *Atlanta Constitution*, July 19, 1890.

106. Bessie Robinson file, AC.

107. "A Female Convict Camp," *Atlanta Constitution*, February 19, 1890.

108. "Grand Jury Presentment," *Atlanta Constitution*, May 3, 1882.

109. Ibid.

110. Dr. R. L. Hope. "A Glimpse into the Life of Fulton County's Poor," *Atlanta Constitution*, January 6, 1895, 11.

111. Ibid.

112. Description of the brickmaking process can be found in Blackmon, *Slavery by Another Name*, 244.

113. "The County Almshouse," *Atlanta Constitution*, August 28, 1884.

114. Hope, "Glimpse into the Life."

115. "Farmer Brown Talks of the Farm," *Atlanta Constitution*, October 8, 1897.

116. Thomas H. Reed, "The Report Made by Thomas H. Reed on 'The Governments of Atlanta and Fulton County, Georgia. 1938," MSS 394, Box 2, Folder 34, AHC.

117. Description of Chastain Arts Center is from my observations during a visit there in August 2007.

118. Examples of white women being sent to jail rather than the almshouse or other convict camps can be found in the files of Emma Wilter, Pearl Ryans, Annie Rawlins, Mary Dido, and Grace Chambers. In other counties white women were also more likely to be sent to jail instead of convict camps. See clemency files of Lizzie Cowart, Jack Davis, Jane Hunter, and Vona Addis. AC.

119. Belle Russell file, AC.

120. Ibid.

121. Myrtle Blake file, AC.

122. "Pardon for a Woman," *Atlanta Constitution*, July 29, 1896.

123. Twelfth Census of the United States, Fulton County, Georgia, 1900.

124. "Grand Jury Presentments," *Atlanta Constitution*, June 25, 1904.

125. Narcissa Reynolds and Cornelia Rake files, AC.

126. Grosz, *Volatile Bodies*, 3.

127. Londa Schiebinger's analysis of late nineteenth-century Western medical understandings of gender reveals the linkages between the legal production of racialized gender categories and scientific thought. She argues that "by the nineteenth century medical men had convinced themselves of the reality of a universal woman. . . . But 'woman' was postulated as a universal only when referring, in fact, to middle-class European woman. . . . White women were considered the most delicate and subject to loss of life; mulatto women were subject to discomfort and suffered 'a thousand little complaints'; and black women, who labored in the fields were thought to breed at an astonishing rate and with remarkable ease." I argue that in the nineteenth and early twentieth centuries "woman" and its traits were also applicable to lower-class white women. See Schiebinger, *Nature's Body*, 183.

128. See Collins, *Black Feminist Thought*, especially chap. 4.

129. "Female Convict Camp."

130. "Women in Stripes," *Atlanta Constitution*, July 22, 1893.

131. Ibid.

132. Ibid.

133. Ibid.

134. AR 1898–99.

135. Ibid.

136. Ibid., 14.

137. AR 1898–99.

138. Lizzie Patterson was assigned to scrub and scour the station house instead of breaking rocks on the quarry immediately before her death in 1883. See "Patterson's Poison."

139. "A Woman in Chains," *Atlanta Constitution*, September 29, 1883.

140. "Stewart's Brigade," *Atlanta Constitution*, February 5, 1879.

141. Ibid.

142. Ibid.

143. "City Chain Gang," *Atlanta Constitution*, August 25, 1882.

144. "Police Points," *Atlanta Constitution*, January 9, 1879.

145. "The City Convicts," *Atlanta Constitution*, June 12, 1879.

146. For accounts of lynching and race riots see Williamson, *Crucible of Race*. He argues that lynching constituted white men's expression of frustration over the inability to achieve sexual liberation without guilt about raping black women or violating passive white femininity. See also Markovitz, *Legacies of Lynching*; McGovern, *Anatomy of a Lynching*; Brundage, *Under Sentence of Death*, and his *Lynching in the New South*; Hair, *Carnival of Fury*; Mixon, *Atlanta Riot*; Baurlein, *Negrophobia*; and Godshalk, *Veiled Visions*. Important studies of violence against black women include a canon of scholarship on Ida B. Wells. In addition to her role as a significant feminist and antiracist activist, her importance as a historical subject lies in her illumination of the relationship between black women's rape and lynching. See McMurry, *To Keep the Waters Troubled*; Schechter, *Ida B. Wells-Barnett*; Giddings, *Ida*; Davidson, *"They Say"*; Feimster, *Southern Horrors*; Bay, *To Tell the Truth Freely*. Other important work on black women, discipline, and gender violence includes Jacquelyn Dowd Hall, "The Mind That Burns in Each Body'"; Carby, "On the Threshold of Woman's Era"; Bakare-Yusuf, "Economy of Violence"; Spillers, "Mama's Baby, Papa's Maybe"; McGuire, "'It Was Like All of Us Had Been Raped'"; Hine, "Rape and the Inner Lives of Black Women"; Rosen, *Terror in the Heart of Freedom*; Gross, *Colored Amazons*; and Lee, *For Freedom's Sake*. On white women as more than symbolic foils for white violence and as instigators of violence or antilynching activists see Glenda Elizabeth Gilmore, *Gender and Jim Crow*; Jacquelyn Dowd Hall, *Revolt against Chivalry*; Blee, *Women of the Klan*; MacLean, *Behind the Mask of Chivalry*; Whites, *Civil War as a Crisis in Gender*; Laura F. Edwards, *Gendered Strife and Confusion*; and Sims, *Power of Femininity*.

147. I do not want to argue that the discourse of protection actually protected all white women from all forms of violence. As Crystal Feimster argues, white patriarchal discourses of protection sometimes served to mask white men's violence against white women. She also includes accounts of "disorderly" white

women being subjected to mob violence, including whipping, and cites an example from Calhoun, Georgia. As with the case of southern punishment, white women's exposure to such violence was rare compared with black women's. Between 1880 and 1930, twenty-six white women were lynched compared with 130 black women. See Feimster, *Southern Horrors*, chap. 6.

148. On race as a metalanguage see Higginbotham's important "African-American Women's History."

149. Bakare-Yusuf, "Economy of Violence," 316.

150. Hartman, *Scenes of Subjection*, 62.

151. Spillers, "Mama's Baby, Papa's Maybe," 68. Key theoretical works on the body include Foucault, *Discipline and Punish*, and his *History of Sexuality*; Judith Butler, *Bodies That Matter*; Grosz, *Volatile Bodies*; Schiebinger, *Nature's Body*; Sterling, *Sexing the Body*; and Scarry, *Body in Pain*.

152. Weheliye, "Pornotropes," 72.

153. Angela Y. Davis and Dent, "Prison as a Border," 1236.

154. Kaplan, *Reproducing Slavery*.

155. See Glenda Elizabeth Gilmore, *Gender and Jim Crow*, esp. chap. 3; Jacquelyn Dowd Hall, *Revolt against Chivalry*.

156. Kantrowitz, *Ben Tillman*, 105.

157. Ibid.

158. On the codification of white womanhood see chapter 4. Martha Hodes argues that during Reconstruction poor white women, especially those charged with interracial sex, were sometimes vilified in popular discourse and subject to violence; nevertheless white supremacist vigilantism continued to be carried out in the name of white female protection. By the 1880s, however, poor white women were incorporated into the discourse of moral purism. See Hodes, "Sexualization of Reconstruction Politics."

159. Higginbotham, "African-American Women's History."

160. On woman as other see Simone de Beauvoir's classic *The Second Sex* in which she classically argues, "Those époques that regard woman as the *Other* are those that refuse most bitterly to integrate her into society as a human being" (71). While de Beauvoir convincingly argues that woman's status as other relegated her to the outskirts of society as a human being, black women were "hyper-other," positioned in opposition to normative constructions of masculinity and femininity; this radical limitation of their recognizability within the human family rendered them subject to the violence described herein.

161. Higginbotham links black women's double labor burden to violence arguing, "They bore and nursed children and performed domestic duties—all on top of doing field work. Unlike slave men, slave women fell victim to rape precisely because of their gender. . . . Gender, so colored by race, remained from birth until death inextricably linked to one's personal identity and social status" ("African-American Women's History," 258).

162. On the hyperexpendability of convicts see reference to Matthew Mancini's argument in note 243 below.

163. Lichtenstein, "Twice the Work of Free Labor?," 159.

164. *Proceedings*, 130.

165. Ibid., 122, 130, 138, 144–45.

166. Rachel Crowder file, AC.

167. Punishment Report 1885.

168. Ibid.

169. Punishment Report 1886.

170. *Proceedings*, 130.

171. For one account of the whipping of male prisoners see David Charles Berry, "Free Labor He Found Unsatisfactory," 9.

172. Byrd, *Report of Special Inspector*, 23–24.

173. Ibid., 24.

174. *Proceedings*, 122.

175. Patricia Hill Collins and Alice Walker are among the black feminist scholars who have influentially analyzed the particular role of black women's bodies in pornographic representation. According to Walker, "where white women are depicted in pornography as 'objects,' black women are depicted as shit," "Coming Apart," 10. Walker's characterization of black women as dehumanized and rendered waste reflects the magnitude of violation that imprisoned black women endured as well as their relegation to the periphery of gendered constructs of humanity. The forced use of bathroom facilities alongside men was, in this instance, part of their gendered undoing and therefore fits within a long historiography of racial sexual representation and dehumanization. In this historical context, the pornographic structure of convict camp life did not merely render black women waste, although the cheapness of leasing convict laborers made them relatively disposable to camp authorities, and their nonnormative gender positioning signaled and reinforced this disposability. The pornographic organization of the camp signaled both disposability and advanced productivity. Convict leasing is exposed here as a structure of pornographic violence; yet this particular historical context of carceral terror does not necessarily evidence pornography's inherent violence. Mireille Miller Young's *A Taste for Brown Sugar* examines black women and pornography, providing a groundbreaking and dramatic reinterpretation of the porn industry, revealing how black women have manipulated historically entrenched stereotypes of racialized sexuality and contested sexualized labor exploitation over the course of its complex long twentieth-century history.

176. Spillers, *Black, White, and in Color*, 156, 164.

177. Press coverage of Eliza Randall from the *Atlanta Constitution* includes the following: "Court and Capital," February 3, 1888; "Found Guilty of Murder," December 23, 1887; "Her Neck Saved," February 2, 1888; "From Our Notebook," February 25, 1891; "Man and Murderess," June 2, 1891; "A Novel Suit," June 3, 1891; "He Was a Convict Guard," June 23, 1891." National coverage of Randall includes "A Woman's Death Sentence Commuted," *Washington Post*, February 23, 1888; and "Good Stories for All," *Boston Globe*, May 28, 1898.

178. Eliza Randall file, AC.

179. "Found Guilty of Murder." References to her sexual abuse appear in Eliza Randall file, AC.

180. "A Novel Suit."

181. Punishment Report 1892.

182. Prison Camp Hospital Weekly Registers 1893, RG 21-1-9, GAA.

183. "Good Stories for All."

184. Du Bois, *Some Notes on Negro Crime*, 4–5.

185. Anonymous, "The Life Story of a Negro Peon, Obtained from an Interview with a Georgia Negro," in Hamilton Holt, *Life Stories of Undistinguished Americans*, reprinted in Lerner, *Black Women in White America*, 153.

186. Ibid., 154.

187. Ibid.

188. For another important account of Crawford and black women's labor in Georgia convict camps see LeFlouria, "'Hand That Rocks the Cradle Cuts Cordwood.'"

189. *Atlanta Constitution*, August 19, 1903.

190. Drawing from Jennifer Morgan and Iris Marion Young, Janell Hobson argues that while normative femininity may imply weakness, even disability, strength in a woman construes abnormality, something attributed to sideshow circuits and black women. See Hobson, *Venus in the Dark*, 12.

191. "Only Woman Blacksmith in America Is a Convict," *Atlanta Constitution*, August 19, 1903. Emphasis added.

192. Halberstam, *Female Masculinity*, 1.

193. Kellor, *Experimental Sociology*, 106.

194. Ibid.

195. Carby, "Policing the Black Woman's Body in an Urban Context," 740.

196. On Kellor and cultural accounts of black criminality see Muhammad, *Condemnation of Blackness*.

197. Kellor, *Experimental Sociology*, 106.

198. Anne McClintock argues compellingly that agency cannot be reduced to context. This caution is well heeded. While it would certainly be wrong to reduce Crawford to "a victimized drudge, exhibited as the embodiment of female degradation and male dominance," it would also be a mistake to "confer" agency retrospectively in the context of extreme violence. See McClintock, *Imperial Leather*, 141.

199. "Only Woman Blacksmith."

200. Mamie De Cris file, AC; "Mamie De Cris, Diamond Queen, Whipped by Prison Officials," *Atlanta Constitution*, August 8, 1903.

201. "Mamie De Cris, Diamond Queen."

202. "Dr. I. H. Adams on Whipping of Woman," *Augusta Chronicle*, August 19, 1903.

203. "I Refused Warden's Advances, Told of Them, and He Lashed Me," *Atlanta Constitution*, August 12, 1903.

204. Ibid.

205. "Mamie De Cris, Diamond Queen."

206. "'Brutally Flogged, I Was Sent Staggering into the Fields,' Declares Miss Mamie De Cris," *Atlanta Constitution*, August 12, 1903.

207. "Prison Farm Management," *Atlanta Constitution*, August 16, 1903.

208. "Miss De Cris' Lashing to Be Probed," *Atlanta Constitution*, August 10, 1903.

209. "Moore after Details of De Cris Whipping," *Atlanta Constitution*, August 11, 1903; "Miss De Cris' Lashing to Be Probed"; "One Resigns," *Boston Daily Globe*, August 10, 1903.

210. "Moore after Details of De Cris Whipping."

211. "I Refused the Warden's Advances."

212. Mrs. John E. Donaldson, "Mrs. Donaldson Writes of Mamie DeCris' Case," *Atlanta Constitution*, August 12, 1903.

213. Mamie De Cris file, AC.

214. Hartman, "Venus in Two Acts," 10.

215. Anonymous, "Life Story of a Negro Peon," 153.

216. Prison Camp Hospital Weekly Registers 1888 and 1890, RG 21-1-9, GAA.

217. Du Bois, *Some Notes on Negro Crime*, 4–5.

218. Prison Camp Hospital Weekly Registers 1889, RG 21-1-9, GAA.

219. Susannah Gilbert file, AC.

220. Baptist, "'Cuffy,' 'Fancy Maids,' and 'One-Eyed Men,'" 15.

221. Pateman, "Women and Consent," 162.

222. Ibid.

223. McClintock, *Imperial Leather*, 15.

224. Ibid., 16. For a theoretical and historical view of black women's practices of dissemblance see Hine, "Rape and the Inner Lives of Black Women."

225. H. V. M. Miller, "Report of the Principal Physician to the Penitentiary," October 1890, in PK 1888–1890, 5.

226. Ibid.

227. Sharpe, *Monstrous Intimacies*, 38.

228. Feimster, *Southern Horrors*, 159. Feimster provides an extraordinary analysis of the significance of the lynching of black women who were perceived as cultural threats to the white supremacist social order based upon their widespread representation as gendered others as well as their resistance to relationships of domination in domestic labor and political contexts.

229. McKittrick, *Demonic Grounds*.

230. Morgan, *Laboring Women*, 7–8.

231. Rosen, *Terror in the Heart of Freedom*.

232. For a thorough historical analysis of debt peonage that continues to loom large see Daniel, *Shadow of Slavery*.

233. "The Georgia Prison Camp," *St. Louis Globe-Democrat*, August 19, 1887, 6.

234. Hartman, "Venus in Two Acts," 2.

235. Bernstein, *Racial Innocence*, 34.

236. Ibid., 34.

237. Roberts, *Killing the Black Body*, 5–6.

238. "I found that this rape of helpless Negro girls and women, which began in slavery days, still continued without let or hindrance, check or reproof from church, state or press until there had been created this race within a race—and all designated by the inclusive term of "'colored.'" (Wells, *Crusade for Justice*, 70).

239. On omission and proaction in the context of black subjectivity and rape law see Hartman, *Scenes of Subjection*.

240. Ibid., 87.

241. Angela Y. Davis, "Reflections on the Black Woman's Role," 123.

242. Of course constraints on prosecutions against white men for the rape of black women outside of the convict camp were also formidable. They included prohibitions on black testimony against white defendants and the threat of white supremacist terror facing black women who would have brought such charges. See Sommerville, *Rape and Race*.

243. Historians including Matthew Mancini have argued that a fundamental difference between slavery and convict leasing was the expendability of the convict laborer. Because convicts were valuable not as individuals, but as "aggregates," the death or release of an individual imprisoned man or woman did not represent a significant loss to a lessee. Mancini argues that this increased the economic incentive to abuse prisoners, or to work them to death or until they were incapacitated. See his *One Dies, Get Another*, esp. chap. 1.

244. Carby, *Reconstructing Womanhood*, 39.

245. Jacquelyn Dowd Hall, "The Mind That Burns in Each Body," 333.

246. Bessie Lockhart file, AC.

247. Ibid.

248. Ibid.

249. Ibid.

250. Amanda Hill file, AC.

251. "'Brutally Flogged, I Was Sent Staggering." The headlines of most of the articles about Mamie De Cris included first-person quotes about her ordeal, another reflection of the importance of her interior sentiments.

Chapter Three

1. "Address of Josephine St. P. Ruffin, President of the Conference," NACW Records, Reel 1.

2. Ibid.

3. Ibid.

4. Quoted in Schechter, *Ida B. Wells*, 115.

5. The following is a sampling of articles from the *Atlanta Constitution* that focus on black women's criminality and insanity during the period 1894–96: "Out on Bond," March 9, 1895; "A Female Highway Robber," April 2, 1894; A Hornet's Nest: Women Resist Officer Mercer and Bit His Arm," April 19, 1894; "A Sad Case," July 1, 1894; "In the Local Field: Minor Happenings of the Day in Court," April 26, 1895; "In the Local Field," July 14, 1895; "With Their Favorite Weapon: Three Negresses Hold a Woman and Kill Her with a Razor," November 27, 1895; "Fought the Officers: A Number of Negro Women Attack an Officer," November 30, 1895; "The Evidence of Crime," December 15, 1895; "'She Sold Cunjer Bags': A Negro Woman Arraigned before Justice Foute Yesterday," January 3, 1896; "Local News in Brief: Social, Criminal, Religious and Other Happenings," January

7, 1896; "Judge's Busy Day," January 9, 1896; "Found on the Tracks: Old Negro Woman Picked Up in Dangerous Place," March 14, 1896; "Crazier Than Carr: A Negro Woman Imagines She's a Horse and Eats Grass," May 20, 1896; "Women Playing with Guns: A Negress at Valdosta Accidentally Killed," July 3, 1896; "Rural Life in Georgia," August 4, 1896; "Child in the Penitentiary: Little Negro, Nine Years Old, Convicted of Murder," September 8, 1896; "Minor News Notes of a City Day," October 23, 1896; "Old Woman Steals Dresses: Negress Sixty-Four Years Old Locked in Station House on Serious Charges," December 12, 1896; "Stole Her Friend's Money," December 8, 1896; "Hattie Lay's Work: Remarkable Swindle of an Old Negress New in the Station House," December 14, 1896.

6. "Address of Josephine St. P. Ruffin."

7. For this important analysis see Shaw, "Black Club Women." Shaw argues that black women's voluntary organizations were part of a long history of independent, proactive community formation and consciousness building, rather than merely reactionary responses to racism. See also Shaw, *What a Woman Ought to Be and Do.*

8. See Spillers, "Mama's Baby, Papa's Maybe."

9. Ibid., 80.

10. Carby, "On the Threshold of Woman's Era," 265.

11. On what Evelyn Brooks Higginbotham has termed "the politics of respectability" and imbedded notions of racial pathology in uplift ideology, see her *Righteous Discontent* and Gaines, *Uplifting the Race.*

12. For debates on uplift ideology and the politics of respectability, see Carby, *Reconstructing Womanhood,* and her "Policing the Black Woman's Body"; Gaines, *Uplifting the Race*; Higginbotham, *Righteous Discontent*; Hunter, *To 'Joy My Freedom*; Mitchell, *Righteous Propagation*; Glenda Elizabeth Gilmore, *Gender and Jim Crow*; and Walcott, *Remaking Respectability.*

13. On the rift between Terrell and Wells, see McMurry, *To Keep the Waters Troubled,* 249–50; Schechter, *Ida B. Wells-Barnett,* 118; and Bay, *To Tell the Truth Freely,* 228–30.

14. Letter from Booker T. Washington to Hugh Mason Browne, August 21, 1908. In Harlan and Smock, *Booker T. Washington Papers,* 552–53.

15. Chautauqua Circle Meeting Agendas, 85th Anniversary Program, Chautauqua Circle Collection, Box 2, AUC.

16. Selena Sloan Butler, "Heredity," *Spelman Messenger,* June 1897, Microfilm, Robert Woodruff Library, Atlanta University Center.

17. "Minutes of the National Association of Colored Women Annual Convention 1896," NACW Records, Reel 1.

18. Ibid.

19. "Report of the Minutes of the Woman's Club of Atlanta for the Six Months Ending June 30, 1896," ibid.

20. "Yearly Report of the Woman's Club of Atlanta, 1896," ibid.

21. On the mammy trope, which represented black women as idealized maternalist figures toward white children and neglectful mothers to their own children, see Morton, *Disfigured Images*; White, *Ar'n't I a Woman?*; Collins, *Black*

Feminist Thought; and Wallace, *Black Macho*. For an analysis of the role of the home in black uplift programs see Mitchell, *Righteous Propagation*.

22. Selena Sloan Butler, *Chain-Gang System*. Although convict leasing would not be abolished and replaced systematically with public chain gang labor until 1906, during this period convict labor camps were commonly termed "chain gangs."

23. Ibid., 4.

24. Untitled, *Savannah Tribune*, May 6, 1905.

25. Ibid.

26. "Horrors of the Chain Gang," *Savannah Tribune*, October 23, 1897.

27. Ibid.

28. Spillers, "Mama's Baby, Papa's Maybe," 65.

29. Painter, *Southern History*, 131. Painter is building upon Susan Griffin's analysis of the pornographic; see her *Pornography and Silence*. For another compelling analysis of white supremacy's pornographic power see Jacquelyn Dowd Hall's analysis of rape as "folk pornography" in her *Revolt against Chivalry*, 150.

30. Painter, *Southern History*, 131.

31. Selena Sloan Butler, *Chain-Gang System*, 4.

32. Ibid., 4.

33. Ibid., 2.

34. "Annual Meeting Minutes 1896," NACW Records, Reel 1.

35. Ibid. On Frances Willard, Ida B. Wells, and the controversy over Willard's initial public sympathies about the threat of rape against white women, see Schechter, *Ida B. Wells-Barnett*, and Bederman, *Manliness and Civilization*.

36. "Annual Meeting Minutes 1896."

37. For an account of black women's convictions for moral crimes in city court, see chapter 1.

38. Henry R. Butler, "Our Need for a Reformatory," *Spelman Messenger*, May 1900, Microfilm, Robert Woodruff Library, Atlanta University Center.

39. Ibid.

40. Machlachlan, "Women's Work," 387.

41. First Quarter Bulletin, Georgia Local Committee on Interracial Cooperation, 1926, Butler Papers, Box 1, Folder 9.

42. *Spelman Messenger*, March 1905. Robert Woodruff Library, Atlanta University Center, Microfilm.

43. Marable and Mullings, *Let Nobody Turn Us Around*.

44. Gore, *Radicalism at the Crossroads*, 74. Gore's brilliant account of the significance of the Ingram case and the mass-based campaign that emerged in her defense provides valuable insight on the long historical significance of Georgia's gendered system of criminal punishment.

45. Mary Church Terrell, "First Presidential Address to the National Association of Colored Women, Nashville, Tennessee, 15 September 1897," Terrell Papers, Box 28, Reel 20.

46. Terrell describes researching the convict lease system for the first time in 1907 in her *Colored Woman*, 267.

47. Charles R. Douglass, "Comment," in Mary Church Terrell, *Progress of Colored Women: An Address Delivered before the National American Women's Suffrage Association at the Columbia Theater, Washington, D.C.* (Washington, D.C.: Smith Brothers, 1898), 4. Consulted in African American Pamphlet Collections, Rare Book and Special Collections Division, Library of Congress, Washington, D.C.

48. Mary Church Terrell, *Progress of Colored Women,* 13.

49. Mary Church Terrell, "Greetings from the National Association of Colored Women to the National Council of Women," 1900, Terrell Papers, Reel 21.

50. "Georgia's Convict Problem," *Washington Post,* June 22, 1897, 6.

51. PK 1897.

52. Labeling this logic as "circular" is intentional and not meant to dismiss it as empty or illegitimate since it was clearly compelling, reasonable, and rational for the purpose of maintaining white supremacy.

53. Mary Church Terrell, "Third Annual Address to the National Association of Colored Women," Buffalo, New York, 1901, Terrell Papers, Box 28, Reel 20.

54. Ibid.

55. Terrell, "Peonage in the United States," 310.

56. Terrell, *Colored Woman,* 207.

57. Ibid., 267.

58. Ibid., 317.

59. Terrell, "Peonage in the United States," 314.

60. Ibid.

61. Angela Y. Davis, "From the Prison of Slavery to the Slavery of Prison: Frederick Douglass and the Convict Lease System," 91.

62. Ibid.

63. Letter to Mary Church Terrell, September 17, 1907, and letter from Andrew B. Humphrey of the Republican Club, October 3, 1907, Terrell Papers, Box 4, Reel 4.

64. Letter from the secretary of the *Atlanta Independent* to Mary Church Terrell, December 3, 1907. Mary Church Terrell Papers.

65. "Lucy Laney Was Fined in Recorder's Court," *Atlanta Independent,* November 30, 1907.

66. Ibid.

67. Elizabeth Lindsey Davis, *Lifting as They Climb,* 26.

68. "Lucy Laney Was Fined in Recorder's Court."

69. Ibid.

70. Terrell, *Colored Woman,* 215.

71. Ibid.

72. Ibid., 207.

73. On Rebecca Latimer Felton's life and career see Felton, *My Memories of Georgia Politics,* and Talmadge, *Rebecca Latimer Felton.*

74. "Speeches, Sermons, Etc.," Felton Papers, Box 14.

75. Talmadge, *Rebecca Latimer Felton,* 98.

76. Felton, *Country Life in Georgia,* 120–21.

77. Felton describes the petition as the effort that "paved the way for the Reformatory movement, and started the rolling ball that eventually broke up the convict lease system." WCTU, *A Petition to the Honorable Senators and Members of the House of Representatives* (Atlanta, 1887), Felton Papers, Box 10.

78. SR 1905, 6; SR 1908–9, 10.

79. For more on the long history of Progressive Era prison reform see Freedman, *Their Sister's Keepers.*

80. Georgia WCTU Convention Minutes, 1890, Georgia WCTU Records, Series 5, Box 23.

81. Ibid.

82. Ibid.

83. Ibid.

84. "At the Convict Camp," *Atlanta Constitution*, June 15, 1891.

85. Georgia WCTU Convention Minutes, 1894 and 1903, Georgia WCTU Records, Series 5, Boxes 3 and 4.

86. "Credit for the Reformatory," *Atlanta Constitution*, February 12, 1900.

87. Whites, *Gender Matters.* For an important account of gender conflict, representation, and labor activism in urban Atlanta see Jacquelyn Dowd Hall, "Private Eyes, Public Women."

88. For a full analysis of Felton as women's rights activist see Whites, "Rebecca Latimer Felton" and her *Gender Matters*; and Feimster, *Southern Horrors.*

89. "Confronted by Woman's Edition Reporters, Police Chief Beavers Breaks Long Silence," *Atlanta Constitution* (Special Women's Edition), June 4, 1913.

90. Ibid.

91. Glenda Elizabeth Gilmore, "'Melting Time,'" 153.

92. Here I am drawing from Saidiya Hartman's analysis of the problematics of redressing the pained body in her *Scenes of Subjection.*

93. "Confronted by Woman's Edition Reporters," Georgia Federation of Women's Clubs, GAA.

94. National Prison Association of the United States, *Report of the Proceeding*, 1886, 311.

95. Ibid., 312.

96. Ibid.

97. Ibid.

98. Rebecca Latimer Felton, Notes from Convict Leasing Speech, Felton Papers, Box 10.

99. Ibid.

100. Ibid.

101. Whites, *Gender Matters*, 188.

102. Felton, *Country Life in Georgia*, 79.

103. Rebecca Latimer Felton, Untitled Speech, Felton Papers, Box 10.

104. Whites, *Gender Matters*, 187.

105. Jacquelyn Dowd Hall, "'Mind That Burns in Each Body,'" 333.

106. Rebecca Latimer Felton, "The Convict System of Georgia," *Forum* 2 (1887), 484.

107. Ibid, 484.

108. Felton, Untitled Speech.

109. Ibid.

110. Hartman, *Scenes of Subjection*, 97.

111. WCTU, *Petition to the Honorable Senators*.

112. Rebecca Latimer Felton, "The Problems That Interest Motherhood: Read before the Georgia Sociological Society, Atlanta, June 1902," in her *Country Life in Georgia*, 281–82.

113. Ibid.

114. Ibid.

115. "Lynch 1,000 Weekly, Declares Mrs. Felton," *Atlanta Constitution*, Felton Papers, undated, Series 4, Box 21.

116. Ibid.

117. On black women as threats to the urban social landscape, see Hunter, *To 'Joy My Freedom*; Carby, "Policing the Black Woman's Body" and "Sexual Politics of Women's Blues"; and Gross, *Colored Amazons*.

118. Feimster, *Southern Horrors*, chap. 5.

119. On Felton's campaign to change the age of legal consent see Feimster, *Southern Horrors*.

120. Georgia WCTU Convention Minutes, 1906, 1908, and 1909, Georgia WCTU Records, Series 2, Box 9. Emphasis in original

Chapter Four

1. Selena Sloan Butler, *Chain-Gang System*, 2.

2. Hattie Johnson to Wiley Williams, November 2, 1912, Johnson file, AC.

3. Hartman, *Scenes of Subjection*, 101; Cheryl Hicks thoroughly analyzes African American women's ideas about morality and respectability in her *Talk with You Like a Woman*.

4. On the inadequacies of reforms that do not seek to eliminate or reduce prisons and policing regimes see Angela Y. Davis, *Abolition Democracy*.

5. Georgia State Assembly, "Employment of Convicts; System of Penology Act," September 19, 1908, Georgia Legislative Documents, GALILEO Digital Initiative Database, http://neptune3.galib.uga.edu/ssp/cgi-bin/legis-idx.pl?sessionid =7f000001&type=law&byte=104256260 (hereafter "Employment of Convicts"). Emphasis added.

6. Aggregate number of women imprisoned on misdemeanor chain gangs is derived from the following record collections: AC and GAA.

7. Georgia State Assembly, "An Act to Create a System of Parole or Conditional Pardons of Prisoners Convicted of Crime and for Other Purposes," September 9, 1908, Georgia Legislative Documents, GALILEO Digital Initiative Database, http://neptune3.galib.uga.edu/ssp/cgi-bin/legis-idx.pl?sessionid=7f000001 &type=law&byte=104249401 (hereafter "Act to Create a System of Parole").

8. In this historical instance parole did not entail release, but instead constituted a gendered regime of carceral servitude in which black women were

exclusively subject to domestic captivity and cultural and social policing. This institution may have historical relevance for analyses of late twentieth- and early twenty-first-century regimes of "gender responsive" imprisonment. Although it is important to note that these regimes emerged in quite different political and economic contexts, both sustain(ed) and expand(ed) broader prison systems and subject(ed) women of color to structures of violence, dislocation, capitalist exploitation, and familial estrangement. For important abolitionist critiques of the late twentieth-century gender responsive prison movement, see Braz, "Kinder, Gentler, Gender Responsive Cages," and Shaylor, "Neither Kind Nor Gentle."

9. Angela Y. Davis "Reflections on the Black Woman's Role," 116.

10. Daina Ramey Berry, *"Swing the Sickle for the Harvest Is Ripe,"* 16.

11. Ibid., 17.

12. Glenn, *Forced to Care*, 36.

13. Kathleen M. Brown, *Good Wives, Nasty Wenches*, 108.

14. "Employment of Convicts."

15. Spillers, "Mama's Baby, Papa's Maybe," 80, and her "Interstices," 78.

16. My thinking on race and gender as mutually constitutive is indebted to black feminist elucidations of the inextricability of these categories in the production of human legibility. In addition to the numerous works referenced throughout the book, several analyses that have informed my thinking in this area include White, *Ar'n't I a Woman?*; Carby, *Reconstructing Womanhood*; Hammonds, "Black (W)holes"; Higginbotham, "African-American Women's History"; Valerie Smith, *Not Just Race, Not Just Gender*; Cohen, "Deviance as Resistance"; Morgan, *Laboring Women*; McKittrick, *Demonic Grounds*; and Painter, *Southern History*.

17. Lichtenstein, *Twice the Work of Free Labor*, 177.

18. Jones, *Labor of Love, Labor of Sorrow*, 303.

19. Rodriguez, *Forced Passages*, 41.

20. See Hunter, *To 'Joy My Freedom*; Hickey, *Hope and Danger in the New South City*; and Machlachlan, "Women's Work."

21. Jacquelyn Dowd Hall, "O. Delight Smith's Progressive Era," 173.

22. Hickey, *Hope and Danger in the New South City*, 29.

23. Jacquelyn Dowd Hall, "O. Delight Smith's Progressive Era," 178.

24. Ibid., 180.

25. Hickey, *Hope and Danger in the New South City*, 39.

26. Ibid.

27. Pateman, *Sexual Contract*, 131.

28. Hunter, *To 'Joy My Freedom*, 110.

29. Ibid., 228.

30. Hickey, *Hope and Danger in the New South City*, 18.

31. Hunter, *To 'Joy My Freedom*, 218.

32. Bederman, *Manliness and Civilization*.

33. Dittmer, *Black Georgia*, 17.

34. Ibid., 20. For an analysis of the relationship between the development of segregation and antiblack violence, see also Mixon, *Atlanta Riot*.

35. Arnesen, "'Like Banquo's Ghost, It Will Not Down,'" 1630.

36. Ibid., 1631.

37. Glenda Elizabeth Gilmore, *Gender and Jim Crow*, 3.

38. Godshalk, *Veiled Visions*, 38; Dittmer, *Black Georgia*, 130.

39. On the Atlanta race riot see also Godshalk, *Veiled Visions*; Mixon, *Atlanta Riot*; Baurlain, *Negrophobia*.

40. As part of the history of racialized and gendered violence in the early twentieth century, it is important to note that the 1920s marked the growth of the second Ku Klux Klan, "the most powerful movement of the far right that America has yet produced," which was centrally concerned with white women's chastity and the protection of the home. See MacLean, *Behind the Mask of Chivalry*, xi.

41. Godshalk, *Veiled Visions*, 55.

42. AR 1905–6, p. 8.

43. AR 1905–6, p. 23.

44. Although the chain gang system was not instituted until 1908, convict lease camps were sometimes called chain gangs during the era of the convict lease system.

45. AR 1907–8, p. 10.

46. "Employment of Convicts."

47. Letter from Franklin to Turner, October 7, 1908, and letter from Turner to Franklin, October 8, 1908, Vona Addis file, AC.

48. Letter to Governor Hoke Smith from W. A. Charters, November 11, 1908, Jane Hunter file, AC.

49. Petition, October 24, 1908, Vona Addis file, AC.

50. Commutation Order, November 6, 1908, ibid.

51. "Shackling of Woman Argued Before Court," *Augusta Chronicle*, March 30, 1909.

52. Letter from Alderman Young to Prison Commission, April 7, 1910, Kate O'Dwyer file, AC.

53. Letter from S. J. Tribble to Prison Commission, April 9, 1910, ibid.

54. Ibid.

55. Commutation Order, January 2, 1911, Maude Davis file, AC.

56. "Dr. Broughton Discusses the Story of Maud Davis," *Atlanta Constitution*, February 27, 1911.

57. Prison Commissioner R. E. Davison, Commutation Order, January 2, 1911, ibid.

58. On black women as perceived agents of disease, see Hunter, *To 'Joy My Freedom*.

59. Table of incarceration by race and gender in AR 1936.

60. Carby, *Reconstructing Womanhood*, 739–40.

61. On black women's "deportation" to the South, see Hicks, *Talk with You Like a Woman*. In addition to Hicks and Carby, important analyses of black women and criminalization in the turn-of-the-century urban North include Gross, *Colored Amazons*; Blair, *I've Got to Make My Livin'*; and Muhammad, *Condemnation of Blackness*. Invaluable analyses of race, gender, and migration to the urban North

include Farah Jasmine Griffin, *Who Set You Flowin'?*, and Blair, *I've Got to Make My Livin'*.

62. "Dr. Broughton Discusses the Story of Maud Davis," *Atlanta Constitution*, February 27, 1911.

63. Prison Commissioner R. E. Davison, Clemency Recommendation, January 2, 1911, Maude Davis file, AC.

64. Margaret Harris file, AC.

65. Ibid.

66. Judith Butler, *Gender Trouble*, 2.

67. Lichtenstein, "Good Roads and Chain Gangs," 86.

68. Dorsey, *To Build Our Lives Together*, 150.

69. Godshalk, *Veiled Visions*, 13.

70. Feimster, *Southern Horrors*, 164.

71. Dittmer, *Black Georgia*, 111.

72. Lucy Jackson, Stella Kemp, and Lizzie McConnell files, AC.

73. Trial transcript, n.d., Minnie Smith file, AC.

74. Ibid.

75. Lichtenstein, "Good Roads and Chain Gangs," 93.

76. Ibid.

77. Henderson, *Politics of Change in Georgia*, 67–69.

78. Punishment Reports 1901–9.

79. Dittmer, *Black Georgia*, 88.

80. Ibid.

81. Annie Tucker file, AC.

82. "Probe Committee to Urge Reforms at State Prison," *Atlanta Constitution*, June 30, 1915; "Prison Farm Conditions 'Absolutely Disgraceful' Declares Health Board," *Atlanta Constitution*, July 8, 1915.

83. "How Georgia Cares for Boys, Helpless Convicts, and Female Prisoners," *Atlanta Constitution*, June 25, 1911.

84. AR 1917, 3.

85. Ibid.

86. Helen Drew file, AC.

87. Ibid.

88. AR 1910.

89. "Act to Create a System of Parole."

90. Ibid.

91. Ibid.

92. Mary Moore file, AC. A combination of factors led to the racially exclusive domestic parole system. White women were less likely to be arrested and convicted of felony charges that would have resulted in parole-eligible sentences. They were sometimes paroled to families, and they were sometimes given pardons or commutations instead of parole. Only sixteen white women who submitted clemency applications after 1909 were imprisoned for felony charges, and were therefore eligible for parole. Of those, ten were granted parole, and of those, four were paroled to family; the remaining six were granted pardons or commutations. By

contrast, 86 of the 129 black women who submitted parole-eligible clemency applications were paroled to employers. AC.

93. Georgia Prison Commission, Parole Affidavit, Rosa Lee McLendon file, AC.

94. Mattie Jane Price file, AC.

95. Georgia Prison Commission, Parole Affidavit, Rosa Lee McLendon file, AC.

96. See clemency files of Queen Kelly, Eula Williams, Susan Drayton, Anna Darcy, Martha Harris. AC.

97. The different labor expectations for white women and black women at Milledgeville were described in chapter 2.

98. Hunter, *To 'Joy My Freedom*, esp. chap. 10.

99. On the emergence of disciplinary institutions targeting black women migrants in the urban North see Carby, "Policing the Black Woman's Body," and Mumford, *Interzones*. On Progressive Era reform focused on white women, wayward girls, and urban amusements see introduction, note 40.

100. Hunter, *To 'Joy My Freedom*.

101. W. B. Bennett to Prison Commission, January 7, 1926, Florida Grimes file, AC.

102. Sallie Washington file, AC.

103. Parole Transfer Petition, undated, Carrie Scott file, AC.

104. Ibid.

105. Marion Felts to Hon. R. E. Davison, August 25, 1921, Carrie Scott file, AC.

106. J. E. Holliman to Prison Commission, August 25, 1921, Carrie Scott file, AC.

107. Marion Felts to H.G. Bell of the Prison Commission, August 29, 1921, Carrie Scott file, AC.

108. Parole Affidavit, April 16, 1925, Rosa Lee McLendon file, AC.

109. Prison Commission's Clerk to Mattie Jane Price, April 24, 1925, Mattie Jane Price, AC.

110. Jones, *Labor of Love, Labor of Sorrow*, 127.

111. On plantation mistresses as domestic managers see Glymph, *Out of the House of Bondage*.

112. Elsa Barkley Brown, "'What Has Happened Here.'"

113. See clemency files of Martha Harris, Eula Williams, Annie Darcy, and Mary Scott. AC.

114. Queen Kelly file, AC.

115. Mosley to Prison Commission, ibid.

116. Bertha Simmons file, AC.

117. Emma Wimms file, AC.

118. Ibid.

119. Ibid.

120. Letter from Clerk of Court, September 9, 1923, Emma Wimms file, AC.

121. Barnes to Prison Commission, October 31, 1922, ibid.

122. Ibid.

123. Hartman, *Scenes of Subjection*, 115, see also chap. 5.

124. Barnes to Prison Commission, February 4, 1925, Eliza Martin file, AC.

125. Julia Anderson to Prison Commission, Septmber 1, 1911, Julia Anderson file, AC.

126. Letters from Julia Anderson to Prison Commission, August 1911 to June 1912, Julia Anderson file, AC.

127. Glymph, *Out of the House of Bondage*, 37.

128. Mrs. J. L. Archer to Prison Commission, May 1, 1923, Mattie Reid file, AC.

129. Ibid. Emphasis in original.

130. Mattie Reid to Prison Commission, May 4, 1923, Mattie Reid file, AC.

131. Mrs. E. A. Barker to Prison Commission, May 4, 1923, ibid.

132. Mrs. Smith to Mr. Simmons, April 19, 1925, Mattie Jane Price file, AC.

133. On the mammy as a "controlling image" and myth see Patricia Hill Collins, *Black Feminist Thought*, chapter 4, and Morton, *Disfigured Images*.

134. Mrs. Smith to Prison Commission, April 19, 1925, Mattie Jane Price file, AC.

135. Ibid.

136. See Hunter, *To 'Joy My Freedom*, 78.

137. T. A. McCord to Prison Commission, May 10, 1925, Isabelle Elders file, AC.

138. Eliza Martin to Prison Commission, November 5, 1925, Eliza Martin file, AC.

139. Sylla Stinson to Prison Commission, January 27, 1925, Sylla Stinson file, AC. Emphasis added.

140. On the "long and drawn out" manumission process see Campbell, "How Free Is Free?," 149.

141. Emma Wimms to Prison Commission, date illegible, Emma Wimms file, AC. On black women and the politics of respectability see Higginbotham, *Righteous Discontent*. For more on working-class and imprisoned black women's struggles to be seen as respectable in the urban North see Hicks, *Talk with You Like a Woman*.

142. Williams, *Alchemy of Race and Rights*, 8.

143. Cheryl I. Harris, "Whiteness as Property," 1730.

144. Ibid.

145. Ibid., 1736.

146. Ibid.

147. Hine, "Rape and the Inner Lives of Black Women"; McGuire, *At the Dark End of the Street*.

148. Hunter, *To 'Joy My Freedom*, especially chapter 10.

149. I use the term "gender-nonconforming" deliberately, to suggest that the black female body was subject to forced "queering" by state regimes of violence and exploitative capitalist labor demands.

150. Federici, *Caliban and the Witch*, 115.

151. Spillers, "Mama's Baby, Papa's Maybe," 67.

152. Statistics drawn from all clemency files for women during the period 1909–36. AC.

153. Ella Pride file, AC.

154. Here, as in previous examples from black women's experiences of punishment in this account, we see an example of the convict labor system's accordance with Ruth Wilson Gilmore's specific definition of racism: "the state-sanctioned or extralegal production and exploitation of group-differentiated vulnerability to premature death." See Ruth Wilson Gilmore, *Golden Gulag*, 28.

155. Ibid.

156. Charlotte Walker file, AC.

157. Dora Holly file, AC.

158. Ibid.

159. Feminist legal theorists who have discussed male standards of reasonableness and legal structures of resistance to women's rape claims include Estrich, *Real Rape*; and MacKinnon, "Rape."

160. Carrie Scott file, AC.

161. Ibid.

162. Ibid. Emphasis added.

163. Victoria Clowden file, AC.

164. Lena Bell Warren file, AC.

Chapter Five

Quoted lyrics for Rainey and Smith songs draw from Angela Y. Davis, *Blues Legacies and Black Feminism: Gertrude "Ma" Rainey, Bessie Smith, and Billie Holiday.*

1. Residence listed in Fourteenth Census of the United States, 1920. Neighborhood description from information contained in Sanborn Map Company, "Insurance Maps of Albany Including Putney, Dougherty County, Georgia, April 1920 Sheet 29."

2. Address and profession reported in Fourteenth Census of the United States, 1920.

3. Ibid.

4. Carrie Williams et al. file, AC. Mrs. Wooten's address as well as family profession data reported in Fourteenth Census of the United States, 1920. Legal records list the girls under varying names including Gladis Trumbick/Gladys Tomlin and Carrie Williams/Theresa Williams. Neighborhood description from information contained in Sanborn Map Company, "Insurance Maps of Albany Including Putney, Dougherty County, Georgia, April 1920 Sheet 6."

5. Affidavit of Clayton Jones, Albany City Court Judge, March 12, 1919, Carrie Williams et al. file, AC.

6. Ibid.

7. Petition for Pardon, undated, ibid.

8. I borrow this phrase from Deborah Gray White's groundbreaking history of black women's organizing, *Too Heavy a Load*. Stella Wooten's occupation listed in Fourteenth Census of the United States, 1920.

9. Fred Moten, *Hughson's Tavern*, 57–58.

10. Snorton, *Nobody Is Supposed to Know*, 16.

11. Kelley, "'Slangin' Rocks . . . Palestinian Style.'"

12. Hartman, *Scenes of Subjection*, 125.

13. Angela Y. Davis, "The Meaning of Emancipation According to Black Women." Davis provides an analysis of the range of economic conscriptions—convict leasing, peonage, domestic service—as well as the prevalence of rape that pervaded black women's lives, making freedom exceedingly remote.

14. By this I mean to account for a rupture of relations of power that are structured through the mutual constitution of race and gender, a relation that fundamentally alters the character and experience of violence and exclusion. See Crenshaw, "Mapping the Margins."

15. Affidavit of W. J. Pinson, Superintendent of Dougherty County Convict Camp, March 19, 1919, Carrie Williams et al. file, AC.

16. Sara Ahmed, "Killing Joy," 573.

17. Petition for Clemency, undated, Williams et al. clemency file, AC.

18. Robinson, *Black Marxism*, 73.

19. Spillers, "Mama's Baby, Papa's Maybe," 67.

20. "sabotage, n." OED Online. September 2015. Oxford University Press. www.oed.com/view/Entry/169373?rskey=HfMphh&result=2&isAdvanced=false.

21. Ibid. Oxford English Dictionary entry for "sabotage" (1918) cites Edward Samuel Farrow, *A Dictionary of Military Terms*, for this definition.

22. Mike Davis, "Stop Watch and the Wooden Shoe," 83.

23. Ibid., 85.

24. Hill, *Men, Mobs, and Law*, 151.

25. Baxandall, "Elizabeth Gurley Flynn," 98.

26. Angela Y. Davis, *Women, Race, and Class*, 165.

27. Referring to black feminism or black feminist epistemologies is not meant to impose a label or identity upon historical actors that they would not have used, but instead it is intended to situate practices, ideas, and cultural expressions within a broader framework and historical tradition of challenges to legal doctrine, gender regulation and normativity, and structures of harm.

28. Kelley, *Freedom Dreams*, 4–5.

29. Kelley, *Race Rebels*, 9.

30. Du Bois, *Black Reconstruction*; Davis, *Abolition Democracy*; Glymph, "Du Bois's *Black Reconstruction*."

31. "Women in Stripes," *Atlanta Constitution*, August 6, 1893, 8.

32. Ibid.

33. PK 1888–1897; AR 1897–1936.

34. Pearl Williams file, AC.

35. "Women in Stripes," 4.

36. Central Register of Convicts, 1866–79, RG 21-3-27, GAA.

37. L. M. Roberts trial testimony, Rachel Crowder file, AC.

38. Sam Frederick, trial testimony, Rachel Crowder file, AC.

39. "Five Women Escape," *Atlanta Constitution*, July 18, 1893, 7.

40. "Women in Stripes," 4.

41. "Five Women Escape," 7.

42. The widespread punishment for sodomy was fifteen lashes; however, it was almost as common for imprisoned men to be whipped twenty-five times. Punishment Reports, E. H. Jackson's Camp, 1906–8.

43. On prison sexual culture and shifting ideas about sex in prison, see Kunzel, *Criminal Intimacy*.

44. Punishment Reports, Chattahoochee Camp, 1886.

45. James C. Scott, *Weapons of the Weak*, 29.

46. Camp, *Closer to Freedom*, 2.

47. Punishment Reports of individual camps, 1886.

48. Punishment Reports of individual camps, 1885–1908.

49. Hartman, *Scenes of Subjection*, 50.

50. Punishment Reports of individual camps, 1885–1908.

51. Statistic drawn from review of all applications for clemency submitted by women from 1900–1943, AC. The percentage of white women who submitted letters was considerably higher, at 22 percent.

52. Margo, *Race and Schooling in the South*, 7–8. Margo demonstrates that black literacy rates varied by age and gender. By 1910 nearly 70 percent of southern black men between the ages of 15 and 24 were literate, compared with approximately 80 percent of black women in the same age range. In the 25–34 age group, the rate for black men in the South remained at about 70 percent, while the literacy rate for black women was almost 10 percent lower.

53. State of Georgia Executive Department Letter to R. H. Lewis, December 7, 1918, Lena Bell Warren file, AC.

54. Lena Bell Warren to R. H. Lewis, February 24, 1919, Lena Bell Warren file, AC.

55. Ibid.

56. Lena Bell Warren to R. H. Lewis, August 24, 1919, Lena Bell Warren file, AC.

57. Ibid.

58. Ibid.

59. Lena Bell Warren to R. H. Lewis, March 27, 1921, Lena Bell Warren file, AC.

60. Commutation order, Lena Bell Warren file, AC.

61. Lethia Higdon file, AC.

62. The clemency files of Mattie Randall, Kate Malone, Martha Thomas, Addie Mae Paschal, Mabel Lemon, Annie Lane, Lethia Higdon, and Leila Everett all contain references to the average Negro intellect or character. AC.

63. Emma Wimms file, AC. Capitalization in original.

64. Ella Gamble file, AC.

65. Ibid.

66. Letter from Janie Mays to Mr. Hertwig, January 18, 1909. Janie Mays file, AC.

67. Punishment Reports, Chattahoochee Camp, 1885 and 1889.

68. For an explanation of offstage/onstage politics and hidden transcripts, see James C. Scott, *Domination and the Arts of Resistance*; and Kelley, *Race Rebels*.

69. Letter from Jos. Vernes, March 1, 1909, Janie Mays file, AC.

70. Janie Mays to H. Hertwig, January 18, 1909, ibid.

71. Letter from Jos. Vernes, March 1, 1909, ibid.

72. Punishment Reports, Old Town Camp, 1885 and 1886.

73. Amanda Hill to S. E. Massengale, Amanda Hill file, AC. Hill refers to him as Mason (not Massengale).

74. Ibid.

75. Hartman, *Scenes of Subjection*, 126.

76. Ibid.

77. Hine, "Rape and the Inner Lives of Black Women," 41.

78. Stepto, *From Behind the Veil*, 5.

79. On writings by imprisoned women and men as neoslave narratives see Rodriguez, *Forced Passages*, and James, *New Abolitionists*. I do not intend to read these clemency letters through the criteria applied by Rodriguez or James, however, since, as Rodriguez argues, contemporary writings by prisoners reflect a subversion of slave narrative formulas: "Imprisoned radical intellectuals, writers, and activists frequently dislodge the structure of the neoslave narrative, speaking into an iconic void in which their names, bodies, and biographies lack popular recognition" (208).

80. Stepto, *From Behind the Veil*, 3. Emphasis in original.

81. Erica Edwards, *Charisma*, 7.

82. Kelley, *Race Rebels*, 13.

83. Jayna Brown, *Babylon Girls*, 15.

84. "Sing Sing Prison Blues," on Bessie Smith, *Bessie Smith* Vol. 2.

85. Angela Y. Davis, *Blues Legacies*, 24.

86. Foucault, "Proper Use of Criminals," 433.

87. Foucault, "About the Concept," 177.

88. "Sing Sing Prison Blues," on Bessie Smith, *Bessie Smith* Vol. 2.

89. Ibid.

90. Daphne Brooks, *Bodies in Dissent*, 162.

91. Michelle R. Scott, *Blues Empress in Black Chattanooga*, 2.

92. Ibid., 135.

93. Ibid.; Herzhaft, *Encyclopedia of the Blues*.

94. On Dylan see Bogdanov, Woodstra, and Erlewine, *All Music Guide*, 522; and Herzhaft, *Encyclopedia of the Blues*, 195. On Spivey's broad influence see Daphne Duval Harrison, *Black Pearls*, 20.

95. On Lomax's recording of women at Parchman in 1936, see liner notes to *Jailhouse Blues*. Lyrics and liner notes from *Jailhouse Blues* reprinted with permission from #1316, Rosetta Reitz Papers, 1929–2008, DRRBML.

96. Oshinsky, *Worse Than Slavery*, 176.

97. Liner notes to *Jailhouse Blues*, DRRBML.

98. Ibid.

99. Clyde Woods, *Development Arrested*, 29–30.

100. Georgia Department of Public Welfare, "Crime and the Georgia Courts: A Statistical Analysis," 1924, AHC; AR 1928.

101. "Booze and Blues," on Ma Rainey, *Ma Rainey*, Vol. 2.

102. Stella Kemp file, AC.

103. Address and occupation reported in Fifteenth Census of the United States, 1930.

104. On the city as a multidimensional sphere of both pleasure and patriarchal exploitation for women at the turn of the century see Meyerowitz, *Women Adrift*; Peiss, *Cheap Amusements*; Ewen, *Immigrant Women*; and Odem, *Delinquent Daughters*.

105. Birtha Riley, Untitled Song, DCC. Spelling in original.

106. "Woman's Trouble Blues," on Bessie Smith, *Bessie Smith*, Vol. 2.

107. Ibid.

108. Edward Brooks, *Bessie Smith Companion*, 199.

109. On black women's blues and migration see Carby, *Cultures in Babylon*; and Farah Jasmine Griffin, *Who Set You Flowin'?*

110. Perry, "Cultural Studies," 920.

111. "Jail-House Blues" on Bessie Smith, *Bessie Smith*, Vol. 1.

112. On Toni Morrison and rememory see Caroline Rody, "Toni Morrison's *Beloved*."

113. "Mr. Dooley, Don 'Rest Me," on *Jailhouse Blues*, DRRBML.

114. "No Mo Freedom," on *Jailhouse Blues*, DRRBML.

115. Ibid.

116. "No Mo Freedom," on *Jailhouse Blues*, DRRBML.

117. Angela P. Harris, "Race and Essentialism," 583.

118. Williams, *Alchemy of Race and Rights*, 3.

119. Ibid., 8.

120. Caleb Smith, *The Prison and the American Imagination*, 167.

121. "Penitentiary Blues," on *Jailhouse Blues*, DRRBML.

122. "Big Man from Macamere," on ibid.

123. "Go Way Devil, Leave Me Alone," on ibid.

124. Birtha Riley, Untitled Song, DCC. Spelling in original. "Roal" here presumably means work.

125. "Chain Gang Blues," on Ma Rainey, *Ma Rainey*, Vol. 3.

126. Transcribed from the recording of "Georgia Stockade Blues" on Martin, *Sara Martin Volume 3*.

127. "Penitentiary Blues," on *Jailhouse Blues*, DRRBML.

128. Alma Hicks, "Long Line," DCC.

129. For a powerful analysis of Spillers's theorization of flesh and liberation see Crawley, "Stayed/Freedom/Hallelujah," in which he argues powerfully, "Black flesh knows this truth, the truth about the necessity of *otherwise* possibilities."

130. Transcribed from the recording of "Go Way Devil, Leave Me Alone," on *Jailhouse Blues*, DRRBML.

131. Anonymous, "Homesick Blue," DCC, Spelling in original.

132. Wynter, "Beyond Miranda's Meanings," 480.

133. McKittrick, *Demonic Grounds*, xxvi.

134. Walter Jackson (Tangle Eye) and unidentified singers, "Rosie (V)." Mississippi Prison Recordings, Parchman 1947, 2/48, T797.0, Track 3.

135. "Five Women Escape," 7.

136. See Jayna Brown's important discussion of "Cabaret" in her *Babylon Girls*, 235.

137. "Blood Hound Blues," on Spivey, *Victoria Spivey Volume 3*.

138. Ibid.

139. Ibid.

140. Ibid.

141. Ibid.

142. "Dangerous Blues," on *Jailhouse Blues*, DRRBML.

143. Ibid.

144. Ibid.

145. Birtha Riley, "Peas and Bread," DCC. Spelling in original.

146. On haunting as sociological phenomenon see Gordon, *Ghostly Matters*.

147. "Susie Gal," on *Jailhouse Blues*, DRRBML.

148. Lewis Jenkins's Works Progress Administration (WPA) narrative printed in Baker and Baker, *WPA Oklahoma Slave Narratives*, 222.

149. Information about the recording process is from the liner notes of *Jailhouse Blues*.

150. Oshinsky, *Worse Than Slavery*.

151. "Ricketiest Superintendent," on *Jailhouse Blues*, DRRBML.

152. Weick, "History of Rickets in the United States."

153. This represents a gendered vision of abolition democracy; see Angela Y. Davis, *Abolition Democracy*.

154. Moten, *In the Break*, 85.

155. "Anybody Here Wants to Buy Some Cabbage?" on *Jailhouse Blues*, DRRBML.

156. "Where Have You Been John Billy?" on *Jailhouse Blues*, DRRBML. Pone bread refers to corn or flour bread/biscuits cooked in a skillet.

157. Ibid.

158. "How'm I Doin It" on *Jailhouse Blues*, DRRBML.

159. "I Gotta Man in New Orleans" on *Jailhouse Blues*, DRRBML.

160. "How'm I Doin?" on *Shakin' the Africann*.

161. Wade, *Beautiful Music*, 155.

162. Ibid., 169.

163. Ibid., 177.

164. Ibid., 170.

165. Ibid., 176.

166. Ibid., 176; Courlander, *Negro Folk Music*, 108.

167. Jayna Brown, *Babylon Girls*, 60.

168. "Mistreatin' Daddy," on Bessie Smith, *Bessie Smith* Vol. 1.

169. M. B. Barnes, "Ham Bone Boiled," DCC. Spelling in original.

170. Clyde Woods, *Development Arrested*, 18. On the significance of naming as a long-standing black tradition of social protest, see Angela Y. Davis, *Blues Legacies*, chap. 4.

171. For groundbreaking insights on racial and sexual knowledge, queer politics, and criminalization, see Cathy Cohen, "Deviance as Resistance" and Regina Kunzel, *Criminal Intimacy*.

172. Ruth Wilson Gilmore, "Fatal Couplings," 16.

173. Carby, "Sexual Politics of Women's Blues," 13.

174. Redmond, *Anthem*, 1.

175. "Woman's Building at the Georgia State Farm Burns," *Atlanta Constitution*, December 8, 1900, 2.

176. Ibid.

177. "Female Convicts Confess Arson," *Atlanta Constitution*, January 17, 1901, 3.

178. On Allagood's harassment and possible rape of imprisoned women see the story of Mamie De Cris in chapter 2.

179. AR 1901.

180. "Female Firebugs Now on Trial," *Atlanta Constitution*, January 19, 1901, 3.

181. "Charge of Arson Wouldn't Stand," *Atlanta Constitution*, January 20, 1901, 12.

182. Ibid.

183. "Must Serve Ten Years in the Pen," *Atlanta Constitution*, January 11, 1898.

184. "Woman Firebug Takes Poison," *Atlanta Constitution*, January 13, 1898.

185. "In Behalf of Mrs. Traylor," *Atlanta Constitution*, January 14, 1898; Mary Traylor file, AC.

186. "Charge of Arson Wouldn't Stand," *Atlanta Constitution*, January 20, 1901, 12.

Conclusion

1. Atlanta Office of Cultural Affairs, "History of the Center."

2. "The Cemetery Discovered Near Chastain Park," *Atlanta Magazine*, October 24, 2014.

3. See Kimberlé Williams Crenshaw, Priscilla Ocen, and Jyoti Nanda, "Black Girls Matter"; African American Policy Forum, "#Say Her Name." In "A Herstory of the #BlackLivesMatter Movement" Alicia Garza describes the co-founding of #BlackLivesMatter with Patrisse Cullors and Opal Tometi as a demand for black freedom rooted "in the labor and love of queer Black women" and the persisting invisibility of black queer women in racial justice movement priorities and politics. Watershed protests against police brutality targeting black women took place in San Francisco, Chicago, New York, and New Orleans on May 21, 2015.

4. Jacquelyn Dowd Hall, *Revolt against Chivalry*, 151–52.

5. Williams, *Alchemy of Race and Rights*, 8.

6. Blackmon, *Slavery by Another Name*. On the impact of the Cold War on civil rights and race relations see Glenda Elizabeth Gilmore, *Defying Dixie*; Dudziak, *Cold War Civil Rights*; Von Eschen, *Race against Empire*.

7. "State Board of Corrections Act," Acts and Resolutions of the General Assembly of the State of Georgia—General Laws, 1946, Georgia Legislative Documents Collection Database.

8. Douglas Blackmon argues convincingly that federal investigations responding to Cold War pressure account for the major demise of convict labor; see his *Slavery by Another Name*, chap. 17. Alex Lichtenstein argues that public pressure, conditions on federal aid for road construction, and evolving theories of penology contributed to convict labor's elimination in Georgia. He cites Mervyn LeRoy's

1932 Academy Award–nominated film, *I Am a Fugitive from a Chain Gang* as one example of intense popular scrutiny of the system; see Lichtenstein *Twice the Work of Free Labor*. Matthew Mancini rejects previous arguments that "humanity" or southerners' activism ended the chain gang; see his *One Dies, Get Another*. For a summary of these debates see Perkinson, "'Between the Worst.'"

9. "City of Homerville—Council; Meetings; Municipal Court" Law No. 201 (House Bill No. 149) Local and Special Acts and Resolutions of the General Assembly of the State of Georgia. 1991," Georgia Legislative Documents Collection Database. Emphasis added.

10. Colbert, Ivey, College Park, Ila, Blairsville, East Point, Lincolnton, Turner, Avondale, Baconton, Chatsworth, Elijah, Hazelhurst, Tazewell, Woodbine, Wrightsville, Carlton, McDuffie, Lula, East Dublin, Eastman, Chattahoochee Plantation, Claxton, Rochelle, Cuthbert, Dallas, Aragon, Avon, Albany, Fanin, Elberton, Decatur, Jesup, Oconee, Wadley, Omaha, Esphesus, Elizabeth, Franklin, Rome, Long, Ambrose, Newton, Lula, Hart, Thomaston Charters. "Local and Special Acts and Resolutions of the General Assembly of the State of Georgia," ibid.

11. Charters of the City of Griffin 1957, 1960, 1973, ibid.

12. Charters of the City of Moultrie, 1964, 1968, 1980, ibid.

13. For example, only in September 2014, in the wake of revelations that imprisoned women were subject to a pattern of coerced sterilization in California prisons did Governor Jerry Brown sign Senate Bill 1135 banning the sterilization of women prisoners without their consent. On the long history of punishment and the reproductive control of black women see Roberts, *Killing the Black Body*; and Ocen, "Punishing Pregnancy."

14. On the afterlife of slavery, see Hartman, *Lose Your Mother*. Quoted in a letter from Angela Y. Davis to Ericka Huggins printed in Angela Y. Davis, *If They Come in the Morning*, 112.

Bibliography

Manuscript Collections

Athens, Georgia
  Hargrett Rare Book and Manuscript Library, University of Georgia
    Rebecca Latimer Felton Papers, 1851–1930
Atlanta, Georgia
  Auburn Avenue Research Library on African American Culture and History
    Selena Sloan Butler Papers
  Fulton County Superior Courthouse
    Criminal Writs, 1870–1920
  James G. Kenan Research Center, Atlanta History Center
    Annual Reports of the Chief of Police of the City of Atlanta, Georgia
    Atlanta Police Department Court Docket, 1886–87
    Fulton County Recorder's Court Dockets, 1871–72; 1878–79; 1885–86
  Manuscript, Archives, and Rare Book Library, Emory University
    Georgia Woman's Christian Temperance Union Records, 1888–1982
  Robert W. Woodruff Library, Archives/Special Collections, Atlanta University
      Center
    Chautauqua Circle Collection, 1913–70
    Neighborhood Union Atlanta, Georgia, Minutes, 1908–61
    Selena Sloan Butler File
Durham, North Carolina
  David M. Rubenstein Rare Book & Manuscript Library, Duke University
    Rosetta Reitz Papers
Jackson, Mississippi
  University of Mississippi Archives and Special Collections
    David L. Cohn Collection
Morrow, Georgia
  Georgia Archives
    Annual Reports of the Georgia Prison Commission, 1897–1936
    Applications for Clemency, Convict and Fugitive Papers, 1858–1942
    Central Register of Convicts, 1817–1987
    Convict Daily Ration and Clothing Records, 1884–1909
    Convict Punishment Reports, 1901–9
    Corporal Punishment Monthly Reports (Whipping Reports), 1884–89
    Georgia Federation of Women's Clubs, Fifth District Records, 1896–1972
    Georgia Legislative Documents Collection
    Individual Convict Camp Registers, 1871–1910

Miscellaneous Records, 1816–1909
Prison Camp Hospital Weekly Registers, 1888–1907
Reports of the Principal Keeper of the Penitentiary, 1852–97
Savannah, Georgia
Georgia Historical Society
Iva Roach Benton Papers

Federal Census Records

Twelfth Census of the United States, 1900 [database online]. State farm, Baldwin Georgia, Roll 178; Page 3A; Enumeration District 0106; FHL microfilm 1240178.

Twelfth Census of the United States, 1900 [database online]. Buckhead, Fulton County, Georgia, Roll 197; Page 8A; Enumeration District 32; FHL microfilm 1240197.

Fourteenth Census of the United States, 1920 [database online]. Albany, Dougherty, Georgia, Roll T625_254; Page 3A; Enumeration District 59; Image 226.

Fourteenth Census of the United States, 1920 [database online]. Albany, Dougherty, Georgia, Roll T625_254; Pages 14A-14B; Enumeration District 61; Images 318–319.

Fifteenth Census of the United States, 1930 [database online]. Atlanta, Fulton, Georgia, Roll 362; Page 30B; Enumeration District 0076; Image 325.0.

Microfilm Editions

Mary Church Terrell Papers, 1851–1962, Manuscript Division, Library of Congress, Washington, D.C.

Records of the National Association of Colored Women's Clubs, 1895–1992, Part 1, edited by Lillian Serece Williams. Bethesda, Md.: University Publications of America.

Digital Collections

Georgia Legislative Documents Collection. http://dlg.galileo.usg.edu /CollectionsA-Z/zlgl_information.html.

Mississippi Prison Recordings, 1947 and 1948, Camp B, Parchman Farm (Mississippi State Penitentiary), Alan Lomax Archive, Cultural Equity Association http://research.culturalequity.org/get-audio-ix.do?ix=recording &id=10268&idType=sessionId&sortBy=abc.

Sanborn Insurance Maps. Sanborn Fire Insurance Company. "Insurance Maps of Albany including Putney, Dougherty County, Georgia, April 1920," Sheets 6 and 29. University of Georgia Libraries Map Collection, Athens, Georgia, presented in the Digital Library of Georgia.

Periodicals

Atlanta Constitution   Chicago Tribune   Spelman Messenger
Atlanta Independent   Forum   St. Louis Dispatch
Atlanta Magazine   Nineteenth Century   Washington Post
Augusta Chronicle   Savannah Tribune

Articles, Books, and Recordings

African American Policy Forum. "#Say Her Name: Resisting Police Brutality against Black Women." Social Media Guide. July 16, 2015. http://www.aapf .org/sayhernamereport.

Ahmed, Sara. "Killing Joy: Feminism and the History of Happiness." *Signs* 35 (Spring 2010): 571–94.

Alexander, Ruth. *The "Girl Problem": Female Sexual Delinquency in New York, 1900–1930*. Ithaca, N.Y.: Cornell University Press, 1995.

Als, Hilton, Jon Lewis, Leon F. Litwack, and James Allen, eds. *Without Sanctuary: Lynching Photography in America*. Santa Fe: Twin Palms Press, 2000.

Anonymous. "The Life Story of a Negro Peon, Obtained from an Interview with a Georgia Negro." In *The Life Stories of Undistinguished Americans, as Told by Themselves*, edited by Hamilton Holt. New York: James Pott, 1906. Reprinted in Gerda Lerner, ed., *Black Women in White America: A Documentary History*, 150–55. New York: Vintage, 1972.

Apel, Dora. *Imagery of Lynching: Black Men, White Women, and the Mob*. New Brunswick, N.J.: Rutgers University Press, 2004.

Arnesen, Eric. " 'Like Banquo's Ghost, It Will Not Down': The Race Question and the American Railroad Brotherhoods, 1880–1920." *American Historical Review* 99 (1994): 1601–33.

Atlanta Office of Cultural Affairs. "History of the Center." Accessed February 3, 2007. http://bccaatlanta.com/index.php?pid=44.

Ayers, Edward L. *The Promise of the New South: Life after Reconstruction*. New York: Oxford University Press, 1992.

———. *Vengeance and Justice: Crime and Punishment in the Nineteenth Century American South*. New York: Oxford University Press, 1984.

Bakare-Yusuf, Bibi. "The Economy of Violence: Black Bodies and the Unspeakable Terror." In *Feminist Theory and the Body*, edited by Janet Price and Margaret Shildrick, 311–23. New York: Routledge, 1999.

Baker, T. Linsday, and Julie P. Baker, ed. *The WPA Oklahoma Slave Narratives*. Norman: University of Oklahoma Press, 1996.

Baldwin, James. *The Evidence of Things Not Seen*. New York: Henry Holt and Company, 1985.

———. *The Price of the Ticket: Collected Nonfiction, 1948–1985*. New York: St. Martin's Press, 1985.

Baptist, Edward E. " 'Cuffy,' 'Fancy Maids,' and 'One-Eyed Men': Rape, Commodification, and the Domestic Slave Trade in the United States." *American Historical Review* 106 (2001): 1619–51.

Baurlain, Mark. *Negrophobia: A Race Riot in Atlanta, 1906.* San Francisco: Encounter, 2001.

Baxandall, Rosalyn Fraad. "Elizabeth Gurley Flynn: The Early Years." *Radical America* 8 (January–February 1975): 97–115.

Bay, Mia. *To Tell the Truth Freely: The Life of Ida B. Wells.* New York: Hill and Wang, 2009.

Beckles, Hilary. *Afro-Caribbean Women and Resistance to Slavery in Barbados.* London: Karnak House, 1988.

Bederman, Gail. *Manliness and Civilization: A Cultural History of Gender and Race in the United States, 1880–1917.* Chicago: University of Chicago Press, 1995.

Berry, Daina Ramey. *"Swing the Sickle for the Harvest Is Ripe": Gender and Slavery in Antebellum Georgia.* Urbana: University of Illinois Press, 2007.

Berry, David Charles. "Free Labor He Found Unsatisfactory: James W. English and Convict Lease Labor at the Chattahoochee Brick Company, 1885–1909." *Atlanta History* 36 (1993): 5–15.

Blackmon, Douglas A. *Slavery by Another Name: The Re-Enslavement of Black Americans from the Civil War to World War II.* New York: Doubleday, 2008.

Blair, Cynthia. *I've Got to Make My Livin': Black Women's Sex Work in Turn-of-the-Century Chicago.* Chicago: University of Chicago Press, 2010.

Blassingame, John W. *Black New Orleans, 1860–1880.* Chicago: University of Chicago Press, 1973.

Blee, Kathleen. *Women of the Klan: Racism and Gender in the 1920s.* Berkeley: University of California Press, 1991.

Bogdanov, Vladimir, Chris Woodstra, and Stephen Thomas Erlewine. *All Music Guide to the Blues: The Definitive Guide to the Blues.* San Francisco: Backbeat, 2003.

Braz, Rose. "Kindler, Gentler, Gender Responsive Cages: Prison Expansion Is Not Prison Reform." *Women, Girls, & Criminal Justice* (2006): 87–91.

Brooks, Daphne. *Bodies in Dissent: Spectacular Performances of Race and Freedom, 1850–1910.* Durham, N.C.: Duke University Press, 2006.

Brooks, Edward. *The Bessie Smith Companion: A Critical and Detailed Appreciation of the Recordings.* Wheathampstead, UK: Cavendish Publishing, 1982.

Brown, Elsa Barkley. " 'What Has Happened Here': The Politics of Difference in Women's History and Feminist Politics." *Feminist Studies* 18, no. 2 (Summer 1992): 295–312.

Brown, Jayna. *Babylon Girls: Black Women Performers and the Shaping of the Modern.* Durham, N.C.: Duke University Press, 2008.

Brown, Kathleen M. *Good Wives, Nasty Wenches, and Anxious Patriarchs: Gender, Race, and Power in Colonial Virginia.* Chapel Hill: University of North Carolina Press, 1996.

Brown, Mary. *Eradicating This Evil: Women in the American Anti-Lynching Movement, 1892–1940.* New York: Garland Press, 2000.

Brundage, W. Fitzhugh. *Lynching in the New South.* Urbana: University of Illinois Press, 1993.

———. *Under Sentence of Death: Lynching in the South.* Chapel Hill: University of North Carolina Press, 1997.

Burns, Robert Elliott. *I am a Fugitive From a Georgia Chain Gang!* New York: Vanguard Press, 1932.

Bush, Barbara. *Slave Women in Caribbean Society, 1650–1838*. Bloomington: Indiana University Press, 1990.

Butler, Anne M. *Gendered Justice in the American West: Women Prisoners in Men's Penitentiaries*. Urbana: University of Illinois Press, 1999.

Butler, Judith. *Bodies That Matter: On the Discursive Limits of Sex*. New York: Routledge, 1993.

———. *Gender Trouble: Feminism and the Subversion of Identity*. New York: Routledge, 1990.

Butler, Selena Sloan. *The Chain-Gang System*. Tuskegee, Ala.: Normal School Steam Press Print, 1897.

Byrd, Phillip G. *Report of the Special Inspector of Misdemeanor Convict Camps of Georgia*. Cambridge, Mass.: Harvard University Press, 1997.

Cahill, Ann J. *Rethinking Rape*. Ithaca, N.Y.: Cornell University Press, 2001.

Camp, Stephanie. *Closer to Freedom: Enslaved Women and Everyday Resistance in the Plantation South*. Chapel Hill: University of North Carolina Press, 2004.

Carby, Hazel V. *Cultures in Babylon: Black Britain and African America*. New York: Verso, 1999.

———. "On the Threshold of Woman's Era": Lynching, Empire, and Sexuality in Black Feminist Theory." *Critical Inquiry* 12 (1985): 262–77.

———. "Policing the Black Woman's Body in an Urban Context." *Critical Inquiry* 18 (1992): 738–55.

———. *Reconstructing Womanhood: The Emergence of the Afro-American Woman Novelist*. New York: Oxford University Press, 1987.

———. "The Sexual Politics of Women's Blues." In *Cultures in Babylon: Black Britain and African America*, 22–39. New York: Verso Press, 1999.

Chauncey, George. *Gay New York: Gender, Urban Culture, and the Making of the Gay Male World 1890–1940*. New York: Basic, 1994.

Childs, Dennis. "'You Ain't Seen Nothin' Yet': Beloved, the American Chain Gang, and the Middle Passage Remix." *American Quarterly* 61 (2009): 271–97.

Clinton, Catherine. *The Plantation Mistress*. New York: Pantheon, 1983.

Cohen, Cathy J. "Deviance as Resistance: A New Research Agenda for the Study of Black Politics." *Du Bois Review* 1, no. 1 (2004): 27–45.

Collins, Patricia Hill. *Black Feminist Thought: Knowledge, Consciousness, and the Politics of Empowerment*. New York: Routledge, 2000.

———. "Pornography and Black Women's Bodies." In *Gender Violence: Interdisciplinary Perspectives*, edited by Laura L. O'Toole and Jessica R. Schiffman, 395–99. New York: New York University Press, 1997.

Courlander, Harold. *Negro Folk Music, U.S.A*. New York: Columbia University Press, 1968.

Cox, Ida. *Ida Cox: The Complete Recorded Works Vol. 4*. Document Records, 1995. DOCD-5325.

Crawley, Ashon. "Stayed/Freedom/Hallelujah." *Los Angeles Times Review of Books*, May 10, 2015.

Crenshaw, Kimberlé W. "Mapping the Margins: Intersectionality, Identity Politics, and Violence against Women of Color." *Stanford Law Review* 43 (July 1991): 1241–99.

Crenshaw, Kimberlé Williams, Priscilla Ocen, and Jyoti Nanda. "Black Girls Matter: Pushed Out, Overpoliced, and Underprotected." African American Policy Forum/Center for Intersectionality and Social Policy Studies. Last modified February 4, 2015. http://www.aapf.org/recent/2014/12/coming -soon-blackgirlsmatter-pushed-out-overpoliced-and-underprotected.

Curtin, Mary Ellen. *Black Prisoners and Their World, Alabama 1865–1900.* Charlottesville: University of Virginia Press, 2000.

Dailey, Jane, Glenda E. Gilmore, and Byrant Simon, eds. *Jumpin' Jim Crow: Southern Politics from Civil War to Civil Rights.* Princeton, N.J.: Princeton University Press, 2000.

Daniel Pete. *The Shadow of Slavery: Peonage in the South, 1901–1969.* Urbana: University of Illinois Press, 1972.

Davidoff, Leonore. "Gender and the 'Great Divide': Public and Private in British Gender History." *Journal of Women's History* 15 (2003): 11–27.

Davidson, James West. *"They Say": Ida B. Wells and the Reconstruction of Race.* New York: Oxford University Press, 2004.

Davis, Angela Y. *Abolition Democracy: Beyond Prison, Torture, and Empire: Interviews with Angela Y. Davis.* New York: Seven Stories Press, 2005.

———. *Blues Legacies and Black Feminism: Gertrude "Ma" Rainey, Bessie Smith, and Billie Holiday.* New York: Vintage, 1998.

———. "From the Prison of Slavery to the Slavery of Prison." In *The Angela Y. Davis Reader*, edited by Joy James, 74–96. New York: Blackwell Publishers, 1998.

———. *If They Come in The Morning: Voices of Resistance.* New York: Third Press, 1971.

———. "The Meaning of Emancipation according to Black Women." In *Women, Race, and Class*, 87–98. New York: Random House, 1981.

———. "Reflections on the Black Woman's Role in the Community of Slaves." In *The Angela Y. Davis Reader*, edited by Joy James, 111–28. New York: Blackwell Publishers, 1998.

———. *Women, Race, and Class.* New York: Random House, 1981.

Davis, Angela Y., and Gina Dent. "Prison as Border: A Conversation on Gender, Globalization, and Punishment." *Signs* 26 (Summer 2001): 1235–41.

Davis, Elizabeth Lindsey. *Lifting as they Climb.* Washington, D.C.: National Association of Colored Women, 1933.

Davis, Mike. "The Stop Watch and the Wooden Shoe: Scientific Management and the Industrial Workers of the World." *Radical America* 8, no. 6 (January–February 1975): 69–97.

Day, Ken Gonzales. *Lynching in the West: 1850–1935.* Durham, N.C.: Duke University Press, 2006.

Dayton, Cornelia Hughes. "Rethinking Agency, Recovering Voices." *American Historical Review* 109 (2004): 827–43.

de Beauvoir, Simone. *The Second Sex*. New York: Vintage, 1949.

Dittmer, John. *Black Georgia in the Progressive Era*. Urbana: University of Illinois Press, 1977.

Dorsey, Allison. *To Build Our Lives Together: Community Formation in Black Atlanta, 1875–1906*. Athens: University of Georgia Press, 2004.

Doyle, Don H. *New Men, New Cities, New South: Atlanta, Nashville, Charleston, Mobile, 1860–1910*. Chapel Hill: University of North Carolina Press, 1990.

Du Bois, W. E. B. *Black Reconstruction in America 1860–1880*. New York: Free Press, 1935.

———. *Some Notes on Negro Crime Particularly in Georgia (Report of the Social Study Made under the Direction of Atlanta University; Together with the Proceedings of the Ninth Conference for the Study of Negro Problems Held at Atlanta University on May 21, 1904)*. Atlanta: Atlanta University Press, 1904.

Dudziak, Mary. *Cold War Civil Rights: Race and the Image of American Democracy*. Princeton, N.J.: Princeton University Press, 2000.

Duggan, Lisa. *Sapphic Slashers: Sex, Violence, and American Modernity*. Durham, N.C.: Duke University Press, 2000.

Duval Harrison, Daphne. *Black Pearls: Blues Queens of the 1920s*. New Brunswick, N.J.: Rutgers University Press, 1998.

Edwards, Erica. *Charisma and the Fictions of Black Leadership*. Minneapolis: University of Minnesota Press, 2012.

Edwards, Laura F. *Gendered Strife and Confusion: The Political Culture of Reconstruction*. Urbana: University of Illinois Press, 1997.

Edwards, Rebecca. *Angels in the Machinery: Gender in American Party Politics from the Civil War to the Progressive Era*. New York: Oxford University Press, 1997.

Enstad, Nan. *Ladies of Labor, Girls of Adventure: Working Women, Popular Culture and Labor Politics at the Turn of the Twentieth Century*. New York: Columbia University Press, 1999.

Estrich, Susan. *Real Rape: How the Legal System Victimizes Women Who Say No*. Cambridge, Mass.: Harvard University Press, 1987.

Evans, Jessica. "Feeble Monsters: Making Up Disabled People" In *Visual Culture: The Reader*, edited by Stuart Hall and Jessica Evans, 274–88. London: Sage Publications, 1999.

Ewen, Elizabeth. *Immigrant Women in the Land of Dollars: Lift and Culture on the Lower East Side, 1890–1925*. New York: Monthly Review Press, 1985.

Faubion, James D., ed. *Power: Essential Works of Foucault, 1954–1984*. New York: New York Press, 1994.

Faust, Drew Gilpin. *Mothers of Invention: Women of the Slaveholding South in the American Civil War*. Chapel Hill: University of North Carolina Press, 1996.

Federici, Silvia. *Caliban and the Witch: Women, the Body, and Primitive Accumulation*. New York: Autonomedia, 2004.

Feimster, Crystal. *Southern Horrors: Women and the Politics of Rape and Lynching*. Cambridge, Mass.: Harvard University Press, 2009.

Felski, Rita. *The Gender of Modernity*. Cambridge, Mass.: Harvard University Press, 1995.

Felton, Rebecca Latimer. *Country Life in Georgia in the Days of My Youth*. New York: Arno Press, 1980.

———. *My Memories of Georgia Politics*. Atlanta: Index Printing, 1911.

Fierce, Mildred C. *Slavery Revisited, Blacks and the Southern Convict Lease System, 1865–1933*. New York: Africana Studies Research Center, Brooklyn College, City University of New York, 1994.

Fink, Gary, and Merle Reed, eds. *Race, Class, and Community in Southern Labor History*. Tuscaloosa: University of Alabama Press, 2003.

Fischer, Kirstin. *Suspect Relations: Sex, Race, and Resistance in Colonial North Carolina*. Ithaca, N.Y.: Cornell University Press, 2002.

Foner, Eric. *Reconstruction: America's Unfinished Revolution*. New York: Harper and Row, 1988.

Foucault, Michel. "About the Concept of the Dangerous Individual in Nineteenth-Century Legal Psychiatry." In *Power: Essential Works of Foucault, 1954–1984*, vol. 3, edited by James D. Faubion, 176–200. New York: New York Press, 1994.

———. *Discipline and Punish: The Birth of the Prison*. New York: Vintage, 1977.

———. *The History of Sexuality*. New York: Pantheon Books, 1978.

———. "The Proper Use of Criminals." In *Power: Essential Works of Foucault, 1954–1984*, vol. 3, edited by James D. Faubion, 429–34. New York: New York Press, 1994.

Fox-Genovese, Elizabeth. *Within the Plantation Household: Black and White Women of the Old South*. Chapel Hill: University of North Carolina Press, 1988.

Freedman, Estelle. *Their Sisters' Keepers: Women's Prison Reform in America, 1830–1930*. Ann Arbor: University of Michigan Press, 1984.

Gaines, Kevin. *Uplifting the Race: Black Leadership, Politics, and Culture in the Twentieth Century*. Chapel Hill: University of North Carolina Press, 1996.

Garza, Alicia. "A Herstory of the #BlackLivesMatter Movement." *Feministwire*, October 7, 2014. Accessed December 2014. http://www.thefeministwire.com/2014/10/blacklivesmatter-2/.

Georgia General Assembly. *Proceedings of the Joint Committee Appointed to Investigate the Condition of the Georgia Penitentiary*. 1870; reprint, New York: Arno Press, 1974.

Giddings, Paula. *Ida: A Sword among Lions, Ida B. Wells-Barnett and the Campaign against Lynching*. New York: Harper Collins, 2008.

———. *When and Where I Enter: The Impact of Black Women on Race and Sex in America*. New York: Harper Collins, 1984.

Gilmore, Glenda Elizabeth. *Defying Dixie: The Radical Roots of Civil Rights, 1919–1950*. New York: W. W. Norton, 2008.

———. *Gender and Jim Crow: Women and the Politics of White Supremacy in North Carolina, 1896–1920*. Chapel Hill: University of North Carolina Press, 1996.

———. " 'A Melting Time': Black Women, White Women, and the WCTU in North Carolina, 1880–1900." In *Hidden Histories of Women in the New South*, edited by Virginia Bernhard, Elizabeth Hayes Turner, and Betty Brandon, 153–72. Columbia: University of Missouri Press, 1994.

———. ed. *Who Were the Progressives?* Boston: Bedford/St. Martin's Press, 2002.

Gilmore, Ruth Wilson. "Fatal Couplings of Power and Difference: Notes on Racism and Geography." *Professional Geographer* 54 (February 2002): 15–24.

———. *Golden Gulag: Prisons, Surplus, Crisis, and Opposition in Globalizing California.* Berkeley: University of California Press, 2007.

Glenn, Evelyn Nakano. *Forced to Care: Coercion and Caregiving in America.* Cambridge, Mass.: Harvard University Press, 2010.

Glymph, Thavolia. "Du Bois's *Black Reconstruction* and Slave Women's War for Freedom." *South Atlantic Quarterly* 112 (Summer 2013): 489–505.

———. *Out of the House of Bondage: The Transformation of the Plantation Household.* Cambridge, Mass.: Harvard University Press, 2008.

Godshalk, David Fort. *Veiled Visions: The 1906 Atlanta Race Riot and the Reshaping of American Race Relations.* Chapel Hill: University of North Carolina Press, 2005.

Goldsby, Jacqueline. *A Spectacular Secret: Lynching in American Life and Literature.* Chicago: University of Chicago Press, 2006.

Gordon, Avery. *Ghostly Matters: Haunting and the Sociological Imagination.* Minneapolis: University of Minnesota Press, 1997.

Gore, Dayo F. *Radicalism at the Crossroads: African American Women Activists in the Cold War.* New York: New York University Press, 2011.

Grant, Donald L. *The Way It Was in the South: The Black Experience in Georgia.* Athens: University of Georgia Press, 1993.

Gregory, James N. *The Southern Diaspora: How the Great Migrations of Black and White Southerners Transformed America.* Chapel Hill: University of North Carolina Press, 2005.

Griffin, Farah Jasmine. *Who Set You Flowin'?: The African American Migration Narrative.* New York: Oxford University Press, 1995.

Griffin, Susan. *Pornography and Silence: Culture's Revenge against Nature.* New York: Harper and Row, 1981.

Gross, Kali. *Colored Amazons: Crime, Violence and Black Women in the City of Brotherly Love, 1880–1910.* Durham, N.C.: Duke University Press, 2006.

Grossman, James. *Land of Hope: Chicago, Black Southerners and the Great Migration.* Chicago: University of Chicago Press, 1991.

Grosz, Elizabeth. *Volatile Bodies: Toward a Corporeal Feminism.* Bloomington: University of Indiana Press, 1995.

Gunning, Sandra. *Race, Rape and Lynching: The Red Record of American Literature.* New York: Oxford University Press, 1996.

Hahn, Steven. *A Nation under Our Feet: Black Political Struggles in the Rural South from Slavery to the Great Migration.* Cambridge, Mass.: Harvard University Press, 2003.

Hair, William Ivy. *Carnival of Fury: Robert Charles and the New Orleans Race Riot of 1900.* New Orleans: Louisiana State University Press, 1976.

Halberstam, Judith. *Female Masculinity*. Durham, N.C.: Duke University Press, 1998.

———. *Skin Shows: Gothic Horror and the Technology of Monsters*. Durham, N.C.: Duke University Press, 1995.

Hale, Grace Elizabeth. "Deadly Amusements: Spectacle Lynchings and Southern Whiteness, 1890–1940." In *Varieties of Southern History New Essays on a Region and Its People*, edited by Bruce Clayton and John Salmond, 63–78. New York: Greenwood Press, 1996.

———. *Making Whiteness: The Culture of Segregation in the South, 1890–1940*. New York: Pantheon, 1998.

Hall, Jacquelyn Dowd. "Disorderly Women: Gender and Labor Militancy in the Appalachian South." *Journal of American History* 73 (1986): 354–82.

———. "'The Mind That Burns in Each Body': Women, Rape, and Racial Violence." In *Powers of Desire: The Politics of Sexuality*, edited by Anne Snitow, Christine Stansell, and Sharon Thompson, 328–49. New York: Monthly Review Press, 1983.

———. "Ola Delight Smith's Progressive Era: Labor, Feminism, and Reform in the Urban South." In *Visible Women: New Essays on American Activism*, edited by Nancy A. Hewitt and Suzanne Lebsock, 166–98. Urbana: University of Illinois Press.

———. "Private Eyes, Public Women: Images of Class and Sex in the Urban South, Atlanta, Georgia, 1913–1915." In *Work Engendered: Toward a New History of American Labor*, edited by Ava Baron, 243–72. Ithaca, N.Y.: Cornell University Press, 1991.

———. *Revolt against Chivalry: Jessie Daniel Ames and the Women's Campaign against Lynching*. New York: Columbia University Press, 1979.

Hall, Stuart, David Held, Don Hubert, and Kenneth Thompson, eds. *Modernity: An Introduction to Modern Societies*. Oxford, UK: Blackwell Publishers, 1996.

Hammonds, Evelyn. "'Black (W)holes' and the Geometry of Black Female Sexuality." *differences* 6(2–3): 126–45.

———. "Toward a Genealogy of Black Female Sexuality: The Problematic of Silence." In *Feminist Genealogies, Colonial Legacies, Democratic Futures*, edited by J. Alexander and C. T. Mohanty, 170–82. New York: Routledge, 1997.

Harlan, Louis R., and Raymond W. Smock, eds. *The Booker T. Washington Papers, Vol. 9, 1906–1908*. Urbana: University of Illinois, 1980.

Harris, Angela P. "Race and Essentialism in Feminist Legal Theory," *Stanford Law Review* 20, no. 3 (1990): 581–616.

Harris, Cheryl I. "Finding Sojourner's Truth: Race, Gender, and the Institution of Property." *Cardoza Law Review* 18 (1997): 309–409.

———. "Whiteness as Property." *Harvard Law Review* 106 (1993): 1707–91.

Harris, Sharon M. *Executing Race: Early American Women's Narratives of Race, Society, and the Law*. Columbus: Ohio State University Press, 2005.

Hartman, Saidiya. *Lose Your Mother: A Journey along the Atlantic Slave Route*. New York: Farrar, Straus and Giroux, 2007.

———. *Scenes of Subjection: Terror, Slavery, and Self-Making in Nineteenth Century America*. New York: Oxford University Press, 1997.

———. "Venus in Two Acts." *small axe* 26 (2008): 1–14.

Henderson, Harold Paulk. *The Politics of Change in Georgia: A Political Biography of Ellis Arnall*. Athens: University of Georgia Press, 1991.

Herzhaft, Gerard. *Encyclopedia of the Blues*. 2nd ed. Fayetteville: University of Arkansas Press, 1997.

Hewitt, Nancy. *Southern Discomfort: Women's Activism in Tampa, Florida, 1880s–1920s*. Urbana: University of Illinois Press, 2001.

Hickey, Georgina. *Hope and Danger in the New South City: Working-Class Women and Urban Development in Atlanta, 1890–1940*. Atlanta: University of Georgia Press, 2003.

Hicks, Cheryl. *Talk with You Like A Woman: African American Women, Justice, and Reform in New York, 1890–1935*. Chapel Hill: University of North Carolina Press, 2010.

Higginbotham, Evelyn Brooks. "African American Women's History and the Metalanguage of Race." *Signs* 17 (1992): 251–72.

———. *Righteous Discontent: The Women's Movement in the Black Baptist Church, 1880–1920*. Cambridge, Mass.: Harvard University Press, 1993.

Hill, Rebecca. *Men, Mobs, and Law: Anti-Lynching and Labor Defense in U.S. Radical History*. Durham, N.C.: Duke University Press, 2008.

Hine, Darlene Clark. "Rape and the Inner Lives of Black Women in the Middle West." *Signs* 14 (1989): 261–92.

Hobson, Janell. *Venus in the Dark: Blackness and Beauty in Popular Culture*. New York: Routledge, 2005.

Hodes, Martha Elizabeth. "The Sexualization of Reconstruction Politics: White Women and Black Men in the South after the Civil War." *Journal of the History of Sexuality* 3 (1993): 402–17.

———. *White Women, Black Men: Illicit Sex in the Nineteenth Century South*. New Haven, Conn.: Yale University Press, 1997.

hooks, bell. *Feminist Theory: From Margin to Center*. Cambridge, Mass.: South End Press, 1984.

Hunter, Tera. *To 'Joy My Freedom: Southern Black Women's Lives and Labors after the Civil War*. Cambridge, Mass.: Harvard University Press, 1997.

Jailhouse Blues: Women's A Capella Songs from the Parchman Penitentiary. New York: Rosetta Records, 1987. RR1316.

James, Joy. *The New Abolitionists: (Neo)Slave Narratives and Contemporary Prison Writings*. Albany: State University of New York Press, 2005.

———. *Resisting State Violence: Radicalism, Gender, and Race in U.S. Culture*. Minneapolis: University of Minnesota Press, 1996.

———. *Shadowboxing: Representations of Black Feminist Politics*. New York: Palgrave, 1999.

Jaynes, Gerald D. *Branches without Roots: Genesis of the Black Working Class in the American South, 1862–1882*. New York: Oxford University Press, 1982.

Jenkins, Wilbert L. *Seizing the New Day: African Americans in Post-Civil War Charleston*. Bloomington: Indiana University Press, 1998.

Jones, Jacqueline. *Labor of Love, Labor of Sorrow: Black women and the Family from Slavery to the Present*. New York: Basic, 1985.

Judson, Sara Mercer. "'Leisure Is a Foe to Any Man': The Pleasures and Dangers of Atlanta during World War I." *Journal of Women's History* 15 (2003): 92–115.

Kaba, Mariame. "Nobody Matters Less Than Black Girls . . ." *U.S. Prison Culture*, December 20, 2013. http://www.usprisonculture.com/blog/2013/12 /20/nobody-matters-less-than-black-girls/.

Kantrowitz, Stephen. *Ben Tillman and the Reconstruction of White Supremacy*. Chapel Hill: University of North Carolina Press, 2000.

Kaplan, Sara Clarke. *Reproducing Slavery: Black Feminism and the Politics of Freedom*. Minneapolis: University of Minnesota Press (forthcoming 2016).

Kelley, Robin D. G. *Freedom Dreams: The Black Radical Imagination*. Boston: Beacon Press, 2002.

———. *Race Rebels: Culture, Politics, and the Black Middle Class*. New York: Free Press, 1994.

———. "'Slangin' Rocks . . . Palestinian Style': Dispatches from Occupied Zones of North America." In *Police Brutality: An Anthology*, edited by Jill Nelson, 21–60. New York: W. W. Norton, 2000.

Kellor, Frances. *Experimental Sociology*. New York: Macmillan, 1901.

Kolchin, Peter. *First Freedom: The Responses of Alabama's Blacks to Emancipation and Reconstruction*. Westport, Conn: Greenwood Press, 1972.

Kousser, J. Morgan, and James M. McPherson, eds. *Region, Race, and Reconstruction: Essays in Honor of C. Vann Woodward*. New York: Oxford University Press, 1982.

Kunzel, Regina. *Criminal Intimacy: Prison and the Uneven History of Modern American Sexuality*. Chicago: University of Chicago Press, 2008.

Lee, Chana Kai. *For Freedom's Sake: The Life of Fannie Lou Hamer*. Urbana: University of Illinois Press, 2000.

LeFlouria, Talitha. *Chained in Silence: Black Women and Convict Labor in the New South*. Chapel Hill: University of North Carolina Press, 2015.

———. "'The Hand That Rocks the Cradle Cuts Cordwood': Exploring Black Women's Lives and Labor in Georgia's Convict Camps, 1865–1917." *Labor: Studies in Working-Class History of the Americas* 8 (2011): 47–63.

Lerner, Gerda. "The Rape of Black Women as a Weapon of Terror." In *Black Women in White America: A Documentary History*, edited by Gerda Lerner, 172–93. New York: Random House, 1992.

———, ed. *Black Women in White America: A Documentary History*. New York: Vintage, 1972.

Lichtenstein, Alex. "Good Roads and Chain Gangs in the Progressive South: 'The Negro Convict is a Slave.'" *Journal of Southern History* 59 (1993): 85–100.

———. *Twice the Work of Free Labor: The Political Economy of Convict Labor in the New South*. New York: Verso Press, 1996.

———. "Twice the Work of Free Labor?" In *Race, Class, and Community in Southern Labor History*, edited by Gary M. Fink and Merle E. Reed, 146–65. Tuscaloosa: University of Alabama Press 2003.

Litwack, Leon F. *Been in the Storm so Long: The Aftermath of Slavery*. New York: Knopf, 1979.

———. *Trouble in Mind: Black Southerners in the Age of Jim Crow*. New York: Knopf, 1998.

Lyons, Beverly Bunch. *Contested Terrain: African American Women Migrate from the South to Cincinnati, 1900–1950*. New York: Routledge, 2001.

Machlachlan, Gretchen Ehrman. "Women's Work: Atlanta's Industrialization and Urbanization, 1870–1929." Ph.D. diss., Emory University, 1992.

MacKinnon, Catherine. "Rape: On Coercion and Consent." In *Toward a Feminist Theory of the State*, 171–83. Cambridge, Mass.: Harvard University Press, 1989.

MacLean, Nancy. *Behind the Mask of Chivalry: The Making of the Second Ku Klux Klan*. New York: Oxford University Press, 1994.

Mancini, Matthew J. *One Dies, Get Another: Convict Leasing in the American South, 1866–1928*. Columbia: University of South Carolina Press, 1996.

Marable, Manning, and Leith Mullings. *Let Nobody Turn Us Around: Voices of Resistance, Reform, and Renewal, An African American Anthology*. 2nd ed. Lanham, Md.: Rowman and Littlefield, 2009.

Markovitz, Jonathan. *Legacies of Lynching: Racial Violence and Memory*. Minneapolis: University of Minneapolis Press, 2004.

Martin, Sara. *Sara Martin Volume 3, 1924–1925*. Document Records, 1995. DOCD-5397.

Mbembe, Achille. "Necropolitics." *Public Culture* 15 (2003): 11–40.

McClintock, Ann. *Imperial Leather: Race, Gender and Sexuality in the Colonial Conquest*. New York: Routledge, 1995.

———. "'No Longer in a Future Heaven': Gender, Race, and Nationalism." In *Dangerous Liaisons: Gender, Nation, and Postcolonial Perspectives*, edited by Anne McClintock, Aamir Mufti, and Ella Shohat, 89–112. Minneapolis: University of Minnesota Press, 1997.

McGovern, James R. *Anatomy of a Lynching*. Baton Rouge: Louisiana State Press, 1982.

McGuire, Danielle L. *At the Dark End of the Street: Black Women, Rape, and Resistance—A New History of the Civil Rights Movement from Rosa Parks to the Rise of Black Power*. New York: Alfred A. Knopf, 2010.

———. "'It Was Like All of Us Had Been Raped': Sexual Violence, Community Mobilization, and the African American Freedom Struggle." *Journal of American History* 91 (2004): 906–31.

McKitrick, Eric L. *Andrew Johnson and Reconstruction*. Chicago: University of Chicago Press, 1960.

McKittrick, Katherine. *Demonic Grounds: Black Women and the Cartographies of Struggle*. Minneapolis: University of Minnesota Press, 2006.

McMillen, Neil R. *Dark Journey: Black Mississippians in the Age of Jim Crow*. Urbana: University of Illinois Press, 1989.

McMurry, Linda O. *To Keep the Waters Troubled: The Life of Ida B. Wells*. New York: Oxford University Press, 1998.

McPherson, James M. *The Struggle for Equality*. Princeton, N.J.: Princeton University Press, 1964.

Meyerowitz, Joanne. *Women Adrift: Independent Wage-Earners in Chicago, 1880–1930*. Chicago: University of Chicago Press, 1988.

Miller-Young, Mireille. *A Taste for Brown Sugar: Black Women in Pornography*. Durham, N.C.: Duke University Press, 2014.

Mitchell, Michelle. *Righteous Propagation: African Americans and the Politics of Racial Destiny after Reconstruction*. Chapel Hill: University of North Carolina Press, 2004.

Mixon, Gregory. *The Atlanta Riot: Race, Class, and Violence in a New South City*. Gainesville: University Press of Florida, 2005.

Moitt, Barbara Bernard. *Women and Slavery in the French Antilles, 1635–1848*. Bloomington: Indiana University Press, 2001.

Montgomery, David. *Beyond Equality: Labor and the Radical Republicans, 1862–1872*. Urbana: University of Illinois Press, 1981.

Moore, Alice. *St. Louis Women Vol. 1: St. Louis Bessie and Alice Moore*. Document Records, 1994. DOCD-5290.

Morgan, Jennifer. *Laboring Women: Reproduction and Gender in New World Slavery*. Philadelphia: University of Philadelphia Press, 2004.

Morrison, Toni. *Beloved*. New York: Vintage, 1987; reprint, 2004.

Morrissey, Marietta. *Slave Women in the New World: Gender Stratification in the New World*. Lawrence: University of Kansas Press, 1988.

Morton, Patricia, ed. *Discovering the Women in Slavery: Emancipating Perspectives on the American Past*. Athens: University of Georgia Press, 1996.

———. *Disfigured Images: The Historical Assault on Afro-American Women*. Westport, Conn.: Praeger, 1991.

Moten, Fred. *Hughson's Tavern*. New York: Leon Works, 2008.

———. *In the Break: The Aesthetics of the Black Radical Tradition*. Minneapolis: University of Minnesota Press, 2003.

Muhammad, Khalil Gibran. *The Condemnation of Blackness: Race, Crime, and the Making of Modern Urban America*. Cambridge, Mass.: Harvard University Press, 2010.

Mumford, Kevin. *Interzones: Black/White Sex Districts in Chicago and New York in the Early Twentieth Century*. New York: Columbia University Press, 1997.

Muñoz, Jose Esteban. *Disidentifications: Queers of Color and the Performance of Politics*. Minneapolis: University of Minnesota Press, 1999.

Myers, Martha. "Gender and Southern Punishment after the Civil War." *Criminology* 33 (1995): 17–46.

———. *Race, Labor, and Punishment in the New South*. Columbus: Ohio State University Press, 1998.

National Prison Association of the United States. *Reports of the Proceeding*. New York: C. G. Burgoyne's Quick Print, 1884–86.

Nelson, Scott Reynolds. *Steel Drivin' Man, John Henry: The Untold Story of an American Legend*. New York: Oxford University Press, 2006.

Novack, Daniel A. *The Wheel of Servitude: Black Forced Labor after Slavery*. Lexington: University of Kentucky Press, 1978.

Ocen, Priscilla. "Punishing Pregnancy: Race, Incarceration, and the Shackling of Pregnant Prisoners." *California Law Review* 100 (2012): 1239–1311.

Odem, Mary. *Delinquent Daughters: Protecting and Policing Adolescent Female Sexuality in the United States, 1885–1920*. Chapel Hill: University of North Carolina Press, 1995.

Oshinsky, David. *Worse Than Slavery: Parchman Farm and the Ordeal of Jim Crow Justice*. New York: Free Press, 1996.

Osofsky, Gilbert. *Harlem: The Making of a Ghetto*. New York: Harper and Row, 1966.

Painter, Nell Irvin. *Exodusters: Black Migration to Kansas after Reconstruction*. New York: W. W. Norton, 1992.

———. *Southern History across the Color Line*. Chapel Hill: University of North Carolina Press, 2002.

Pateman, Carole. *Sexual Contract*. Stanford: Stanford University Press, 1988.

———. "Women and Consent." *Political Theory* 8 (1980): 149–68.

Peiss, Kathy. *Cheap Amusements: Working Women and Leisure in Turn-of-the-Century New York*. Philadelphia: Temple University Press, 1986.

Perkinson, Robert. " 'Between the Worst of the Past and the Worst of the Future': Reconsidering Convict Leasing in the South." *Radical History Review* 71 (1998): 207–16.

———. *Texas Tough: The Rise of America's Prison Empire*. New York: Metropolitan, 2010.

Perry, Imani. "Cultural Studies, Critical Race Theory, and Some Reflections on Methods." *Villanova Law Review* 50 (2005): 915–24.

Rabinovitz, Lauren. *For the Love of Pleasure: Women, Movies, and Culture in Turn-of-the-Century Chicago* New Brunswick, N.J.: Rutgers University Press, 1998.

Rabinowitz, Howard N. *Race Relations in the Urban South: 1865–1890*. Athens: University of Georgia Press, 1978.

———, ed. *Southern Black Leaders of the Reconstruction Era*. Urbana: University of Illinois Press, 1982.

Rachleff, Peter. *Black Labor in Richmond, 1865–1890*. Philadelphia: Temple University Press, 1989.

Raiford, Leigh. "The Consumption of Lynching Images." In *Only Skin Deep: Changing Visions of the American Self*, edited by Coco Fusco and Brian Williams, 267–73. New York: Harry Abrams, 2003.

Rainey, Gertrude "Ma." *Ma Rainey: The Complete Recorded Works Vols. 1–5*. Document Records, 1998. Vol. 1: DOCD-5581; Vol. 2: DOCD-5582; Vol. 3: DOCD-5583; Vol. 4: DOCD-5584; Vol. 5: DOCD-5156.

Redman, Don. *Shakin' the Africann*. United Kingdom: Hep Records, 2002. HEP CD 1001.

Redmond, Shana. *Anthem: Social Movements and the Sounds of Solidarity in the African Diaspora*. New York: New York University Press, 2013.

Roberts, Dorothy. *Killing the Black Body: Race, Reproduction, and the Meaning of Liberty*. New York: Pantheon, 1997.

Robinson, Cedric J. *Black Marxism: The Making of a Radical Tradition*. Chapel Hill: University of North Carolina Press, 1999.

Rodriguez, Dylan. *Forced Passages: Imprisoned Radical Intellectuals and the U.S. Prison System*. Minneapolis: University of Minnesota Press, 2006.

Rody, Caroline. "Toni Morrison's *Beloved*: History, 'Rememory,' and a 'Clamor for a Kiss.'" *American Literary History* 7 (1995): 92–119.

Rogers, William Warren, and Robert David Ward. *Convicts, Coal, and the Banner Mine Tragedy*. Tuscaloosa: University of Alabama Press, 1987.

Rose, Willie Lee. *Rehearsal for Reconstruction*. Indianapolis: Bobbs-Merrill, 1964.

Rosen, Hannah. *Terror in the Heart of Freedom: Citizenship, Sexual Violence, and the Meaning of Race in the Postemancipation South*. Chapel Hill: University of North Carolina Press, 2009.

Rouse, Jacqueline A. *Lugenia Burns Hope: Black Southern Reformer*. Athens: University of Georgia Press, 1989.

———. *To Better Our World: Black Women in Organized Reform, 1890–1920*. New York: Carlson, 1990.

Santiago-Valles, Kelvin. "'Still Longing for de Old Plantation': The Visual Parodies and Racial National Imaginary of US Overseas Expansionism, 1898–1903." *American Studies International* 37 (October 1999): 18–43.

Saville, Julie. *The Work of Reconstruction: From Slave to Wage Laborer in South Carolina, 1860–1870*. New York: Cambridge University Press, 1994.

Scarry, Elaine. *The Body in Pain: The Making and Unmaking of the World*. New York: Oxford University Press, 1985.

Schechter, Patricia A. *Ida B. Wells-Barnett and American Reform, 1880–1930*. Chapel Hill: University of North Carolina Press, 2001.

———. "Unsettled Business: Ida B. Wells against Lynching, or, How Antilynching Got Its Gender." In *Under Sentence of Death: Lynching in the South*, edited by W. Fitzhugh Brundage, 292–317. Chapel Hill: University of North Carolina Press, 1997.

Schiebinger, Londa. *Nature's Body: Sexual Politics and the Making of Modern Science*. London: Pandora, 1994.

Schwalm, Leslie A. *A Hard Fight for We: Women's Transition from Slavery to Freedom in South Carolina*. Urbana: University of Illinois Press, 1997.

Scott, David. *Conscripts of Modernity: The Tragedy of Colonial Enlightenment*. Durham, N.C.: Duke University Press, 2004.

Scott, James C. *Domination and the Arts of Resistance: Hidden Transcripts*. New Haven, Conn.: Yale University Press, 1990.

———. *Weapons of the Weak: Everyday Forms of Peasant Resistance*. New Haven, Conn.: Yale University Press, 1985.

Scott, Joan W. "Gender: A Useful Category of Historical Analysis." *American Historical Review* (1986): 1053–75.

Scott, Michelle R. *Blues Empress in Black Chattanooga: Bessie Smith and the Emerging Urban South*. Urbana: University of Illinois Press, 2008.

Sernett, Milton. *Bound for the Promised Land: African American Religion and the Great Migration*. Durham, N.C.: Duke University Press, 1997.

Shakur, Assata. *Assata: An Autobiography*. Chicago: Lawrence Hill, 1987.

Shapiro, Karin A. *A New South Rebellion: The Battle against Convict Labor in the Tennessee Coalfields, 1871–1896*. Chapel Hill: University of North Carolina Press, 1998.

Sharpe, Christina. *Monstrous Intimacies: Making Post-Slavery Subjects*. Durham, N.C.: Duke University Press, 2010.

Shaw, Stephanie. "Black Club Women and the Creation of the National Association of Colored Women." *Journal of Women's History* 3 (1991): 10–25.

———. *What a Woman Ought to Be and Do: Black Professional Workers during the Jim Crow Era*. Chicago: University of Chicago Press, 1996.

Shaylor, Cassandra. "Neither Kind nor Gentle: The Perils of 'Gender Responsive Justice.'" In *The Violence of Incarceration*, edited by Phil Scranton and Jude McCulloh, 145–63. New York: Routledge, 2009.

Sims, Anastasia. *The Power of Femininity in the New South: Women's Organizations and Politics in North Carolina, 1880–1930*. Columbia: University of South Carolina Press, 1997.

Sing, Nikhil Pal. *Black Is a Country: Race and the Unfinished Struggle for Democracy*. Cambridge, Mass.: Harvard University Press, 2004.

Smith, Bessie. *Bessie Smith: The Complete Recordings Vols. 1–5*. New York: Columbia Records, 1991. Vol. 1: C2K47091; Vol. 2: C2K47471; Vol. 3: C2K47474; Vol. 4: C2K52838; Vol. 5: C2K 57546.

Smith, Caleb. *The Prison and the American Imagination*. New Haven, Conn.: Yale University Press, 2009.

Smith, Clara. *Clara Smith: The Complete Recorded Works Vols. 1 and 3*. Document Records, 1995. Vol. 1: DOCD-5364; Vol. 3: DOCD-5366.

Smith, Mamie. *Mamie Smith: The Complete Recorded Works, Vol. 4*. Document Records, 2005. DOCD-5360.

Smith, Valerie. *Not Just Race, Not Just Gender: Black Feminist Readings*. New York: Routledge, 1998.

Smith-Rosenberg, Carroll. "Female World of Love and Ritual: Relations between Women in Nineteenth-Century America." *Signs: Journal of Women and Culture in Society* 1 (Autumn 1975): 1–29.

Snorton, C. Riley. *Nobody Is Supposed to Know: Black Sexuality on the Down Low*. Minneapolis: University of Minnesota Press, 2014.

Snyder, Tom, ed. *120 Years of American Education: A Statistical Portrait*. Washington, D.C.: National Center for Education Statistics, 1993.

Somerville, Siobhan. *Queering the Color Line: Race and the Invention of Homosexuality in America*. Durham, N.C.: Duke University Press, 2000.

Sommerville, Danielle Miller. *Rape and Race in the Nineteenth-Century South*. Chapel Hill: University of North Carolina Press, 2004.

Sontag, Susan. "Regarding the Torture of Others." *New York Times Magazine,* May 23, 2004.

Southern, David W. *The Progressive Era and Race: Reaction and Reform, 1900–1917.* Wheeling, Ill.: Harlan Davidson, 2005.

Spillers, Hortense. *Black, White, and in Color: Essays on American Literature and Culture.* Chicago: University of Chicago Press, 2003.

———. "Mama's Baby, Papa's Maybe: An American Grammar Book." *Diacritics* 17 (1987): 64–81.

Spivak, John L. *Georgia Nigger.* New York: Brewer, Warren, and Pubnam, 1932.

Spivey, Victoria. *Victoria Spivey Volume 3.* Document Records, 2000. DOCD-5038.

Stampp, Kenneth M. *The Era of Reconstruction.* New York: Knopf, 1965.

Stanley, Amy Dru. *From Bondage to Contract: Wage Labor, Marriage and the Market in the Age of Slave Emancipation.* Cambridge: Cambridge University Press, 1998.

Stepto, Robert. *From behind the Veil: A Study of Afro-American Narrative.* Urbana: University of Illinois Press, 1979.

Sterling, Anne Fausto. *Sexing the Body: Gender Politics and the Construction of Sexuality.* New York: Basic, 2000.

Talmadge, John E. *Rebecca Latimer Felton: Nine Stormy Decades.* Athens: University of Georgia Press, 1960.

Taylor, Montana. *Montana Taylor: The Complete Recorded Works.* Document Records, 1995. DOCD-5053.

Taylor, William Banks. *Brokered Justice: Race, Politics, and Mississippi Prisons, 1798–1992.* Columbus: Ohio State University Press, 1993.

Tentler, Leslie Woodstock. *Wage-Earning Women: Industrial Work and Family Life in the United States, 1900–1930.* New York: Oxford University Press, 1979.

Terborg-Penn, Rosalyn. *African American Women in the Struggle for the Vote, 1850–1920.* Bloomington: Indiana University Press, 1998.

———. "Discontented Black Feminists: Prelude and Post-script to the Passage of the Nineteenth Amendment." In *Decades of Discontent: The Women's Movement, 1920–1940,* edited by Lois Scharf and Joan M. Jensen, 261–78. Westport, Conn.: Greenwood, 1983.

Terrell, Mary Church. *A Colored Woman in a White World.* New York: Humanity, 2005. First published 1940.

———. "Peonage in the United States: The Convict Lease System and the Chain Gangs." *Nineteenth Century* 62 (1907): 306–22.

———. *The Progress of Colored Women: An address delivered before the National American Women's Suffrage Association at the Columbia Theater, Washington, D.C., February 18, 1898, on the Occasion of its Fiftieth Anniversary.* Washington, D.C.: Smith Brothers Printers, 1898.

Thompson, Heather Ann. "Blinded by a 'Barbaric' South: Prison Horrors, Inmate Abuse, and the Ironic History of American Penal Reform." In

The Myth of Southern Exceptionalism, edited by Matthew Lassiter and Joseph Crespino, 74–98. New York: Oxford University Press, 2010.

Tindall, George. *The Emergence of the New South*. Baton Rouge: Louisiana State University Press, 1967.

Trotter, Joe William. *The Great Migration in Historical Perspective: New Dimensions of Race, Class, and Gender*. Bloomington: Indiana University Press, 1991.

Trouillot, Michel-Rolph. *Silencing the Past: Power and the Production of History*. Boston: Beacon Press, 1995.

Von Eschen, Penny. *Race against Empire: Black Americans and Anticolonialism, 1937–1957*. Ithaca, N.Y.: Cornell University Press, 2000.

Wade, Stephen. *Beautiful Music All around Us: Field Recordings and the American Experience*. Urbana: University of Illinois Press, 2012.

Wagner, Bryan. *Disturbing the Peace: Black Culture and the Police Power after Slavery*. Cambridge, Mass.: Harvard University Press, 2009.

Walcott, Victoria. *Remaking Respectability: African American Women in Interwar Detroit*. Chapel Hill: University of North Carolina Press, 2001.

Walker, Alice. "Coming Apart." In *The Womanist Reader*, edited by Lalyi Phillips, 3–11. New York: Taylor & Francis, 2006.

Walker, Donald R. *Penology for Profit: A History of the Texas Prison System 1867–1912*. College Station: Texas A&M University Press, 1988.

Wallace, Michelle. *Black Macho and the Myth of the Superwoman*. New York: Dial Press, 1978.

Washington, Booker T. "The Standard Printed Version of the Atlanta Exposition Address." In *The Booker T. Washington Papers, Vol. 3: 1889–95*, edited by Louis R. Harlan, 578–83. Urbana-Champaign: University of Illinois Press, 1974.

Waters, Andrew, ed. *On Jordan's Stormy Banks: Personal Accounts of Slavery in Georgia*. Winston-Salem, N.C.: John F. Blair, 2000.

Weheliye, Alexander G. "Pornotropes." *Journal of Visual Culture* 7(1): 65–81.

Weick, Sister Mary Theodora. "A History of Rickets in the United States." *American Journal of Clinical Nutrition* 20 (November 1967): 1234–41.

Weinstein, Laura. "The Significance of the Armagh Dirty Protest." *Éire Ireland* 24 (2007): 11–41.

Wells, Ida B. *Crusade for Justice: The Autobiography of Ida B. Wells*. Edited by Alfreda Duster. Chicago: University of Chicago Press, 1991.

Welter, Barbara. "The Cult of True Womanhood: 1820–1860." *American Quarterly* 18 (1966): 151–74.

White, Deborah Gray. *Ar'n't I a Woman? Female Slaves in the Plantation South*. New York: W. W. Norton, 1985.

———. *Too Heavy a Load: Black Women in Defense of Themselves, 1894–1994*. New York: W. W. Norton, 1999.

Whites, LeeAnn. *The Civil War as a Crisis in Gender, 1860–1890*. Athens: University of Georgia Press, 1995.

———. *Gender Matters: Civil War, Reconstruction, and the Making of the New South.* New York: Palgrave Macmillan, 2005.

———. "Rebecca Latimer Felton and the Wife's Farm: The Class and Racial Politics of Gender Reform." *Georgia Historical Quarterly* 76, no. 2 (Summer 1992), 354–72.

Wiegman, Robyn. *American Anatomies: Theorizing Race and Gender.* Durham, N.C.: Duke University Press, 1995.

Williams, Kidada E. *They Left Great Marks on Me: African American Testimonials of Racial Violence from Emancipation to World War I.* New York: New York University Press, 2012.

Williams, Patricia J. *The Alchemy of Race and Rights.* Cambridge, Mass.: Harvard University Press, 1991.

Williamson, Joel. *After Slavery.* Chapel Hill: University of North Carolina Press, 1965.

———. *The Crucible of Race: Black White Relations in the American South since Emancipation.* New York: Oxford University Press, 1994.

———. "Wounds Not Scars: Lynching, the National Conscience, and the American Historian." *Journal of American History* 83 (1997): 1221–53.

Wilson, Theodore Branter. *The Black Codes of the South.* Tuscaloosa: University of Alabama Press, 1965.

Wood, Amy Louise. "Lynching Photography and the Visual Reproduction of White Supremacy." Special issue, *American Nineteenth Century History* 6 (2005): 373–99.

Woods, Clyde. *Development Arrested: The Blues and Plantation Power in the Mississippi Delta.* New York: Verso, 1998.

Woodward, C. Vann. *The Origins of the New South, 1877–1913.* Baton Rouge: Louisiana State University Press, 1951.

———. *The Strange Career of Jim Crow.* New York: Oxford University Press, 1957.

Wright, R. F. *Special Report of R.F. Wright on Misdemeanor Convicts of the State of Georgia.* Atlanta: Franklin Publishing, 1897.

Wynter, Sylvia. "Beyond Miranda's Meanings: Un/Silencing the 'Demonic Ground' of Caliban's 'Woman.'" In *The Routledge Reader in Caribbean Literature,* edited by Alison Donnell and Sarah Lawson Welsh, 476–82. New York: Routledge, 1996.

Index

Abbott, Stella, 190
Abuse, 14, 56, 90, 93, 101, 122, 138, 150,
  182, 192–93; black male convicts
  and, 127; convict leasing and, 14,
  111, 118, 124, 126, 140, 170; domestic
  forms of, 3, 190, 193, 233, 241;
  imprisoned black women's, 14,
  135–36, 152–53, 190, 251; legal forms
  of, 33; physical forms of, 127, 193;
  sexual forms of, 150, 210, 277
  (n. 179); white women and, 190
Activism, 15, 129, 133, 144; black
  women's, 10, 15, 122; labor, 263, 284
  (n. 87); southerners and, 297–98
  (n. 8); white women's, 15
"Act to Create a System of Parole or
  Conditional Pardons of Prisoners
  Convicted of Crime and for Other
  Purposes," 174
"Act to Provide for the Future
  Employment of Felony and
  Misdemeanor Male Convicts upon
  the Public Roads of the Several
  Counties of the State . . . To Amend
  Section 1039 of the Code so far as
  the Same Relates to Females," 158
Addis, Vona, 167–68
Adultery, 43, 72, 167
African Methodist Episcopal Church
  (AME Church), 28
Alabama, 133, 241, 262 (n. 32)
Albany, 195–96, 255
Alchemy of Race and Rights, 223
Alexander, Thomas, 32
Allagood, Captain, 100–102, 104,
  246–47, 297 (n. 178)
Ambiguity, 21, 22, 139, 254; black
  women's gendered forms of, 92,

  161; blues women's prison songs
  expressions of, 225, 254
Americus, 132
"Another Man Done Gone," 241–42
Antilynching movement, 114
Archer, Mrs. J. L., 183–84
Arkansas, 133
Arnall, Ellis, 172
Athens, 60, 169
Atkinson, William Y., 125, 129
Atlanta, 13, 28–31, 38, 40–44, 60–61,
  69, 73, 78–81, 83–85, 113, 126, 130–31,
  146, 161–65, 219, 265 (n. 38), 284
  (n. 87); black Americans in, 177;
  black women's entrenchment as
  domestic workers in, 34, 163, 188,
  247; city services of, 79; convict
  labor in, 80, 83, 85; courts of, 29–30,
  130, 265 (n. 40); criminal process in,
  130; discourses of, 40; downtown
  of, 162; imprisoned women, rock
  breaking in, 95; industrial progress
  of, 126; judge of, 80; local press of,
  40–41, 165; residential segregation
  law of, 164; sheriff of, 248; white
  female workforce in, 161–62, 170;
  white households in, 131, 247; white
  male job and profit access in, 170
Atlanta Chautauqua Circle, 124
"Atlanta Compromise," 13
Atlanta Constitution, 32–49 passim,
  54, 93, 95–97, 120, 127, 139, 144, 173,
  246, 266 (n. 67), 267 (n. 83), 268
  (nn. 106, 109), 280–81 (n. 5)
Atlanta jail, 84, 147
Atlanta race riot, 57, 165, 287 (n. 39)
Atlanta stockade, 85, 131, 172
Atlanta University, 170

Automobile, 12, 21, 158, 170
Autonomy, 11–12, 178, 182, 211, 221;
  bodily manifestations of, 3, 194,
  211, 232; fragmentation and, 11;
  imprisoned black women and, 3,
  12, 178, 182, 194, 211, 216, 221, 236;
  modernity and, 11; moral forms
  of, 182; sexual theories of, 216, 236;
  white collective absolute forms of, 11
Autry, Sarah, 63–64, 66–67, 79,
  106, 210

Baker, Mrs. G. R., 195
Baker, Sophia, 43
Baldwin County, 44
Baptist, Edward E., 107
Baptist Missionary Society, 135
Baptists, 28
Baptist Women's Home Missionary
  Society, 135
Barnes, Mrs. E. J., 182, 186
Bartow Iron Works Camp, 63–64,
  67, 70
Battles, G. F., 181
Baxandall, Rosalyn, 201
Beauty, 20, 47, 237; black girls'
  appropriation of, 199; black
  women convicts as lacking, 20;
  blues women depicting black
  female forms of, 237; white women
  prisoners', 33, 47, 52
Beauvoir, Simone de, 114, 276 (n. 160)
Bederman, Gail, 57
Belcher, May D., 135
Bell, George H., 101–2
Berry, Daina, 159
Berry, John, 80
Bibb County jail, 191
"Big Man from Macamere," 224
Bishop, Hattie, 195–96, 200
Black, Mattie, 75–76
Black, Pearl, 72
Black abjection, 3, 57, 161, 190, 245;
  blues feminist refusal of, 245;

female-specific forms of, 57, 90–91,
  97, 190, 251; gender ambiguity
  and the production of, 21, 161;
  home and, 190; photographic
  representation of, 22; sexist
  discursive forms of, 187, 251;
  violence of, 57; white supremacist
  foundations in, 65
Black dehumanization, 160, 202;
  gender undoing and, 277 (n. 175);
  modernity as premised upon, 3;
  production of, 160; women's death
  and, 202
Black education, 138; radical
  condemnation of, 135
Black female deviance, 3, 14, 19–20,
  77, 120–21, 127, 134, 251; assumption
  of, 77, 120, 141, 147, 152; black
  feminist work against, 120, 123;
  carceral entrenchment of, 5, 20,
  38, 187; circular logic of, 38, 134;
  construction of, 3, 20, 40–41, 121,
  251; juridical production of, 56;
  maternal form of, 36, 51; racist
  mythologies of, 120, 141; symbolic
  forms of, 121, 127; transnational
  narrative of, 39
Black female lasciviousness, 15, 81, 102,
  111, 261
Black feminist refusal, 65, 205, 212,
  233; blues critique investment in,
  254; blues politics as ostentatious
  form of, 212; bodily acts that
  stage, 64–65; epistemologies of,
  205–6, 254; gendered disciplining
  of imprisoned black women and,
  253–54; prison rule-breaking as acts
  of, 209; sonic sabotage of juridical
  power through, 213–14; survivance
  and, 205; temporality and, 205;
  white supremacy and, 13
Black infrapolitics, 202
Black life, 3, 32, 41, 55–56; carceral
  disregard for, 3, 31–32, 56;

expendability of, 41, 115; queer descriptions of, 40

Blackman, Leila, 74–75

Black parent-teacher association, 124

Black radical: collective critique, 220; critical catalogue, 214; political imaginary, 211–12; tradition, 200–201

Blake, Myrtle, 80–81

Blues, the, 211–23; black feminist radicalism of, 236; conditions that produced, 218; danger and, 219; epistemology of, 217, 243; imprisonment and, 219–20, 223, 244; leisure and, 219; loneliness and, 219–20; revival of, 215; self-fashioning within, 244; staccato and, 222, 237; women artists political articulation via, 221; working-class politics of, 216

"Blues the World Forgot," 218–19, 221

Boatwright, Lizzie, 73, 91, 126–28, 136–37

Bohnefeld, Mary, 144–45

Bolden, M. M., 93–94

Bolton broom factory camp, 70

Borders, 228; black radical transcendence of, 201; certainty of, 9; U.S. and its, 38

Boston Globe, 94

Bowers, Mamie, 80

Boyd, Mary, 76

Brer Rabbit, 34

Brock, Anna, 51

Brooks, Edward, 220

Brooks, Lula, 203

Brown, Elsa Barkley, 180

Brown, Evelyn, 76

Brown, John T., 63–64, 68–69, 71–72

Brown, Joseph M., 18

Brown, Kathleen, 159–60

Brown, Sterling, 231

Browne, Hugh Mason, 124

Bruffey, E. C., 95

Brunswick and Albany Railroad, 69, 72

Brutality, 4, 65, 132, 134; black incarcerated women and, 128, 134, 136, 152, 171, 185, 189, 223, 225, 264 (n. 30); male convicts and, 127, 136; police and, 297 (n. 3); white female subjects and, 109, 125

Buckhead, 84

Burgess, James, 90

Burgess, Leila, 90, 126, 206, 210

Burns, John, 171–72

Bush, Callie, 77

Butler, Henry R., 130–31

Butler, Selena Sloan, 14–15, 42, 94, 119, 122–33, 136–37, 140–41, 156

Byrd, Phillip, 32, 91, 126–27, 131, 134

Cages, 86, 170–71, 211; geography of, 211; sight of, 170

Campbell, Doyle, 178–79

Campbell, Mary, 44, 57

Camp de Emmel, 41–42, 85

Capital accumulation, 87, 92

Captivity: archive of, 111; black women's, 8, 17–18, 28, 41, 56, 62, 64, 74, 78, 93–94, 99–100, 113, 147, 183, 199, 200–202, 209–10, 212, 235, 243, 245, 251, 257; blues women's theorizing resistance to, 216, 220–22, 226, 228, 230–31, 235–36; conditions of, 205; contested terms of, 183, 194, 202–4, 209, 247, 253; domestic service and, 169, 176, 285–86 (n. 8); domestic violence and, 226; escape from, 208, 210; estrangement and, 117; historical continuity and, 67, 265 (n. 33), 267–68 (n. 72); logic of, 100; pain of, 2, 253; parole as, 186; radical dreams to dismantle, 201–2; release from, 208, 211; structures of, 3; weaponry of, 202

Carby, Hazel, 7–8, 12, 97, 115, 122–23, 169, 285 (n. 117), 286 (n. 16), 287–88 (n. 61)

Carcerality, 9, 157, 227, 231; black female aesthetic innovations amidst, 231; black women's objection to, 157; capital's deep connections to, 255; performative nature of, 9; practice of, 9; public sites of, 35; racially specific gendered order of, 251; southern institution of, 157, 231

Carceral logic, 156, 194; antiblackness of, 156; criminalized women's sabotaging of, 194; imprisoned women's critical revealing of, 200; patriarchal dimensions of, 156; twentieth-century forms of, 217

Carceral state, the, 9, 16, 38, 75, 155, 185, 251; black women's confrontations with, 3, 11, 253; history of, 264 (n. 30); white supremacy and, 252

Caribbean, 39

Carmichael, Frank, 165

Carolinas, the, 133

Carpenter, Nellie, 74

Cartoonists, 38–39; American imperial conquest and, 39; black children depicted by, 38; imprisoned black women depicted by, 19–20

Central Georgia Land and Lumber Co. camp, 70

Chain gang, 3–4, 9, 26–29, 125, 139, 143–155 passim, 219, 254–55, 262 (n. 29), 264 (n. 28), 282 (n. 22), 287 (n. 44); auto and, 12; black girls on, 42, 199; black women on, 4, 10, 14, 30, 32, 35, 41–42, 45–46, 55, 57, 63, 72–74, 88, 121, 126–27, 148, 155–60, 163–64, 166, 171–73, 176, 252, 256, 260 (n. 8), 285 (n. 6); brutal conditions of, 4, 35, 72–73, 126–27, 139, 157, 171–73, 241; county roads and, 4, 157–58, 170, 172; gendered racial construction of, 4, 15, 126–27, 157, 160, 163–64, 166–71; labor exploitation under, 161, 163, 226; popular cultural representations

of, 231, 297–98 (n. 8); slavery's gendered continuities with, 159; white women exempted from, 4, 30, 57, 84, 148, 158, 160, 163–64, 166–71, 255

"Chain Gang Blues," 224

Chain gang law, 1908, 158, 160, 167, 188

Chain-Gang System, The, 125–26

Chastity, white women's, 11, 114, 252, 287 (n. 40)

Chatham County, 79, 100

Chattahoochee Brick Company camp, 70, 73–74, 78, 81, 90, 93, 106, 143, 209

Cherokee county, 49

Chevrolet, 28

Chickamauga River, 77

Childbirth: as compulsory, 25, 115, 117; death during, 46, 106; documentation of, 104, 108–9, 111, 172; imprisoned black women's, 17, 104, 108, 127, 172; portrayed as illness, 108–9, 111, 172; shackling during, 256

Clark, Kate, 206

Clark, Matt, 63

Clarke County chain gang, 167–68

Clemency, 8, 14, 18–23 passim, 45, 52–57 passim, 80, 103–4, 115–17, 157, 167–69, 171, 187, 206–7, 209, 271 (n. 23); applications for, 18, 21, 31, 49, 52, 55, 75, 103–4, 106, 115, 169, 206, 209–11, 248, 288–89 (n. 92); files for, 53, 209–10, 269 (n. 1), 290 (n. 152), 293 (n. 62); grounds for, 45, 52, 171, 173; letters seeking, 211, 294 (n. 79); petition for, 18, 52, 60, 190–91, 193, 210; records of, 21, 116–17, 270 (n. 8)

Cleveland, Lizzie, 203

Clowden, Victoria, 193

Clubwomen: black, 14–15, 118, 121–25, 139, 141, 149, 210; white, 15, 49, 141, 162

Cobb, Eliza, 17–27, 36, 46–49, 52–53, 56–57, 106, 210

Cobb County, 59–60

Cobb County chain gang, 171
Cohen, Cathy, 244, 286 (n. 16), 296
  (n. 171)
Cohn, David, 233
Cole, Arthur, 47
Cole, Della, 44, 57
Coleman, Essie, 172
Coleman, E. W., 47–50
Commercial Telegraphers Union of
  America, 162
Committee to Investigate the
  Penitentiary, 89
Congressional Library, 136
Conscription, 11–12, 199, 292 (n. 13)
Convict camp facilities, forced
  cogender use and, 91–92, 169–70,
  277 (n. 175)
Convict labor regime, 3, 110, 154;
  reactions against, 3
Convict lease camps, 4, 10, 26, 46, 66,
  287 (n. 44); black women and, 10,
  88; deadly conditions of, 157; white
  women and, 4, 8
Convict leasing system, 4, 14–15,
  26–27, 68, 262 (n. 29), 264 (n. 28),
  282 (n. 46); abolition of, 121, 132,
  136, 140–41, 148; activism against,
  14–15, 73, 94, 119–55, 136, 142;
  archive of, 141, 149; black children
  and, 46, 55, 112, 142; black women's
  experience under, 14, 57, 68, 73, 89,
  94, 118, 121–25, 129, 133–34, 137, 147,
  152, 160, 253, 292 (n. 13); end of,
  4, 131, 157, 172, 282 (n. 22); era of,
  170, 287 (n. 44); expendable labor
  and, 280 (n. 243); death under,
  65, 67, 144–45; gendered regime
  of, 66, 68, 115, 122, 140, 149, 164;
  inception of, 89; infrastructure of,
  29; investigations of, 28, 140–41;
  modernization project of, 46, 67,
  126; mothers and, 55, 68, 115; reform
  and, 27; sexual violence pervasive
  to, 94, 111, 129, 131, 141, 277 (n. 175),
  292 (n. 13); spectacle of, 67

Conyers, Susan, 44, 57, 73
Cook, Swanie, 190
Cotton States and International
  Exposition, 13
Crawford, Mattie, 95–100, 118, 127,
  278 (n. 188)
Criminalization, 136–37, 219, 251;
  black children and, 68; black
  critiques of, 136–37, 223; black
  women and, 12, 15, 27, 121, 137, 190,
  220, 222, 251, 287–88 (n. 61); racial
  disparity in, 190, 251; white women
  and, 15, 190
Criminal legal system, 3, 15, 132;
  changes in, 15; gendered racism
  of, 132
Criminal punishment, 121, 147, 192,
  200, 216, 251, 256, 264 (n. 30), 282
  (n. 44); blues women's insight into,
  16, 216, 220, 222, 224, 236, 244–45;
  ethos of, 200; gendered racial
  regulation and, 12–13; lexicon of,
  256; record of, 192; reproductive
  control of black women and, 298
  (n. 13)
Critical race feminism, 16, 202
Crowder, Rachel, 90, 203
Crowfoot Alley, 34
Crozier, L. Graham, 49–50
Cuba, 39
Cubbo, Mamie, 73
Cultural pathology, black, 38; females
  and, 64; uplift ideology and, 281
  (n. 11)
Cureton, Hubbard, 32, 65, 89, 91
Cursing, 36–38, 94, 100, 130, 204, 209;
  arrest for, 37; charge of, 36, 38;
  crime of, 130; whipped for, 94

Dade Coal Mines camp, 270 (n. 11)
Dade County Coal Mines, 58, 70
Dahlonega, 47
"Dangerous Blues," 232–33, 236
Daniel, Norah, 204–5
Darcy, Annie, 51

Index 323

Darktown, 36–37

Darnell, John, 31, 65, 70

Davis, Angela Y., 87, 114, 136–37, 159, 199, 202, 285 (n. 4), 292 (n. 13), 296 (n. 171), 298 (n. 14)

Davis, Emma, 30, 57

Davis, Maude, 168–69

Davis, Mike, 201

Davison, R. H., 168–69

Dean, Wyley, 45–46

Decatur Street, 219

De Cris, Mamie, 100–104, 118, 280 (n. 251), 297 (n. 178)

Degradation, 127–28, 150, 153; gendered language of, 127; imprisoned black women's plight as, 128, 151

Delaney, Tom, 226

Demonic, the, 228–30; black female subjects absence/presence as contribution to, 230; computer science and, 229; peripheral reordering by, 230; philosophical multiplicity of, 229; physics and, 229; potentiality of, 230; second law of thermodynamics challenged by, 229. *See also* Katherine McKittrick; Sylvia Wynter

Dent, Gina, 87

Desire, homosexual, 6, 40

Determinism, 229; causal form of, 229; scientific articulation of, 229–30

Discipline, 27, 44, 189, 261 (n. 22), 275 (n. 146); behavioral control and, 204; conversion and, 146; moral forms of, 93; subject fit for, 214

Disease, 4, 64–66, 76–77, 113, 200, 235; black prisoners and, 4, 65–66, 76–77, 129; black women figured as, 149, 287 (n. 58); incarcerated childbirth as, 108; prisons as space of, 68, 76, 129, 172–73, 200, 270 (n. 6)

Disorderly conduct, 30–31, 34, 130–31, 138

Dispossession, 200, 217, 257

Dixon, Sarah, 76

Docility, 39, 177, 189, 200; carceral enforcement of black female forms of, 177, 207–11; imprisoned black women's strategies of, 207–8, 210–11

Domestic carceral sphere, 16, 156–94; expansion of the prison regime through, 160; gendered exploitation of labor via, 161, 182; violence of, 183; white expectations and satisfaction as central to, 188; white women's role and control over black female labor restored by, 180, 183

Domestic manager, 180, 182, 185; white women as, 180, 289 (n. 111)

Domestic servants, 2, 9, 34, 178, 189, 208

Donaldson, Mrs. John E., 103

Dougherty County, 196, 199, 200

Dougherty county chain gang, 196, 199

Douglass, Charles R., 133

Douglass, Frederick, 133

Drinks, Fannie, 76

Du Bois, W. E. B., 13, 94, 106, 202

Du Bois sawmill camp, 17, 24, 70

Dylan, Bob, 215, 240

Edwards, Erica, 212

E. H. Jackson's camp, 204

Elders, Isabelle, 185–87

Emmel, Jack, 41–42

Eugenics, 135, 153

Everyday: abandonment, 220; acts of resistance, 3; ethics, 217; forms of resistance, 205; goals, 26; judicial terror, 220; life, 26, 217, 222; rebellion or defiance walk, 235; resistance, 139

Everydayness, 220, 222; torturing imprisoned black women as, 127

Evidence, 1, 14, 43–54 passim, 90, 104–7, 122, 128–29, 131, 147, 151, 154, 174, 179, 207; investigations uncovering of, 65; lack of, 45–47, 49, 51–52, 105, 107, 191; medical forms of, 46, 53, 104; photographic form of, 18–22; standards for, 21, 54

Expansionism, U.S., 39

Farmer, Mollie, 53–54, 57

Fears, Mary Lou, 17

Fecal impaction, 76, 271 (n. 22)

Feimster, Crystal, 109, 154, 275–76 (n. 147), 279 (n. 228)

Felton, Rebecca Latimer, 15, 140–44, 147–55, 162, 283 (n. 73), 284 (nn. 77, 88), 289 (n. 119)

Felton, William H., 142

Fitzgerald, Ella, 212

Florida, 133, 136

Floyd County, 73

Floyd County Board of Commissioners of Roads and Revenue, 75

Flynn, Elizabeth Gurley, 201

Forgery, 43, 100, 175

Fort, William A., 69

Foster, K. R., 102, 247

Foucault, Michel, 27, 105, 213–14, 261 (n. 22), 263 (n. 11)

Freedom, 16, 194, 254–55; black dreams and visionings of, 114, 187, 199–200, 202, 215, 224, 228, 230–31, 236, 297 (n. 3); black women and, 5–6, 20, 22, 28, 94, 110, 129, 135, 138, 183–84, 194, 206, 208–11, 292 (n. 13); consent and, 107; domestic servitude and, 186, 206; individual forms of, 107; slave women's war for, 202; twentieth-century notions and practices of, 182; white control and, 17, 265 (n. 33); white male delineation of, 245; white women and, 23–24, 168

Fugitivity, 196, 199

Fulton Bag and Cotton Mills, 163

Fulton County, 28, 42, 66, 78, 84

Fulton County convict camp, 168

Fulton county women's stockade, 131

Gaines, Kevin, 123

Gainesville, 45

Gamble, Ella, 73–74, 208–9

Gammon, W. M., 75

Gault, Martha, 21–25, 27, 43, 56, 80

Gee, Jack, 220

Gendered racial terror, 3, 8, 9, 12, 14, 15, 57, 67, 86, 87, 88, 92, 114, 128, 221, 227, 231, 246, 251, 253, 256, 257

Gender ideology, 4–5, 8, 10, 13, 67, 141, 256; black women's critique of, 10, 157; carceral life and, 4–5, 8, 141, 157, 251; racial formation of, 4–5, 140, 157; slavery's history and, 13, 50, 67, 176, 261 (n. 25); white femininity and, 13, 50; white supremacy of, 5, 10, 52, 150, 160

George D. Harris's convict camp, 106

Georgetown, 50

Georgia, 1, 4, 12–16, 26, 28–29, 31, 36, 40, 42, 45–47, 51, 55–56, 60–61, 66, 69–70, 72, 77, 81, 84, 92, 95, 101–2, 109, 124, 126, 131–32, 134, 138, 140–44, 148–49, 159, 164–65, 195, 217, 219, 231, 254–55; black girls in, 42; black women in, 18, 28–29, 31, 43, 46, 55–56, 63, 72–73, 81, 90, 92–93, 100, 104–5, 109, 113–14, 119, 127, 131–32, 134, 136, 138, 140–41, 155, 157–58, 163, 177–78, 203, 206, 220, 250, 256, 278 (n. 88); carceral authorities of, 46, 158, 248; early twentieth-century and, 47; economy of, 13–14, 69, 170; elites of, 47, 50; modernization of, 12, 69–70, 170–71; nineteenth-century and, 42, 72; prisoners in, 10, 32, 43, 46, 55–56, 63, 66, 69, 72–73, 77, 79, 81, 90, 92–93, 100, 113–14, 119, 127, 131–32, 136, 140–42, 155, 157–58, 190, 203, 231; prison reform in, 166; punishment system of, 2–4, 15–16, 26, 55–56, 63, 66, 69–70, 73, 76–77, 81, 86, 89–90, 92–94, 100–102, 104–5, 108, 113–14, 119, 126–27, 129, 132, 134, 136, 140–41, 155, 160–61, 164, 171, 189, 206, 209–10, 220, 254, 256–57, 262 (n. 69),

272 (n. 45), 282 (n. 44); roads in, 12, 160–61, 170, 172, 297–98 (n. 8); state legislature of, 142, 148, 152, 175; state violence in, 14, 102, 171–72; symbolic significance of, 13–14, 164; white women in, 77, 84, 100, 124, 134, 140–42, 158, 160, 162–63, 166, 170–71, 188, 275–76 (n. 147)

Georgia Air-Line railroad, 69, 72

Georgia and Alabama Railroad, 69

Georgia Commission on Interracial Cooperation, 124

Georgia Federation of Women's Clubs, 49–50

Georgia General Assembly, 157, 174

Georgia House of Representatives, 101–2

Georgia Legislature, 175

Georgia Nigger, 172

Georgia Prison Commission, the, 1, 32, 54, 82–83, 103, 115–16, 136, 158, 165, 167, 173–76, 178–86, 208–9, 247; affidavit to, 18; chairman of, 18, 74; letter to, 19, 22–24, 54, 74–75, 103, 156, 173, 176, 178–79, 181–84, 186, 208; officers of, 83; petition to, 54; reports to, 176, 180, 182; secretary of, 2, 167; telegram to, 54

Georgia Representative, 101

Georgia State Capitol, 124

"Georgia Stockade Blues," 224

Georgia Western railroad, 69

Gibson, Lucy, 44

Gilbert, Susannah, 54–55, 106, 210

Gilmore, Glenda, 10, 123

Gilmore, Ruth Wilson, 245, 291 (n. 54)

Glenn, Evelyn Nakano, 159

Glymph, Thavolia, 202

Glynn county, 79

"Go Away Devil, Leave me Alone," 224

Godbee, Edna, 190

Godshalk, David, 165

Goff, Hattie, 222, 243, 246

Gordon, John B., 60

Gore, Dayo F., 132, 282 (n. 44)

Grant, Alexander, and Co. convict camp, 32, 65, 69

Grant, Alexander & Co., 32, 69

Grant, William D., 70

Graysville lime quarrying camp, 70, 77

Great Migration, The, 177–78

Green, Joe, 75–76

Griffin News, 84

Grimes, Florence, 178

Gross, Kali, 12, 273 (n. 97)

Guilt, 18, 46, 50, 218–19, 222–25, 244, 254; blues women's confounding of, 218–19, 222–25, 244, 254; burden of, 18; convicted black women and, 46, 53, 115–16; white men's lack of, 275 (n. 146); white women and, 50

Gunn, J. F., 179

Habersham County, 167

Haines Normal and Industrial Institute, 138

Hale, Grace, 10

Hall, Jacquelyn Dowd, 162, 252, 261 (n. 26); 282 (n. 29)

Hall, Vera, 240–42

Halpert, Herbert, 216, 234, 241, 245

Harper, Anderson, 191

Harper, Frances E. W., 122

Harper, Mrs. E. E., 146

Harris, Cheryl, 188

Harris, George D., 63–64, 66–67, 106

Harris, Joel Chandler, 34

Harris, Margaret, 169

Harrison, Pearl, 80

Hartman, Saidiya, 14, 56, 105, 109, 111, 114, 152, 271 (n. 24), 284 (n. 92)

Hawaii, 39

Heard, Laura, 203, 206, 210

Henderson, E., 51

Henderson, Rose, 54, 76, 129

Hendley, Anna, 76

Henry, W. M., 2, 7

Hicks, Alma, 227

Hicks, Cheryl, 12, 285 (n. 3), 287–88 (n. 61)

Higdon, Lethia, 208, 293 (n. 62)

Higginbotham, Evelyn Brooks, 123, 275 (n. 161), 281 (n. 11)

High, Raymond, 182

Hill, Amanda, 54, 117, 209

Hill, Mrs. R. B., 75

Hill, Rebecca, 201

Hine, Darlene Clark, 211

Holliman, J. E., 179

Holly, Dora, 191, 210

Homes for wayward women, 178

Hope, R. L., 76, 78

Hopkins, Pauline, 122

Horne, Mrs. E., 49–50

House of the Good Shepherd for fallen women, 50

Houston, 215

Howard, Lucy, 203

Hudson, Ella, 203

Hughes, Evaline, 47

Hutchins, G. R., 18

Hunter, Alberta, 215

Hunter, Jane, 167–68

Hunter, Tera, 13–14, 35, 72, 123, 163, 178, 202, 285 (n. 117)

Hypersexuality, black females assumed, 147, 149; disease and, 149; myth of the black male rapist and, 149

I am a Fugitive from a Georgia Chain Gang!, 171–72

Illness, 4, 26, 73, 75–76, 172; black prisoners and, 4, 26, 73, 75–76; childbirth as, 108–9; feigning of, 35, 178, 205–6; imprisoned black women and, 35, 76, 205; old age and, 73; prison records of, 76, 111, 172

Industrialization, 39, 144, 196, 256, 262–3 (n. 39)

Industrial Workers of the World (IWW), 201

Infanticide, 17, 24, 43, 47, 53, 98, 268 (n. 105); all-white juries and cases of, 18; black female lechery as motor for, 51; black women and,

46, 51–55, 270 (n. 9); normative femininity and, 46; poor white women and, 51, 207; prosecution of, 51, 55; race and disparate sentence length for, 53; racial-sexual bias in cases of, 53; white babies and, 47–49, 268 (n. 106)

Infrastructure, 12–14, 67, 78; black women's role in, 12, 78, 250; intrastate transport and, 157; prisons and, 3, 29, 78, 82, 183; private forms of, 12; public forms of, 12, 77; southern development and, 12–14, 67, 161

Ingram, Rosa Lee, 132, 282 (n. 44)

Innocence, 17, 23, 46, 52, 54, 153, 187, 207, 223; binary construction of, 223; blues women's troubling of, 219, 222–23, 225; declarations of, 171, 187, 218; imprisoned black women's rejection of, 243, 254; presumption of white male, 1–2; white female infantilization and, 24; white women's perceived, 51; women's claims to, 211

Insubordination, 100–101, 204, 206, 209, 211; imprisoned women's veiled history of, 209–10; whippings for, 209

International Cotton Exposition, 13

Interracial sex, 15, 149–54; opposition to, 150; prohibitions against, 162; violence and, 150–52; white women and, 150, 276 (n. 158)

Invert, the, 6, 89; black women as, 6, 8, 89

Jacks, John, 120

Jackson, Walter, 231

"Jail-House Blues," 212, 221, 227

Jailhouse Blues: Women's A Capella Songs from the Parchman Penitentiary, 216

Jails, 3, 9, 200, 246, 254; visits to, 142, 146

James, Sarah, 203

Jarbon, Louisa, 203

Jim Crow modernity, 3, 11–12, 28, 67, 111, 189, 195, 199; absolute difference and, 252; binary foundations of, 81; black imprisoned women and challenges to, 200, 253; carceral production of, 251; domesticity and white femininity linked by, 189; gender categorization constructed during, 87, 251; gendered racial labor dynamics of, 71; nonviolent treatment of white women during, 102; racial separation defining, 80; racial terror and, 88, 252; white male sexual assault of black women as strategic control of terrain within, 111

Johnson, Emma, 1–2, 7

Johnson, Hattie, 73, 156–57, 161, 187

Johnson, Joe, 43

Johnson, Leana, 237

Johnson, Lula, 73

Johnson, Sarah, 76

Jones, Jacqueline, 180

Jones, Mamy, 34, 57

Jones, Violet, 41, 57

Jordan, Samuel B., 181–82

Kelley, Robin D. G., 202, 212, 293 (n. 68)

Kellor, Frances, 97–98, 278 (n. 196)

Kelly, Queen, 181

Kemp, Joe, 219

Kemp, Newt, 219

Kemp, Stella, 171, 219

Kicks, Adolphus, 75–76

Kinsey, Molly, 28

Kriese City convict camp, 84

Ku Klux Klan, 60, 116, 87 (n. 40)

Kunzel, Regina, 244, 260 (n. 13), 272 (n. 67), 296 (n. 170)

Labor extraction, 39, 67, 114, 159, 226; colonial mastery and, 39; women in bondage and, 159, 226

Lanier, Mr. and Mrs., 47

Laney, Lucy, 137–39

LaPlace, Pierre, 229

Larceny, 43–45, 79, 156, 168, 171, 247; black women sentenced to chain gangs for, 44–45, 156, 171; petty crimes of, 43–44, 169; women convicted for, 43–45, 79, 156, 168; working-class white women sentences for, 79, 168

Laurens county, 79

Lea, Nora, 204

Leflouria, Talitha, 262 (n. 35)

Leniency, 18–19, 74, 117, 213; appeals for, 18–19, 117; Bessie Smith commentary on, 213; black women's perceived maternal dysfunctionality as basis of, 42, 53, 117; black women's presumed guilt requiring alternative grounds for, 53; mobilizations for executive, 21; racialized conditions that justified judicial forms of, 73; sexual force and, 117; white women's ease in garnering, 51, 53, 75

Lessees, 21, 29, 73, 75, 152; complaints of, 72–73; trial of, 129

Lewis, Hazel, 172

Lewis, Robert H., 207

Lindsay, Louisa, 51, 54

Link, Martha, 55

Literacy rates, black, 122, 206, 293 (n. 52)

Litwack, Leon, 10

Lockhart, Bessie, 115–17

Lomax, Alan, 231, 234, 241

Lomax, John A., 216, 240–41, 294 (n. 95)

Lomax Family Iconic Song List, 228, 241

Long, Laney, 62, 76

"Long Line," 227

Louisiana, 107, 133, 147

Lowe, Rebecca Douglas, 49–50

Lucas, Annie, 73

Lynch mobs, 109
Lynn, Eliza, 203

Macon, 182
Macon and Augusta Railroad, 69
Macon and Brunswick Railroad, 66, 90
Maddox, Adaline, 142, 148
Maddox, Colonel, 38–39, 61, 203–4
Maddox, W. H., 82, 94
Mammy, the, 39, 81, 146, 187, 281–82
    (n. 21), 290 (n. 133); black female
    defiance of, 185, 187; colonized
    nations as, 39
Manumission, 186, 290 (n. 140)
Marshall, Annie, 76
Martin, Eliza, 182, 186
Martin, Sara, 215–16, 224–26, 245
Maryland, 50
Masculine dress, forced imposition of,
    99, 127–28
Masculinity, black women's racially
    constructed and forced proximity
    to, 9, 88, 95, 97, 100, 103, 118,
    127–28, 159, 253
Massachusetts, 135
Matthews, J., 19, 24
Maxwell, James, 65–66, 90
Mays, Janie, 208–9
McCarthy, Pauline, 30
McCord, T. A., 185–86
McKittrick, Katherine, 229–30, 286
    (n. 16)
McMillen, Neil, 10
Memphis, 132
Milledgeville State Prison Farm, 1,
    3–4, 16–18, 21–22, 26, 31, 42–43,
    48–50, 52, 54, 70, 73–74, 76, 82–83,
    86, 95, 100, 102, 115, 142, 148, 164,
    167, 169, 172–74, 176, 178–79, 181,
    183–86, 189, 191, 193, 203, 207–10,
    246–48, 256–57, 263 (n. 4), 289
    (n. 97)
Miller, H. V. M., 108
Miller, Stephen, 71
Miller-Young, Mireille, 277 (n. 175)

Mills, Maggie, 53
Minor laws, 42, 267 (n. 89)
Minstrelsy, 215
Miscegenation, 141, 150
Mississippi, 16, 133, 216, 262 (n. 32)
Missouri, 120
Mitchell, Margaret, 13
Mitchell, Michele, 123
Mitchell, Susie, 204
Mitchell County chain gang, 173
Modernization, southern, 12, 67, 157,
    195, 262 (n. 29), 265 (n. 33); black
    children and, 46; black women as
    resources for, 205; convict leasing
    and, 46, 70, 157, 265 (n. 33)
Monk, J. F., 186
Moore, Mary, 175–76
Moreland, Amelia, 76
Morgan, Jennifer, 261 (n. 25), 262
    (n. 27), 266–67 (n. 72), 286 (n. 16)
Morgan, Pleasant, 42, 57
Morgan, Susan, 44
Morris, Leta, 73
Morris, Mrs. Charles, 155
Morris, Nancy, 58, 62–63, 269 (n. 1),
    270 (n. 11), 270 (nn. 18–19), 271
    (n. 23)
Morton, Julia, 75
Mosley, Alicia, 181
Moten, Fred, 196–98
"Mr. Dooley Don 'Rest Me," 222, 243
Murder, 1, 22, 46, 53, 191, 251;
    allegation of, 191, 193; attempting
    to, 43, 190; black women convicted
    of, 1, 43, 46, 55, 90, 93, 132, 190–91,
    203–4, 209, 248; blues songs about,
    243; charge of, 192, 207; intent to,
    21; sentenced to death for, 93; trial
    for, 191–92; white women and, 76
Murderer, black women portrayed as,
    59, 71, 73

Nashville, 125, 247
National American Woman's Suffrage
    Association (NAWSA), 133

National Association for the
Advancement of Colored People
(NAACP), 132
National Association of Colored
Women (NACW), 15, 73, 119, 253
National Committee to Free the
Ingram Family, 132
National Conference of Colored
Women, 119
National Council of Women, 134
National Prison Association (NPA),
125
Negation, 87, 200, 236; modernity and,
200; productivity of, 21; regimes of
captivity and, 236
Neglect, 4, 65; black convicts and,
55, 115, 117, 171; imprisoned black
women's experience of, 57, 115, 205;
medical forms of, 26, 55, 57, 117,
171, 205
Negress, 21, 36, 266 (n. 67)
Neoslave narratives, 211, 294 (n. 79);
imprisoned intellectual production
as, 294 (n. 79)
Neoslavery, 9, 182, 184, 261 (n. 22);
carceral state as form of, 75, 159, 261
(n. 22); gendered regime of, 67–68
Neuralgia, 77, 270 (n. 18)
New South, the, 3, 9–10, 13, 164;
economic progress of, 13;
formation of, 9–10; gendered labor
exploitation in, 3; state violence
and, 3; white men in, 179; white
supremacist defense of, 50–51
New York, 42, 169, 267 (n. 89)
Nineteenth Century, The, 137
Nonbeing, black women's, 160;
domestic labor and, 160; road labor
and, 160; unbearable flexibility of,
160
Normativity, gender, 21, 67, 147, 154,
253; black female negation and,
21, 67, 147, 253; black feminist
interrogations of, 202, 292 (n. 27);
counternormativity and, 41, 97;

sexual forms of, 6, whiteness
constituted by, 67; white women as
paragon of, 67, 154
North Carolina, 146
Northeastern railroad, 69
Northen, William, 143
North Georgia Railroad, 89

Oberlin College, 132
O'Dwyer, Kate, 167–68
Old South, 39–40, 205
Old Town Camp, 70, 73, 90, 129, 209
Oshinsky, David, 233
Overseer, convict camp, 25, 28, 31, 41,
60, 64, 66, 91–92, 100, 203; beatings
by, 60, 91–92, 151; imprisoned black
women and, 19, 66, 91–92, 151
Overwork, 4, 55, 73, 171; black
prisoners and, 4, 55, 171;
incarcerated pregnant black women
and, 73

Pacific Islands, 39
Painter, Nell, 128, 282 (n. 29)
Parchman Farm (Mississippi
Penitentiary), 215–16, 219;
recordings from, 221, 226, 243
Parks, Cammie, 53
Parole, 2–3, 75, 115–17, 169, 285–85
(n. 8); black women under, 158–60,
174–93, 206–10, 252; carceral space
of, 16; laws enacting, 158, 174; racial
exclusivity of, 288–89 (n. 92).
See also domestic carceral sphere
Parole Act, 1908, 175–77
Pateman, Carole, 107, 162–63
Pathologization, 154, 220; black female
bodies and, 266–67 (n. 72); concern
and, 154; dominant narratives of,
220
Patriarchy, white supremacist, 24,
107–8, 122, 136, 156, 163, 226, 257;
black women's challenges to, 11, 122,
136, 202; built landscape of, 199;
domestic practices of, 38

Patterson, Lizzie, 30, 41, 57, 72, 85, 275
  (n. 138)
"Peas and Bread," 233
"Penalty of Being a Woman, The," 162
Pendergast, Pearl, 40, 82
"Penitentiary Blues," 223–24, 226
Penn, Zachariah, 64
Peonage, 94, 136, 262 (n. 29), 292
  (n. 13); as induced by debt, 110, 135,
  279 (n. 232)
"Peonage in the United States," 135,
  137, 140
Perjury, 43, 207; blacks and, 207;
  females convicted for, 43
Personhood, 20, 24, 254, 263 (n. 10);
  blacks and, 20, 24, 110, 114, 254;
  whites and, 9
Philadelphia, 12, 273 (n. 97)
Philippines, the, 39
Pickaninny, imaginaries of, 39, 111, 113
Pitts, Elizabeth, 54–55
Plantations, 3, 68–70, 82, 146, 179;
  agrarian economy of, 12; enslaved
  black female labor on, 17, 68,
  159; enslaved resistance on, 205;
  household of, 68, 183, 272 (n. 52);
  tropes of, 146; white femininity
  produced by, 68, 183, 289 (n. 11);
  white nostalgia for, 63, 69–70
Pneumonia, 59, 76, 270 (n. 6)
Police, 17, 29, 31, 40–41, 45, 52, 90, 144,
  158, 190–91, 218–19; black women
  violated by, 251; blues women's
  satirical portraits of, 243; chief of,
  144; contemporary protests against
  violence by, 297 (n. 3); dockets of,
  14; raid by, 43
Police station, 144, 190
Policing, 6, 36, 144, 189, 217, 219,
  251–52, 285 (n. 4); black women
  and, 29, 38, 98, 200, 245, 267 (n. 98);
  moral forms of, 128, 168
Politics: black women's, 123–24, 156,
  216, 243, 281 (n. 12), 290
  (n. 141); blueswomen's disavowal

of normative forms of, 212,
  216; challenges to, 162, 200, 240;
  dominant political processes
  negation of, 110, 123, 144, 153–54;
  imprisonment and, 15, 125, 144,
  206; queer women's leadership and
  invisibility within, 297 (n. 3); the
  sexual and, 15; strategies of, 187,
  200. See also respectability politics
Polk county convict camps, 66
Poole, Annie Laurie, 165
Positionality, 213, 226; black girl
  subversive displays of, 195; black
  queer performances of, 226; blues
  women's lyrical persona and,
  213; incarcerated black and white
  women's differential forms of, 81
Postbellum: convict labor, 158; defeat,
  70; era, 25; phenomenon, 50;
  politics, 87; poverty, 50; south, 20
Potts, Captain, 90
Pregnancy, 17, 55, 73, 104, 106, 172,
  187, 273 (n. 84); compulsory form
  of, 115, 117; disregard for, 157
Premodernity, 126, 133
Price, Mattie Jane (Honey Ann), 180,
  185, 187
Pride, Ella, 190–91, 210
Principal keeper, 29, 31–32, 43, 63, 66,
  68–71, 108; penitentiary conditions
  and, 63, 65–66, 270 (nn. 6–7);
  women's imprisonment and, 32, 48,
  70–71, 108
Prison administrators, 18, 21, 109, 169
Prison Commission of Georgia, 18
Prison matron, 22, 144–45
Pritchett, Dolly, 47–56, 207, 268 (n. 111)
Probation, 175
Probation Act, 1913, 175
Probation officer, 175; white women
  as, 144
Progressive era, 20, 136, 155, 162, 219;
  antiblackness of, 20, 35, 97, 136;
  challenges to, 219; reform and, 77,
  178, 284 (n. 79), 289 (n. 99)

"Progress of Colored Women, The,"
133
Puerto Rico, 39
Purity, 20, 53, 102, 153, 162–63; poor
white womens', 50–51, 162–63;
protecting white feminine forms
of, 53, 87, 102

Quarantine, 149
Queer, 35, 39–41, 64, 267 (n. 82);
blackness and, 40–41, 51; black
women as, 5–7, 40, 88, 97–98, 226,
244, 290 (n. 149), 297 (n. 3)
Queerness, 40–41, 97; black female
forms of, 6–7, 98

Rabinowitz, Howard, 10
Race relations, 254, 297 (n. 6); future
of, 110; nadir of, 20, 120; southern,
251
Racial subordination, 3, 57, 67, 87, 110,
114, 161, 181, 188, 232, 251–52, 266–67
(n. 72); black women's challenging
of, 110, 163, 188; blues music as
a system against, 244; carceral
form of, 262 (n. 29); discursive
mobilization of black women in
support of, 87, 251; legislative
entrenchment of, 251; narrative
justification for, 5, 251; patriarchal
forms of, 232, 251; white women's
reinforcement of paroled black
women's, 163, 181
Racism, 154, 281 (n. 7); definition
of, 291 (n. 154); scientific form of,
35, 39
Rainey, Gertrude "Ma," 215–19, 222,
224–25, 232, 245
Rake, Cornelia, 80–81
Randall, Eliza, 93–95, 277 (n. 177)
Rape, imprisoned black women's, 15,
24–26, 36, 63, 92, 104–35, 149–54,
191, 199, 210, 226, 233–36, 260–61
(n. 19), 275 (n. 146), 280 (nn. 239,
242), 282 (n. 29), 291 (n. 159);

acceptability of, 71; archival veiling
of, 104–6, 140; convict camps and
systemic, 104–6, 114–16, 128, 131,
204, 210; denial of, 114; forced
reproduction and, 104, 109, 115,
117; imminent threat of, 43, 109;
inescapability of, 233; innuendo
and, 24; inviolability and perceived
inability for, 109, 116, 140;
magnitude of, 104–6, 137; pandemic
of, 55, 131, 233; reporting of, 104;
tacit sanctioning of, 114; ubiquity
of, 25, 203, 292 (n. 13); white guard
perpetration of, 106, 114, 128, 211,
297 (n. 178); white male supremacy
and, 68, 106, 109, 114
Reagon, Bernice Johnson, 216
Rearrest, 167, 175
Reconstruction, 10, 20, 70, 100, 165,
253; black women during, 88, 100;
failure of, 137; poor white women
and, 276 (n. 158)
Redmond, Shana, 246
Reed, Thomas, 79
Reid, Mattie, 183–85, 187
Reimprisonment, 175, 183; threat of,
183; women subjected to, 16
Release, 2, 4, 31–32, 34, 42, 47, 50, 52,
62–63, 65, 73–77, 80, 117, 145,
168–69, 172, 182, 185–86, 191, 208, 219;
black children and, 21, 199–200;
black convict labor expendability
and, 280 (n. 243); ideology of black
women as nonrapeable resulting
in rape as nullified justification
for, 36; incarcerated black women's
relationships after, 63; parole as
continuance of servitude and
incarceration and not, 160, 174–76,
187, 285–86 (n. 8); rape as obstacle
to, 116; white documented support
of black convicts as necessity for,
31, 168, 178, 181, 208, 211; white
women's tendency to receive early,
4, 8, 169, 175–76, 187

Remorse, 212; blues women's performative rejection of, 212; lack of, 187, 213

Republican Club of New York City, 137

Respectability politics, 12, 123, 156, 187, 199–200, 240, 243, 290 (n. 41); challenges to, 237, 240, 243; class and, 123, 187, 290 (n. 41); conventions of, 156, 242; debates on, 281 (n. 12); flouting norms of, 237, 242; gender categories and, 187; imprisoned blues singers rejection of, 243–44, 254; moral tenets of, 12, 185, 285 (n. 3); protective strategy of, 243, 253–54

Reynolds, Narcissa, 80–81

Rheumatism, 45, 77, 79, 270 (n. 19)

Richardson, Flora, 51–54, 57

Richmond County, 79

Richmond County's brickmaking camp, 73

Riley, Birtha, 219, 224, 233, 246

Rising Fawn iron ore mines camp, 66, 70, 270 (n. 4)

Rivers, Florence, 74

Roberts, Dorothy, 266–67 (n. 72), 298 (n. 13)

Roberts, Oran, 69–70

Robinson, Bessie, 77

Robinson, H. G., 185–86

Robinson, Sarah, 54–55

Rodriguez, Dylan, 9, 294 (n. 79)

Rosen, Hannah, 110

Rosetta Records, 216, 245

Ruffin, Josephine St. Pierre, 119

Russell, Belle, 79–80

Sabotage practice: black women's, 3, 15–16, 196, 199–202, 204, 206; blues women's feminist soundscapes of, 212–48; gendered interference with carceral conditions as, 195–212, 253

Sanford, Vince, 1

Scott, Carrie, 179, 192

Scott, Henry, 192, 199

Scroggins, Miss, 47

Segregation, 10, 139, 162, 164–65, 196; antiblack violence and, 286 (n. 34); black organizations against, 132; economic advancement predicated on, 7, 165; historical era of, 7; laws of, 164; penal logic of, 10; penal reform and, 155; prison labor and, 249

Self-defense, black women's acts of, 2, 189–93, 213, 232

Self-representation, 102, 206; discursive strategies of, 206; white women's practice of as oppositional to characterizations of black women, 102

Senate Chamber of Atlanta, 169

"Send Me to the 'Lectric Chair," 212–13

Sentience, 21, 49, 118, 147; white denial of black capacity for, 115, 118, 147, 151; white imaginary, black women in the, 21, 109–10, 121, 127, 252

Sexual exploitation, 102, 260–61 (n. 19); paroled black women's silence on, 183; pervasiveness of, 260–61 (n. 19); religious reformers views on, 162; threat of, 102; violent forms of, 183, 237

Sex work, 36, 162; blues narratives about, 236

Sibley Jane Elizabeth, 144

Silence, 104, 119, 135, 206, 217; black women's letters seeking clemency strategic deployment of, 206; collective organizing as effective breaking of, 119, 129; imprisoned women's tactical use of, 211; literacy and, 206; prisoners' forced forms of, 129; sonic disruption of sexual forms of, 217; as technique which violently sustains rape, 236

Simmons, Bertha, 181

Simpson, Fred, 204

"Sing Sing Prison Blues," 212, 214

Slave, the, 89; circumbscribed agency of, 109; female nonpersonhood of, 109; fragmented identity of, 56; subject position of, 211

Slave narratives, 211; literary tradition of, 211

Slavery, 7–8, 28, 67, 69, 75, 135, 149–50, 189, 251, 261 (n. 25), 262 (n. 29); 265 (n. 33); 280 (n. 243); archetypes from, 39; black women under, 10, 67–68, 75, 89, 159, 183; efforts to limit abuse under, 56; formal eradication of, 67; gender logics produced under, 67, 159, 176; historical continuity and, 158–59, 251; history of, 67; labor under, 17, 49, 75, 176, 183; racist rhetorics originating in, 136; radical modes of eroding, 202; symbolic vestiges of, 146, 176; transition from, 25; white supremacist purpose of, 28; woman as ideological category produced under, 152

Smith, J. E., 22, 178–79

Smith, Minnie, 171

Smith, Nancy, 45–46, 57

Smith, Ola Delight, 162

Smith and Taylor's farm camp, 70

Snorton, C. Riley, 260 (n. 15), 291 (n. 10)

Sociality, black women's, 200, 220–21, 254

"Some Notes on Negro Crime Particularly in Georgia," 13, 94

Song, 62, 146, 210–11, 213, 215–24, 228, 231–45, 254, 294 (n. 95); black children's, 234; black female body satirized in, 237; dance and, 212; deep knowledge of, 244; gender reference in, 226; group form of, 216, 234, 236; home and, 235; masculine prisoner subject of, 241; men's prison blues tradition and,

228; misogynist violence as theme for, 235–36; prison-themed, 212, 227, 235–36; protagonist of, 213; punishment-themed, 224; southern roots and routes of, 241. *See also* blues, the

Souls of Black Folk, The, 13

Southern, David W., 35–36

Southern Association of College Women, 42

Southern carceral regime, the, 3, 159–61, 163, 183, 201; black women's alternative networks forged within, 194; consolidated racial-gender logics generated by, 181; contemporary prison industries and, 256; disruptions within, 201; replication of slavery's gendered economies by, 159; turn-of-the-century and, 161; violence of, 163, 183; woman as white produced by, 2–3, 160, 188

Southern industrial capitalism, 28, 200, 255, 272 (n. 48); chain gang's endurance and, 200, 255; gendered-racial-carceral development of, 4, 161, 196, 200; transition to, 272 (n. 48); urban girls and women and, 200, 262–63 (n. 39)

Southern legal system, 13, 55; black women's oppression within, 136–37

Southern Lumber Company chain gang, 172

Southern penal regime, 5, 7, 55, 86, 94, 110, 157, 160; black women's terrorizing by, 177, 257; white women's protection from, 164

Southern punishment, 8, 10–11, 27, 121, 125, 133, 140, 148, 155, 157, 189–90, 200, 221, 231, 243, 251, 254, 261 (n. 22), 262 (n. 29), 264 (n. 30), 275–76 (n. 147), 282 (n. 44); black women's blues renderings of, 16, 214, 216, 221, 226, 241; black women's violent experience of, 2–5,

7, 11–13, 35, 38, 70, 86, 89,
127, 134, 159–60, 189, 206, 214,
219, 226, 241, 243, 252, 262
(nn. 32, 35), 265 (n. 40), 275–76
(n. 147), 282 (n. 44), 291 (n. 154);
cultural history of, 231; demand
for chain gang labor and, 254–56;
expressive forms of protest against,
16, 134, 241; horrific conditions of,
33, 133, 166, 221; modern technique
of, 27, 90, 133; multivalent discourse
on, 155; raced gender constructions
as formed by, 4–5, 8, 10–13, 27, 30,
51, 80, 90, 100, 104, 127, 134, 140–41,
148, 166–68, 251, 275–76 (n. 147),
282 (n. 44); records of, 31, 51, 204;
sonic imaginary of, 241. *See also*
neoslavery
Sparta, 28
Special Committee on the Condition
of the Criminals, 73
Special Report on Misdemeanor
Convicts, 71
Spelman College, 119, 124, 132
Spelman Messenger, 124, 130
Spillers, Hortense, 87, 92, 226, 260
(n. 13), 264 (n. 24), 295 (n. 129)
Spivak, John, 172
Spivey, Victoria, 203, 215–16, 232, 245,
294 (n. 94)
Spivey Records, 215
Standard Oil Alley, 195, 199–200
State farm, the, 22, 42, 57, 82, 116,
173–74, 176, 178, 180, 184–85; black
women's brutal experience on, 57,
82, 116, 173–74, 184–85; children
born at, 112–13; sexual violence at,
116; white women and, 8, 22, 54, 57
State Federation of Colored Women's
Clubs, 42
Steed, Walter, 115–17
Sterilization, 153; banning of, 298
(n. 13); calls for black girls', 165;
imprisoned women coerced into,
298 (n. 13)

Stevens, Henry, 70
Stevens, John, 3
Stevens, Lucinda, 31, 57
Stewart, Andrew, 85
Stinson, Sylla, 186, 203
Stockade, 31, 41–42, 60, 85, 173
Stone Mountain, 60
Stubbs, Sarah, 30, 57
Subservience, 189, 207; black
circumscription within, 189;
conveyance of, 207; rupturing of
black women's coerced form of, 200
Summerlain, Annie, 203
Sumter chain gang, 72
Surveillance, 35, 38, 158, 252, 261 (n. 22);
carceral constancy of, 158, 233

Taylor, Mrs. J. H., 181–82
Temperance movement, 122, 141–44
Tennessee, 133
Terrell, Mary Church, 14–15, 94,
122–23, 131–41, 281 (n. 13), 282
(n. 46)
Terrell, Joseph, 50, 101, 103
Texas, 69–70, 133, 215
Texas blues sound, 215, 232
Theft, 21, 196, 199; black girls and,
196, 199; minor forms of, 44; petty
form of, 34
Thomas, Ann, 34, 57
Thomas, Florida, 42, 57
Thomas, Mattie Mae, 223, 226
Thomas, Rosa, 44, 57
Thurman, Lucy, 123, 125, 130
Tifton County, 172
Torture, 73, 91, 136, 171, 205, 210; black
women and, 109, 127, 204; carceral
rituals of, 27–28, 204; public
spectacle of, 261 (n. 22); resistance
to, 253; sexualized forms of, 68, 204;
social death and, 14; white women
and, 152
Trawick, Hattie, 44
Tribble, S. J., 168
Trumbick, Gladis, 195, 200, 291 (n. 4)

Tuberculosis, 76, 173
Tucker, Annie, 171–72
Turner, Joseph, 66, 74, 165–67, 208
Turner, Martha, 203
Turner, Mary, 109
Typhoid, 59, 172, 270 (n. 6)

Uncle Remus, 34
Unfreedom, 14, 57, 186
Uplift ideology: debates on, 281
    (n. 12); pathology in, 281 (n. 11);
    racial, 124, 131, 187, 243
Upson County, 19
Urban north, the, 11, 169, 177, 262–63
    (n. 39), 264 (n. 30), 267 (n. 82);
    black female struggles for respect
    and public worth in, 290 (n. 141);
    black women migrants to, 11,
    69, 177; disciplinary institutions
    targeting black women in, 289
    (n. 99); male identification as queer
    in, 267 (n. 82); penitentiaries in,
    264 (n. 30); turn-of-the-century,
    287–88 (n. 61)

Valdosta, 109
Vaudeville, 215
Veal, Savannah, 54
Vice, 42, 154; black women and, 97,
    123, 154; legislation of, 178; sexual
    forms of, 42, 154
Vines, Martha, 36–38, 57

Walcott, Victoria, 132
Walker, Alice, 277 (n. 175)
Walker, Charlotte, 191, 210
Walker, Clifford, 115–17
Walker, Lula, 1–3, 7
Walker, Mollie, 203
Wallace, Ella, 34, 57
Walton County, 73
Warden, 4, 19, 22, 100, 178–79, 181,
    207–8, 246–48; sexual assault by,
    233, 246–48; white women as
    domestic form of, 4

Warren, Lena Bell, 193–94
Washington, Booker T., 13, 123–24
Washington, D.C., 132; Board of
    Education in, 132
Washington, Dinah, 212, 215
Washington, Margaret Murray, 123, 125
Washington, Mary, 75
Washington County, 156
"Wash Me and I Shall Be Whiter
    Than Snow," 146–47
Wells, Ida B., 114, 120, 122–23, 275, 281
    (n. 13), 282 (n. 35)
White, Alice, 203, 232
White, Eva, 216, 222, 224, 246
White, Mattie, 80
White, Mollie, 129, 205–6
White County, 45
White farms, 3, 48, 135; marital gender
    inequality on, 144, 149; paroled black
    female labor on, 3, 175, 182, 185
White home, the, 38, 178, 189; black
    women's contestations of oppressive
    labor conditions within, 35, 178;
    historical regulatory function
    of, 189; idealized black female
    subservience and, 35; paroled black
    women's compulsory domestic
    labor within, 160, 174, 176–77. See
    also domestic carceral sphere
Whiteness, property rights in, 188,
    196, 199
White private individuals, 3–4, 16,
    68–69, 158; compulsory black
    convict labor for, 4, 16, 68–69, 158
"Whiter Than Snow," 146
Whites, LeeAnn, 149–50
White slavery, 136
White supremacists, 207–8; as self-
    appointed experts in Negro manner
    and character, 207–8
White women's vulnerability: chivalry
    and, 24; conceptions of, 5, 24, 26,
    50–51, 109, 122, 140, 148, 150, 163,
    165, 169, 187; myth of the black
    male rapist and, 141, 165, 192